EDUCATION and

COLLECTIVE BARGAINING

Readings in Policy and Research

Anthony M. Cresswell

Northwestern University

Michael J. Murphy

The University of Utah

**A University Counsel
for Educational Administration
and Phi Delta Kappa Publication**

distributed by

McCutchan Publishing Corporation
2526 Grove Street
Berkeley, California 94704

© 1976 by McCutchan Publishing Corporation
All rights reserved

Library of Congress catalog card number 76-46121
ISBN 0-8211-0227-3

Printed in the United States of America

Contents

Preface   ix

Introduction   xiii

Part I. The Environment of Collective Bargaining   1

Overview   3

Readings

  1. Why They Organize   12
       Gus Tyler

  2. Teacher Negotiation: History and Comment   22
       Ross A. Engel

  3. The Need for Limitation Upon the Scope of
     Negotiations in Public Education, I   33
       John H. Metzler

  4. The Need for Limitation Upon the Scope of
     Negotiations in Public Education, II   52
       William F. Kay

5. Determinants of Attitudinal Militancy Among
   Teachers and Nurses   78
      Joseph A. Alutto and James A. Belasco

6. The Local Community and Teacher Strike Solidarity   95
      Albert I. Goldberg

7. Correlates of State Public Employee Bargaining Laws   109
      Thomas A. Kochan

Part II. The Collective Bargaining Process   129

Overview   131

Readings

8. Models of Cooperation and Conflict   143
      Martin Patchen

9. A Certainty-Equivalent Model of Bargaining   174
      Edward Saraydar

10. An Interactive Model of Collective Bargaining
    in Public Education   200
       Anthony M. Cresswell

11. Collective Negotiations and Teachers: A Behavioral
    Analysis   214
       Donald Hellriegel, Wendell French, and
       Richard B. Peterson

12. Comment on "Collective Negotiations and Teachers"   240
       William J. Moore

13. Toward a Theory of Collective Negotiations   262
       A. William Vantine

14. Perception of Power in Conflict Situations   279
       H. Andrew Michener, Edward J. Lawler, and
       Samuel B. Bacharach

Part III. Impasse Resolution and Strikes   295

Overview   297

Readings

15. The Limits of Collective Bargaining in Public
    Employment   308
        Harry H. Wellington and Ralph K. Winter, Jr.

16. The Role and Consequences of Strikes by Public
    Employees   332
        John F. Burton, Jr. and Charles Krider

17. Why Teachers Need the Right To Strike   357
        Albert L. Shanker

18. Impasse Issues in Teacher Disputes Submitted to
    Factfinding in New York   363
        Barbara Doering

19. Preintervention Effects of Mediation versus Arbitration   382
        Douglas F. Johnson and Dean G. Pruitt

20. The Chapter Chairman and School Grievances   400
        Alan M. Glassman and James A. Belasco

Part IV. Economic, Political, and Organizational Outcomes 411

Overview 413

Readings

21. The Influence of Collective Bargaining on Teachers'
    Salaries in New York State   425
        David B. Lipsky and John E. Drotning

22. The Effect of Teachers' Organizations on Salaries
    and Class Size   452
        W. Clayton Hall and Norman E. Carroll

23. Teacher Salaries and School Decentralization   464
        Robert N. Baird and John H. Landon

24. Negotiations at the Crossroads: Increased
    Professionalization or Reinforced Bureaucracy   476
        Michael J. Murphy and David Hoover

25. Collective Bargaining and School Finance Reform
     Michael J. Murphy, Clifford Barton, and
     Richard P. Mills

26. Political Implications of Public Employee Bargaining
     Thomas M. Love and George T. Sulzner

Preface

Collective bargaining and labor relations have assumed a position of major importance in the sphere of educational policy and administration. In many of the large industrialized states the process of bargaining and contract administration in schools is well developed. In other states bargaining is less pervasive but is nonetheless high on the list of concerns of public officials, educational administrators, school board members, and teachers. It has been estimated that there are close to 2,000 agreements in effect between classroom teachers and school boards, with over 700,000 teachers covered by these agreements (see William R. Hazard, "Collective Bargaining and School Governance," *Southwestern University Law Review* 5 (1973), pp. 83-117). This total does not include agreements covering non-instructional employees. In some bargaining states, statutes regulating collective bargaining in the schools are being studied and updated by legislatures. In many states without bargaining laws, legislation is being drafted or debated. At one time, the United States Congress had before it two bills which would federalize the educational bargaining system. Enactment of pending legislation will undoubtedly speed the already rapid spread of bargaining.

The importance of bargaining to education is reflected in the

amount of literature which has emerged. Like most emergent litera-
tures, however, there are serious deficiencies. Many of the best empirical and theoretical analyses of bargaining in schools and elsewhere
are scattered. It is difficult for practitioners and scholars alike to
build systematic knowledge about the nature and mechanisms of bargaining when the building blocks are in such a diverse literature.
Without a foundation of understanding, however, it is likely that the
practice of bargaining will remain at a level of intuition and folklore.
A prime objective of this book is to bring together some of the best
analytical perspectives on a complex topic.

A second purpose of this collection is to present the readings in
a framework which itself facilitates understanding and encourages further inquiry. The book is arranged into four parts:

Part I   The Environment of Collective Bargaining
Part II   The Collective Bargaining Process
Part III   Impasse Resolution and Strikes
Part IV   Economic, Political, and Organizational Outcomes

Preceding Part I is a short introduction. Its purpose is to provide a
perspective for viewing collective bargaining as a system and to set
forth some of the editors' impressions after a large-scale review of the
literature. Each of the four parts will follow a similar format: a short
overview by the editors followed by six or seven selected readings.

Two structures guided the evaluation and selection of the articles from among the nearly 500 reviewed. One was our conception of
collective bargaining as a social system. The other was our desire to
emphasize theoretical and conceptual literature. We attempted also
to strike a balance between general works and studies dealing specifically with bargaining in schools. By presenting such a mixture, we
hope to interest schoolpeople in the considerable amount of valuable
bargaining research which has been drawn from other institutional
contexts as well as present a review of collective bargaining in educational settings. The introduction and overviews attempt, in part, to
establish the link between bargaining theory and research in general
and bargaining and research in education.

There are at least three audiences for this collection. Growing
numbers of graduate students in educational administration will be
taking courses in labor relations. This volume should be useful in

these courses. Because the orientation is to theoretical and analytical works, it could also be used in collective bargaining courses outside of schools of education. In addition, the level of interest in labor relations in education is high among school administrators and others in government and politics. We would, therefore, expect substantial interest from practitioners in education and others in policy-making positions.

The impetus for this collection came from the work of a Task Force on Collective Bargaining Simulation sponsored by the University Council on Educational Administration. The job of the Task Force was to create an in-basket type collective bargaining simulation for use as an instructional tool in educational administrator training. Part of the instructional packet included a bibliography of readings to supply an analytical basis for the students in the simulation. The work on that bibliography led to this collection. We are indebted to Jack Culbertson and L. Jackson Newell of UCEA for their support in this effort, and to John Horvat, Burt Knighton, and Gerald Mansergh, members of the Task Force, for their review of our bibliographic work and concurrence with our estimate of need for conceptual and empirical content in teaching about collective bargaining. Also we should thank Fred Frank of UCEA who urged elaboration of our Task Force bibliographic summaries and arranged for their publication.

And finally, special thanks to Welthy Murphy who spent tedious months at a sewing-table desk converting readings from diverse journals to a common editorial format.

Evanston   A.M.C.
Salt Lake City   M.J.M.

Introduction

Collective bargaining in education is a process made up of many highly interactive events and activities. Though it is convenient at times to limit one's conception of collective bargaining to events which occur at a table where two sides oppose each other, it is in reality part of a much more complex system. Behavior at the bargaining table is constrained and directed by a host of environmental or contextual factors. Laws constrain the matters which may be discussed. Economic, social, and political conditions influence the behavior of parties involved. The nature of the employing organization, its decision structure and authority system, color the discussions and contribute to the issues being negotiated. Member and organizational needs of unions influence the generation of issues and the ease with which they can be resolved.

One can also view collective bargaining from the standpoint of its outcomes. Collective bargaining sessions produce, among other things, agreement or impasse. They establish wage rates and affect the nature and structure of organizational life. These outcomes interact with the bargaining processes and contexts which are determinants of future events in the system.

Just as it provides a useful way of considering collective bargaining, a systems approach also provides a mechanism for ordering the literature of collective bargaining. It insistently reminds the inquirer not to focus his attention on one piece of the action.

Using this dynamic or interactive perspective as an entry point, we have identified four major types of statements about collective bargaining. First, those dealing with contextual determinants or inputs. These include statements about the attitudes and collective motivations of teachers; the political and organizational environments in which teachers find themselves; and the legal setting in which the bargaining process functions.

Second, we have identified a series of conceptual writings which portray elements of the bargaining process qua process. These statements refer to aspects of the exchange process we call collective bargaining. Third, we have collected a series of writings which refer to the problems of disagreement and impasse. These readings are included partly because the trauma and violence often associated with them demands attention, but also because they are an integral part of the bargaining process, and influence its outcomes.

Finally, we have selected statements about the economic, political, and organizational outcomes of collective bargaining. Not all of these statements are as theoretically or empirically rigorous as we might have wished, but they do illustrate our contention that collective bargaining does have enormous consequences.

The Environment of Collective Bargaining

Our review of the research and theoretical literature on the context of bargaining suggests to us some important general conclusions. These are summarized below. They will be elaborated later in discussion and illustrated selected readings.

1. The social and political environment seems to be growing more open to collective bargaining in education. Fewer and fewer articles appear as the years go by dealing with the evils of bargaining and how it must be exorcised from the body of education. It is also clear that the legal framework in which bargaining occurs is becoming more and more tolerant of teachers' needs to organize and bargain collectively. At the time of this writing some 36 states have provisions for collective bargaining. Four states even have legitimized teachers' rights to strike.

2. Teacher militancy as a movement seems to be giving way to teacher unionism as an institution. Bargaining has become less an ideological crusade and more a routine operation of well-organized unions and associations. This institutionalization process carries with it certain advantages and problems. On the one hand, it stabilizes bargaining relationships and tends to minimize the emotional component. On the other hand, it creates an organization which has needs and problems of its own including maintenance needs common to any organization.

3. Courts, legislatures, and boards of education seem as yet unsure of appropriate responses to the teacher militancy movement and the institutionalization which seems to follow. They are unable to devise uniform strategies to contain it or acquire understanding to direct the relationship constructively.

4. We seem to be moving from a fragmented, pluralized system of educational decision making to one in which the principal relationship is between two strong parties. It is perhaps a major difference between a pluralist political system and a bargaining system that the latter has difficulty accommodating multiple parties and interests. In education, bargaining seems to be establishing two strong parties, one representing management and board of education interests, the other representing the interests of organized teachers. In the process other parties with interests in educational decision making find they must work through one of these two parties.

5. The literature on teacher union activity seems to stress two major sources or motivating drives. One is that teachers feel they are not receiving their just economic rewards; the other is that teachers are not happy with their present organizational status and will not be satisfied until they have achieved greater influence over the decision mechanisms of the schools employing them. If true, this means that teachers will not enter a maintenance phase in their bargaining relationship with school boards; once they can influence wage rates and working conditions, they will push for more say in instructional matters. Defining the scope of negotiations will be particularly difficult for educational bargaining.

6. Finally, the literature on the context of teacher militancy and collective bargaining suggests that teacher militancy occurring at this time is in part attributable to the general growing militancy of society. Teachers have been influenced by success in the civil rights movement and other aggressive expressions of aggrieved groups.

The Collective Bargaining Process

Models can take many forms. They can be static and descriptive or they can be dynamic. Our investigation of the collective bargaining literature has turned up some of each. Models can also be simple. The most elemental are two-variable models. On the contrary, they can be very complex, seeking to take in the entire bargaining process, i.e., macromodels. We encountered no macromodels which attempted to account for context or for very many output variables. Several of the best models were those which attempted to account for the behavior of bargainers regarding concessions made during the bargaining process. These explanatory models are essentially built around distributive bargaining or pure conflict. All of these models highlight the importance of learning which occurs during the bargaining process, that is, they focus on changes in behavior of one bargainer as a result of his change in perception or learning about the position of an opponent. Partial models deal with more limited variables and are not interactive. They attempt basically to explain variance in bargaining behavior or outcomes using a set of independent variables. Most of these variables can be categorized as perceptions of opponent power, good will, or information differentials.

Impasse Resolution and Strikes

The large literature on strikes and impasse resolution reveals that this is still a preoccupying concern to those studying educational bargaining. The impasse represents the most visible and potentially most traumatic part of the bargaining process. Analyses of strikes and debates about strikes have not produced uniform conclusions or useful data on the functional and dysfunctional aspects of strikes in the public sector. The same can be said for mediation, factfinding, and arbitration. The general impression one gets from the literature is that, aside from fear of political distortions stemming from strikes, a more strike tolerant literature is emerging.

Relative to a third-party intervention mechanism, the literature seems fairly supportive. Most research studies to date suggest that impasse resolution mechanisms in the industrialized states have been employed with success. They also suggest they have been employed often. Data taken from New York state, for instance, reveals that in 1969 and in 1970 over one-half of the school districts ended up employing some form of third-party reconciliation in their attempt to arrive at contract settlements. This probably says more about the immaturity of the process of bargaining in education than about the nature of impasse resolution mechanisms.

Most of the literature is strongly biased on the matter of teacher strikes. Some would allow teachers the right to strike and to form a free collective system similar to the private sector. Others vociferously argue for a situation in which teachers are prohibited from striking and a third-party impasse mechanism is substituted (e.g., mediation and arbitration). The arguments in favor of teacher strikes are the following:

1. Teacher strikes represent no immediate danger to public health and safety.

2. Strikes occur anyway and it requires a good deal of societal and legal energy to police illegal strikes.

3. Available impasse resolution mechanisms are simply not adequate to the task, and are not able to infuse the bargaining relationships with the necessary motivation to settle. The threat of mediation or arbitration is in no way a substitute for the threat of a strike or a lockout. In short, free collective bargaining is impossible without the right to strike.

The arguments against teacher strikes flow from the assumption that decisions which affect teachers are not simply two-party issues, but rather are part of a more complex pluralistic process of educational decision making. In this argument, teachers are only one of many interest groups seeking to affect distribution of scarce educational resources. Allowing teachers to strike gives them an unfair advantage in political deliberations.

Economic, Political, and Organizational Outcomes

Many explanations have been offered for the rapid unionization of teachers and consequent collective bargaining. Some argue that the motive force is economic deprivation. Others suppose that wage rates are a minor issue and focus on organizational dissatisfaction, bureaucratic conflict, decision deprivation, managerial caprice, and the like.

Given the abundance of explanatory variables, it seems reasonable for researchers to be interested not only in contextual variables but in outcomes as well. Have teacher unions sought to increase economic returns to teachers? Have they succeeded? Have unions reduced organizational incongruence? Have they curbed administrative malpractice?

A strong positive effect of teacher militancy and collective bargaining on wage rates has not been clearly established. Present evidence suggests the influence has been slight. The literature also reveals that the attempt to isolate union influence on teacher wage rates is bound up in very difficult research problems.

1. There is considerable spillover from unionized to nonunionized districts in teacher wage rates. Teacher salary scales are commonly exchanged among adjacent school districts within states as well as across state lines. Since the teacher wage rate may be expected to be competitive in the same way other wage rates are, it is likely that they are interactive.

2. Measurement of the level of union activity is difficult. A simple dichotomized variable (negotiating or not negotiating) seems a very poor measure of the amount of leverage being applied to drive the wage rate up.

A second major conclusion is that teachers are having and will continue to have a considerable impact on the decision and policy structures in education. Several researchers have found that the decision structure of schools and school systems has been altered by the presence and activity of teacher unions.

In general, however, the literature in Part IV is disappointing both in scope and in rigor. Little research is reported that would help estimate the impact of collective bargaining on managerial behavior, for instance. A similar research void is apparent with regard to governance or political consequences.

PART I

The Environment of Collective Bargaining

Overview

The processes and outcomes of collective bargaining in education are important to many people. Some are employees of the school district whose lives are enriched or made more difficult as a consequence of bargaining. Some are students whose educational services may be affected. Others are property owners whose local property tax is partly determined at the bargaining table. Still others are elected public officials who must cope with economic and political consequences of bargaining. And some are citizens whose goal of greater involvement in educational decisions may seem threatened by bargaining.

These groups and others have an interest in collective bargaining; to a greater or lesser extent, achievement of aspirations may be subject to bargaining outcomes. Naturally, these groups may try to influence the course of bargaining. This influence may be direct or indirect; it may be exercised in the public policy arena or by buttonholing the negotiating parties.

Interested parties not participating in the negotiations form a group of onlookers whose influence is manifest at the table in a variety of ways. For example, taxpayers are increasingly resistant to school budget changes which adversely affect their tax rate; they

lobby for "more efficient" use of their tax dollars. School administrators, board members, and union leaders are conscious of taxpayer
concerns, and agreements are cast in the shadow of this restive group.

Though interest group analysis is one way to think about the
context of collective bargaining in education, it is by no means the
only way. Bargaining is influenced by many conditions and events in
its environment. General social, economic, and demographic conditions affect bargaining. For instance, events at the table are conditioned by the attitudes of the local community toward teachers and
their demands. Community attitudes may determine in a given instance whether a teachers' union will press demands or risk the consequences of a strike. If the community is perceived as sympathetic to
teacher demands or can be made sympathetic to teacher demands,
the union will be more aggressive and also more willing to strike. Certainly, behavior of the United Federation of Teachers in New York
has been modified in recent years as a result of the excruciating 1968
teacher strike in which traditional alliances were destroyed and community support for UFT was eroded. The Goldberg paper (reading 6)
discusses some important dimensions of this union behavior-commu-
nity attitude dynamic.

Conditions of the market place (supply, demand, and inflation)
certainly affect the position of parties at the bargaining table. The
present surplus of teachers has altered the stance and power base of
teachers' unions. School boards know that there are three unemployed teachers available as replacements for every teacher on their
present staff. As a consequence, job security is emerging as a major
issue for the bargaining table as working teachers seek to insulate
themselves from the pressures created by the army of unemployed
teachers.

Changes in composition of the teaching force also condition
bargaining. Younger teachers, especially, were influenced by a growing social militancy (campus protests, civil rights marches, and the
like). Militant behavior is increasingly accepted as a legitimate response to the failure of social institutions. Numerous authors suggest
a linkage between this social conditioning and attitudes and behavior
in the teachers' union movement. Tyler (reading 1), Engel (reading
2), and Alutto and Belasco (reading 5) elaborate various aspects of
this line of thought.

The environment may also influence public policy relative to collective bargaining. As Kochan (reading 7) points out, public policy may be viewed as intervention strategies—attempts to see that collective bargaining serves the larger public interests. In the private sector, also, major legislative milestones clearly reveal attempts to cause desired adjustments in collective bargaining practice. For example, in the early 1900s the aim of legislation was to constrain organizing and other union activities. Judicial opinion was similarly inclined. The Sherman Antitrust Act was first actively used to try to retard the development of employee organizations. In the 1920s and 1930s public sentiment began to be more favorably disposed to unions. This attitude was reflected in the Norris-LaGuardia Act of 1932 and the Wagner Act (National Labor Relations Act) of 1935. As a result of these federal legislative acts, employers were required to bargain collectively with employees. Employees were given a number of rights and few constraints were placed on the behavior of unions. In 1947, after a rash of strikes and activities on the part of organized labor following World War II, the national mood was one of concern for the growing and unregulated power of labor unions. The Taft-Hartley Act amended the National Labor Relations Act with restrictions on labor unions. In 1959, after Senate investigations revealed corruption and undemocratic union practices, the Landrum-Griffin Act (Labor Management Reporting and Disclosure Act) was passed. This act was an attempt to reduce the power of labor bosses and to make labor unions more responsive to member needs and interests. The history of federal legislation in collective bargaining demonstrates public policy attempts to establish equal bargaining power positions; regulations have changed over time according to perceptions of the power or abuse of power by either management or labor. A similar process of dynamic regulation seems to be unfolding in the public sector.

Events and practices in private sector bargaining influence bargaining in education, as do events and practices in public sector bargaining generally. Private and other public sector bargaining, therefore, constitutes a contextual input to bargaining in education. There are many ways this influence is exerted. Obvious among them is the fact that regulations governing public sector bargaining (including education) are frequently modeled on private sector legislation (though work stoppages are generally prohibited in the public services, and union security clauses are generally more restricted).

Legislation introduced in the United States Congress offers the possibility that public sector bargaining will be brought under federal control, with the likelihood that differences in practice between the two sectors will be further reduced. (One bill, which has the support of both the AFT and NEA, would strike the provision in the National Labor Relations Act which excludes public employees from coverage. NLRA coverage has recently been expanded to hospital personnel.)

A slightly more subtle, but nonetheless significant, private-to-public sector influence comes through personnel export. The growth of public sector union and collective bargaining has been rapid. Before 1960 bargaining was rare in the public sector. No state legislation existed, nor was it demanded. In 1975, a mere fifteen years later, thirty-six states had bargaining laws. Public employee relations commissions, rosters of mediators and arbitrators, and other trappings of bargaining management systems are much in evidence. Where did the negotiators, mediators, arbitrators, and others necessary to collective bargaining come from? A large number expanded private sector practices, or simply transferred. The result is a system heavily staffed with people who learned their craft in private sector bargaining. Naturally they brought with them attitudes and approaches derived from their private sector experience. Usually they fit private sector solutions to public sector problems. Present bargaining is always conditioned by prior events. Decisions made by government, the courts, and regulatory agencies create a precedential web circumscribing bargaining space. The way things came to be often determines the way they will continue to be. In collective bargaining we know that previous contract terms usually set the floor for future contract negotiations. Unions oppose attempts to remove or reduce previous contract gains with great vigor.

A climate of growing public acceptance of unionism, especially for public employees, is an important factor. In this opinion environment, it is easier for formerly nonunionized groups to accept the propriety of forming their own organization. In reading 1, Tyler characterizes this phenomenon as an evolution of attitudes about labor organizations and suggests that it involves a group self-awareness as well as a climate. In reading 2, Engel traces the process of evolution by noting the changes in policy statements of the National Education Association during the 1960s. During this period the NEA moved from an anti-union position to one accepting the concept of teacher strikes. It is difficult to say whether the militancy of teachers and other public employees helped forge the changes in public opinion or vice versa. But it is clear that the two processes are related. (See also Kassalow 1969.)

Militancy in labor organizations is related also to militancy in other components of the society. It is fostered by a pervasive attitude that institutions in general and schools in particular are not functioning properly. Civil rights and student protest movements may have helped to legitimatize the concept of militancy for public employees. (See Corwin 1968.) Bureaucratic authority structures of the schools were seen as obstacles to improvement, and not vulnerable to anything less than a strong and militant teacher organization. Thus, not only did a general acceptance of militancy provide a fertile ground for the growth of teacher unions, but the pressures on the schools for change and improvement reinforced the role of the teacher organization as reformer. To achieve the reform and improve the lot of the teacher, the union was forced to compete directly for authority with the traditional school governance structure. This set the stage for much of the conflict that has accompanied the growth of collective bargaining in education and relates directly to scope of bargaining discussed in readings 3 and 4.

Growth of teacher unionism is related to individual aspirations as well as to organizational and political concerns. Both Corwin (1968) and Horvat (1968) point out, although from different perspectives, that militancy is connected to the desires of individual teachers for professional status and power as well as for economic rewards. The prevailing professional norms of peer regulation and individual autonomy were (and are) in stark contrast to the subservient role of teachers in many school systems. Militancy can be seen as an effort to achieve professional status through collective action, rather than as a "nonprofessional" activity as it is sometimes characterized. In addition to seeking higher professional status, teachers and other government employees could be characterized as suffering from relative deprivation in terms of income. That is, the teachers felt that they received less income than other workers with comparable education or status. The sense of deprivation may occur as well in other areas. In reading 5, Alutto and Belasco find a relationship between teachers' decisional deprivation and their attitude toward militant behavior.

Status inconsistency or deprivation can be related to militancy as well. Teachers who perceive their professional responsibilities as indicative of a higher status than their income or authority will be more likely to take action to improve their status. These tendencies are likely to be augmented by high expectations for the schools. That is, if the schools are looked upon as solvers of social problems, teachers may seek status commensurate with this high responsibility. The relationships between personal aspirations, status, and union militancy, suggested as sociological determinants of militancy, are treated in Cole's study of rank-and-file support of teachers for their union (Cole 1968). The social status of teachers and their position in the authority structures of schools interact with the development of unionism and militancy. Knowledge of unionizing forces aids in understanding the process of bargaining and particularly the conflicts over major issues.

An important element of collective bargaining is the legal context. State laws allow collective bargaining and require boards of education to bargain with elected teacher bargaining agents. State laws also specify how bargaining agents are elected, what matters may be negotiated and how bargaining impasses are to be treated. They specify the form of collective interaction and whether boards and teacher unions may enter into a written contract which can be enforced.

The legal context of collective bargaining includes not only local, state, and federal statutes, but court decisions, attorney generals' rulings, and decisions by state and federal regulatory bodies. But collective bargaining poses other legal problems. Many states have established civil service systems to regulate appointment, promotion, and dismissal of public employees. In that these matters are frequently subject to negotiation as well, a question of legal precedence may arise. Because economic matters are negotiated, and because revenue and expenditure powers of governmental agencies are restricted, there is sometimes a question of whether the school board can be forced into an agreement which may be in conflict with expenditure restrictions.

And, of course, collective bargaining and the statutes, rulings, and opinions which support it, have created many serious challenges for the doctrines of sovereignty and delegation of authority which underlie the American system of local government.

The question of whether boards can negotiate salaries, benefits, and certain conditions of employment is being resolved, de facto if not always de jure. Thirty-six states provide a legal basis for some form of collective bargaining; negotiation is reported in all states.

Currently, major legal debates revolve around two questions: scope of bargaining (including management rights) and post-impasse procedures. Part III takes up strikes and impasse resolution alternatives. In Part I we have included two statements (readings 3 and 4) which reflect different perspectives in the scope-of-bargaining debate.

Proponents of a broad scope model of bargaining for education argue that it is essential for the unions to participate in the determination of policy which affects their ability to perform their job. There is a combination of professional and economic arguments. On the economic side, working conditions are closely related to wages. Improvements in working conditions are sought by unions and can be traded off, presumably, for increases in wages. The union is assumed to seek the maximization of the satisfaction of its members through improving both wages and working conditions. But in professional occupations like teaching, the employees can argue that their ability to function properly and deliver the necessary educational services is affected by educational policy. School organization, curriculum, and administrative procedures become conditions of employment, in this view, right along with hours and fringe benefits. All aspects of educational policy thereby become negotiable. Kay's article (reading 4) elaborates and provides justification for this point of view.

On the other side of the argument, public sector negotiations are held to involve pluralistic decision making. Public policy should be worked out in a process involving all interested groups. The public employer usually represents only those groups which are active. But on any given issue, only a segment of the public will have an interest and therefore be active. The rest will be indifferent, but in favor of labor peace. If all issues are open for bargaining an imbalance will again result. The union has the strike to reinforce its demands, while the interested groups have only their ability to pressure the government and counterbalance other groups which would rather accept the union's position to preserve labor peace. This argument is put forth by Metzler (reading 3) and developed by Wellington and Winter (reading 14).

Another environmental feature of importance, especially for bargaining in education, is the level of public satisfaction with the services being provided by the government agency. In the case of the schools, there is currently widespread dissatisfaction with the quality of education. As a result there is a concomitant pressure for reform. Because the schools provide a service, rather than goods, educational reform involves changes in the manner in which those services are provided. These changes are connected directly to the working conditions of the teachers and thus to the collective bargaining process. This connection produces two effects of interest. One, as we mentioned earlier, is that the teachers can use their advocacy of reform as a means of gathering increased public support for their bargaining position. Thus, persons dissatisfied with the current state of schooling can be recruited to support the teachers, even though they may know little of the teachers' specific proposals. Where reform issues emerge, such as decentralization of the New York City schools in 1967-68, the unions emerge as a powerful interest group on one side of the question. In these cases the strike or threat of strike can distort the political process and produce results not in the general public interest, or not supported by a majority of the public. Kay argues that the current laws and court decisions reserve enough power to the employer to maintain the public interest. But this view is not shared by Metzler. With the current state of knowledge it is not possible to ascertain which structures or legal provision will produce the best decision process. The readings included in Part I do not answer that question, but rather identify the issues and offer proposals.

We have focused on the issue of scope of bargaining in the belief that it is a central issue to the state of collective bargaining. The centrality of this issue is another example of the interaction of the processes of collective bargaining with their environment. As the study of the history of collective bargaining shows, there has been a progression of issues in the development of collective bargaining in the private sector, beginning with the right to organize and the right to bargain. This same sequence is being repeated to a large degree in the public sector. So, what is a highly salient issue now will almost certainly be settled and uninteresting later. As the patterns of public opinion and the acceptance of certain practices changes, so do the issues. Moreover, there is an evolution of structures as well. Organizations to regulate bargaining, arbitrate impasses and grievances, and mediate conflict have grown up in the private sector. We can expect organizations to emerge to deal with the same components of public sector labor relations as well. Changes in political decision-making processes in government will also affect the manner in which employers bargain, resulting in changes in the relative distribution of power. These readings are not intended to provide definitive or permanent answers to the issues or problems raised. We acknowledge that to be impossible. Instead the intent is to identify some important relationships and point the way for further analysis.

References

Cole, Stephen. "The Unionization of Teachers: Determinants of Rank-and-File Support." *Sociology of Education* (Winter 1969): 66-87.

Corwin, Ronald G. "Teacher Militancy in the United States: Reflection on Its Sources and Prospects." *Theory Into Practice* VII (April 1968): 96-102.

Horvat, John J. "The Nature of Teacher Power and Teacher Attitudes Toward Certain Aspects of this Power." *Theory Into Practice* VII (April 1968): 51-56.

Kassalow, Everett M. "Trade Unionism Goes Public." *The Public Interest*, no. 14 (Winter 1969): 118-30.

Reading 1

Why They Organize

Gus Tyler

"The 4122 employees at UN Headquarters in New York moved a step closer to a strike today," read a news dispatch of July 28, 1971, "despite a pledge by Secretary-General Thant of at least an eight percent increase for non-professional staffers."

The item milestoned the internalization of public employee unionism. Taking place at the UN, under the generally benign handling of the diplomatic U Thant, the confrontation climaxed a rising drama of militancy on the part of government workers.

The natural question is: What went wrong at the UN to cause its employees to unionize and to threaten a strike? The same question recurs every time any public employees organize, especially if they are white-collar, educated, and sophisticated. The assumption is that such people, unlike the blue-collared, horny-handed sons of toil, are not naturally inclined toward unionism and certainly not toward parading on the picket line. Hence, the inevitable search for the special circumstance or provocation that moves the traditionally genteel civil servant to become militant.

Reprinted by permission from *Public Administration Review* 32, no. 2 (March/April 1972), pp. 97-101.

This probe for the particular reason behind public employee unionism is nothing new. In the past, when other sectors of the labor force unionized, there was always the digging for details, for the immediate causes of the conflict. As a result, the forest (the underlying reason) was obscured by the trees (the immediate cause). In every case, of course, there were grievances, for what worker or group of workers, competing for goods, services, or status is without grievances? But in many cases, the newly voiced grievance is of ancient duration, and, moreover, unionization frequently occurs at a time when the weight of traditional oppression is being lifted. In almost every case, among the first to rebel (unionize) are the better paid, better situated employees, while the very last to organize are the most deprived and aggrieved. The cycles of unionism seem to come not when a new outrage is perpetrated against employees, but when the class or subclass is ready—and times are propitious.

The Historical Compulsion To Organize

Underlying the reasons why public employees unionize is the universal reason why people organize. Thousands of years ago Aristotle offered a clue when he stated in his *Politics* that "man is, by nature, a political animal." By "political," the Greek sage did not mean that all men, by nature, run for office or even vote. He meant— since he spoke Greek—that all men tend to gather in a *polis*, in a natural grouping where through a process of *politics* in a *polity*, they work out their *policies,* enforced by a *police*. This varied play on words assumes that man is instinctively—by nature—a herd animal, a creature of the *polis,* congregating compulsively with those of his kind.

This Aristotelian concept is commonly accepted in regard to tribes, city-states, nations, or subgroups such as ethnic conclaves or even religious sects. For some reason, perhaps because it is secondary in the development of man, the same idea of man, the political animal, is not applied as readily to the work *polis,* the occupation that certain people hold in common. Yet, there is abundant history to prove that the work *polis* is a continuing force in bringing men and women together into societies, fraternities, guilds, associations, and unions. Such organizations do not necessarily begin as instruments of overt conflict. They come into being as extended families (often deriving family name from the occupation: smith, carpenter, weaver, tyler), living in tight little neighborhoods, protected by family deities, indulging in special occupational high-days and holidays, coming to one another's aid in life, and burying one another in a communal cemetery after death. In sum, historically, the politics (the *polis*) of the craft or trade precedes its economics (the division of income).

In the ancient cities of Sumeria the first class to organize was the priesthood; in possession of then arcane knowledge about weather, irrigation, and the management of group conflict, it set up a tight fraternity with restricted admission and even more restricted mysteries to be shared with none outside the closed circle. The warriors formed their "union," called the nobility, with inherited power and wealth restricted to lords and ladies. The professionals organized their colegii: medicine, teaching, law. While their class institutions were not called "unions," they were "unions" in all but name. For a fuller discussion of this concept, see Tyler (1968).

But the lesser occupations also organized, especially among the more skilled: the labor aristocracy. In ancient Mesopotamia, "the citizens when working for the temple were organized in groups or guilds under their own foremen" (Frankfort 1956). Among the early Hebrews, "families employed in the same craft formed clans that later grew into guilds [that] . . . tended to bond together for common social, economic and cultural benefit" (Duckat 1968). In ancient Greece, "the tradition was that a craft belonged to a family or clan" (Landtman 1938). In Rome there were the colegii of occupational groups that "gave them more force in time of need for safeguarding their common interests. . . . Each organization had its protecting god, *genius colegii*. . . . The organization of workmen was, at the same time, a burial society. . ." (Durkheim 1933). In Medieval Europe, guilds were organized to aid members "in sickness, helpless old age, poverty, commercial failure, loss by shipwreck and fire and other distress, and after their death . . . the expense of their burial and of masses and prayers for the repose of their souls" (Davis 1961). In subsequent centuries they became more interested in the economic *now* than in the spiritual *hereafter,* prescribing rules like: "no one who is not of the guild may trade in the said town."

No doubt, each of these organizations—whether in Mesopotamia or Medieval Europe—had its special moments for grievances, complaints, work stoppages, and social pressuring. But the continuing reason for these organizations was the communal compulsion, the eternal urge for birds of a feather to flock together.

In societies with caste systems (legal or informal), a coming together of the folk in the craft or trade was compulsively easy. They were related by blood and lived, worked, prayed, sang, danced, wooed, and died on the same turf—literally. In more fluid and open societies, such as the United States, the coming together of the occupational clan has been more difficult. But whenever any sector of the labor force became sufficiently aware of its collective presence and power, it sooner or later organized to make itself seen and heard.

What is true of occupational as well as political groups is also true of ethnic, sexual, age groups. In short, the Aristotelian imperative about man's natural *political* instinct to herd in his *polis* underlies unionism, as it does cities, states, tribes, religions, and movements of women and children.

Stages of Labor History in the United States

In 20th century America there have been three major periods of union development, signalling the emergence of three different, though related, parts of the labor force. The first period, from 1900 to the mid-1930s, reflected the unionization of the skilled craftsman; the second, from the mid-1930s to the mid-1950s, saw the rise of the semi- and unskilled in mass manufacture; the third, which started with the mid-1960s, voices the aspirations of the white-collar and service-economy employee, very heavily engaged in public employment. Each period corresponds to the awakening of a class—or better, subclass—in the labor force.

For the first three decades of the century the American trade unions were composed overwhelmingly of workers in building and construction, in railroading, and in the graphic trades. In other industries, where unionism had a foothold, the sectors enjoying organization were those employing skilled craftsmen: machinists in the metal trades, cutters in the apparel industry, tool and die-makers.

Why were the more highly skilled the first to organize in any grand way? Because they were aware of their collective presence and, hence, their power potential. They held skills that were in relatively short supply; they were more literate; they shared a pride of craft bordering on snobbery; they were of earlier immigrant stock and hence felt more confident and sure-footed on American soil. The craftsman-mechanic was the kingpin of the blue-collar world and, most important, he knew it.

During World War I the American economy began to change, breaking down complex tasks into simplified pieces and moving each piece on to a moving belt to be handled by semiskilled men with brief training. Much of the new labor supply was drawn from recent European arrivals or from the rural South and West. For a full decade, 1920 to 1930, this "new" class of workers in mass manufacture grew as the auto, rubber, steel, and allied industries expanded to become the giants of the American economy.

It took a full decade for this new class to mature, to become aware of its collective presence and power potential. It was propelled into action by both a negative and a positive charge. The negative was the Great Depression with its traumatic impact on all workers in the United States; the positive was the New Deal with its encouragement to labor to unionize for collective bargaining.

Thus, during this second period in American labor history a massive new tier was added to the movement, but by 1955 unionism began to lose steam. Once more, a quiet economic revolution in the American economy was changing the nature of the labor force and thereby creating a vast new class that still had to mature for unionization. This class became statistically visible in the post-World War II years as white-collar outstripped blue-collar employees, as workers engaged in dispensing services outnumbered those engaged in producing commodities, and as the number of public and professional employees rose dramatically.

What brought about this change, one of whose outstanding characteristics was the unparalleled increase in the civil service, especially at the state and local level? While, as we shall see, the reasons were many, one was basic, namely, automation. America issued from World War II—as it did from World War I—with a new sort of economy derived from improved productivity. The symbol after the first war was the assembly line; the symbol after the second was the computer.

The expectation was that "automation," guided by "cybernation," would displace labor—especially blue-collar workers—and create unemployment. Some people were disemployed in one place but many others were employed elsewhere: on balance, the labor force grew, even more rapidly than the population. The goods-producing sector did not expand rapidly, but the service sector grew faster than the labor force and the population.

How did this happen? The answer lies, foremostly, in "expanded aggregate demand" for goods and services—a demand that had been accumulating during the war years. In addition, when World War II ended, major unions insisted that, with overtime eliminated or reduced, hourly wages should go up to compensate for lost overtime. At the same time, working families began to cash in their savings bonds and to indulge needs and desires that had been denied in the war years. Finally, with the surtax lowered, there was more in the pay envelope for spending. The demand for goods and services from the private personal sector rose.

Hence, the expanded productivity by automated workers was balanced by enlarged demand from consumers. Each worker could produce more, but the same worker, as consumer, could buy more. Consequently, the number of workers in the goods-producing sector did not decline; indeed, the number in manufacture *increased*, although at a slower speed.

The Rise in the Service Sector

The pent up demand turned to the service sector. The demand for services was not limited to the private sector, but extended to the public sector. The New Deal habit had led people to expect things from government. While the stimulus for many programs had come from the federal government, from the top, the actual implementation of these programs took place at the local level, at the bottom. States, counties, cities, and school districts expanded their budgets and payrolls, sometimes alone, sometimes in partnership with other levels of government, often with federal funding and prodding.

A "service" in high demand was education, both public and private. In 1930 public and private school expenditures were $3.2 billion; ten years later the amount was the same. But by 1950 (post-World War II) expenditures were at $8.7 billion (3.4 percent of the Gross National Product) and then continued to rise to $65.8 billion in 1970 (7.1 percent of the GNP). Overwhelmingly, the educational expenditure is in public, as distinct from private, schools: of the 57.9

million pupils enrolled in both in 1968, 49.9 million were in public institutions.

The demand for education was spurred by several concurrent developments. First was the need for educated workers to fill openings in a white-collar economy: for professionals, technicals, and kindred; for clericals and programmers; for bureaucrats and social workers. Even in manufacture, white-collar workers were moving in heavily. Between 1960 and 1969 the number of production workers (blue-collar) in manufacturing rose by about 17 percent, while the number of nonproduction workers (white-collar) rose by 25 percent.

Second, since to fill these jobs workers needed education, or at least a diploma, a college degree became as desirable as the high school certificate had been in prior years, and the more people there were with education, the more there were reaching out for even more (higher) education.

A third pressure on education was the big bulge of young in the population curve after World War II. Some 14 million veterans returned home, married, and produced a baby boom that hit kindergartens in the early 1950s and colleges in the 1960s and 1970s.

In the 1960s the schools were given a special chore: to be the prime instrument for the racial integration of America. In a society that was nonintegrated in housing and employment, the schools were to integrate education, with the hope that out of the classroom would come the model relations for the rest of the society. As this idea developed, it meant more than racial integration in a classroom; it came to mean open admissions, scholarships, headstarts, and changes in curricula. The school was viewed as the place where America would begin to cope with its two most difficult problems: race and poverty.

For all these reasons—automation, high purchasing power, rising expectations, demand for professional skills, the need for education, a numerous generation of young, mounting funds to purchase health services, a desire to combat poverty and racism—the labor force changed its make-up in the post-war years.

The rise in public employment was part of this general shift in the labor force that created a large "new class." Actually, the word "new" is an overstatement, since these occupations were in existence before World War II. The newness applies to their emergence as a numerous and vital entity in the economy. For more than a decade the growth of this class was unnoted and unnoticed. Indeed, it was not until the early 1960s, when the public employee, most notably the teachers, began to unionize and strike, that some observers began to pay attention to the civil servant as a power, as well as a presence.

Forces Influencing Public Employee Unionization

What was it that led to their unionization?

Although each subgroup of public employees undoubtedly had its special reasons to organize, there was an all-inclusive cause for their striking out in the 1960s. By that time the public employee was a large class in popular demand. Together with his confreres in the changed labor force—white-collar, service, professional, nonprofit— the public employee was a major presence. He was in the same position as the mass production worker in the 1930s: numerous, needed, and neglected. In the 1960s the public employee repeated the history of the industrial employee thirty years before and of the craftsman sixty years before: having discovered his collective presence, he moved—like a teenager come of age—to express his collective power.

In the 1960s the political climate was propitious for public employee organization: the new President John F. Kennedy issued Executive Order 10988 making it federal policy to grant recognition to unions of government employees. "As a catalyst to union organizing in the federal civil service, it was to prove comparable to the original National Labor Relations Act—the Wagner Act of 1935—in the private sector" (Perlman 1971). The election of JFK, like the election of FDR, encouraged a union air.

Actually, the Kennedy Order gave national expression to a mood already in the making at lower levels. The son of Senator Robert Wagner (Wagner Act), the then Mayor of New York City, Robert F. Wagner, issued Executive Order no. 49 in 1958 that permitted "employees to participate, to the extent allowed by law, through their freely chosen representatives in the determination of the terms and conditions of their employment." In the policy declaration was a commitment to "further and promote, insofar as possible, the practice and procedures of collective bargaining in accordance with the patterns prevailing in private labor relations."

The next year, 1959, Wisconsin became the first state to enact a public sector labor relations law which made collective bargaining mandatory for municipalities. In subsequent years (1958 to 1969), twenty other states passed some form of legislation dealing with public employees.

By the mid-1960s a third force came into being to stimulate public employee unionism: the civil rights movement. Indeed, in many situations—most notably the strike of sanitation men in Memphis when Martin Luther King, Jr., was assassinated—the labor and civil rights movements are almost indistinguishable.

Ninety per cent of the sanitationmen in Memphis are Negroes. In fact, government at all levels is the largest single employer of minority groups. This is not necessarily in order to set a good example, but also because of economic factors which restrict government's efforts to compete in the job market. Government has become, in the economists' jargon, the employer of last resort. In the great cities of the nation, the two most important domestic problems—the civil rights struggle and the struggle for economic improvement of minority groups by means of collective bargaining—are really one and the same movement. (Anderson 1969)

For the public employee, then, the time to go union came in the 1960s: (1) a large class became aware of its own image; (2) a congenial political ambience encouraged movement; and (3) the civil rights movement inspired Negroes who were numerous in public and nonprofit employment to organize.

As a consequence of public employee upsurge, the fastest growing unions in the United States are the American Federation of Government Employees, the American Federation of Teachers, and the American Federation of State, County, and Municipal Employees. But the full strength of unionism among public employees cannot be accurately measured by merely adding the membership of the three national unions above. Many traditional unions, such as Transport Workers, Teamsters, Carpenters, Maritime Workers, Electrical Workers, and Firefighters, count civil servants among their members. Equally significant are the millions of public employees who belong to organizations such as the National Education Association, the American Nurses' Association, the various Police Benevolent Leagues, and the numerous Civil Service Associations. Although the latter disclaim the title of "union," they are unions in all but name: they elect bargaining representatives, negotiate contracts, process grievances, and—finally—either strike outright or indulge in the subtle strike known as a "job action."

Why, in summary, do *they* organize? For the same reason that boys and girls become men and women. They grow up and demand adult status. The grievances that employees raise, the hopes they voice, the recognition they demand, the influence they seek in the larger society—all these are part of growing up. It's as natural as life itself.

References

Anderson, Arvid. "Current Trends, Recent and Predicted Developments." *Perspective in Public Employee Negotiations*, edited by Kenneth D. Warner. Chicago: Public Personnel Association, 1969, p. 1.

David, John P. *Corporations.* New York: Capricorn Books, 1961, p. 148.

Duckat, Walter. *Beggar to King.* Garden City, N.Y.: Doubleday, 1968, pp. XV-XVI.

Durkheim, Emile. *The Division of Labor in Society.* New York: Free Press, 1933, p. 11.

Frankfort, Henri. *The Birth of Civilization in the Near East.* Garden City, N.Y.: Doubleday, 1956, p. 69.

Landtman, Gunnar. *The Origin of Inequality of the Social Classes.* Chicago: University of Chicago Press, 1938, p. 88.

Perlman, David. "The Surge of Public Employee Unionism." *American Federationist* 78 (June 1971): 1.

Tyler, Gus. *The Political Imperative, The Corporate Character of Unions.* New York: Macmillan, 1968, chap. 3.

Reading 2

Teacher Negotiation: History and Comment

Ross A. Engel

Boards of education and school superintendents have to appreciate the context within which teachers are now developing militant organizations to promote collective bargaining. The teachers' position today is reminiscent of labor in the period prior to the passage of the Wagner Act. In private industry before 1935, workers had to strike for recognition, but after 1935 the National Labor Relations Board developed machinery in which petitions, elections, determination of the appropriate bargaining unit, and finally recognition became a substitute for the strike. Now, basically, the only time strikes make the news is when contracts expire and the unions declare, "no contract, no work."

In the public schools, machinery has not yet been created to accommodate mature collective negotiations to the needs of employees. However, machinery is rapidly being developed in many states which will serve to take the pressure off of board members and school administrators, who at present are required to develop their own election and recognition procedures. This direction will be par-

Reprinted by permission from *Journal of Law and Education* 1, no. 3 (July 1972), pp. 487-95.

ticularly important to the school administrator who finds himself caught between the opposing forces of the American Federation of Teachers (AFT), AFL-CIO, pressuring for collective bargaining, and the National Education Association (NEA) desiring professional negotiations.

Teachers are concerned with many of the changes that are occurring in the educational picture. They want protection from physical assault; they do not want neighborhood community groups to run their local school; and they want the board of education to maintain uniformity and standardization in personnel assignments, pay, and working conditions. They want an income adequate to send their own children to college, without the need to "moonlight."

The teacher is now mobilizing collective strength through either the NEA or the AFT. Teachers demand an opportunity to improve their professional as well as economic status and working conditions. Through their employee organizations, they hope to find a nearly equal voice with boards of education and school superintendents in developing educational policies. They now insist on a full right to bargain on these items at negotiation sessions. No longer are they satisfied to petition the board for a *chance* to be heard. Teacher organizations use bargaining power to reach settlements, including threats of strike, sanctions, and the employment of other techniques to effect a written contract.

Teachers have had years of employment under paternalistic conditions and have participated in "company union" types of organizations in which superintendents, principals, and supervisors were in the same "bargaining unit." As evidence of teachers' desire to establish an identity, administrators are being asked to leave the "teacher" organizations.

Because of the dynamic changes in the educational scene, teachers will continue to become more militant and join unions as long as community issues create unrest in the schools and threaten security. Evidence is available that public school teachers want to take a hand in decision making as it affects their assignments, conditions of work, and their professional futures. They are not asking to run the schools, but they want their views heard and heeded.

In many cities where school authorities have tended to underestimate mounting anxiety and hostility, teachers have resorted to strikes, sanctions, boycotts, walkouts, and other means of withdrawing services. Because of this, the AFT and the NEA have both abandoned their earlier positions, a reluctance to use the extreme bargaining power, strike, in the negotiation of new contracts. Whether the technique is called a strike or "sanction," the results are the same. The lessons learned during the last five years of strikes by teachers is that threatening employees with injunctions, or calling them disloyal or "in violation" of the laws, has had little impact so far as prevention of strikes or withdrawals from work.

At present, the National Education Association and its state and local affiliates are competing with the expanding American Federation of Teachers for recognition of exclusive negotiation rights in many school districts. These two organizations, which started out as friendly rivals around the time of World War I, have now embarked upon active and often bitter competing organizing campaigns. This change in attitude has occurred since the AFT affiliate, the United Federation of Teachers of New York City, was the victor over the NEA in a major election held in December, 1961. That action placed approximately 45,000 teachers in the AFT camp and triggered the AFT to other victories over the NEA in Philadelphia, Detroit, and other major cities.

At the present time, NEA has over 1,000,000 members, most of whom are classroom teachers, but it also includes some administrators and principals. The AFT has more than 250,000 members and does not permit the membership of administrative and supervisory personnel. The different approaches result in somewhat different strategies of negotiation, as well as divergent viewpoints concerning the role of the superintendent in negotiations.

The NEA views the role of the superintendent as supplying information and data impartially to both the NEA and the board of education as discussions are launched leading to a contract. The AFT, on the other hand, looks to the superintendent of schools as the chief administrative officer of the organization and bargains with him as the representative of the board. This is probably better, since it prevents the board from actually becoming involved in administrative functions. The board can establish the parameters for negotiation and reserve final decisions.

The NEA was founded originally in 1852 as the National Teachers Association. Fifty years later it still had only about 2,000 teachers as members. After World War I, school superintendents began to pay attention to NEA's membership problems, because teachers appeared to be growing more interested in the affairs of the American Federation of Teachers, which had been founded in 1916.

With the help of school superintendents, memberships in NEA increased from about 10,000 at the end of World War I to 120,000 in 1922. Thereafter, growth was steady, except for the depression years. In the 1950s, the average gain in membership was about 40,000 per year.

The NEA is a strong organization with a headquarters staff in Washington, D.C. It has close ties with the United States Office of Education and with state departments of education through its affiliate state organizations.

Since the 1961 victory of the AFT in New York City, the NEA has begun to work diligently in order to gain recognition from school districts as the bargaining agent for teachers. It has begun to employ the same tactics in bargaining and organizing used by the AFT since 1960, despite the fact that a few years ago NEA described these same techniques as the "rankest unionism."

NEA still prides itself on the fact that it is a professional organization, not a union, although it is beginning to act very much like a strong union. NEA describes its negotiations as professional and denies that it is engaging in collective bargaining of the type that generally characterizes the activities in private industry operating under the Taft-Hartley Act.

The NEA appears to be playing a dual role in the face of the growing strength of the AFT. It tries to be both a professional- and union-type organization. It now permits its locals to make decisions excluding administrative staff from the collective agreement, despite the fact that principals and administrators are generally NEA members.

While collective bargaining for public employees is relatively new, union membership for teachers dates back to 1916 when the American Federation of Teachers was organized and became affiliated with the American Federation of Labor. In the early days of the AFT's existence, NEA was not unfriendly. Members in both groups thought that the role of the NEA should be concerned with the professional side of teachers' activities—how to improve teaching —while the AFT should concern itself primarily with improving the economic status of teachers.

During World War I, teachers flocked to join the new union and by 1919 membership had increased to 10,000. NEA leaders saw this gain in AFT membership as a threat to their organization. Beginning in 1920, many school district superintendents insisted that job applicants join the NEA as a condition of employment. As a result of this pressure, AFT membership declined from 10,000 to 3,500 in 1927. During the depression years, membership again rose as teachers worried about insecurity and arbitrary discharge. During World War II, the American Federation of Teachers took resolute action to drive Communists out of their ranks. After World War II, teachers continued to join the AFT in greater numbers and by 1958 membership had increased to 55,000.

The founders of the AFT originally believed that public school teachers should not be permitted to strike. Instead, they offered their members the support of organized labor and assured them that allies among labor unions would offset the loss of bargaining power because of the denial of the right to strike. More recently, AFT has attempted to win closed shop agreements. In the working agreement with the Butte, Montana, Board of Education, an appropriate clause was developed, reading in part:

Any teacher who fails to sign a contract which includes the provisions in this Union Security Clause and who fails to comply with the clause shall be discharged on the written request of the Union . . . except any teacher who now has tenure shall not be discharged, but shall not receive any of the benefits or salary increase negotiated, but shall continue to be employed without contract from year to year on the same terms and conditions as such teacher was employed during the year 1955-1956. (Department of Health, Education, and Welfare 1964)

When subjected to court review, the clause was thrown out by the State Supreme Court of Montana in 1959.

The present AFT position on use of the strike as a bargaining tool is this:

. . . numerous boards of education have refused to grant the right to a representative election in accordance with established policy . . . whereas, even after the establishment of collective bargaining, certain school boards often fail to bargain in good faith, therefore, be it resolved: that the AFT recognize the right of locals to strike under circumstances. (Forty-Seventh Annual Convention of the American Federation of Teachers)

The NEA originally condemned strikes and, as recently as 1962, stated its opposition to them. In 1965, NEA deleted references to strikes and softened its policy against them. In the NEA convention in July 1967, the board of directors stated that the "NEA will in the future give full support to striking local affiliates."

From a practical point of view, the power to strike appears to be vested in the AFT or NEA local chapter. Despite the fact that the NEA condemned an earlier strike undertaken by the AFT in New York City, it failed to criticize the action of its own affiliate in Newark, when in February 1966 the Newark Teachers Association struck in the face of a court order. While the power to strike is vested in a local, the NEA nationally still controls the use of sanctions, mass resignations, and blackballing a district. An example was the NEA invoking statewide sanctions in Florida in 1967, followed by state-wide mass resignations.

It becomes necessary, no matter what a person's view of either the NEA or AFT, to take a look at just what is meant by the term "collective bargaining," heard frequently in the news these days. Can it be employed in a public sector such as education? Is it legal for school districts or boards of education to participate?

Those who question the right of public school teachers to negotiate and bargain collectively most frequently express their basic objection by contending that negotiation and collective bargaining constitute a serious invasion of school board authority. To understand this objection, it is vitally important to understand that the terms negotiations and collective bargaining have a legal connotation much different than merely providing various groups the opportunity to appear before or, in some other fashion, to present their requests to a school board. School boards have permitted this type of activity for many years.

In order to react to the validity of the assertion that collective bargaining does constitute a serious invasion of school board authority, it seems necessary to outline fully what collective bargaining means legally. What constitutes good faith collective bargaining has been determined to a large extent by the federal courts and the National Labor Relations Board in interpreting section 8(d) of the National Labor Relations Act (NLRA) which by its specific language imposes a duty on employers and unions to "meet at reasonable times and confer in good faith with respect to wages, hours and other terms and conditions of employment." It goes on to explain that "such obligation does not compel either party to agree to a proposal or require the making of a concession." (See Cohen 1966.)

It is possible that, if state statutory language differs from that of the NLRA, there could be an interpretation of good faith bargaining somewhat different than the description which follows. It seems certain, however, that no state legislation calling for negotiation will require, by way of bargaining approach, more than does the NLRA and the decisions interpreting the responsibility imposed by the Act.

Good faith bargaining often does require, in reaction to demands that are not acceptable, the offering of reasons for rejection and some counter proposals. It requires recognition by both parties, not merely formal but real, that collective bargaining must be a shared process in which each party has a right to play an active role. In this area there has been a recent interesting development. In December 1964, the NLRB in the *General Electric Company* case (150 NLRB no. 36, 57 LRRM 1491) dealt with what is familiarly known as the Boulwarism approach.

In this instance, the employer listened to and analyzed the demands and arguments offered by the union, and then made an offer to it, which included everything the employer found to be warranted. Nothing was held back for later negotiations, and the company took the position that the offer would not be changed unless new information indicated that adjustments were warranted. The company did not say "take it or leave it" but did make it clear it would not change its position unless significant new information was presented. It made it clear that it would take a strike rather than make any change.

The NLRB condemned this type of bargaining on the ground that it was a mere formality and transformed the role of the employer to merely that of an adviser. Collective bargaining does not mean that the public employer must ultimately capitulate to demands. It does not mean that there is a necessity to make some concessions as an outgrowth of every demand. Good faith bargaining does not sanction an administrative body or a court undertaking to exercise its wisdom to determine if a particular proposal was reasonable or unreasonable.

The United States Supreme Court, in interpreting the meaning of good faith bargaining under the National Labor Relations Act, has recognized three categories of proposals (*NLRB v. Wooster Division of Borg Warner Corp.* (1958) 356 US 342):

1. Those that are illegal and, therefore, cannot be bargained about.
2. Those that may be bargained about if the parties voluntarily wish to do so.
3. Those that are mandatory and must be bargained about.

Proposals that come within the category of wages, hours, and other terms and conditions of employment fall within the mandatory area. Certainly falling within the conditions of employment would be such things as assignments during out-of-school hours to supervision of extracurricular events, class loads, class size, use of teacher assistants, and rest periods.

It would appear that decisions on curriculum content could technically be viewed as remaining solely the prerogative of administration and the school board. In this respect, however, it would seem wise for the school board not to adopt too literal an approach. It would probably be better to adopt the attitude that bargaining does not necessarily mean capitulation. This approach in the long run would probably cause no harm, and to allow discussions could perhaps be of benefit to both parties.

It is significant that the United States Supreme Court recognized that a party cannot be forced to bargain on certain matters over which neither party has jurisdiction or control. This principle answers objections of those who argue that public employee bargaining is blocked by statutes which may impose budget limitations, by such things as state salary laws and state tenure, retirement and pension laws. The principle recognizes that it would be improper to ignore the problem of public employee bargaining colliding with existing statutes. This recognition, however, requires an appreciation of what it means to collide with the statutes. For example, even if there are state tenure laws setting forth reasons for "for cause" discharge, it would still be possible to bargain for an intermediate grievance procedure.

In determining whether there has been good faith bargaining, it must be recognized that it is necessary to evaluate the facts. This can be difficult, because it requires an evaluation of the parties' attitudes as reflected in their conduct during negotiation. In connection with this, it is significant to note the comments of Chairman McCulloch of the National Labor Relations Board:

The decision does not hold that an employer may not after appropriate bargaining make a fair and final offer to the union representing his employees. It does not hold that an employer may not criticize union leaders for proposals. It does not hold that an employer may not communicate with his employees. Those who tell you differently do you a disservice. (1965 Annual Conference of Texas Industry)

The evaluation of good faith has meant that certain types of conduct are held to be sufficient of themselves to establish a lack of good faith bargaining. A refusal to discuss or provide data necessary to intelligent discussions of a subject within the mandatory area of bargaining is an example. So, also, is insistence upon including in a contract a proposal that is outside the scope of mandatory bargaining. It is apparent that when the school board undertakes collective bargaining, as defined, it undertakes burdens which it does not assume if it does not bargain collectively. The assumption of these burdens does not mean that the board has delegated away its authority. When employers were first confronted with the statutory necessity of bargaining collectively, they complained that they were being forced to delegate their authority. The courts did not agree with them. The courts recognized that they did assume additional burdens, but they still retained ultimate authority to make final decisions.

In the public employee field, the state legislative bodies determine if there shall be bargaining, and if it shall be permissive or mandatory. It represents a decision that employee relations will be benefited. It does not appear that this decision can be denied through the argument that the provision for bargaining will result in forcing a school board to delegate away its authority or abrogate its responsibility in any way.

In the public employee field, the push of employees to join employee organizations, whose goals are betterment of employment conditions, has been gaining momentum since the end of World War II. Such employees have not automatically been given the same rights as industrial workers. Hurdles have been erected by judicial decisions and in some cases by legislators.

A legislative hurdle which is fast disappearing is the denial of the right to join an employee organization or union on the ground of inconsistency with government employment. To the extent that this attitude still exists, it would seem possible to challenge it as a First Amendment constitutional interference with the right of freedom to assemble. A greater obstacle today is the denial of the opportunity to bargain collectively.

The only logical justification for prohibiting public employees from joining employee organizations which have goals similar to labor unions would seem to be a finding that such organizations generally seek to force their employee members to do something which is inconsistent with the position of the employee as a government worker. This is generally not true. The arguments in support of the attitude that the public employer should not be required to bargain collectively with public employees can be summarized as follows:

1. The fixing of conditions of work in the public service is a legislative function.

2. Neither the executive nor legislative body may delegate such function to any outside group.

3. The legislature or executive body must be free to change the conditions of employment at any time.

These arguments are based upon a misconception of what is actually meant by good faith collective bargaining, as it has been defined.

Any discussion concerning the right of teachers to engage in collective bargaining should not end without some mention of the legality of public employees' use of certain activities intended to exert pressure upon school boards, with the objective of attaining certain contract goals—primarily through the right to strike. To date the judicial position on this method of exerting pressure is uniform. All courts and authorities agree that the right does not exist. As far as striking against school boards is concerned, there is an additional point besides the illegality stated by courts. Teachers cannot forget that they work in an area where it is of the utmost importance that young people be encouraged to respect the ultimate authority of school personnel. Even with good cause, teachers risk loss of this respect when they go on strike so long as strikes are illegal for them.

There currently remains the question as to whether, other than through fact finding, there is any effective pressure that teachers can exert in place of the strike. The NEA has proposed sanctions. Under this suggestion teacher organizations encourage teachers not to return a signed contract, and advise teachers not to accept jobs in the troubled area. These actions are viewed as only minimally effective.

As we look to the future, it definitely appears that the tide is running in favor of granting public employees more bargaining rights, and that this trend cannot be stopped for long by school boards. As a result, boards of education might very well stop trying to label provisions for collective bargaining illegal and turn their attention toward working out procedures which will make of public employee bargaining something which is beneficial. They must realize that there are legitimate pressures in collective bargaining. Although the pressure does not require capitulation, it should create an atmosphere which will insure give-and-take in the form of responses to demands, and will often result in counterproposals and full explanations when demands are rejected. This process has worked in the private sector and is calculated to produce some logical and positive compromises.

Finally, it seems important to draw to the attention of those school boards that feel collective bargaining means capitulation, the philosophy expressed by the United States Supreme Court in a 1964 decision (*Fiberboard Paper Products Corp. v. NLRB* (1964) 379 US 203). The Court stated that collective bargaining does not connote capitulation and that it has a very important function. The Court commented that although it is not possible to say whether a satisfactory solution can be reached, the national labor policy is founded upon a determination that the chances are good enough to warrant subjecting issues to the process of collective bargaining.

If boards of education engage in collective bargaining and work out satisfactory procedures, there is every reason to believe that there will be an improved climate within which better education for children can be attained.

References

Cohen, Sanford. *Labor in the United States* (2d ed.). Columbus, Ohio: Charles E. Merrill, 1966.
Department of Health, Education, and Welfare. *Teachers Negotiate with Their School Boards.* Washington, D.C.: The Department, 1964. OE-23036, Bulletin no. 40.

Reading 3

The Need for Limitation Upon the Scope of Negotiations in Public Education, I

John H. Metzler

Introduction

Collective negotiation for public employees, which is now common in over three-fifths of the states, is here to stay. This is important to note in any discussion of collective bargaining in education, in order to ensure that there is no intent to reverse the evolution of negotiations. Educational reform must take place if schools are to serve large sectors of the nation and win the support they need. This, too, is important to note, so that educational change does not become an innocent victim in a struggle for power. However, educational reform is much more apt to be restricted by bargaining—not encouraged. We are in the midst of critical changes for decision making in setting policy for and managing the schools, but by collective bargaining we stand more chance of devising restrictive work rules and protections against pupil contact than we do of improving education.

There is no question that teachers, through their organizations, ought to or will be involved in decision making about educational

Reprinted by permission from *Journal of Law and Education* 2, no. 1 (January 1973), pp. 139-54.

reform. A good mechanism can be devised for this, but the pragmatics of collective bargaining dictate that it is not collective negotiations.

Obviously, a realignment of power is occurring between teachers and administrators. However, it must not negate their basic roles. There is a redistribution of functions taking place and a change from unilateral to bilateral decision making. Even if roles are being redefined, though, superintendents and principals must remain the managers—the executives who carry out policy. Policy should be recommended by faculty, or faculty and administration together, and approved by the board of education. However, it cannot safely be left to the art of compromise, to collective bargaining.

The educational process will be better served if the scope of bargaining among boards of education and teachers' organizations is limited. Even if this contention is incorrect, far less damage will occur as a result of limitations than the damage that will occur if the contention proves correct and there are no limitations.

Regardless of theory to the contrary, once a benefit accrues to a sizable number of members of the bargaining unit from an existing contract, it is most difficult to change that benefit in a subsequent contract. Thus, with an unlimited scope for negotiation, almost irreparable harm could occur before the mistake can be remedied.

The natural consultation and involvement that flows from collective bargaining can accelerate teacher involvement to aid a school system. However, limited scope of bargaining can avoid the stifling effect of restrictive work rules and inordinate unnecessary expense that are likely consequences of the usual pattern of teacher negotiations.

The basic question involving the scope of negotiations in collective bargaining is whether the interests of children are served by the active intervention of collective bargaining in program development and educational processes. To resolve this, several factors must be considered in order to determine logically the proper scope of bargaining.

The Imposition Upon Education of the Private Sector Model of Collective Bargaining

"Negotiations" could be defined as mutual discussion and arrangement of the terms of a transaction or agreement. "Mutual discussion" implies a meeting between two or more parties. Where do the parties come from; what are the events and the causes of their coming together?

There was a long period in American history during which the total forces of society—the government, the law and the courts—combined in an attempt to stamp out and stop the trade union movement. Workers were jailed, leaders were hanged, police brutality was common; yet the movement was not wiped out. In the next period, government accepted the existence of trade unions, but the force of law rested with management. Although the period was marked by wholesale jailing of workers and their leaders and often the use of brute force, the movement remained in existence.

The third period began with the advent of the Wagner Act of 1935, which required that management negotiate with unions chosen by the workers. Its effect was not evolutionary, it was convulsive. Bloodshed, murder, conspiracy, all condoned by the elite leaders of the nation, had failed to stop America's workers from building a union movement.

There are, broadly, two types of unions. One is the craft union, with examples such as the bricklayers, sheet metal workers, and painters. It is based on a geographic area. Frequently, it is stronger than any or many of the individual employers comprising its jurisdiction. There is apt to be a floating labor supply, with a hiring hall operated by the union. Rather severe competition among the employer elements in this group is likely. Interestingly enough, this is the type of union upon which the American Federation of Labor was built and which, regardless of the force of government exerted against it, remained in existence.

The second type is the industrial union. Although it was not born with the passage of the Wagner Act of 1935, its growth was so dramatic once the government guaranteed that negotiations must take place, that its growth is often measured from 1935. It can be visualized as being contained within the four walls of a factory, its local leadership is apt to be unpaid, there is a stability to the work force, and less power of the leader over the members than in a craft union. There seems little doubt that this type of union required the Wagner Act for its growth and, in many cases, probably requires the Wagner Act to continue its existence.

The collective bargaining process rests upon these two types of unions and their power relationship with their employers. How does the process function? Visualize two wheels which exert pressure upon each other. Each has a source of power which causes it to operate; each has a form of friction which restrains it. The grinding wheels operate against each other, resulting in a jointly produced product different than that which began the journey between them.

Contract negotiations function in the same manner. A variety of forces flow through and are exerted upon each party, creating pressures which result in a contract. The pressure is the essential point, not the discussion nor the logic. Occasionally, if the existing pressure fails to produce agreement, a strike, a lockout, a boycott or some other form of additional pressure is introduced into the situation.

Negotiations take place only between equals. These equals might be Russia and the United States, husband and wife, or union and management. For negotiations to occur there are two essential requirements: (1) the parties must be, legally or otherwise, equals and (2) each party must be able to utilize pressure to induce the other to compromise.

The settlement of disputes among collectively organized equals inevitably is an adversary relationship, regardless of protestations of desire to the contrary. This is the process which was lifted from the private sector of the economy and, occasionally with modification, imposed almost haphazardly upon the public sector.

Obviously, the model does not work equally well, nor does it exert the same pressure, in all segments of the private economy. There are those industries in which the union is dominant and others where management is dominant. The effects of the imperfections of the model in the private economy are costly. Prices may become high and consumers stop buying. There can be a job loss. However, in the apparent majority of cases, wages do increase, the standard of living of the union member does become better and, with the aid and assistance of technology and increased demand, jobs are increased.

This model does not fit as well the public sector of the economy, however. The effect of imperfection in the model in education is magnified because it has immediate community-wide repercussions in every instance. In the private economy the effect is economic and often rather removed from the community as a whole.

What Does the Law Say?

The New Jersey statute is much like that of most states having a statute and provides that the majority representative of the employees and the designated representative of the public employer must negotiate in good faith with respect to "terms and conditions of employment." What these "terms and conditions" embrace is not specified in the law.

In New Jersey, the law does not expressly vest in its public employee relations agency the power to decide what are negotiable items and the courts have clearly established this lack of authority (NJSA 34, 13A-5.3). Hence, disputes about what is negotiable must be left to the courts to determine. The courts have yet to come up with definitive rulings. They have established no guidelines.

For all practical purposes, public employers have to battle it out by themselves to determine what is or is not negotiable. The same "no-man's land" prevails in the other states with comparable administrative boards. Public employers and employee organizations must negotiate and bargain in good faith. That's about all most statutes really say. What issues are negotiable and what constitutes good faith bargaining remain in most jurisdictions to be hammered out on a case basis.

In each of the states where making and maintaining contractual relations is a statute's goal, determination of negotiable issues becomes important. As to these laws, it is necessary to look mainly for the exclusions. A few spell them out. Thus, with respect to state employees in Hawaii (GERR RF* 51:2011-2016, Act 171, 1970, as amended, §9), Vermont (GERR RF 51:5411-5417, ch. 27, 1969, as amended, §§904(b), 905(a)), and Washington (GERR RF 51:5611-5613, §§41.56.00-41.56.900, ch. 108, 1967, as amended, §41.56.100), civil service merit systems are declared non-negotiable. A few state laws do the reverse by asserting non-negotiable management rights and prerogatives. New Hampshire's law has such reservations (GERR RF 51:3811-3812, ch. 98-c, 1969, §98-C:7). Delaware forbids negotiating for binding grievance arbitration by teachers' organizations and boards of education (GERR RF 51:1712-1713, ch. 40, title 14, 1969, §4008(c)).

Keep in mind that the two largest teachers' organizations contend that any school board policy or practice even remotely affecting teachers' interests and livelihoods is or should be negotiable. Where, as in most states, the statutes are silent, bitter disputes as to negotiability usually must end up in the courts. If laws are not revised to

---

*Government Employee Relations Report, Reference File.

restrict the scope of bargaining, anticipate a welter of court decisions as time marches on.

Administrative agencies can say with authority only what the high courts of each state let them say. Hence, in New Jersey, by judicial edict (*Burlington County Evergreen Park Mental Hospital v. Dorothy Cooper and the Public Employment Relations Commission* (Supreme Court of New Jersey, July 24, 1970)) the Public Employment Relations Commission can decide nothing about permissible, mandatory, or prohibited issues for collective bargaining. Factfinders assigned by the state agency are, at the time of this writing, forbidden by the agency from issuing a recommendation on any item not in the contract and declared by one of the parties to be a non-negotiable item.

The Labor Mediation Board of Michigan sanctions union security clauses such as the agency shop or a modified union shop even in education and gives them precedence over tenure laws (*Southgate Community School District and Linda Morrison* (Michigan Employment Relations Commission, Case no. C69 B-18, Feb. 6, 1970; on appeal to Supreme Court)). New Hampshire, whose law does not apply to teachers, also sanctions union security clauses for other public employees (GERR RF 51:3811-3812, ch. 98-C, 1969, §98-C:31, IV), as does Delaware (GERR RF 51:1711-1712, ch. 13, title 19, Del. Code §§1301-1313).

The New York State statute permits their agency to adjudicate negotiable items (GERR RF 51:4111-4119, §108, §205.3(g)). There is one notable decision which, in effect, states that layoffs attributable to lack of funds do not have to be negotiated (*City School District of the City of New Rochelle and New Rochelle Federation of Teachers, Local 280, AFT* (Public Employment Relations Board of the State of New York, Case no. U-0240, U-0249, U-0251, July 1, 1971 and July 29, 1971)). The impact is, however, negotiable. The New York agency has also ruled (in the same case) that a local school board decision to curtail staff did not constitute a negotiable item.

A recent decision of the New York State Court of Appeals left the door almost wide open as to what has to be negotiated (*Board of Education of Union Free School District no. 3 of Town of Huntington v. Associated Teachers of Huntington, Inc.* (State of New York Court of Appeals, March 16, 1972)). Its gist: that any matter connected with terms and conditions of employment must be regarded as a negotiable issue unless some state statute contains an explicit prohibition against bargaining on it. The court rejected the opposite contention in the case before—that is, that a public agency is prohibited from negotiating in any subject unless the law expressly requires it to negotiate.

Apart from this generalization, the court addressed itself to the issues that were raised by the local school board as being non-negotiable. These were:

1. Board reimbursement for costs of replacing teachers' glasses, dentures, etc., lost or damaged through the course of employment;

2. Reimbursement for loss or damage to clothing or other personal effects, except automobiles;

3. Reimbursement of 50 percent of tuition or costs for outside courses related to teachers' assigned subjects;

4. A special automatic salary increase effective for the last year prior to retirement; and

5. Arbitration of disputes arising over the discipline or discharge of tenure teachers.

The court decided that every one of these was a proper subject for mandatory negotiation.

Few state or local agencies have built-in revenue producing functions. To get money to finance the payrolls, most are dependent on the legislatures of county or local governments. Consequently, approval of the agency having authority over their appropriations is frequently necessary to implement the wage, salary, and other economic provisions of labor agreements. There are the usual exceptions. In Hawaii, for example, where there are statewide negotiations with an association representing all public school teachers, salaries and fringe benefits are the only contract provisions necessitating legislative approval (Act 171, 1970, as amended, §10(b)). Connecticut requires that a school board contract be submitted to the municipal government for possible veto before it can finally be accepted (GERR RF 51:1614-1616, title 10, ch. 166, 1958, as amended, §10-153(d)). There are others.

An occasional state law, such as Pennsylvania's, attempts to define mandatory and permissive bargainable issues (GERR RF

51:4711-4719, 1970, art. VII). A recent labor board decision further spelled out many items (*Pennsylvania Labor Relations Board v. State College Area School District* (Case no. PERA-C-929-C, Oct. 14, 1971)). This was then changed somewhat by a later appeal to the same labor board, which had changed personnel (*Pennsylvania Labor Relations Board v. State College Area School Directors* (Case no. PERA-C-29-C, June 26, 1972)).

The law applying to the scope of involvement of teachers varies widely. In the state of Washington, negotiations are mandated over "policies relating to but not limited to curriculum, textbook selection, in-service training, student teacher programs" (GERR RF 51:5613-5614, § 28.72.010-.090, ch. 28.72, revised Code of Washington, § 28.72.030). In Minnesota "education policies" are excluded from the topics of negotiation (GERR RF 51:3211-3219, SB 4, 1971, as amended, § 179.50-179.58, and § 148.21-148.24, § 3(18)). There is the broad middle category of state statutes, New Jersey's among them, and these statutes are most susceptible to dispute because of their ambiguity. In fact, this ambiguity has led to the calendar being declared both negotiable (*Burlington County College Faculty Association v. Board of Trustees, Burlington County College* (Superior Court of New Jersey, May 25, 1972) and non-negotiable (*Carl Moldovan et al. v. Board of Education of the Township of Hamilton* (Decision of N.J. Commissioner of Education, June 8, 1971).

What Has Actually Occurred in Negotiations?

As a practical matter, what has happened is that to some degree almost anything is negotiable. Recognition of a union means much more than a polite acknowledgment of its existence. Unions have been created to do something about something. Their right to function has been held by the courts to be guaranteed by the First Amendment of the United States Constitution, and the Fourteenth Amendment prohibits any state from enacting a law prohibiting a labor organization from functioning at all.

This inherent right of existence, however, does not vest in any union the power to demand and get its own way. Indeed, the term, "to negotiate," means to seek rather than to command. "Meeting and conferring" with employers are all that some public employees' organizations are allowed to do under a number of state laws. By

such meetings and conferences the organizations are in fact negotiating, even though nothing concrete eventuates.

Some employer agencies still take the cavalier attitude that few
of the typical union demands are negotiable. When they do so, they
are dead wrong most of the time.

In public employment, teachers' organizations have been leaders
in organized labor's fight to open up the range of bargainable issues
to include almost every conceivable item that would even remotely
affect their terms and conditions of employment. Many observers
believe their crusade is intended to make them partners in public
education and to destroy the existing employer-employee relationship. It is not uncommon for a teachers' organization to persist in
demanding an equal voice in the selection of school principals and
superintendents, that no policy of the board be changed without
negotiation, and that all matters of curriculum be negotiated.

Regardless of law, there are three basic areas in a contract:
money, managerial decision making, and the rights of the parties.
The more the public employees are comparable to private industry
blue-collar workers, the more their demands and consequent agreements concentrate on money and the rights of the parties. The more
"professional" the public employee, the more managerial decision
making is demanded. In a tax conscious society, the public employer
is faced with a dilemma of higher cost or loss of managerial control.
His dilemma is especially acute when he is offered an opportunity to
trade one off for the other.

What an employees' organization may propose in the way of
model agreement is one thing. What is finally negotiated into an actual agreement by a local bargaining unit may bear little perceptible
resemblance to the original model. Periodically, a potent state teachers' association published a working paper containing what is characterized as a sample agreement. A recent edition details thirty-seven
articles and five appendices, using a total of seventy-one single-spaced
pages. In addition, this model agreement has an index that refers to
633 separate and distinct items, ranging from academic freedom to
censorship, from curriculum improvement to class size, from teaching hours and teaching load to workshops—not to mention salaries,
economic benefits, leaves, and a variety of special payments.

You could look long and hard to find any negotiated teachers'
agreement in that state or anywhere that covers all the main issues

set forth in the sample agreement. The list does, however, provide a succinct outline of what one major organization considers proper subjects for collective negotiation. As typical clauses, proposals included in the sample agreement range from minute trivialities to issues of great import. Two trivialities: x number of days off with pay to attend the marriage of a member of the immediate family; private closet space with lock and key to store coats, overshoes, and personal articles. Two major issues: proposed reduction in number of teachers must be negotiated, with the association right to veto the reduction implied; the current agreement must be reopened for renegotiation of any section when any new state or federal funds are allocated to the school district. There is a considerable difference between the hopes and realities when one inspects what the state organization proposes and what the local organization secures. Manifestly, the local associations either do not try to negotiate every item proposed by their parent or, if they did try on some items, they must have been unsuccessful.

The danger that is repeatedly appearing in contracts is that a naive board of education will agree to a definite contract commitment which it cannot fulfill. In a New Jersey city, the contract contained an article, reading:

The goal for class size will be to maintain academic classes not in excess of 25 pupils. Immediate steps will be taken to assure that no academic class will be maintained at a level in excess of 30 pupils for the school year 1970-71.

At the beginning of the new school year, some classes still had more than thirty students. The teachers' association grieved, charging an explicit contract violation. Its grievance went to an arbitrator under a clause providing for final and binding arbitrable awards relating to contract interpretation.

The school board's defense was that the class size numbers were only supposed to provide guidelines pointing to the ultimate target of classes with no more than twenty-five students and that it was impossible, without additional space, to comply with the guidelines.

The arbitrator ruled against the board. His award stated, in substance, that the phraseology of the class size article was clear and definite. Accordingly, he could not look elsewhere to determine an alleged intent contrary to the precise contract language. The arbitrator ordered the board to comply fully with its class size article within forty-five days after the issuance of his decision (*Trenton Education Association and Trenton Board of Education* (AAA Case no. 14-39-0203-71-J, Jan. 14, 1972)). The arbitrator's award is now being appealed to the courts.

The issue is not the arbitrator's award, since, under the terms of the contract, he was probably correct. The issue is the fact that the board, inexperienced in negotiations, made a commitment which it could not keep.

In another instance, the teachers' organization successfully negotiated a complicated system of combined verbal and written tests to qualify persons for appointment as principal. Selection of individuals for promotion was to be made from among the top few names on the qualified list. Soon thereafter, there was an outbreak of violence in the city and great racial unrest. One of the issues was that of insufficient black principals. The board, when it next appointed principals, appointed several blacks who were not at the agreed upon place on the list.

The teachers' organization appealed the action. Eventually, the commissioner of education, later upheld by the courts, ruled that a written contract between a teachers' organization and a board of education is not enforceable under such circumstances (*Porcelli v. Titus* (App. Div. 1970) 108 NJ Super 301, cert. denied (1970) 55 NJ 310).

Fast moving community events created a situation in which it was unwise to wait until a lengthy contract expired in the hope of renegotiating it. The potential harm to the educational process was judged to be greater from community antagonisms than from a broken agreement with the teachers' organization. Was it? No one can say with certainty, but a scope of bargaining limited strictly to salaries and economic fringe benefits would aid in avoiding this type of confrontation.

Another primary problem, not considered when the private sector model was imposed upon public education, is the style of negotiation necessary.

By its very nature, a board of education is a public body comprised of individuals who function individually. As a vote is necessary, sufficient numbers of the individuals join and comprise a majority for that specific decision. For that decision, those individuals are the board.

When this board then becomes involved in negotiation, the negotiator for the board must, of necessity, receive inconsistent or indefinite direction by this group of individual public bodies coming together in different majorities on different issues. He can have only problematic confidence with regard to goals, strategies, and tactics. Both the teachers' organization and the board require a form of political approval for the negotiated agreement.

It requires a skillful, experienced negotiator to function under such circumstances. Individual board members, because they believe it to be their responsibility to the citizens, attempt to conduct negotiations themselves, without the experience required to make them a match for the negotiator from the teachers' organization.

With an unlimited scope for bargaining, effective management of the schools is diluted, often with catastrophic consequences. If the primary consideration of the law is the education of youth, the scope should be limited to an area in which the board member can effectively function in carrying out the statutory mandate of a board of education.

What Has the Law Failed To Consider?

Generally, the law has failed to recognize the differences existing between the public and private sectors of the economy as it has imposed the private sector collective bargaining model upon the public sector. These differences have often been commented upon, but their effect has been underestimated.

The lack of a profit motive reduces immeasurably the inducement to compromise, both on the part of the board and on the part of the teachers. Of the four states which permit teachers a limited right to strike—Alaska, Hawaii, Pennsylvania, and Vermont—only Pennsylvania, with over 500 school districts, provides the laboratory conditions to study the legal strike (art. X).

Pennsylvania law also limits the scope of negotiations (art. VII). In other states, which either limit the scope of negotiations or permit it to be clouded by ambiguities, there is no right to strike, but strikes occur. The penalties for the illegal strike range from mild to excessively harsh. Regardless of the degree of penalty, it cannot but inhibit the desire to strike. Under these circumstances, it would be quite unsound to equate a limited scope of negotiations with strike potentiality. Strike potentiality must exist whenever the adversary relationship of collective bargaining exists.

This is not intended as an argument against either collective bargaining or the right to strike. It is intended to dispose of the false argument that an unlimited scope of negotiations will reduce strikes.

In education, the law has failed to recognize the monolithic structure of the organizations competing to represent the teachers, compared to the uniquely individual existence of each of the many boards of education. When negotiations begin, the teachers' organizations are far more ready than the boards and consistently remain ahead. Thus, many state legislatures have inadvertently provided the impetus for creating a partnership to control education—a partnership composed of a teachers' organization and a local board of education. However, the very nature of one partner, the teachers' organization, is one of state and national direction, while the other partner remains local in character.

This cannot be equated with union-management relations in the private sector. The "partnership" in the private sector is related only to the subjects for bargaining as established by case-by-case-decisions of the National Labor Relations Board. In the public sector, the scope of negotiations may include almost any subject the teachers' organization can prevail upon the board to bargain. And the boards, cost conscious and tax supported, practice the false economy of performing their own negotiations—in far too many cases committing themselves to agreements they cannot keep, providing for a partnership in controlling education rather than local lay control of education, and, occasionally, providing not a partnership, but teachers' organization control.

The question to be resolved as to what should be the scope of negotiations must be inspected by determining a different question: what in education lends itself to being resolved by the adversary relationship inherent in collective negotiations? Earlier mention was made of the 633 items in a model agreement. These can actually be grouped into three main headings: (1) teachers' organization interest, such as make-up of the bargaining unit, rights of entry to and utilization of buildings, the inclusion of the agency or union shop clause, and the right to protect the agreement; (2) individual teacher interest, such as salaries, free time, considerations for promotion, transfers and assignments, protection against arbitrary board or administrative action through utilization of a grievance procedure, use of lounges, and a variety of fringe benefits, such as paved parking lots, file cabinets, and economic benefits directly affecting the teacher;

(3) general concerns, including many areas categorized as educational or at the very least on the periphery of educational concerns, which might include class size, disciplinary procedures, school calendar, books, supplies, grading, utilization of specialists and aides, and the like.

A few years ago, Bakke (1967) explored the division of the teacher's role into the employment relationship of the teacher to the board and the professional relationship of the teacher to education and concluded:

Our rights as teachers to personal and professional representation and control over our own affairs and the legitimate interests of unions and associations to extend their membership, influence and power have got to be integrated with the right of the whole people through their elected or appointed boards of education to have a powerful voice in choosing the kind of education they want and in deciding what they are willing to pay for it, and what that comes to in terms of employment.

This is as good a division as one can secure for determining what should be and should not be negotiable. Utilizing this division, most if not all those areas of individual interests become negotiable. Most of the teachers' organization interests can also be considered negotiable.

The role of management in education must be inspected to aid in determining what is negotiable. The work of the manager—planning, organizing, directing, coordinating, and controlling—is performed in education as it is performed in industry. It is the responsibility of the manager to make sure that the goals of the organization are met and he both devises a set of guidelines to aid him and then performs a specific task to accomplish the goals. To perform his tasks, the education manager must follow principles of efficiency, of authority, of minimal and opportunity costs, and of discriminating supervisory evaluation.

The question of what should be the scope of bargaining should be answered by an analysis of the effect of these negotiations upon the educational process. It is essential to provide a system which will permit the managerial function to be performed as efficiently as possible for the ultimate good of the educational process.

This does not mean that teachers should not be involved in other areas of decision making. There is probably no book on educational administration written in the last twenty-five years which does not advocate a type of consultative participation plan. Unfortunately, there have been very few boards or administrators who have taken this so seriously as to establish a mechanism by which it is done broadly or with any regularity—except in those tasks which require large amounts of detailed work or detailed knowledge.

It would seem, however, that the only means by which educational issues can be wholly removed from the arena of conflict is by enforcing the concept that the teacher, as a professional, must have an active voice in determining educational questions. This could be accomplished by utilizing the negotiations procedure, including advisory or binding arbitration, in combination with an agreed structure for consultative decision making. Consultative decision making is the process of informing and influencing decisions with data, opinions, and advice. It is both a deliberate search for help and a willingness to listen to unsolicited ideas.

Given the acceptance by both parties of the mechanism for structured consultation and its incorporation in the agreement between the parties, disputes as to whether teachers have had sufficient involvement in determining educational policies can be resolved within the grievance procedure. The questions, "Was the professional staff involved sufficiently in the educational decision-making process? Did their views carry sufficient weight? If not, how can this be remedied?," can be grieved by the teachers' organization, with the right of final determination by an arbitrator. The arbitrator should not have the power to settle the educational issue which properly should be resolved within the educational community.

Such a procedure was negotiated into three contracts in New Jersey, immediately prior to the passage of the state's statute on public employment bargaining in 1968. With that passage, the teachers' organization forced the deletion of the plans from the contracts.

The plans did not exist long enough to make any judgment about their effectiveness. The teachers' organization looked upon them as a threat to the organization. In addition, the organization has been unsuccessful at negotiating a substitute. Nor have they successfully negotiated into a contract subjects which were to be resolved internally within the participative plan.

At present, the state teachers' organization involved is advocating an instructional council comprised of teachers and administrators. There would be no limitation upon the subjects the council could consider and it would report to, and make recommendations to, both the local teachers' organizations and the boards. Either could refuse to follow the recommendation. If a board refuses, the matter can be arbitrated.

Obviously, the concept of an instructional council, as proposed, would drastically change the employer-employee relationship and would shift control of education from the community to the education profession and arbitrators.

The unique characteristics of education should dictate which decisions should be grievable—which areas of decision making should be negotiable. If an attempt is made to determine these characteristics, the following must be included:

1. The teacher is both a professional and a salaried employee;

2. As both, the educational level of the collective group is considerably higher than that of almost any other group organized for collective action;

3. Much of the work of the teachers does not lend itself readily —at least it has not done so in the past—to accurate evaluation by either those outside the profession or within the profession;

4. The school management, the administrators, are well trained in modern educational practices, but considerably less trained in modern business practices and human relations skills;

5. The transformation of research in education into practice requires an inordinate amount of time, probably because there is little direct relationship between those who do the research and those who utilize the findings of research directly in the educational process;

6. The profession of teaching and the public school system are supported by public funds raised through public taxation; and

7. The work of the profession has traditionally been controlled by the non-professional—the lay public school board, which performs an unpaid, voluntary civic function.

It should be apparent that determining the scope of bargaining cannot be done on an item-by-item approach. Rather, a theory and a philosophy must be constructed that may be applied to each item, in order that the totality of the agreement and its day-by-day administration come within the framework of the theory and philosophy.

The essential question is: Is there something so unique about education and those who are professionals in education that its process can function without some individual directing others, coordinating the work of others—someone who plans, organizes, and controls the work? This is the task of a manager.

It is also necessary to consider the process of decision making. A comparison of the process of decision making in industry with the process of decision making in education reveals a correlation and analysis not frequently considered.

For example, industry essentially operates as does the military, with someone in command possessing the authority to reach a unilateral decision. Regardless of the means by which he reaches that decision—whether by committee recommendations, delegation of authority to others, or advice of associates—he cannot escape the responsibility of having to say eventually, "This is it. This is what we are going to do." In other words, there is no other person who has co-equal status with him. Consequently, when the decision is reached, all those who participated in the process of reaching that decision, regardless of the attitude they might have had previously, must accept it because of command authority.

There is, however, one glaring exception to this in industry and that is the area of personnel decision making. Here the government, by law, has decreed that a union has equal authority with the company to establish hours, wages, and working conditions. Consequently, once co-equal status is present, the decision making process is changed.

If co-equal status permits bilateral determination of all issues in education, as desired by both teacher organizations, the resolution of each issue must rest in the conflict of the adversary relationship.

Under these circumstances, disruption of the educational process will be increased by extending the scope of bargaining and will be decreased by limiting the scope.

The problem of decision making and the unique characteristics of education combine to provide two basic guidelines to determine the scope of negotiations:

(1) Management must be unfettered in making decisions, even if it is required to have many of its decisions subject to the grievance procedure; and

(2) Decision making in education can be analyzed to determine which

decisions *must* be retained to the unilateral action by the board or by the administrators and which can be either shared or turned over to the teachers for their unilateral action.

These guidelines make one assumption: local lay control of education will, and should, continue. Thus, in reverse, they obviously assume that control of education should not be turned over to the education profession.

A few examples should suffice to illustrate the application of these guidelines:

1. In the areas of teacher organization concern, such items as building access and utilization should be on a permissive basis, not one of indiscriminate right. Items such as the "union shop" or the "agency shop" are dependent upon legal interpretation and individual value judgment. However, they are probably negotiable. The teacher organization, if it has a right to exist, has a right to negotiate upon those items which aid it in existing.

2. In areas of promotion, assignment, and transfer, the teachers might have the right to negotiate a mechanism for drawing their desires and aspirations to the administrator for his consideration. They might have the right to grieve the action taken by the administrator on the grounds that he acted either capriciously or discriminatorily. However, the decision as to who should be promoted, transferred, or assigned is one which should be made in a broad context of criteria and, therefore, retained to the administration and the board.

3. The teacher should not be able to block evaluation, nor should he be able to restrict the type of evaluation, as long as such evaluation is made in an ethical manner. He should not be able to dictate the type of evaluation nor its utilization. He might properly be able to grieve the specific evaluation made of him.

4. A fourth, and last, example: The board and administration must retain sufficient flexibility to utilize new or experimental educational ideas and programs, such as modular scheduling or the increasingly available educational technology. The board should not, therefore, define the length of the work day, or teaching hours or teaching load, in terms which might prevent change from taking place. A "book of rules" in a school system can be just as devastating as the "book of rules" among railroad labor or the civil service

employees of Italy. Obviously, these examples are not meant to imply that salaries, direct economic benefits, or a grievance procedure are not to be negotiated.

The final caution to use in determining the scope of negotiations is the blunt, pragmatic fact that most of the agreements in existence have or will have a form of advisory or binding arbitration. This means that many, if not most, of the subjects negotiated into the agreement will be subject to an appeal to an agency beyond the board and an agency which is unprepared and unsuited to determining educational questions. In a recently decided case in New Jersey, the judge wrote:

. . . the American Arbitration Association may be well qualified to "arbitrate" compensation, hours of work, sick leave, fringe benefits and the like, but they and their panels possess no expertise in arbitrating the maturation level of a 7th grade student in the elementary schools of Rockaway Township . . . (*The Board of Education of the Township of Rockaway v. Rockaway Township Education Association and Joseph Youngman* (Superior Court of New Jersey, Docket no. C 2148-71, Sept. 25, 1972))

Reference

Bakke, E. W. "Teachers, School Boards, and the Employment Relationships." *Employer-Employee Relations in the Public Schools,* edited by R. E. Doherty. Ithaca, N.Y.: State School of Industrial and Labor Relations, Cornell University, 1967.

Reading 4

The Need for Limitation Upon the Scope of Negotiations in Public Education, II

William F. Kay

To study the limitations upon the scope of bargaining for teachers, the problems of other public employees cannot be ignored. In fact, the constraints upon teacher negotiations are essentially the same as those upon collective bargaining for all public employees. Generally, these fall into one of the following categories: statutory limitations which exist in the express language of the various collective bargaining statutes; legal and practical limitations on the fiscal and managerial authority of public employers; pre-existing employment laws, rules, and regulations; management rights directed by pre-existing laws, rules, and regulations; limitations upon the obligation to bargain any changes in working conditions; and, finally, the limitation upon public employees' right to strike.

These constraints on the bargaining process are real and are legal in nature. They are rooted in the fact that the entire government employment context is a creature of law and, as such, the employment context exists as a maze of legislative fiats and agency regulations. Onto this pre-existing employment system, the concept of collective

Reprinted by permission from *Journal of Law and Education* 2, no. 1 (January 1973), pp. 155-75.

bargaining has been superimposed, without regard to the conflicts thus set in motion.

The other source of nonsubstantive limitations on bargaining stems from the long-held concept that public employment is inherently different from private employment. This concept, which is sometimes expressed in terms of "the public trust," is a restraint basically philosophical in nature. Public employers frequently express to public employee unions that their reluctance to bargain on certain items is due to the fact that the decision-making authority is vested in them as a public trust—a trust that cannot be shared with the employees.

The fallacy of this concept is that the same individuals who define themselves as holding a public trust, are frequently not accountable to the public. Moreover, when they are asked to share this same trust with the public, their response often is negative. This is due to the fact that governmental service has grown extensively over recent years, and individuals who are the public employers are frequently insulated from the general public by a silent bureaucracy. It is for this reason that the "public trust" concept—as a limitation to bargaining—is more illusory than real. This is especially true for those public employers who are not elected by the public, but instead are appointed officials.

These factors indicate that the major battle ground concerning whether there should be a broad scope of bargaining will center in the upper level management ranks of public employment. Employee demands expose the fact that these administrators are all too frequently the actual policy-makers, not the various governing boards and elected officials. These demands also expose management decisions to the scrutiny of the actual employer and the citizenry. More frequently than not, the pressures of collective bargaining in the public sector have forced the official employer to assert his governmental authority, much to the consternation of the nonelected bureaucrats who were the actual policy-makers.

Limitations Contained Within the Collective Bargaining Statute

The first and most obvious of the real restraints on the scope of bargaining for public employees is the express language of the enabling legislation. Many of the state legislatures, in drafting collective bargaining statutes for public employees, chose to employ language other than that which has been the established standard in the private sector. That standard, as set forth in the National Labor Relations Act, defines the obligation to bargain as "to meet at reasonable times and confer in good faith with respect to wages, hours, and other terms and conditions of employment. . . ." (29 USC § 141 et seq.; Act of June 23, 1947, Pub. L. no. 101, 80th Cong., 1st sess., amended by Pub. L. no. 902, 80th Cong., 2nd sess.)

A number of state legislatures have chosen a more limited definition. For example, the Minnesota Public Employees Relations Act of 1971 reduces the scope of bargaining for professional employees by this additional limiting language:

In the case of professional employees, the terms means the hours of employment, the compensation therefor, and the economic aspects relating to employment, but does not mean educational policies of the school district. . . . (§ § 179.51-179.57, 1951L, as amended by ch. 839, 1965L, as repealed by § § 179.61-179.77, 1971L, § 179.63(18))

A public employer is not required to meet and negotiate on matters of inherent managerial policy, which include, but are not limited to, such areas of discretion or policy as the functions and programs of the employer, its overall budget, utilization of technology, the organizational structure and selection and direction and number of personnel. (§ 179.66)

The Nevada statute and the Montana legislation are also good examples of expressed statutory language which limits the scope of bargaining.*

---

*Nevada Local Gov. Employee-Management Rel. Act, NRS 288, as amended by 1971L, § 288.150, reads: "Each local government employer is entitled, without negotiation: (a) To direct its employees; (b) To hire, promote, classify, transfer, assign, retain, suspend, demote, discharge or take disciplinary action against any employee; (c) To relieve any employee from duty because of lack of work or for any other legitimate reason; (d) To maintain the efficiency of its governmental operations; (e) To determine the methods, means and personnel by which its operations are to be conducted; and (f) To take whatever actions may be necessary to carry out its responsibilities in situations of emergency. Any action taken under the provisions of this subsection shall not be construed as a failure to negotiate in good faith." Also see Montana Statutes, HB 455, 1971L, which reads: ". . . to discuss matters relating directly to the employer-teacher relationship such as salary, hours and other terms of employment, and to negotiate and bargain for agreement on such matters. The matters of

The courts and the labor boards in states which have statutory language measurably different from the private sector standard have predictably established mandatory subjects of bargaining for public employees which are substantially different from those in the private sector. For example, the Pennsylvania Public Employees Relations Act (SB 133, 1970L), which has the standard private sector language —"wages, hours, and other terms and conditions of employment. . . ." (§701)—also contains limiting language regarding managerial policy and conflicting state laws."* This additional language has produced an expected result. In the first major test on the scope of bargaining before the Pennsylvania Labor Board (*Pennsylvania Labor Relations Board v. State College Area School District*, Case no. PERA-C-929-C (October 1971), the Board ruled that the items at issue—including planning time, assignments, work space, class size, calendar, access to personnel files—were all nonbargainable.

Similar results have occurred in other states where language defining the scope of bargaining is substantially different from private sector standards. The Kansas statute (Kan. Professional Negotiations Act, KSA 1970, Supp. 72-5413) was tested in *National Education Association of Shawnee Mission, Inc. v. Board of Education of Shawnee Mission Unified School Board no. 512, Johnson County, Kansas* (District Court, Division no. 1, no. 48462 (December 1971)). That decision restricted bargaining for the Kansas teachers, and specifically eliminated from the bargaining process all matters of

---

negotiation and bargaining for agreement shall not include matters of curriculum, policy of operation, selection of teachers and other personnel, or physical plant of schools or other school facilities."

*Section 702 reads: "Public employers shall not be required to bargain over matters of inherent managerial policy which shall include but shall not be limited to such areas of discretion or policy as the functions and programs of the public employer, standards of services, its overall budget, utilization of technology, the organizational structure and selection and direction of personnel. Public employers, however, shall be required to meet and discuss on policy matters affecting wages, hours and terms and conditions of employment as well as the impact thereon upon request by public employee representatives." Section 702 states: "The parties to the collective bargaining process shall not effect or implement a provision in a collective bargaining agreement if the implementation of that provision would be in violation of, or inconsistent with, or in conflict with any statute or statutes enacted by the General Assembly of the Commonwealth of Pennsylvania or the provisions of municipal home rule charters."

"educational policy." A similar result relating to teachers was recently handed down by the Nebraska Supreme Court.*

State statutory language not only restricts the scope of bargaining but also leads to a multiplicity of disputes, because public employees find difficulty accepting a standard different from the private sector. They see the inconsistency in a logic which states that an
employee of the municipal golf course cannot strike while the employees of a private utility may strike; and they cannot accept the
logic which tells them that the employees in a national transportation industry can have a broader scope of bargaining than do the professional employees of a school system. The obvious means of
removing such restrictions is through the legislative process, by specifically avoiding any language which strays from the standard contained in the National Labor Relations Act—a standard which has
been defined by decisions and a standard which adequately protects
the inherent right of management to direct the operation of the
enterprise.

Limited Authority of Employer

A second major limitation on bargaining originates from the
limited authority which is often vested in the public employer. One
of these elements of limited authority centers around his fiscal
autonomy. Unlike the private sector, the public employer gathers his
"income" from a multitude of sources, and quite frequently the public employer shares his fiscal authority with other governmental
agencies, with different jurisdictions, and with the electorate. Or, as
is often the case, the public employer with whom the employees

---

*School District of Seward Education Association v. School District of
Seward, 199 NW2d 752 (Neb. 1972), at 759; LLRp. 6 §952. The Nebraska Supreme Court stated: "Without trying to lay down any specific rule, we would
hold that conditions of employment can be interpreted to include only those
matters directly affecting the teacher's welfare. Without attempting in any way
to be specific, or to limit the foregoing, we would consider the following to be
exclusively within the management prerogative: The right to hire; to maintain
order and efficiency; to schedule work; to control transfers and assignments; to
determine what extracurricular activities may be supported or sponsored; and to
determine the curriculum, class size, and types of specialists to be employed."
199 NW2d at 757.

bargain is devoid of any revenue producing authority, as are many school boards.

An excellent example of this problem can be demonstrated in the recent dispute in the nation's capitol between the local teachers' union and the school board. The major element in this dispute was money. However, neither the elected school board nor the officials of the District of Columbia government had the authority to set wages or regulate "income," since such power was vested in the U.S. Congress. This situation, needless to say, only exacerbated the dispute. The District of Columbia teachers' dispute demonstrates what is all too often the situation in public employment bargaining—the employer has limited authority and jurisdiction over certain employment areas and, therefore, the same limitations are placed on the bargaining process. This problem of limited employer authority can best be demonstrated by reviewing a series of public employment bargaining disputes in Michigan as brought to light by refusal to bargain charges filed with that state's Employment Relations Commission. Section 10(a) of MSA § 17.455, Public Acts 1965, reads in part: "It shall be unlawful for a public employer or an officer or an agent of a public employer . . . to refuse to bargain collectively with the representatives of its public employees. . . ."

A number of these problems arose in Michigan upon adoption of local government budgets, since the adoption of the budget, which is generally the only document pinpointing the priorities of government activities, puts an end to any meaningful bargaining with employee organizations. The finalization of the budget locks bargaining on economic items into fairly tight limits. It would seem reasonable that the unions would look upon the adoption of a municipal budget during bargaining as a unilateral act by the employer which would constitute a statutory refusal to bargain. This is what happened in 1966, when the Saginaw Fire Fighters Association engaged in bargaining with the city representatives who made a counterproposal on wages which was not accepted by the union negotiators. Shortly thereafter, the city council adopted its budget with funds insufficient to finance more than its final wage offer. The union filed a refusal to bargain charge. (*City of Saginaw,* 1966 Labor Op. 465, Case no. C66 F-73.)

The question presented was whether the adoption of a budget terminated the city's duty to bargain on economic issues, and

whether or not the city council was the actual employer with whom
the union was bargaining. The city council contended that it had
independent statutory authority to act beyond the role of the "employer," whom they defined as the designated department heads
which were negotiating with the union. The trial examiner's report,
as incorporated into the board's final decision, found that ". . . the
negotiating team must receive instructions from the governing body
. . . if its concessions and tentative commitments are to be meaningful, but it need not, and probably cannot, be vested with final authority to bind the public employer, since that would seem to involve an illegal delegation of the law-making power of the City
Council." (*City of Saginaw*, 1966 Labor Op. at 479.) In effect, this
language gave the city the right to adopt its budget and place severe
restrictions on bargaining. Nevertheless, the city was ordered to continue bargaining in good faith with the union. This schizophrenic
approach was apparent in the trial examiner's analysis of the problem. The city violated its good faith duty to bargain under the Public
Employees Relations Act, but was in good faith compliance with the
city charter.*

A similar issue arose later in *School District of North Dearborn
Heights* (1967 Labor Op. 673, Case no. C67 F-60), where the teachers' union filed a refusal to bargain claim which was not sustained.
The parties had completed bargaining when the negotiator for the
school board received, by telephone, the unanimous consent of the
school board on a final salary package. Later, in a public meeting, the
school board rejected the agreement. The Labor Board found no
refusal to bargain since ". . . the Board of Education relies on the
statutory requirement that a board of education act only via resolu-

---

City of Saginaw, 1966 Labor Op. at 484 reads: The problem as stated by
the trial examiner was that: "The super-imposition of a comprehensive collective
bargaining law onto the labyrinth of statutes, charters, ordinances and other
forms of regulation of local government operations presents many real or apparent conflicts of law not encountered in the traditional application of collective
bargaining to private industry. This case involves such conflicts in the areas of
delegation of power to negotiators, insistence upon an ordinance in lieu of a
contract, and a refusal to negotiate after adopting the annual budget. Here, the
City's reliance on the finality of a budget as grounds for refusing to bargain was
misplaced, even though the City may be assumed to have acted in good faith
consistent with its own interpretation of the City Charter."

tions adopted during official meetings. If a board of education can act only when in formal session, it is reasoned, then the Board cannot be bound by individually solicited, informal statements of its members as to their approval of the salary schedule" (*School District of North Dearborn Heights,* 1967 Labor Op. at 679).

The *North Dearborn Heights* case was cited later in a major decision of the Commission (the title of the Michigan Labor Mediation Board was changed in 1969 to Michigan Employment Relations Commission, MERC) in *City of Detroit* (1971 MERC Labor Op. 237). The Detroit Police Officers Association had been engaged in bargaining with the mayor and the city's labor relations specialists. Agreement was finally reached on wages and other items. However, the city's Common Council deleted the monies in the budget for the policemen's pay. The mayor vetoed the deletion, but the council overrode his veto. When the DPOA filed a refusal to bargain, the Commission disagreed. Citing *Saginaw* and *North Dearborn Heights,* MERC found no refusal to bargain on mandatory subjects so long as the mayor and Common Council did not refuse to meet with the union after the passage of the budget. Despite the fact that the mayor's representatives did not have latitude to bargain the wage funds which were specifically cut from the budget, the Commission found no violation of the statute so long as the city showed a willingness to return to the bargaining table.

Thus, the diversity of the public employer's fiscal authority in Michigan has limited the bargaining power of the parties and bargaining, *per se.* As evidenced by the Michigan experience, the fragmentation of the employer's authority places heavy restrictions on bargaining. This is especially true for teachers who deal with employers who frequently have no fiscal authority, or who have to share that authority by referendum with the citizens, or who have no control over retirement or fringe benefit systems, or who have no control over the hiring and firing standards (e.g., certification and tenure laws). Teacher organizations have frequently found that the only way to resolve this problem is to confront the actual source of the authority —whether that authority is the legislature, a local fiscal authority, or a governmental agency. Often the employer tactically joins the employee group in this confrontation, since the public employer is not only interested in resolving employee disputes, but also in consolidating its authority as an employer. Employers soon realized that if they

are to bargain with the employees they must have full employment
authority. At the same time these employers realize that if they continue with only limited authority over employees, they also have
limited authority to deal with other problems outside of bargaining.
It is for this reason that many public employers now are working
toward consolidating their authority. However, so long as the fiscal
authority is spread among the several named "employers," and so
long as the concern remains over the improper delegation of fiscal
and decisional authority, the scope of bargaining will be restricted,
not only in the quantitative sense, but in the qualitative sense—the
ability of both parties to deal with each other at arm's length.

Preexisting Employment Laws, Rules, and Regulations

The third barrier to a broad scope of bargaining for teachers and
public employees arises because public employment, prior to the advent of collective bargaining, was governed by rules and regulations
as set forth in state and local law. The new process of collective bargaining was superimposed upon the old employment structure, which
thus set into motion immediate conflicts between the two employment systems. Typical of this type of problem is the case of *Kerrigan
v. City of Boston* (278 NE2d 387 (Mass 1972), LLR 68, 617), where
the Massachusetts Supreme Judicial Court recently decided a conflict
over a health and welfare trust fund. The school committee and the
teachers had previously reached agreement on a trust fund. However,
the city refused to make payment, arguing that such expenditure
would be contrary to state law. The court ordered payment, because
it construed the trust fund benefits to be wages, relying on NLRA
cases and mandatory bargaining required by the NLRB with regard
to that subject. The court implicitly held that since the benefits were
subject to mandatory bargaining, the state law could not excuse that
obligation (278 NE2d at 389).

However, the most instructive analysis of the complexities of
this problem of conflicting laws is found by following the evolution
of decisions of the labor boards of Michigan and New York.

Two areas of special conflict that have caused problems in
Michigan are the various civil service codes and home rule charters. In
City of Escanaba (1967 Labor Op. 701, Case no. C67 B-8), the
Teamsters' local filed an unfair labor practice charge against the city

for refusing to bargain. The respondent denied the charge, asserting in turn that the city had recently passed a home rule ordinance which excluded the town from the state's bargaining act. The MERC upheld the charge on the grounds that the home rule ordinance was adopted after the enactment of the state's bargaining statute and, further, that a public employer is prohibited from enacting a local home rule ordinance to avoid collective bargaining.

A similar attempt to undermine the collective bargaining process was presented in *Township of Redford* (1967 Labor Op. 596, Case no. C67 D-32), when the citizens of the town voted overwhelmingly to establish a civil service system pursuant to the Township Civil Service Act which was enacted during the same legislative session as the bargaining statute. The town refused to bargain with the union, basing its refusal upon the contention that the Civil Service Act divested the township's control over the newly established Civil Service Commission. The MERC resolved the problem by finding that the township had lawfully refused to bargain and that the existing statutory law transferred the wage and fringe benefit determination from the township governing body to the Civil Service Commission. However, after making that determination, the MERC then directed the Civil Service Commission to enter into good faith collective bargaining with the union.*

The most difficult question, however, as to a conflict between a preexisting home rule law and the bargaining statute, was faced by the labor relations policy-makers in *City of Flint and Hurley Hospital* (1970 MERC Labor Op. 348). Flint, as a home rule city, had established through local ordinance a uniform pay plan for all of the employees except policemen and firemen. In order to exempt any employees from the uniform pay plan, such exemption would have to be voted on by the citizens in accordance with the home rule charter. The certified bargaining representative for the local hospital employees, who was refused negotiations on wages and fringe benefits,

---

Township of Redford, 1967 Labor Op. at 605 reads: "The Commission may not, in the light of PERA, simply hold public hearings and make its own studies regarding salaries and benefits: It must bargain to agreement or impasse with an organization representing the employees. So construed, there is no conflict between the Township Civil Service Act and the collective bargaining policy contained in PERA."

filed a charge alleging a refusal to bargain. The MERC held that "The City is obligated to bargain in respect to rates of pay, wages, hours of employment or other conditions of employment without regard to any provisions of the City Charter relating to these mandatory subjects of collective bargaining" (1970 MERC Labor Op. at 365).

The impact of *Hurley Hospital* was evident in *City of Detroit* (1971 MERC Labor Op. 237), a case where the police officers were demanding an increase in benefits from the local retirement system which included police, firefighters, and others. The pension plan was embodied in the City Charter. In response to the request by the police officers, the Mayor arranged a meeting with all interested groups. The police balked at the concept of isolating a mandatory subject of bargaining from the table, and as a result charged a refusal to bargain. The MERC reduced the issue to the fundamental question of whether removal of the retirement question from the collective bargaining process was clearly contrary to the mandate of the state legislature. The MERC applied the doctrine of *Hurley Hospital* and ordered the Mayor to begin bargaining with the police over the issue of pension benefits without any requirement that any such charter change be submitted to and contingent upon the vote of the Detroit electorate.*

City of Flint, 1970 MERC Labor Op. at 348 reads: "The factual situation in *Hurley Hospital* is analogous to the one in the instant case. Here, as in *Hurley Hospital*, the Charter provision applies to city employees other than those represented by the charging party and the charter provisions can only be changed by a favorable vote of the electorate. Also, as in *Hurley Hospital*, the instant case involves a mandatory subject of collective bargaining."

As to pension plans being mandatory subjects of bargaining, this was determined by trial examiner Joseph Bixler in *City of Detroit*. In a rather perfunctory decision manner Bixler found ". . . that pension plans have long been considered a mandatory subject of collective bargaining by the National Labor Relations Board as part of wages, hours and other terms and conditions of employment is well established. *Inland Steel v. NLRB*, 170 F2d 247, 22 LRRM 2506; *Pacific Coast Association of Pulp and Paper Manufacturers*, 133 NLRB 690. There appears to be no reason to regard pension plans as other than a mandatory subject of bargaining under the provisions of PERA that require a public employer to 'confer in good faith with respect to wages, hours and other conditions of employment.' " Bixler also found that the Employment Relations Commission had determined that one mandatory subject of bargaining cannot be isolated from others, and cited *W. K. Kellog Community College* (1969 Labor Op. 40), where the Board stated: "The instance upon resolution of one issue before considera-

A look at the results in Michigan as set forth in *City of Escanaba, Township of Redford, Hurley Hospital,* and *City of Detroit,* shows significant strides toward assuring that the scope of bargaining for public employees is not limited by prebargaining employment laws—especially in the area of civil service ordinances and home rule charters. These cases, and the judicial decisions which stand behind them, have established the right of Michigan employees to bargain on items which might otherwise have been severely limited by the conflicts of the various employment laws.

The New York experience, relative to conflicts with preexisting laws, has been similar to Michigan, as reflected by the decisions of the New York Public Employment Relations Board (PERB) subsequent to a 1969 amendment to the Taylor Law providing for "improper practices"* (section 108, Civil Service Law, added by ch. 391, L. 1947, amended by ch. 392 (Taylor Act) L. 1967, which repealed and replaced the Condon-Waldin Act, amended by ch. 1020, L. 1970, effective May 21, 1970, and ch. 414, L. 1970, effective May 6, 1970, as last amended by ch. 503, L. 1971, effective immediately upon approval on June 17, 1971). A good example of the conflict was brought to light in a PERB General Counsel Opinion (2 PERB 5048 (1969)) to a local school board in May 1969, in a response to a local employer who inquired whether it had to negotiate a grievance

---

tion of others may have been due to inexperience in bargaining. However, this does not excuse the college from its statutory obligation to bargain in good faith."

*Section 209-a reads: "Improper employer practices: It shall be an improper practice for a public employer or its agents deliberately (a) to interfere with, restrain or coerce public employees in the exercise of their rights guaranteed in section two hundred two for the purpose of depriving them of such rights; (b) to dominate or interfere with the formation or administration of any employee organization for the purposes of depriving them of such rights; (c) to discriminate against any employee for the purpose of encouraging or discouraging membership in, or participation in the activities of, any employee organization; or (d) to refuse to negotiate in good faith with the duly recognized or certified representative of its public employees. Improper employee organization practices: It shall be an improper practice for an employee organization or its agents deliberately (a) to interfere with, restrain or coerce public employees in the exercise of the rights granted in section two hundred two, or to cause or attempt to cause, a public employer to do so; or (b) to refuse to negotiate collectively in good faith with a public employer, provided it is the duly recognized or certified representative of the employees of such employer."

procedure with an employee organization if such procedures were already statutorily mandated. The employer felt that a negotiated grievance procedure would be in conflict with, and inconsistent with, the preexisting grievance procedure which was established according to state law. The general counsel advised the employer that there was no conflict between the new right of the employees to negotiate collectively and the preexisting state law.*

The rights imposed by the Taylor Law and previous state laws first came into conflict over the concept of an employees' trust fund. In *New Rochelle Federation of Teachers* (3 PERB 3594 (1970)), the teachers' union charged the city school district with an unfair practice, since the school board refused to execute a written agreement after the parties had agreed to a union welfare trust fund. The school board submitted the proposed declaration of trust to the New York State Department of Education for a legal opinion, which declared that such transmittal of public funds to the union trust fund would constitute a gift or a loan of public funds which was prohibited by the state constitution. The PERB (at 3594-97), however, opted simply to declare the pension trust fund as a term and condition of employment, and further declared that, under the Taylor Law, a trust fund could be incorporated into a collective bargaining agreement—the provisions of the state constitution notwithstanding.

A similar trust fund question arose in *Local 456 International Brotherhood of Teamsters v. Town of Courtlandt* (4 PERB 8300 (S Ct Westchester County 1971)), where the Teamsters had negotiated payments to the trust fund; nonetheless, the employer refused to make a payment to the trust fund based on the opinions of the state comptroller which stated that the town lacked the authority to make

---

*The opinion (2 PERB at 5049) in part reads: "The Taylor Law authorizes a contractual grievance procedure entirely independent of any connection with Article 16. Such a procedure, however, would not replace but would parallel that required by Article 16, and its use would be subject to the election of the particular grievant. The use of such alternative procedure might be made subject to a waiver by such grievant of his rights under Article 16. Under such alternative contractual procedure, the employee organization could have a voice in the selection of final stage arbiters. Thus, no real conflict or inconsistency exists between the Taylor Law and Article 16. A negotiated grievance procedure that provides its own procedural steps in grievance resolution would not conflict with the requirements of Article 16; it would merely add to the basic procedures statutorily mandated."

the agreed upon payments as contrary to the prohibition in the state constitution against conferring a gift upon its employees through payment into a trust fund. Essentially, this was the same issue the PERB had skirted in *New Rochelle Teachers*. The court ordered the payment of the funds by favoring the public policy inherent in the Taylor Law, and read the bargaining law as actually superseding the interpretations of the state's insurance provisions.*

Another area of conflict between the New York collective bargaining statute and preexisting state law related to the dismissal of probationary teachers. In *The Arbitration Between the Associated Teachers of Huntington v. Board of Education, Union Free School District no. 3* (60 Misc2d 433, 3 PERB 8210 (S Ct Suffolk County 1970)), a nontenured teacher was dismissed prior to the end of the school year, but did not meet the standard of the collective agreement which contained a provision mandating that nontenured teachers would be notified of termination of employment by no later than March 1. The state's tenure law provides, in part, that "Teachers . . . shall be appointed by the board of education . . . for a probationary period of three years. The services of a person appointed to any such position may be discontinued at any time during such probationary period . . ." (§ 3012 of the N.Y. Education Law). Even though the school board's dismissal of the teacher did not meet the contractual deadline of March 1, the board refused to arbitrate the dismissal, asserting that the tenure law allowed dismissal at any time during the probationary period. The court rejected this contention.† Moreover,

---

*4 PERB at 8304 stated: "Article 3-A (insurance law) became the law of this State in 1936. At that time, the whole concept of public employer-employee relationships and public employee unions was in its embryonic stage. The Taylor Law came along in 1967 and brought with it a whole new approach to public employer-employee relations. It is well settled that the provisions of the Taylor Law must be applied liberally to effectuate its public benefit purpose. Contractual agreements between a municipality and a union representing its employees are looked upon with favor by the Courts unless sufficient constitutional or statutory objection is shown."

†3 PERB at 8213 reads: "Certainly, after 1967, not only is the subject type of arbitration permissible, but it was mandated by the public policy of this State. . . . This court would be remiss if it stayed the arbitration proceeding herein which is not prohibited by statute and which is in accordance with the public policy of this State."

as to the question of arbitrability, the court applied the private sector standard as established by the U.S. Supreme Court.*

With *Associated Teachers of Huntington* as a foundation, the PERB began to use the private sector standard in their decision framework regarding arbitration of dismissals. In *The Monroe-Woodbury Teachers Association* (3 PERB 3632 (1970), aff'd, 4 PERB 7097 (S Ct Albany County)), the employer refused to negotiate, asserting the right under the state education law which gave the superintendent the absolute right to determine the procedures for evaluating and dismissing probationary teachers. The PERB relied upon *Associated Teachers of Huntington* to decide that the dismissal procedure for probationary teachers is a mandatory subject for bargaining.†

To add to the expanded list of bargaining items, the PERB, in *The West Irondequoit Board of Education* (4 PERB 4606 (1971)), affirmed the private sector standard, finding that the promotional policy and the class size standards were not contrary to education law and were, therefore, mandatory subjects of bargaining which would have to be negotiated to impasse.‡

---

*3 PERB at 8212 reads: "The court finds that there is no prohibition against submitting the question of the procedure used in terminating employment of a nontenure teacher and the best that can be said for respondent's position herein is that there is doubt as to whether the provisions in question may or may not be arbitrable. In such circumstances, the question of arbitrability must be submitted to an arbitrator for resolution as indicated by the United States Supreme Court in *Steelworkers v. Gulf Co.* (63 US 574, 582-83): 'An order to arbitrate the particular grievance should not be denied unless it may be said with positive assurance that the arbitration clause is not susceptible of an interpretation that covers the asserted dispute. Doubts should be resolved in favor of coverage.' "

†3 PERB at 3634 stated that: "Admittedly, the procedures proposed by the Association in Article D do go beyond that required by the Education Law *supra*, but it does not appear that the procedures set forth in Article D contravene the provisions of the Education Law. Simply put, Article D, if included in a negotiated agreement, would require the Employer to follow procedures in the denial of tenure that absent an agreement the Employer would not be required to follow. *Associated Teachers of Huntington v. Board of Education, Union Free School District no. 3, supra.* Accordingly, we agree with the conclusion of the Hearing Officer that Article D as proposed is not barred by existing law and as it deals with a term and condition of employment. We conclude that it is a mandatory subject of negotiations which the Employer must, upon request, negotiate with the Association."

‡4 PERB at 4609-10 decided that: "The first question to be decided in

However, in no case did the bargaining statute and preexisting laws conflict as much as on the question of an agency shop, which arose as a second issue in *Monroe-Woodbury Teachers,* when the teachers filed a refusal to bargain charge against the school board. The employer asserted that negotiating an agency shop would be contrary to state law, and, therefore, not a mandatory subject of bargaining. PERB (3 PERB 3632 (1970)) drew back from its previous approach and agreed with the employer that an agency shop provision was not in harmony with state law and, therefore, a "permissive" subject of bargaining.

Sooner or later the entire question of conflict between prebargaining employment regulations and the collective bargaining statute was bound to arise in the litigative process. In *Associated Teachers of Huntington v. Board of Education* (30 NY2d 122, 282 NE2d 109 (N.Y. 1972)), the Board raised the basic question of whether it could be party to an agreement which provided, among other items: arbitration of cases in which tenured teachers were dismissed, reimbursement for graduate course, and reimbursement pay on the last year of service. The court of appeals posed the singular question as to "whether there is any fundamental conflict between the provisions of the Taylor Law and the provisions of any other statute dealing with the powers and duties of school boards" (30 NY2d at 124). The court majority determined all the items as mandatory subjects of bargaining, finding no conflict between statutes. In addition, it established the standard of the employer's obligation

---

this case therefore, is whether class size and promotional policy are 'terms and conditions of employment.' In the absence of specific legislative history, it makes sense to basically adopt the approach evolved by the court in construing an essentially identical phrase in the National Labor Relations Act, as amended, namely, that any subject with a 'significant or material' relationship to conditions of employment constitutes a 'term and condition of employment' unless it involves decisions concerning the basic goals and direction of the employer. More specifically, in the public sector a proper balance must be struck between the duty of elected officials to make decisions for the entire electorate and the statutory right of employees to negotiated items directly affecting terms and conditions of employment. Without question, class size has a major and tangible impact on teachers' working conditions (most notably, perhaps, on workload), being an internal component of the working environment. As class size is not an expression of a primary policy goal of the basic direction of the respondent, but does have a significant impact on working conditions for teachers, I find that it constitutes a term and condition of employment."

to bargain as "a broad and unqualified one, and there is no reason why the mandatory provision of that act should be limited, in any way, except in cases where some other applicable statutory provision explicitly and definitively prohibits the public employer from making an agreement as to a particular term or condition of employment" (30 NY2d at 126).

Thus, in New York, as in Michigan—where bargaining in the public sector has existed for a longer period than most states—the decisions of the respective labor boards and courts have evolved a substantially broader scope of bargaining. The private sector standards eventually have found acceptance in these decisions as the prebargaining hodgepodge of employment rules have to a significant degree been circumvented, discounted, or ruled to be superseded by the collective bargaining statutes. However, there is no doubt that the prebargaining system of rules and regulations is still a major impediment to a broad scope of bargaining and continues to provide ready-made excuses for employers who wish not to negotiate on specific items. This problem is especially acute in those areas where there is an absence of a collective bargaining statute, or in those states which do not have a decisional mechanism to which the employees' organization can turn in order to resolve this problem. It is in these areas where the public employees are at the mercy of the public employer, since the employee groups cannot walk into a court or agency and assert their collective bargaining rights. They are, thus, without means to argue that collective bargaining supersedes conflicting employment laws and regulations, and this works to restrict unduly the scope of bargaining.

Management Rights by Law—the Michigan Experience

Let us now turn to specific issues, such as promotion standards, subcontracting, recruitment, and residency requirements, to ascertain whether the scope of bargaining in these areas is as broad for the public employees as exists in the private sector. All of the above-mentioned issues have a basic relationship to what has been traditionally known as management rights. Management rights in public employment is a more amorphous concept, simply because much of what is considered to be a management prerogative, as defined by statute, often is not in harmony with accepted management standards in the private sector. Again, if we analyze the experience in Michigan this statutory management rights barrier becomes apparent. Michigan, however, does not statutorily set forth "management rights" in the collective bargaining law (PERA).

One of the most constant questions arising in this area is whether promotional standards can be negotiated. This question first arose in *City of Detroit Board of Fire Commissioners* (1968 Labor Op. 492), when the commissioners attempted to establish new job specifications for top uniformed positions without first negotiating these changes with the local fire fighters. The firemen filed a claim which the MERC found valid by applying the NLRB standard that promotion standards within the bargaining unit are mandatory subjects of bargaining.*

The MERC came to similar conclusions regarding the elimination of bargaining unit work in *Gibralter School District* (1970 Labor Op. 338). When the school board created new supervisory positions outside the bargaining unit for unit members who were previously school counselors, the MERC decided that "action which places bargaining unit work outside of the ambit of the members of the collective bargaining unit without reasonable notice to the union and a chance to bargain thereon, is a violation of the duty to bargain." (In 1970 Labor Op. at 341, the Commission cited the NLRB standard in *Fitzer Television, Inc.,* 131 NLRB 821, 831, 48 LRRM 1165 (1961), enforced, 299 F2d 845 (1962).) Moreover, in *Lenawee County Road Commission* (1970 Labor Op. 912), the MERC applied the same standard and found that where a union represents the job of a janitor-watchman by contract, and there are no bargaining unit employees available to fill the job, the employer may not subcontract the work without first bargaining with the union (1970 Labor Op. at 919). Thus, it was established in Michigan public employment relations that an employer must first notify and negotiate with the union prior to the subcontracting of any work—using either the *Gibralter* theory or the *Lenawee* standard.

Further inroads were made on statutory management rights in

---

*1968 Labor Op. at 493 reads: "It is clear from the decisions of the National Labor Relations Board and the courts that under the National Labor Relations Act, standards and procedures for promotion within a bargaining unit are working conditions which are mandatory subjects of bargaining."

City of Detroit (1971 Labor Op. 211), where the charging parties, nine in all, claimed a refusal to bargain against the mayor for changing the work week from 35 to 40 hours. Despite the claims of the city that it had the right by ordinance to change the hours, the MERC found such unilateral action an unfair labor practice, relying on *City of Detroit Board of Fire Commissioners* and a series of NLRB decisions. (In 1971 Labor Op. at 226, the MERC cited *NLRB v. C. & C. Plywood Corp.*, 385 US 421 (1967); *Hooker Chemical Co.*, 186 NLRB no. 49 (1970); *Southern Materials Co., Inc.*, 181 NLRB no. 153 (1970).)

In a second *City of Detroit* case (1971 Labor Op. 237), following the aforementioned, two very difficult scope of bargaining issues were posed—a residency requirement for Detroit police, and standards for recruitment of new police officers. As to the first issue, the police department had a prior regulation which required all officers to reside in the city. When the union reached agreement with the mayor to eliminate this requirement, the city's Common Council passed an ordinance instituting the residency requirement. The MERC found the residency requirement to be a mandatory subject of bargaining, and required the city, despite the ordinance to the contrary, to bargain with the union over this item (1971 Labor Op. at 241). The second scope of bargaining issue in *City of Detroit* was whether recruitment standards for new police officers would fall within the scope of bargaining as defined by the Commission. In a rare 2-1 split the Commission ruled that items relating to conditions prior to employment were excluded from public employee bargaining. The split turned on the rejection of the NLRB standard. (In 1971 Labor Op. at 242, MERC relied upon *Associated General Contractors*, 143 NLRB 409, 53 LRRM 4299 (1963).)

Even though MERC did not endorse the NLRB standard for negotiating entrance or recruitment standards, their decisions of 1970 and 1971 relative to management rights gave the Michigan public employees most of the bargaining rights that had been established in the private sector. The previous management rights that had been established by law were severely restricted and the public employee now has a right to bargain over promotional standards as set forth in the *Detroit Board of Fire Commissioners* cases; they have the full rights to notice and to bargain over subcontracting as settled in *Gibralter* and *Lenawee*; and they have a right to bargain to impasse over such items as residency requirements and any change in working conditions, notwithstanding existing collective agreements, as found in the two *City of Detroit* cases.

If the Michigan experience holds true, then public employer management rights will evolve to be comparable to those of the private employer. Or, put another way, it appears that decisional bodies will be hard pressed to find overriding reasons for continuing the distinction between private and public management. If the evolutionary course holds true, the public employer will retain the full rights to define the mission of the enterprise—the right to define the goals and the function of the governmental body. However, the other management rights as established by law will more than likely be eroded through the decisional process as the distinction between public and private employment becomes blurred.

Duty To Bargain Any Changes in Working Conditions— the New York Experience

An ancillary question related to the scope of bargaining problem is whether the employer has the duty to bargain any proposed changes in working conditions—whether or not the existing collective agreement speaks to the proposed change. If this employer duty is limited then naturally the scope of bargaining will be proportionately limited.

If, after an agreement is in effect between the parties, the employer—acting under the aegis of what he believes to be state law or inherent management rights—alters some conditions of employment, the question arises as to the exclusive right of the employee organization to negotiate such change. Quite frequently, such changes in working conditions may be tangentially related to the collective agreement. The question then arises as to whether the employee organization should protest such action through the grievance-arbitration mechanism, or whether the union should file a refusal to bargain charge. The relation of this question to the scope of bargaining becomes clear when one considers the two alternative routes. If the union's only recourse is the grievance-arbitration mechanism, then the scope of bargaining will be limited. Only those items included in the collective bargaining agreement would be arbitrable. Management would have a right to change working conditions so long as they did not conflict with the existing collective agreement. If, on the other hand, the employees are able to file a refusal to bargain on the proposed change in working conditions, then any mandatory subject of bargaining would have to be negotiated with the employee representative.

The New York Public Employment Relations Board was faced with this problem soon after the improper practices amendment to the Taylor Law was passed in 1969. In *Board of Education, Union Free School District no. 3, Town of Hempstead, Nassau County* (4 PERB 3659 (1971)), the teachers' group claimed the board of education unilaterally imposed conditions requiring employees on sabbatical leave to be employed for a period of two years upon their return. The board had agreed upon a sabbatical leave provision in the collective agreement; however, pursuant to what it believed to be the mandate of education law, it added the requirement of the post-leave employment. The association did not file a grievance, but instead registered a refusal to bargain claim. The school board countered that the dispute was a matter for the contractual grievance-arbitration mechanism and not a matter within the jurisdiction of the PERB. The PERB concluded that, unlike the bargaining statutes in Wisconsin (Wisconsin State Employment Labor Relations Act, W.S.A. §§111.80-111.94, 1965L, as amended, 1967L) and Hawaii (Collective Bargaining in Public Employment, H.R.S., ch. 89, 1970L), which specify a breach of collective bargaining agreement as an unfair labor practice, the New York Taylor Law had no such provision in its improper practices section. The PERB, therefore, opted not to exercise jurisdiction over the alleged violation of the collective agreement. However, the PERB confronted the issue of whether a breach of contract may also constitute an improper practice. The answer was in the affirmative, as the PERB decided that where the board of education changed existing practices, policies, and procedures without negotiating such change with the representative employees, such change constituted a violation of the board's obligation to negotiate in good faith (4 PERB at 3661).

A similar charge was filed by a group of blue collar employees of the Spencer-Van Etten School District (*Central School District no. 1 of Spencer-Van Etten School District,* 4 PERB 4591 (1971)), who charged the employer with unilaterally granting one employee an additional week's vacation beyond the vacation benefits provided in the collective agreement. This action was found to be more than a violation of the contract—the employer's action constituted individual negotiating of vacation benefits which violated the statutory obligation to negotiate any alterations of terms and conditions of employment.*

At this juncture in the evolution of New York labor relations policy, it appears that the PERB has significantly expanded the scope of bargaining by insisting that any change in mandatory subjects of bargaining must be negotiated with the employee representative—despite the existence of a collective bargaining agreement which may be silent or partially silent on the subject of dispute. This direction of the PERB has limited the "inherent managerial rights"—those established by prior state law—and has expanded the duty of the employer to bargain. By favoring the private sector standard as to a limited PERB jurisdiction over collective bargaining agreement disputes, the New York Labor Board enhanced growth in the scope of bargaining by saying, in effect, that simply because the subject of the dispute is not contained in the collective bargaining agreement, this does not give the employer the right to change working conditions unilaterally.

This approach, as exhibited by the New York experience, is healthy because it forces the employer and the employee organizations into a continuous relationship. In many areas, where there is an absence of a continued relationship, the employee organization is forced to request a multitude of items in its contract proposals in order to prepare for all contingencies. In such instances the employees know that if the contract does not cover the entire waterfront, then they will have no right to be involved subsequently in changes in working conditions. Such an approach only clutters the bargaining table and pressures the employer to broaden the scope of bargaining into every area, which in turn creates a climate for increased disputes in bargaining.

---

*Spencer-Van Etten School District, 4 PERB at 4593 reads: "An employer's obligation to negotiate with the representative of its employees concerning terms and conditions of employment arises when an employee organization is duly recognized or certified. Thereafter, as a general rule, an employer may not unilaterally alter its employees' terms and conditions of employment or conclude private arrangements with employees regarding such matters without breaching its statutory negotiating obligations."

Limitation on Public Employees' Right To Strike

In the final analysis, the scope of bargaining is as broad or as narrow as is the relative strength or weakness of the parties at the table. If the employee organization is a well-organized and disciplined group, then the employer is less likely to be worried about bargainability and more concerned about contract settlement. Of course, the most effective bargaining lever available to any employee organization is the strike, and without that leverage the public employee unions will be relatively weak bargaining advocates, and the scope of bargaining will be restricted. Since most public employees are prohibited by law from striking (4 PERB 3659 (1971); Wisconsin State Employment Labor Relations Act; see also the Vermont statute which provides for teachers a limited right to strike (Labor Relations for Teachers, U.S.A., T. 16, §§ 1981-2018, 1969L)), this proscription is an effective limit on the scope of bargaining. It would seem only fair that public employees who are prohibited from striking should therefore be afforded some other source of leverage to compensate for their inability to strike—such as a mandate that public employers have a higher duty to bargain than private sector employers.

This "higher duty of bargaining" is a decision concept that was written into the New York Taylor Law by PERB on the theory that, in the absence of the public employees' right to strike, the employer has a higher duty to bargain than in the private sector where the right to strike exists. This concept was first established in *City of Troy Uniformed Firemen's Association** and was subsequently accepted by a lower court in a decision involving a strike by the New Rochelle teachers.†

---

*In 2 PERB 3501 (1969), the Board decided that: "Public employees of the State have been granted the right to organize, the right to be represented by employee organizations, to negotiate collectively with their public employer concerning terms and conditions of employment, and the public employer is required to negotiate with such employee organization and to enter into written agreement concerning the terms and conditions so negotiated. The right to strike as part of the negotiating process, however, is denied public employees. Thus, it would appear that public employers in this State under the statutory scheme have a particular responsibility and obligation to negotiate in good faith."

†In *New Rochelle Federation of Teachers, Local 280, American Federation of Teachers, AFL-CIO*, 3 PERB 8146 (1970), the court found that: "The

However, this "higher duty to bargain" has been paid little more than lip service by PERB in the process of defining mandatory subjects of bargaining. Two recent PERB decisions* have combined to narrow what PERB considers to be mandatory subjects of bargaining for public employees. In both instances the PERB expanded the concept of the "mission of the employer"—those items which are not mandatory subjects of bargaining. Thus, with a broad definition of the "mission of the employer," the scope of bargaining has been proportionally narrowed. This trend is most perplexing, especially in light of the theoretical existence of the employer's "higher duty to bargain." It is most difficult to imagine how an employer's "higher duty to bargain" can coexist with a broad definition of the "mission of the company" which limits the scope of bargaining.

Thus, the "higher duty to bargain," which is an employer responsibility to compensate for the prohibition against employee strikes, is apparently nothing more than a hollow concept, and the uncompensated prohibition against public employee strikes still stands as a major impediment to achieving a scope of bargaining equal to that existing in the private sector.

---

fact that strikes by public employees are prohibited does not give a license to public employers to be intransigent in negotiating with their employees or to frustrate the negotiating process. Rather this prohibition would appear to impose a higher duty of good faith negotiating on the part of public employers than employers in the private sector."

*In *Association of Central Office Administrators*, 4 PERB 3058 (1971), and 4 PERB 4509 (1971), and in *City School District of the City of New Rochelle*, 4 PERB 3060 (1971), 4 PERB 3705 (1971), the PERB set forth the standards for the mission of the public employer. In *Association of Administrators* where the question was whether a residency requirement was mandatory subject of bargaining, the PERB's position regarding the mission of the employer was stated as: ". . . management's right to make fundamental policy decisions regarding the operation and goals of the mission is, if anything, more compelling in the public sector where the employer, charged with the management and direction of a governmental enterprise, has the added responsibility of fulfilling a public trust." *Association of Administrators*, at 4509. In *City of New Rochelle* where 140 teaching positions were eliminated without prior negotiations with the teachers, the PERB's response was: "Decisions of a public employer with respect to the carrying out of its mission, such as a decision to eliminate or curtail a service, are matters that a public employer should not be compelled to negotiate with its employees." *New Rochelle*, at 4599.

Summary and Conclusion

The lot of the public school teacher is now inextricably bound with the future of all public employee relations. A restriction on bargaining for one segment becomes a restriction upon all segments of public employment. Of the restrictions on the scope of bargaining for public employees, as enumerated in this discussion, only those limitations which relate to prebargaining employment rules and regulations have been overcome to some degree by employee organizations. The public school teachers and public employees who are engaged in collective bargaining are still faced with severe restrictions which are contained in the express provisions of the various bargaining statutes; they are still confronted with management rights which are dictated by law; they are still frustrated by the limited fiscal and managerial authority of public employers; and they are still limited by the prohibition against strikes. All of these factors have created measurable roadblocks to achieving a scope of bargaining equivalent to that enjoyed in the private sector.

The one area of encouragement for public employees rests with the tendency of state labor boards and courts to eliminate many of the traditional legal impediments which stand in the way of a meaningful collective bargaining process. If the experience in New York and Michigan is to give us a clue to the future of public employment labor relations, then the decision process of the labor boards and courts will eventually evolve a broader scope of bargaining than now exists.

That experience also points to the long-term solution regarding the scope of bargaining. That solution rests with the adoption of statutory language which is comparable to the National Labor Relations Act, and with the establishment of an administrative agency to decide the questions on a case-by-case situation.

On the other hand, if public employers and public agencies attempt to make a clear distinction between private and public employment, and if there is a continued effort to assert managerial rights which are broader than private sector rights, then such positions only invite continued controversy and conflicts. The same is true of any artificial schemes to divide collective bargaining in the public sector into consultations and negotiations. Such an arbitrary division would only increase the disputes in negotiations when attempting to define items appropriate for consultation. Furthermore, if in such a scheme bargaining is limited to mostly wages and money items, then there would be little incentive to bargain and settle at the table. An employee organization would have to increase its monetary demands in order to retain viability since there would be little else to bargain. This would also decrease the number of settlements and increase the disputes.

Thus, if we are to have long-term stability in public employee labor relations, the problem must be attacked in a pragmatic way—that is, use the experience from the private sector to devise an adequate statutory scheme and then allow the administrative agencies to resolve the questions on a case-by-case basis. The guiding principle in such a scheme would be an elimination of any philosophical approach which leads to disputes and encouragement of any elements which lead to stability and settlement.

Reading 5

Determinants of Attitudinal Militancy Among Teachers and Nurses

Joseph A. Alutto and James A. Belasco

In numbers faintly reminiscent of the great organizing drives of the 1930s, teachers, nurses, social workers, and other white-collar workers have been joining unions and even striking in recent years. These actions constitute a sharp departure from the past practices of these occupational groups, members of which have traditionally pursued their occupational objectives through individual efforts or collective activities that have been largely nonmilitant, such as lobbying.

There seem to be many reasons for the change in the attitudes and actions of these white-collar groups. Changing patterns of societal values that legitimate direct confrontation activities may constitute one factor (MacDonald 1967). Another may be the changing makeup of the work force in these occupations, such as an increasing proportion of younger males and minority group members (Belasco and Alutto 1969; Cole 1969). Another factor might have been the spectacular success of the militant actions taken by certain blue-collar unions in the postwar period, particularly in the construction and transportation industries. Yet, although these and other factors

Reprinted by permission from *Industrial and Labor Relations Review* 27, no. 2 (January 1974): 216-27. Copyright 1974 by Cornell University.

have led to increased militancy within many professions, some, such as teachers, appear to be more militant than others, such as nurses, in the pursuit of occupational objectives. Also, within occupational groups, there seem to be wide variations in militancy, with those particularly in the urban areas displaying higher levels of militant behavior.

It is the belief of the authors that these intra- and intergroup variations in militancy may be associated with the nature of both the profession and the specific employing institution. To test this hypothesis, a questionnaire survey was conducted among members of two professions—nurses and teachers—that have been characterized by an increasing number of militant activities. The survey was conducted with a limited sample, examined only a small number of variables, and collected primarily attitudinal rather than behavioral data, so its results obviously do not constitute the definitive study of militancy among white-collar workers. Given the importance of this subject today, however, it is believed that even a partial and preliminary study is of interest.

Organizational Context

The occupational structure of the United States has been strongly influenced by two, often contradictory, trends. On one hand, there has been the growth, in both absolute numbers and status, of a large number of occupational groups clamoring to be recognized as professional (Vollmer and Mills 1966). On the other hand, given the development of a service-oriented economy and the assumption of new social responsibilities by both government and business, many of these rapidly growing occupations have been attached to large-scale bureaucratic organizations (Wilensky 1964; Chamberlain and Cullen 1971). As a result, large numbers of individuals have come to share the "autonomous-independent" orientations of professional groups while existing in the "subordinate-dependent" organizational setting usually occupied by nonprofessional employees. To some extent, the militant collective action of some white-collar groups may be an outgrowth of the tension attributable to this clash between professional ideals and organizational reality.

In addition, a number of factors specific to particular organizational forms may account for the militancy among many professional and quasiprofessional groups. For example, limitations on professional autonomy often emerge in organizations in which decision making is controlled by nonprofessionals (Blau and Scott 1962). In addition, employment in large-scale bureaucratic institutions sharply modifies professional career progressions. Instead of career advancement taking place through systems controlled by professional colleagues, career advancement becomes a matter of progressing through hierarchies in which control is shared with or dominated by nonprofessionals (Scott 1965). All this results in a loss of control over conditions of professional practice (Wilensky 1965).

General organizational characteristics of institutions employing professionals may account for modifications in the degree of professionals' militancy (Kornhauser 1963). These organizational-specific factors may produce two different patterns. First, since different professions are employed by organizations with different structures (e.g., hospitals are structured differently than schools), professional groups may vary in attitudinal militancy because of the nature of their employing organization. In essence, teachers may have different militancy predispositions than nurses because their employing organizations are so different. Second, within each profession, differences among particular employing organizations may result in different levels of attitudinal militancy. For example, teachers employed in different school districts may vary in intensity of militancy due to the differing characteristics of each district, and nurses employed in different hospitals may exhibit varying levels of attitudinal militancy for the same reason.

Research Design

Thus, the purpose of this study was to identify determinants of attitudinal militancy among professionals through a questionnaire survey of nurses and teachers. Specifically, three research questions were examined: (1) Does the nature of particular occupations account for differing levels of militancy? (2) Within a given occupation, are differences in attitudinal militancy associated with variations in employing institutions? (3) Regardless of differences in professions and employing systems, do professionals vary in militancy because of differences among individuals—in either demographic characteristics (such as sex and marital status) or personality and related traits (such as interpersonal trust and professional commitment)?

To gather data on these variables, a questionnaire survey was conducted among the teachers employed in two separate school districts (one rural and one small-city urban) and the registered nurses employed in three general hospitals (religious, county, and community), all in western New York.* Completed questionnaires were received from 414 teachers, representing 70 percent of all those employed in both school districts, and from 482 registered nurses, representing 80 percent of all nurses employed in the three hospitals. This high rate of participation increased the probability that professional personnel from all organizational levels and professional specialties were adequately represented. Furthermore, comparisons of the distributions of demographic (e.g., age, sex) and general organizational (shift, school building, position) characteristics among participants and nonparticipants revealed no significant differences. Information concerning each subject's occupation, employing organization, age, sex, seniority, and marital status was taken directly from completed questionnaires. Each of the variables represented in tables 1 through 4 required the computation of separate indices or scores based on the responses of each subject. These indices resulted from extensive item analyses and questionnaire development reported elsewhere (Hrebiniak and Alutto 1972; Alutto, Hrebiniak, and Alonso

Table 1

Occupational Differences in Attitudinal Militancy

Occupational group	Collective bargaining by professionals	Strikes by professionals	Unions for professionals	Professional associations
Teachers	5.04	2.89	3.48	5.18
Nurses	2.68	4.82	4.25	2.23
F Value[†]	417.65*	275.86*	36.41*	645.30*

*Significant at the .01 level.
[†]1/899 degrees of freedom.

---

*A rural school district was defined as one that does not serve any population center of more than 2,500 people. A community hospital is a general, nonprofit hospital owned and operated by a voluntary association of citizens.

Table 2
Employment Systems and Attitudinal Militancy

Occupational group	Collective bargaining by professionals	Strikes by professionals	Unions for professionals	Professional associations
Teachers				
Urban	4.78	2.73	3.22	4.86
Rural	5.37	3.09	3.81	5.58
F Value‡	8.65*	4.02†	8.21*	10.26*
Nurses				
Religious	2.67	5.16	4.56	2.06
County	2.53	4.55	3.96	2.30
Community	2.88	4.79	4.28	2.33
F Value**	2.40	5.92*	5.32*	3.11

    *Significant at the .01 level.
    †Significant at the .05 level.
    ‡1/414 degrees of freedom.
    **2/482 degrees of freedom.

Table 3
Marital Status, Sex, and Attitudinal Militancy

Demographic characteristic	Collective bargaining by professionals	Strikes by professionals	Unions for professionals	Professional associations
Sex				
Males	5.42	3.64	4.18	5.00
Females	3.51	3.97	3.85	3.37
F Value†	94.92*	2.33	2.97	56.01*
Female by occupation				
Nurses	2.68	4.82	4.25	2.23
Teachers	3.96	2.26	3.31	5.28
F Value‡	85.61*	416.80*	39.67*	438.77*
Marital status				
Married	3.63	3.81	3.03	3.33
Single	3.82	4.00	3.90	3.68
Other	3.83	3.52	3.61	3.93
F Value**	.80	2.35	.62	2.91

    *Significant at the .01 level.
    †1/899 degrees of freedom.
    ‡1/731 degrees of freedom.
    **2/898 degrees of freedom.

Table 4
Age, Seniority, and Personal Characteristics as Predictors
of Attitudinal Militancy*
(n = 901)

Variable‡	Regression coefficient	Multiple R	R^2†
	Attitudes toward collective bargaining by professionals		
Age	.5656	.465	21.7
Organizational commitment	−.4915	.480	23.0
Seniority	−.2717	.489	23.9
Job tension	.1385	.493	24.3
	Attitudes toward strikes by professionals		
Age	−.4572	.402	16.2
Seniority	.3973	.435	18.9
Role conflict	.0475	.442	19.6
Career dissatisfaction	−.0621	.448	20.0
Interpersonal trust	.6432	.452	20.4
	Attitudes toward unions for professionals		
Age	−.1865	.165	2.7
Seniority	−.3118	.207	4.3
Interpersonal trust	−.6264	.218	4.8
Career dissatisfaction	−.0695	.227	5.2
Job tension	.1285	.238	5.7
	Attitudes toward professional associations		
Age			
Career dissatisfaction	.0975	.753	32.8
Seniority	−.2653	.581	33.8
Organizational commitment	−.4240	.585	34.2

*Only results that are significant at the .01 level are reported in this table.

†Cumulative percentage of total variance explained.

‡Two other variables were included in each equation (professional commitment and authoritarianism) but neither was found to be significant at the .01 level for any of the attitudinal militancy measures.

1970, 1973; Kahn et al. 1964). Regardless of occupation, subjects responded to the same questions.

In this article, "attitudinal militancy" refers to the subjects' opinions of strikes by professionals, collective bargaining by professionals, unions for professionals, and professional associations. Individuals evaluated each of these objects by responding to seven-point semantic differential scales that measured the degree to which subjects viewed strikes, unions, collective bargaining, and professional associations with favor or disfavor. Subject scores could range from

1, very unfavorable, to 7, very favorable. It was assumed that the more militant the attitudes of professionals, the more favorable their opinions would be concerning strikes, unions, and collective bargaining, and the less favorable, or at least more uncertain, would be their view of their traditionally less forceful professional associations.

Other Variables

In order to investigate the relationship between personality traits and attitudinal militancy, two measures of personality characteristics were used. The first measured authoritarianism, or each subject's reaction to authority, by means of a shortened thirteen-item version of the California F-scale (Adorno 1950). The second personality characteristic, interpersonal trust, was measured by a six-question scale that tests the degree to which each individual views his social world as either friendly, supportive, and predictable, or hostile, demanding, and unpredictable (Kluckhohn and Murray 1967). It was assumed that the more "trusting" the individual's perceptions of his social environment, the lower would be his level of attitudinal militancy.

It was felt that another relevant variable might be the extent to which employees are dissatisfied with the behavior or attributes they feel are necessary for career advancement. Subjects were presented with a list of thirty-five attributes that might be necessary for career advancement (e.g., having spouse liked by your superior, knowing the right people, having technical skills, showing initiative, being lucky, getting along well with others, etc.). They responded to these thirty-five attributes twice, indicating on a five-point scale how important they believed each item was *currently* and how important they felt it *should be.* For example, when confronted with the trait, "high technical skill," subjects would indicate its perceived current importance and their preference for how important it should be. The degree of career dissatisfaction was computed by adding the absolute difference between responses concerning current and preferred values for each of the thirty-five attributes.

The degree of commitment an individual has to his occupation and employing organization has also been shown to be a central factor in determining attitudes (Hrebiniak and Alutto 1972). Consequently, an index of commitment was constructed for each subject based on total responses to whether or not he would leave his current occupation (professional commitment) or employing system (organizational commitment) if offered inducements such as a slight increase in pay, a slight increase in status, slightly greater creativity, or slightly friendlier colleagues. For each subject there was one score for commitment to profession and a separate score representing commitment to present employing organization (Hrebiniak and Alutto 1972; Alutto, Hrebiniak, and Alonso 1970, 1973; Kahn et al. 1964).

Two additional variables were examined in this research. The first, felt job tension, was measured through use of a scale that indicates how much job-related anxiety or pressure an individual is experiencing (see Kahn et al. 1964; Alutto, Hrebiniak, and Alonso 1970). Finally, in order to determine the degree of perceived role conflict, subjects were presented with a list of ten role activities common to their occupation. Every subject then indicated the percentage of his total job time he *currently* devoted to each activity and the percentage of work time he *preferred* to allocate to each activity. By adding the discrepancies between current and preferred job time allocations, a single comparable index of role conflict was derived for each subject.

Data analysis for this study occurred in two phases, both of which utilized dimensions of attitudinal militancy as the dependent variable. First, a series of analysis of variance tests were conducted, using four independent variables: occupational grouping (teachers, nurses), employment system (two school districts for teachers and three hospitals for nurses), marital status (married, single, other), and sex (males, females). Results of these analyses are presented in tables 1, 2, and 3.

The second phase of analysis involved use of multiple regression techniques to answer the question. "Of the many independent variables examined in this study, which were of greatest relative importance in explaining degrees of attitudinal militancy?" Due to limitations imposed by step-wise multiple regression techniques, included for analysis were only those variables which appeared to approximate a linear continuous range of variation.* Thus, serving as independent

---

*More specifically, it was felt the variables in this stage of analysis would more closely satisfy the traditional regression assumptions of (1) linearity, (2) interval scales of measurement, (3) normal distributions, and (4) relative lack of

variables in the analysis presented in table 4 were age, seniority in employing system, career dissatisfaction, organizational commitment, interpersonal trust, job tension, perceived role conflict, and professional commitment.

Analysis of Variance Series

It is clear from data presented in table 1 that the nature of the occupation is a significant factor differentiating levels of attitudinal militancy. Teachers tended to view collective bargaining ($\overline{X}$ = 5.04) and professional associations ($\overline{X}$ = 5.18) much more positively than did nurses ($\overline{X}$ = 2.68 and 2.23, respectively). On the other hand, nurses viewed strikes by professionals and unions for professionals more positively than did school teachers. The more favorable evaluation of professional associations by the teachers, and of the unions by the nurses, may be explained by the ineffectiveness of the American Nurses Association's attempts to date to engage in collective bargaining, in contrast to the activism and success of many district affiliates of the National Education Association (Alutto 1971; Seidman 1970). In any event, the first research question is answered in the affirmative: levels of attitudinal militancy do vary among professional occupations.

Also, although it might be assumed that a person's attitudes are uniformly positive or negative towards strikes, unions, and collective bargaining, table 1 shows that nurses and teachers in this study demonstrated an ability to respond differentially to the four measures of attitudinal militancy. Again, this might be a result of prior occupational experiences with collective action. For example, the more favorable response of nurses to strikes by professionals may reflect the recent success of some nursing groups in engaging in sick calls and other concerted activities designed to provide for the protection of minimal patient needs while still exerting economic pressure on employers. As the "consciousness" concerning collective action has increased among nurses, the dramatic impact of strike activity may

---

interdependence between predictors. See Nemar (1969); Kelley, Beggs, and McNeil (1969). A step-wise regression technique was selected since there were no prior guidelines for eliminating any regressors and the desire was to generate a relatively parsimonious model for analytical purposes. See Draper and Smith (1970); Wonnacott and Wonnacott (1970); and Brownlee (1965).

have increased its perceived value, particularly when compared with the ineffectiveness of previous activities. On the other hand, since nurses have long been involved in quasibargaining relationships that have not proven very satisfactory, in part due to the historical reluctance of nurses to exercise economic power, their overall evaluation of collective bargaining may have become relatively negative.

In essence, rather than allowing one to identify either teachers or nurses as more militant than the other, data from this study suggest that these groups define militancy quite differently: for teachers, it may mean reliance on collective bargaining, in the sense of collective negotiations through a professional association and little use of the strike; for nurses, however, militancy may currently entail strike action and reliance on unions.

Data presented in table 2 focus on the second research question of whether attitudinal militancy within an occupation is affected by a particular employment system. For teachers, the employing district apparently serves as a good differentiator of attitudinal militancy, but in an unexpected direction: those employed in the urban district consistently revealed less militant attitudes than those teaching in the rural district. Subsequent interviews confirmed this finding. Evidence presented elsewhere suggests that this rural-urban difference may well be a result of the lower degree of participation by teachers in the decision-making structure of the rural district (Alutto and Belasco 1972). In terms of attitudes toward strikes and unions, employment organization also appeared to be related to the attitudinal militancy of professional nurses. It should be noted, however, that in respect to attitudes toward collective bargaining and their professional associations, nurses were consistently negative in evaluating both collective bargaining and their professional associations, regardless of particular institutional affiliations. On balance, however, the second research question is also answered in the affirmative.

The third research question deals with the impact of specific demographic variables on attitudinal militancy. Table 3 reports results of an analysis based on sex and marital status for all 900 subjects. Apparently marital status does not serve as an effective discriminator of attitudinal militancy. A similar conclusion holds with respect to sex and attitudes toward strikes and unions for professionals. There are, however, differences in the attitudes of males and females toward collective bargaining and professional associations, and differences between female teachers and female nurses on all four subjects. Males view collective bargaining and professional associations far more favorably than do females. Female teachers view collective bargaining and professional associations more positively than do female nurses, but they are more negative than nurses in their opinions of strikes and unions.

Thus, the results of the analysis of variance tests recorded in tables 1 to 3 suggest that the most effective bases for differentiating levels of attitudinal militancy are occupational grouping and employing organization.

Personal Characteristics

In an effort to develop a parsimonious predictive model for attitudinal militancy, step-wise multiple regression analysis was employed, using the four attitudinal militancy dimensions as separate dependent variables and several measures of individual differences as independent variables. In this manner, four sets of multiple regression equations were generated to test the extent to which professionals vary in militancy because of differences among individuals with respect to age, seniority, and various personality and attitudinal characteristics.

Table 4 presents the results of this analysis, showing that of the variables tested, age was the single best predictor of attitudinal militancy, accounting for as much as 31 percent of the variance in attitudes toward professional associations. Age was positively correlated with evaluations of collective bargaining (accounting for 21.7 percent of the variance) as well as professional associations, and negatively correlated with evaluations of strikes (accounting for 16.2 percent of the variance) and attitudes toward unions (accounting for 2.7 percent of the variance). Apparently younger teachers and nurses evaluate strikes and unions more favorably than do their older colleagues, whereas the latter hold a more favorable view of collective bargaining activities and traditional professional associations. Furthermore, age accounts for substantially more of the variation of attitudes toward collective bargaining and professional associations than it does toward strikes and unions, indicating that other factors intervene in the relationship between age and attitudes toward the more militant activities of joining unions and striking.

Career dissatisfaction appears as another significant contributor to the prediction of attitudinal militancy, showing up in three of the four sets of equations. Interestingly, the greater the career dissatisfaction of professionals, the more positive the attitudes toward professional associations and the more negative the attitudes toward strikes and unions. Thus, it would appear that older teachers and nurses who become disenchanted with their career development tend to look to their professional associations and not unions for relief.

Length of service with the institution (seniority) is another variable that contributes significantly to the regression equation in all four sets. Despite the presumed close identity of seniority and age, these factors have opposite effects in three of the four equation sets. This result indicates that older, but shorter-service employees, have relatively favorable attitudes toward collective bargaining and professional associations, whereas younger, longer-service employees have more favorable attitudes toward strikes. The first group probably includes both the high mobility professionals and individuals who have recently returned to the occupation, either from another occupation or from maternity or housekeeping activities.

Organizational commitment is another contributor to the explained variance in attitudes toward collective bargaining and professional associations. In both instances, the greater an individual's commitment to his employing organization, the more negative his evaluation of collective bargaining and professional associations.

Felt job tension and interpersonal trust were also significant contributors to more militant attitudes. The greater the degree of job related tension experienced by subjects, the more positively they evaluated collective bargaining and unions for professionals. Rather surprisingly, however, interpersonal trust was positively related to attitudes toward strikes and negatively related to attitudes toward unions.

The data reveal a somewhat different profile of the militant teacher and nurse than prior research may have led one to expect. Those most favorable to collective bargaining may well be older, low-seniority employees who are less committed to the employing organization and who experience greater job tension. Furthermore, the prominence of career dissatisfaction in the equations suggests that many of these older, shorter-service employees do not find their careers satisfactory, and this may contribute to their more militant attitudes. These dissatisfied teachers and nurses, however, do not favor strikes, thus indicating the limits of their militancy, and they are most likely to turn to a professional association to remedy their employment problems. The low amount of variance explained in terms of attitudes toward unions may reflect the low salience of union activities for these two groups of semiprofessionals.

In summary, the independent variables listed in table 4 were relatively uneven predictors of attitudinal militancy accounting for from 5.7 percent to 34.2 percent of attitudinal variance. Furthermore, those predictors do a better job of explaining the less militant concepts of collective bargaining and professional associations (24 percent and 34 percent) than the more militant concepts of strikes (20 percent) and unions (6 percent).

In any event, the data presented in tables 1, 2, 3, and 4 suggest that the most effective discriminators of attitudinal militancy among professional employees may well be (1) characteristics of the particular professional occupation; (2) characteristics of the specific employing institutions in which professional employees are found; and (3) age. Thus, in order to understand professionals' changing attitudes toward militant job behavior, researchers should not assume that members of professional and semiprofessional groups are homogeneous in attitudinal orientation, and these investigators might profitably focus their attention on rather traditional worksite concerns.

Summary and Implications

It has been noted that this study has several limitations. First, it deals only with teachers and nurses, members of semiprofessional occupations. Whether or not our findings can be generalized to more traditional professionals, such as doctors and lawyers, is a question for future research. Also, the survey was conducted in a single geographic area and collected primarily attitudinal rather than behavioral data. Nevertheless, the results do have several interesting implications.

In the first place, the findings suggest that factors specific to particular employing organizations may well be among the most effective predictors of attitudinal militancy among members of professional and semiprofessional occupations (see table 2 and the importance of career dissatisfaction, role conflict, and job tension in table 4). Issues such as job autonomy, participation in decision making, salary, and other conditions of professional practice are likely to have a major influence on the level of attitudinal militancy that surfaces in any given organization. This is consistent with previously reported data concerning teachers (Belasco and Alutto, 1969), nurses (Alutto 1971), and other members of occupational groups. Concern for participation in decision making, for instance, has been widely cited as contributing to the spread of teacher militancy (Nigro 1969; Shils and Whittier 1968). In the same vein, denial of job autonomy, particularly control over matters of professional practice, has been demonstrated to be related to attitudinal militancy for teachers and social workers. This implies that by focusing on the specific needs and concerns of their own professional employees, employing organizations can reduce the level of attitudinal militancy.

One specific organizational factor emerges quite strongly from the multivariate analysis of both occupational groups studied. Career dissatisfaction—that is, dissatisfaction with the behavior or attributes perceived to be necessary for career advancement—ranked as a major contributor to the emergence of attitudinal militancy. It is interesting to note that both nurses and teachers tend to have horizontal occupational structures located in vertical, multilevel organization hierarchies. The absence of professional advancement opportunities forces teachers and nurses to leave, in effect, the actual practice of their profession if they desire to advance along the organization hierarchy—and the administrative positions offering promotion opportunities may require different characteristics for success than those that would contribute to effective teaching or nursing. This suggests the need for employing organizations to provide a differentiated professional hierarchy that would clearly permit several steps of advancement for "practicing" professionals. In education, the concept of differentiated staffing, with the utilization of master teachers and team leaders, is an effort to provide a multilevel professional advancement structure. In medicine, the recent emergence of the nurse/physician role is a similar attempt to provide a multilevel career structure.

In many respects, the situation confronting nurses and teachers closely parallels that which confronted engineers and scientists in the late 1950s. Until that time, the engineering profession had had a flat occupational hierarchy and salary structure that forced ambitious professionals into nonengineering management positions. The career dissatisfactions expressed by engineers at that time, combined undoubtedly with the threat of emergent unionism, led to the creation of dual salary and advancement ladders that permitted engineers and scientists to advance upward in a professional hierarchy that paralleled the management hierarchy in terms of both salary and status. Similar organizational inventions may serve to ease career pressures in the teaching and nursing professions.

Although organizationally specific factors are powerful influences, broad occupational factors are also significant. The findings of this study suggest that professional groups do vary from each other in their levels of attitudinal militancy. Nurses as a group do, in fact, show different attitudes than teachers as a group (see table 1), and these interprofessional differences exist even when sex is held constant (see the comparison of female nurses and teachers in table 3). This suggests the operation of structural factors that may be traced to either some self-selection factor (e.g., females who enter teaching may be different in some critical attributes from females who enter nursing), characteristics of the professional work itself, or simply characteristics of the occupational group (e.g., the relative ineffectiveness of nurses' attempts at collective bargaining in the past due to the structure and functioning of the American Nurses Association and the economic characteristics of the health care industry).

In any event, the clear implication is that members of the two occupations studied cannot be grouped together in matters concerning militant collective action. This suggests, in turn, that different occupational groups might require different statutory procedures regulating their bargaining activities. The New York State Teachers' Association, for instance, has argued most vehemently that the Taylor Law, which regulates the concerted activities of all state and local government employees in New York, is not relevant to the needs of public school teachers. Several states, including Oregon, Washington, and Rhode Island, have enacted labor laws that differentiate not only between nurses and teachers but also between these two professional groups and other occupations found in the public service.* The data

---

*For example, in Washington, teachers are only mandated to meet and negotiate, whereas other employees, including nurses, are mandated to meet, negotiate and sign agreements. For a further summary of relevant laws, see Goldberg (1970).

in this article support this kind of differentiation as a viable public policy.

On the other hand, the relative absence of variation in militant attitudes according to demographic and personal characteristics, other than age, suggests that militancy is a pervasive attitude that is widely distributed throughout the professional population. Employers and legislators who believe that militancy is a phenomenon found only among a few malcontents, whose demands therefore can be ignored, are almost certain to be faced with increased difficulties. The findings of this study support those who argue that changing societal values that legitimatize confrontation and aggressive action in the pursuit of group objectives reinforce, sustain, and may even amplify the attitudinal predisposition of many professionals, who can probably be expected to engage increasingly in militant collective action.

Finally, the heterogeneity in most professional populations suggests the necessity for further research to isolate those concerns most relevant to specific substrata within various occupations. These patterns within professions are of considerable interest to both the researcher who examines individual behavior and the practitioner concerned with managing individual behavior to attain a set of organizational objectives.

References

Adorno, T. *The Authoritarian Personality*. New York: Harper & Brothers, 1950.

Alutto, Joseph. "Professionals and Collective Bargaining: The Case of the American Nurses Association." *Administering Health Systems*, edited by M. Arnold et al. Chicago: Aldine, 1971.

Alutto, Joseph, and Belasco, James. "A Typology for Participation in Organizational Decision-Making." *Administrative Science Quarterly* 17, no. 1 (March 1972): 117-25.

Alutto, Joseph; Hrebiniak, L.; and Alonso, R. "Correlates of Work Related Tensions." *Proceedings of the Industrial Relations Research Association, 23rd Meeting*. Madison, Wis.: The Association, 1970.

Alutto, Joseph; Hrebiniak, L.; and Alonso, R. "On Operationalizing the Concept of Commitment." *Social Forces* (June 1973): 448-54.

Belasco, James, and Alutto, Joseph. "Organizational Impact of Teacher Negotiations." *Industrial Relations* 9, no. 1 (October 1969): 67-79.

Blau, Peter, and Scott, William. *Formal Organizations*. San Francisco: Chandler, 1962.

Brownlee, K. *Statistical Theory and Methodology in Science and Engineering*. New York: John Wiley & Sons, 1965.

Chamberlain, Neil W., and Cullen, Donald E. *The Labor Sector*. New York: McGraw-Hill, 1971.

Cole, Steven. "Teachers' Strikes: A Study of the Conversion of Predisposition in Action." *American Journal of Sociology* 24, no. 5 (March 1969): 506-20.

Draper, N., and Smith, H. *Applied Regression Analysis*. New York: John Wiley & Sons, 1970.

Goldberg, Joseph. "Changing Policies in Public Labor Relations." *Monthly Labor Review* 93, no. 7 (July 1970): 5-10.

Hrebiniak, L., and Alutto, Joseph. "Personal and Role Related Factors in the Development of Organizational Commitment." *Administrative Science Quarterly* 17, no. 4 (December 1972): 555-73.

Kahn, R., et al. *Organizational Stress: Studies in Role Conflict and Ambiguity*. New York: John Wiley & Sons, 1964.

Kelley, F.; Beggs, D.; and McNeil, K. *Research Design in the Behavioral Sciences: Multiple Regression Approach*. Carbondale, Ill.: Southern Illinois University Press, 1969.

Kluckhohn, C., and Murray, H. *Personality in Nature and Society in Culture*. New York: Knopf, 1967.

Kornhauser, W. *Scientists in Industry*. Berkeley: University of California Press, 1963.

MacDonald, Robert M. "Collective Bargaining in the Postwar Period." *Industrial and Labor Relations Review* 20, no. 4 (July 1967): 555-79.

Nemar, Q. *Psychological Statistics*. New York: John Wiley & Sons, 1969.

Nigro, F. *Management-Employee Relations in the Public Service*. Chicago: Public Personnel Association, 1969.

Scott, Richard. "Reactions to Supervision in a Heteronomous Professional Organization." *Administrative Science Quarterly* 10 (June 1965): 65-81.

Seidman, Joel. "Nurses and Collective Bargaining." *Industrial and Labor Relations Review* 23, no. 3 (April 1970): 335-51.

Shils, E. B., and Whittier, C. J. *Teachers, Administrators and Collective Bargaining*. New York: Thomas Crowell, 1968.

Vollmer, Howard, and Mills, Donald. *Professionalism*. Englewood Cliffs, N.J.: Prentice-Hall, 1966.

Wilensky, Harold L. "The Professionalization of Everyone?" *American Journal of Sociology* 70 (September 1964): 137-58.

Wilensky, Harold L. "The Professional Persons in Public Organizations." *Educational Administration Quarterly* 1 (1965): 1-26.

Wonnacott, R. and T. *Econometrics*. New York: John Wiley & Sons, 1970.

Reading 6

The Local Community and Teacher Strike Solidarity

Albert I. Goldberg

Teachers and other service employees, who have regular contact with the public, have become increasingly militant in recent years. Such behavior appears to run counter to the notion that workers who are "involved" in the local community will be less likely to strike than workers who are "isolated" from the community. This notion is often based on the assumption that community sentiments are primarily hostile toward strikes. Instead, those considering militant action may perceive the neighboring community in a variety of ways. This study uses a typology of four local community environments as they are perceived by teachers. It demonstrates that environmental perceptions do not depend on historical factors and describes how they influence union solidarity in a strike situation (the New York City teachers' strike in 1966). Finally, in-group tensions and administrative support are examined as possible intervening variables in the transfer of external community sentiments into strike solidarity among union members.

Reprinted by permission from *Industrial Relations* 13, no. 3 (October 1974), pp. 288-98.

Previous Research

In their cross-national study of the strike propensity of industrial workers, Kerr and Siegel (1954, p. 195) concluded that one of the main explanatory variables was the location of the worker in society. Highly strike-prone industries were found to be those in which workers were "unusually isolated from the general community." (The same relationship was found for British industrial workers by Knowles 1960, pp. 301-18.) Isolation of a work group results in the development of a local occupational community holding common interests and acts to insulate the strikers from critical sentiments held in the general community. Militancy may also be retarded if an isolated work group comes to identify with the general community. See Rimlinger (1959).

Public service workers, such as teachers, are not able to isolate themselves from the community. Their tasks require regular contact with the public, and they usually live within the community. Moreover, a greater degree of responsibility is expected from them, and strikes in the public sector are illegal in most states. Despite this lack of isolation, public service employees have frequently gone out on strike. A case in point is the New York City teachers' union which called strikes in 1960, 1962, 1967, and 1968. In the 1968 strike, which we will examine here, a particularly high level of strike solidarity was reportedly shown by teachers throughout the entire school system (*New York Times,* Sept. 10, 1968, p. 36).

In order to understand the New York City teachers' high strike solidarity, we propose that a local community may come to identify with the striking employees of a particular occupational group. Warner (1963) has presented evidence of such local community support when Yankee City citizens came to identify more with striking workers than with absentee management, and the Illini City studies also portrayed a local community as sympathetic to union activity (Wray 1953, pp. 1-145). While a hostile community can set off processes which may disrupt strike solidarity, a supportive local community can protect the striking group from a more hostile general community. How these perceived local community environments were actually found to affect strike solidarity is the research question examined below.

Sample and Methods

The two sets of data analyzed here were taken from a survey of union chapters of the United Federation of Teachers within New York City schools during the years 1968 and 1969. (These data were collected by the Center for Urban Education, New York City.) Between the time of the collection of these two sets of data, a union strike had been called. The conflict which ensued went beyond the area of normal labor-management relations and engendered hostility between the black community and Jewish teachers. (See Berube and Gittell 1969; Harris and Swanson 1970.) The strike was called by the United Federation of Teachers (UFT), Local 2 of the American Federation of Teachers (AFT). At the time of the 1968 strike, the union claimed a membership of 85 percent of the city's 55,000 teachers; 96 percent of all elementary schools had UFT chapters.

In the spring of 1968, a questionnaire was sent to all union chapter chairmen in the 640 elementary schools of New York City which had active chapters. Replies were received from 62 percent, or 401 chairmen. A second questionnaire was sent to these same schools in the spring of 1969 and responses received from 390 chairmen, or about 61 percent—49 percent of these having also answered the first questionnaire. The second questionnaire repeated some of the key questions from the first and introduced a number of items to gauge the consequences of the strike.

The union chairmen served as informants about union and faculty conditions.* It can be reasonably assumed that the union chairmen were in a particularly advantageous position to accurately report on strike participation and union membership. In addition, the non-professional status of these chairmen—42 percent serving for their first year—would lead most to perceive local community sentiments in a manner similar to the majority of teachers in their schools. It is possible, nevertheless, that chairmen may have overestimated community approval and underestimated community disapproval. However, the concreteness of the items reported should mitigate against

---

*See Barton (1961, p. 3) on the use of such informant data. The primary advantage in using informant data was to make possible the study of 390 separate organizations.

this potential bias. In addition, our analysis was concerned with relative evaluations and was not dependent on the exact level of approval
or disapproval. The findings were distillled from these data as well as
from the author's own observations during the strike.

Results

Local Community Sentiments

Strong criticism was expressed against the strike on a city-wide
level. Mayor John Lindsay believed that the issue was "whether one
group can successfully bring this city to its knees" (*New York Times,*
Oct. 21, 1968, p. 44). The Public Education Association (1968, p.
3), an influential group in New York public education, saw the issue
as a "naked power grab." The New York Civil Liberties Union (1968,
p. 1) described the strike as an effort to undermine local community
control of schools. The *New York Times* (Sept. 10, 1968, p. 46) edi-
torialized that the strike showed "the insensitivity of the professional
education establishment." Thus, little sympathy for the strike was
forthcoming from these larger and more formal institutions of the
city. The character of public employee bargaining in New York City
has been described by Cook (1970).

However, the neighborhood in which the teachers worked was a
community at least as relevant to the teachers as the municipality.
The local community expressed its feelings toward the teachers
through a host of behavioral indicators, ranging from simple verbal
expressions to writing, phoning, joining in some strike activity, or
physically attacking a picket.* The data in table 1 reflect the range
of such sentiments, separated into positive and negative types, as reported by the school chapter chairmen.

In general, the chairmen more often reported positive support
than hostility in their local communities. A sizable majority (68 percent) encountered sympathy from the local community, at least in
the form of verbal support. Active expressions of support included
signing petitions (52 percent), joining picket lines (41 percent), and

_____

*A large demonstration of public support occurred on October 17, 1968,
when 40,000 marchers massed at City Hall. An earlier attempt to demonstrate
against the strike drew 5,000. See the *New York Times,* October 18, 1968, p.
50.

Table 1
Expressions of Approval and Disapproval on the Part of Loyal Parents and/or Residents, as Reported by Chapter Chairmen

Proportion of schools reporting each expression of approval/disapproval (in percentages)	Approval of strike (in percentages)		Disapproval of strike (in percentages)	
60-69	Expressing verbal sympathy	68		
50-59	Signing supporting petitions	52		
40-49	Joining picket lines	41	Demanding that school be kept open	44
30-39	Demanding that school be kept closed	36		
	Offering homes	30		
20-29	Making supportive phone calls	23	Abusing pickets verbally	25
10-19			Distributing hostile leaflets	17
91-09	Writing approving letters	6	Signing condemning petitions	9
			Making abusive phone calls	8
			Writing letters of disapproval	6
			Physically attacking pickets	3

n = 390

offering homes for union activities (30 percent). The main form of disapproval (at 44 percent of the schools) was demands by local residents to keep the schools open. Verbal abuse occurred at 25 percent of the schools, and physical attacks were present at only 3 percent of the schools.

Two separate indices were constructed by adding together these approval and disapproval items. The frequency with which these levels of support or disapproval were reported by union chairmen is shown in table 2. While no forms of approval were reported by 25 percent of the chairmen, 50 percent could find no sign of community disapproval. In turn, while 51 percent of the schools were described as experiencing three or more types of approval, only 19.5

Table 2
Distribution of Approval and Disapproval Expressions

n number of expressions	Percent schools experiencing n number of expressions of approval (in percentages)	Percent schools experiencing n number of expressions of disapproval (in percentages)
0	25	50
1	13	20
2	11	11
3	17	12
4	12	4
5	13	3
6	6	.5
7	3	
	n=390	n=390

percent of the schools were seen as being exposed to three or more forms of disapproval. Contrary to the notion that community residents are generally hostile toward strike activity, in this strike the majority of the chairmen perceived support coming from their local communities. In contrast, fewer chairmen reported incidents of hostility to the strike in their neighborhood.

Community Sentiment and Strike Solidarity

Having demonstrated that community sentiments toward teacher strikes varied, it remains to be seen if these sentiments also had an impact on the strike solidarity of teachers. Teachers were classified as being high on strike solidarity when "almost all" of a school's teachers were reported as strike participants. The indices of perceived community approval and disapproval were then cross-tabulated with the strike solidarity in each school. Figure 1 shows an almost linear relationship between strike solidarity and community approval/disapproval. The incidence of solidarity clearly increases with community approval and declines with community disapproval.*

Community approval and disapproval sentiments concerning the strike were used to create a typology of four distinct local commu-

---

*This analysis is not concerned with the reasons for community hostility. For a description of how different community characteristics can influence union-management relationships, see Derber, Chalmers, and Stagner (1958).

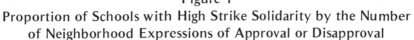

Figure 1
Proportion of Schools with High Strike Solidarity by the Number of Neighborhood Expressions of Approval or Disapproval

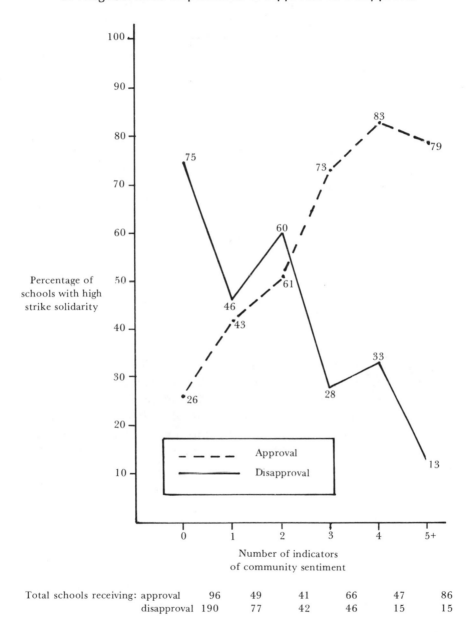

| Total schools receiving: | approval | 96 | 49 | 41 | 66 | 47 | 86 |
| | disapproval | 190 | 77 | 42 | 46 | 15 | 15 |

nity environments which union chairmen perceived. These four environments (shown in table 3) were: (1) a *menacing* environment, in which disapproval was expressed against the strike, combined with few signs of approval; (2) a *passive* environment, in which there were no indicators of disapproval but also few signs of approval; (3) a *mixed* environment, which showed signs of both approval and disapproval, probably reflecting differing opinions among various neighborhood groups; and (4) a *supportive* environment, where approval occurred with little indication of any disapproval.

Table 3
The Proportion of Chairmen Reporting High Strike Solidarity
Within a Typology of Community Environments

Approval indicators	Disapproval indicators	
	Yes (1-6)	No (0)
Low (0-2)	Menacing 29% (127)	Passive 56% (73)
High (3-7)	Mixed 65% (68)	Supportive 85% (131)

Note: Percentages indicate high strike solidarity. The figures in parentheses indicate the number of schools in each type of community environment.

Table 3 also shows the incidence of strike solidarity within each type of local community environment. As shown, the lowest level of strike solidarity occurred in the menacing environment, where only 29 percent of the union chairmen reported high strike solidarity. This is in contrast to the supportive environment where 85 percent of the chairmen reported high strike solidarity. Thus, there was a 56 percent difference in the likelihood of high strike solidarity between the menacing and the supportive community environments. Clearly, the perceived local community environment had a major influence on the ability of the union to maintain strike solidarity among its members.

Historical Union Solidarity

One might ask if strike solidarity in 1968 can be explained by showing that teachers in particular schools have always expressed strong support for the union in the past. Conceivably, the history of unity might also have influenced the chairmen's 1968 perceptions of community sentiments. To address this question, solidarity data available from the previous year's strike were compared with that of 1968 (see table 4).

Table 4
Changes in the Proportion of Schools Reporting High Strike Solidarity in Different Local Community Environments Between the 1967 and 1968 Strikes

Local community environment (1968)	Percent schools with high strike solidarity in 1967	Percent schools with high strike solidarity in 1968	Percent change	Number of schools
Menacing	43	35	−8	84
Passive	43	54	+12	37
Mixed	46	63	+17	46
Supportive	37	87	+50	98

The data in table 4 show that strike solidarity in 1968 changed significantly from that of 1967. While schools in the menacing environment of 1968 showed a slight reduction (8 percent) in their incidence of strike solidarity between 1967 and 1968, schools in the 1968 supportive environment were not held back by the 1967 level of strike solidarity and increased their strike solidarity by 50 percent (see the third column in table 4). Thus, solidarity in 1968 was an accurate reflection of community sentiments *at the time of the 1968 strike* and not of 1967 solidarity.

Another historical influence which might explain the impact of perceived local environments on strike solidarity could be the incidence of prestrike union membership.* Presumably, union members would be more likely to participate in the strike, and, therefore, prior membership of a large proportion of the teaching staff would increase the possibility of strike solidarity at each school. Prestrike unity should be particularly crucial in the menacing environment as

---

*Prestrike membership was taken from the questionnaire administered before the strike and, therefore, was not dependent on retrospective recollection.

it acts to shield the teachers from the effects of antagonistic community sentiments.

The data presented in table 5 demonstrate that prestrike membership positively influenced the likelihood of strike solidarity in three of the local community environments but not in the critical menacing environment. While the association between prestrike membership and strike solidarity (measured by the gamma statistic) was relatively high in the passive, mixed, and supportive environments (.42, .40, and .64, respectively), a very low association was found in the case of the menacing environment (−.07). Thus, contrary to expectations, prestrike unity among teachers did not counteract the effects of a menacing environment at the time of actual conflict.

Table 5

The Relationship Between Strike Solidarity and Three School and Union Factors, by the Four Local Community Environments

School or union factor	Schools with high strike solidarity (in percentages)			
	Menacing	Passive	Mixed	Supportive
Percent of teachers belonging to the union six months before the strike				
84 percent or less	37% (43)	45% (20)	52% (21)	78% (46)
85 percent or more	34% (41)	67% (15)	72% (25)	94% (52)
Gamma	−.07	.42	.40	.64
In-group tensions				
High	17% (87)	33% (27)	50% (36)	69% (26)
Low	50% (36)	68% (28)	83% (29)	90% (97)
Gamma	.66	.62	.66	.59
Principal supports strike				
Very much	38% (64)	62% (34)	72% (53)	92% (106)
Somewhat	25% (24)	50% (8)	—[a]	62% (13)
Neutral or hostile	9% (32)	18% (11)	20% (10)	40% (10)
Gamma	.52	.57	.65	.79

[a]Inadequate number of cases.

Historical solidarity, as measured by both the level of earlier strike solidarity and the existence of prestrike member unity in the 1968 menacing environment, did not help to explain the influence of perceived environments on strike solidarity during the 1968 strike. It is necessary, therefore, to examine processes which developed at the time of the 1968 strike.

Role of In-Group Tensions

Community hostility may have had an impact on strike solidarity if it acted to divide teachers along potential cleavages in each school. In the 1968 strike, our data and direct observations showed that external hostility led to increased tensions among subgroups of teachers from the same schools in the following areas: (1) the hostility differentially affected teachers due to variations in demographic factors, especially differences between black and white teachers; (2) there were disagreements over ways to counter external hostility, with some teachers questioning the legitimacy of strike action (29 percent of the chairmen reported this disagreement in their schools); (3) some teachers identified more with the strike opponents than with their union position. This identification with opponents was particularly evident among younger, more liberal teachers (this was reported as occurring at their schools by 16 percent of the chairmen). Community hostility could thus increase tension among teachers in these areas and, in turn, tend toward a breakdown in strike solidarity.

Evidence of the importance of in-group tensions as the link between external hostility and a decrease in strike solidarity can be found in table 5. In-group tension was measured by an index based on chairmen reports of tensions among white teachers, among black teachers, and between white and black teachers. The index was constructed by adding these three responses. That is, a high level of tension between teachers was reported in 71 percent of the schools in a menacing environment (87 of the 123 schools), 49 percent in a passive environment, 55 percent in a mixed environment, and 21 percent in a supportive environment. Thus, the likelihood of in-group tensions in a school was highly related to perceptions of hostility in the local community.

That these in-group tensions had a substantial impact on strike solidarity can also be seen in table 5. In each of the four types of environment, the schools reporting a low level of in-group tension were more likely to show strike solidarity. While only 17 percent of the schools with high in-group tension in the menacing environment showed high strike solidarity, this increased to 50 percent of the schools in the same environment but without such tensions. This pattern was repeated in substantially the same manner for all four of the local community environments (gamma = .66, .62, .66, and .59).

These data support the proposition that the development of in-group tension is one of the paths by which outside community sentiments can influence the strike solidarity of union members.

Administrative Support of the Strike

A second channel through which the local community may affect the strike solidarity of the teaching staff is through its impact on the teacher's first-line supervisor, the school principal. The position of the school principal is somewhat ambiguous because he is expected to identify professionally with the teaching staff as fellow educators while also acting as the agent of the community in the school. In the case of the 1968 teachers' strike, the principals were massively in support of the strike; 79 percent of the union chairmen reported that their principals were somewhat or very supportive of the strike, and only 16 percent were neutral or hostile.

However, the four community environments had an impact on the degree of principal or administrative support for the strike. While only 8 percent of the principals in the supportive environments were described as hostile or neutral (i.e., 10 of the 129 schools), this proportion increased to 15 percent in the mixed environment, to 21 percent in the passive, and to 27 percent in the menacing environment. Thus, support by principals also reflected sentiments in the local community environment.

That the existence of principal support had a substantial impact on strike solidarity can also be seen in table 5. The gamma statistics showing the strong influence of principal support on the likelihood of strike solidarity in each environment varied little, from .52 in the menacing environment to .79 in the supportive environment. Of particular interest was the low likelihood of strike solidarity (40 percent) in the supportive environment when principals were seen as hostile or neutral. This solidarity level was nearly equal to that of the menacing environment when principals were very supportive (38 percent). Thus, it appears that principal support of the strike was approximately equal to the influence of local community sentiments in determining strike solidarity. Administrative support, however, is itself a reflection of sentiments of the community.

Conclusion

The perceived community environment can have a major impact on the strike solidarity of a service group such as teachers. Contrary to the assumption that the community will always act to discourage strike action, this was found to be only one of several possibilities in the case of the 1968 New York City teachers' strike. When community sentiments toward the strike were arrayed along a continuum from menacing to supportive, the highest level of strike solidarity was found in supportive environments, followed by mixed, passive, and, finally, menacing environments which discouraged union action.

The past history of union strike solidarity failed to account for the degree of solidarity demonstrated in each environment. The incidence of prestrike union membership had some effect on strike solidarity in every environment except the menacing environment, where it did not prevent hostile community sentiments from undermining solidarity.

The process by which perceived local community environments influenced the strike solidarity of teachers was found to develop by way of two intervening factors: (1) the extent to which community sentiments tended to produce tensions among subgroups of teachers and (2) the extent to which community sentiments affected the support given by the school principal to the strike. Both of these factors, in turn, influenced the strike solidarity found among teachers.

References

Barton, Allen H. *Organizational Measurement*. New York: CEEB, 1961.

Berube, Maurice R., and Gittell, Marilyn. *Confrontation at Ocean Hill-Brownsville: The New York School Strikes of 1968*. New York: Praeger, 1969.

Cook, Alice H. "Public Employee Bargaining in New York City." *Industrial Relations* IX (May 1970): 249-67.

Derber, Milton; Chalmers, W. Ellison; and Stagner, Ross. "Environmental Variables and Union-Management Accommodation." *Industrial and Labor Relations Review* XI (April 1958): 413-28.

Harris, Louis, and Swanson, Bert E. *Black-Jewish Relations in New York City*. New York: Praeger, 1970.

Kerr, Clark, and Siegel, Abraham. "The Interindustry Propensity to Strike: An International Comparison." *Industrial Conflict*, edited by Arthur Kornhauser, Robert Dubin, and Arthur M. Ross. New York: McGraw-Hill, 1954.

Knowles, K. G. J. C. " 'Strike Proneness' and Its Determinants." *Labor and Trade Unionism*, edited by Walter Galenson and Seymour M. Lipset. New York: John Wiley & Sons, 1960.

New York Civil Liberties Union. *The Burden of Blame: A Report on the Ocean Hill-Brownsville Controversy*. New York: The Civil Liberties Union, 1968.

Public Educational Association. *A Call to Sanity and Action*. New York: The Association, 1968.

Rimlinger, Gaston V. "International Differences in the Strike Propensity of Coal Miners: Experience in Four Countries." *Industrial and Labor Relations Review* XII (April 1959): 389-405.

Warner, W. Lloyd (ed.). *Yankee City* (vol. 1). New Haven: Yale University Press, 1963.

Wray, Donald E. "The Community and Labor-Management Relations." *Labor Management Relations in Illini City* (vol. 1), edited by W. Ellison Chalmers, et al. Champaign, Ill.: University of Illinois, Institute of Labor and Industrial Relations, 1953.

Reading 7

Correlates of State Public Employee Bargaining Laws

Thomas A. Kochan

In recent years the rapid growth of collective bargaining in public employment has raised policy issues in the public sector to the center of attention in the industrial relations literature. Most research in this area, however, has consisted of qualitative discussions of potential and actual consequences of various policy options. In comparison, there have been few attempts to systematically examine the relationships between public sector policies in the fifty states and the respective milieus in which they were developed. This paper describes an attempt to analyze public sector legislation quantitatively by developing an index of public policy and then relating it to a number of environmental characteristics in each of the states.* The overall

Reprinted by permission from *Industrial Relations* 12, no. 3 (October 1973), pp. 322-37.

*This research was partially financed by grants from the U.S. Department of Labor, Division of Public Employee Labor Relations (contract no. L-72-157), from the National Science Foundation (grant no. 91-358), and from the Center for the Study of Unions and Collective Bargaining of the University of Wisconsin through a grant from the David Dubinsky Foundation. The views expressed are the author's and do not reflect the official positions of any governmental agency.

conclusion is that roughly one-third of the variance in state public sector laws can be accounted for by the environmental characteristics observed.

Theoretical Framework for Public Policy

The majority of the industrial relations literature addresses the *consequences* of public policy and thus implicitly treats policy as an independent variable. We suggest here that it is more appropriate to view policy as an intervening variable between certain antecedent conditions and dependent variables of interest in labor-management relations. That is, for any given aspect of the process or outcomes of labor-management relations that public policy seeks to regulate (e.g., strikes by government employees), there are likely to be both environmental characteristics that are antecedent to public policy and situational or institutional variables that moderate the effects of public policy on these dependent variables (e.g., the way in which strikes are actually handled). By exploring the relationships between a number of environmental characteristics and a measure of public policy, this paper represents a first step in testing the empirical validity of viewing public policy as an intervening variable.

The Concept of Public Policy

Public policy is defined here as the desired goals or targets of the relevant governmental units on some specified set of issues or events.* These goals or targets may be: (1) actively asserted as is the case where a comprehensive set of regulations on the specified issues is established, or (2) passively asserted as is the case where no specified set of regulations exists and the nature of policy must be interpreted from common or civil law. In addition, since we rely on goals or desired outcomes in our definition, the direction of policy (i.e., the substance of the desired outcomes) must be specified. Thus, our

---

*This definition of public policy draws heavily from the discussion of the concept by Sharkansky and Hofferbert (1971, pp. 315-53). The discussion of policy making in Katz and Kahn (1966) was also helpful in drawing the distinction between policy and goals. Finally, the importance of specifying the direction, comprehensiveness, and targets of policy was drawn from Barbash (1970).

concept of public policy can be thought of as having two dimensions: comprehensiveness and direction. Since the public sector policies which have been evolving in recent years are clearly moving toward a formalized collective bargaining relationship between governmental employers and employee organizations, we will evaluate the comprehensiveness of these policies in terms of the degree to which they move toward formalization. Thus, the extent to which the policies provide for a formalized bargaining relationship will serve as our criterion for evaluating the comprehensiveness of the regulations in effect. Because different states have used legislation, executive orders, administrative orders, judicial decisions, or even legal opinions of attorney generals to enunciate policy for public sector labor-management relations, all of these policy expressions are considered in constructing our measure of existing policies in the states.

The Quantitative Index

The myriad of policy issues that confront legislators makes the development of a valid measure of public policy a complicated task. Fortunately, however, some efforts at standardization and classification of the provisions of comprehensive laws have been made and provide us with a starting point for building a quantitative index of the laws. The most comprehensive of these efforts to date is the one prepared by the Division of Public Employee Labor Relations of the U.S. Department of Labor (1971a). It classifies the provisions of state policies into twelve categories, and where appropriate, further divides the provisions within each category into different policy options. From this general classification scheme, an index of comprehensiveness of the laws for five employee groups (police, firefighters, teachers, local and state employees) in each state was developed by assigning ordinal values to the options within each classification and then summing across the classification categories. Where the options within the classifications were limited to either the existence or nonexistence of a provision, the values of one or zero, respectively, were assigned. For those classifications in which more than one option was listed, the discrete options were ordered according to the extent to which they moved toward a more formalized collective bargaining relationship. This criterion is based on the assumption that the more formalized the procedures specified in the law, the more detailed and

comprehensive the regulation of labor policy attempted by the legislation. For example, in the category of bargaining rights, "no provision" received the lowest value (zero) and "required to bargain collectively" received the highest value (four), with three other options
between these two extremes. The entire classification scheme showing the values assigned to each option is presented in table 1.

A number of alternative weighting schemes could be used to
combine the values for each category into an overall index. Since,
however, there is likely to be disagreement among experts concerning
the relative importance of the different categories, it was decided at
this point to simply add up the discrete values to obtain a total index
score. While this procedure is as arbitrary as any other weighting formula, it does have the advantage of being simple, understandable,
and consistent with the literature of scaling.*

Index Values by State

The values for the indices obtained by this scaling procedure are
presented in table 2. In addition, the first column lists the number of
years since the state passed its first comprehensive law governing
public employment labor relations.

Summary Scores for Employee Groups

In table 3 we have summarized across all states the values obtained for the policies in effect as of June 1972 for the five employee
groups. The maximum scale value, noted in table 1, that a policy can
attain is 26. As seen in table 3, firefighters have the highest average
scale value of the employee groups while state employees have the

---

*See, for example, Nunnally (1967). Two checks on the internal consist-
ency of the scale were made and the results provide additional confidence in the
reliability of the index. First, correlations of the values of the individual categories with the total scores for the laws were computed. For the scale to be
internally consistent, these correlations should be positive and quite high. The
average correlation between the separate categories and the total score for all
employee groups is .76. Secondly, the components of the scale were factor analyzed to determine if they cluster well into one factor. If they do not, we cannot
assume that the total score on the index represents a single construct. The results
of these analyses confirmed the unidimensionality of the total score. The average
of the loadings (correlation between the component variables and the overall factor) was .72. Thus, it appears that our scaling procedure provides an adequate
measure of the comprehensiveness of state laws.

Table 1
Index of State Public Sector Bargaining Laws: Scaling Code

Category	Scaling code
Administrative body	0 = no provision 1 = some provision
Bargaining rights	0 = no provision 1 = right to present proposals 2 = required to meet and confer 3 = may bargain collectively 4 = required to bargain collectively
Recognition type and procedure	0 = no provision 1 = recognition other than exclusive 2 = exclusive recognition
Unit determination	0 = no provision 1 = some provision
Rules of procedure	0 = no provision 1 = some provision
Impasse procedures	0 = no provision 1 = mediation 2 = fact finding or advisory arbitration 3 = voluntary binding arbitration 4 = compulsory binding arbitration
Strike policy	0 = no provision 1 = strike prohibited and penalties against striking employees 2 = strikes prohibited 3 = some limited strike rights
Management rights	0 = no provision 1 = some provision
Scope of bargaining	0 = no provision 1 = scope limited to specified items 2 = scope includes wages and other conditions of employment
Unfair labor practices	0 = no provision 1 = provision covering only employees and employers 2 = provision covering both employees and employers
Grievance procedures	0 = no provision 1 = grievance procedures negotiable 2 = grievance procedures required 3 = binding arbitration of grievances required
Union security	0 = no provision 1 = checkoff allowed 2 = maintenance of membership or form of agency shop allowed

Maximum index value = 26

Table 2
State Law Index for Various Employee Groups—June 1972[a]

State	Years since passage of legislation	Police	Fire-fighters	Teachers	Local employees	State employees
Alabama	00	02	05	02	02	02
Alaska	00	06	06	13	06	06
Arizona	00	00	00	01	00	00
Arkansas	00	00	00	00	03	05
California	00	09	05	08	09	07
Colorado	00	00	00	00	00	00
Connecticut	07	21	21	13	21	02
Delaware	02	16	16	13	16	16
Florida	00	02	12	09	06	02
Georgia	01	00	12	05	00	01
Hawaii	02	22	22	22	22	22
Idaho	02	00	12	10	03	00
Illinois	00	02	04	05	05	02
Indiana	00	03	03	03	03	03
Iowa	00	05	05	05	05	05
Kansas	01	18	18	12	18	18
Kentucky	00	00	16	07	03	03
Louisiana	00	01	01	01	01	01
Maine	03	20	20	20	20	18
Maryland	00	00	00	16	00	00
Massachusetts	07	20	20	20	20	18
Michigan	07	19	19	17	17	14
Minnesota	07	21	21	21	21	21
Mississippi	00	00	00	00	00	00
Missouri	05	00	10	01	10	10
Montana	00	00	00	14	00	00
Nebraska	05	18	18	09	18	00
Nevada	03	18	18	18	18	00
New Hampshire	03	15	00	00	00	17
New Jersey	03	21	21	21	21	21
New Mexico	00	06	06	06	06	15
New York	05	17	17	17	17	17
North Carolina	00	00	00	00	00	00
North Dakota	00	08	08	15	08	06
Ohio	00	01	01	01	01	01
Oklahoma	01	15	15	11	00	12
Oregon	09	17	17	09	17	17
Pennsylvania	04	10	10	24	24	24
Rhode Island	11	14	14	15	18	20
South Carolina	00	02	02	02	02	02
South Dakota	03	08	08	14	14	14
Tennessee	00	02	02	02	02	02
Texas	00	02	02	02	02	02

Table 2 (continued)

State	Years since passage of legislation	Police	Fire-fighters	Teachers	Local employees	State employees
Utah	00	03	03	03	03	03
Vermont	05	00	18	15	18	19
Virginia	00	04	04	04	04	01
Washington	05	19	19	10	09	11
West Virginia	00	00	00	00	00	00
Wisconsin	13	22	22	20	20	20
Wyoming	00	00	12	00	00	00

[a]The basic reference used to assign values to the laws was *Summary of State Policy Regulations for Public Sector Labor Relations: Statutes, Attorney General's Opinions and Selected Court Decisions* (Washington, D.C.: Department of Labor, 1971).

lowest. In addition, firefighters have the largest number of laws in the intermediate ranges (10-19). A number of the states falling in this range on the firefighters law (Florida, Georgia, Kentucky, Idaho, and Wyoming) have little bargaining legislation for other public employees. This is perhaps an indication of the political effectiveness of the firefighters as lobbyists. The distribution of the laws governing teachers is the second most comprehensive. Although the teachers also have a large number of laws in the intermediate ranges, these laws are found in different states than the intermediate firefighters laws. For example, Alaska, Connecticut, Delaware, Kansas, Maryland, Montana, North Dakota, Oklahoma, Rhode Island, Vermont, and Washington all have teachers laws that fall within the range of 10-16 on the index, but none of these falls within the same range on the firefighters law.

Table 3
Total Score on the Comprehensive Index
for the Five Employee Groups

Employee group	0-4	5-9	10-14	15-19	20+	Average score	Standard deviation
State employees	26	5	3	10	6	7.8	8.0
Local employees	24	6	2	10	8	8.8	8.3
Firefighters	18	7	7	11	7	9.7	7.8
Police	25	6	2	10	7	8.2	8.2
Teachers	18	9	9	7	7	9.1	7.4

The laws for state, local, and police groups are more highly skewed toward the low end of the scale. Approximately half of the state laws for these groups score less than six on the index as compared to only 36 percent of the state laws for firefighters and teachers. In addition, fewer of the state laws for these groups fall in the 10-14 range of the scale than do the firefighters and teachers laws.

State Characteristics

Only general guidance exists for the choice of those state characteristics that are likely to affect the development of policy in the area of public sector industrial relations—little empirical research has focused specifically on this area. Nevertheless, there has been a large amount of related research on public policy in other areas by political scientists. In general, this research has focused on two sets of variables as antecedents to public policy: (1) characteristics of the economic and social environments of the states, and (2) characteristics of the political systems of the states. For an overview of the studies in this area, see Dye (1970); Sharkansky (1970); or Sharkansky and Hofferbert (1971). These characteristics are normally treated as the two major environmental determinants of public policy in the states. The variables shown to be most significantly related to public policy variables in these studies were chosen here as potential antecedents of state bargaining policies.

Beyond these broad guidelines, characteristics of the states that appeared to be directly relevant to the industrial relations "subenvironment" were considered as potential determinants of state bargaining policies. The industrial relations characteristics included here were (1) wage and employment levels of public employees, (2) degree of unionization among private sector employees in the states, (3) measures of strike activity for both private and public sector employees, and (4) a measure of another law of importance to industrial relations in the states, a right-to-work law.

Relationship Between the Index and State Characteristics

In all, forty-four state variables were considered as potential antecedents to public policy in the states and their correlations with the state laws for the five employee groups were computed. Of these forty-four variables, twenty-five met the predetermined criterion of zero-order correlations above .20 to be included in further analyses. These variables and their correlations with the indices are presented in table 4, along with the correlations between these state characteristics and the number of years since the states passed their first comprehensive bargaining statute. The environmental characteristics are grouped into categories corresponding to measures of state (1) economic or social environments, (2) political system characteristics, and (3) industrial relations subenvironment characteristics.

Economic and Social Characteristics

The zero-order correlations between economic and social characteristics and the indices of public sector laws suggest that more urbanized, industrialized, affluent, and high income states and those with rising per capita incomes were quicker to enact public sector policies and tend to have more comprehensive policies in this area. The variable labeled "percent change in per capita revenue from the federal government" is especially interesting since it reflects the growing role of the federal government in financing programs to deal with urban problems (the intercorrelations of this variable with urbanization and population density are .45 and .68, respectively). This suggests that, as Chamberlain (1968, pp. 18-30) has argued, the growth of activity among public employees in the 1960s is perhaps to some extent a reflection of the urban crises that erupted during this period. One interesting conclusion that comes from the examination of the zero-order correlations is that no relationship exists between the size of the states (measured in terms of size of population) and the nature of the public sector policy. (Although population size was included in the larger correlation matrix, it did not meet the criterion of a correlation of .20 or higher to be in table 4. For all employee groups, the correlation was less than .10, and for the firefighters group, it was actually negative.)

Variations by Employee Groups

In addition to looking at the size of the correlations, further information can be obtained by observing the differences in the correlations for the variables across the five employee groups. Although in general these correlations are quite stable, a few interesting differences can be noted. For example, the correlations between the

Table 4

Zero-Order Correlations of Selected State Characteristics with the Public Employee Bargaining Law Indices and with Number of Years Since Comprehensive State Legislation was Passed–June 1972

State characteristics	Years since passage of legislation	Public employee bargaining law indices				
		Police	Firefighters	Teachers	Local employees	State employees
Economic and social characteristics						
Population density[a]	.30	.36	.30	.39	.39	.33
Percent population urban[a]	.22	.38	.25	.25	.30	.21
Per capita personal income, 1970[a]	.34	.55	.45	.52	.54	.36
Per capita expenditures, 1970[a]	.16	.34	.34	.45	.35	.28
Percent change in urban population[a]	-.17	-.02	-.02	.03	-.05	-.23
Percent change in per capita income, 1960-1970[a]	.31	.38	.24	.33	.39	.37
Percent change in per capita revenue from federal government, 1960-1970[a]	.30	.33	.24	.41	.37	.31
Industrialization factor[b]	.34	.38	.24	.33	.39	.37
Affluence factor[b]	.10	.38	.34	.30	.31	.19
Political system characteristics						
Centralization of state legislatures[c]	-.26	-.28	-.16	-.38	-.31	-.27
Interparty conflict in state legislature, 1963[c]	.44	.46	.40	.46	.50	.38
Pressure group conflict in state legislature, 1963[c]	.13	.18	-.07	.06	.13	.22
Number of years state has had merit system[d]	.07	.21	.28	.08	.07	.08
Governor's appointive power[d]	.12	.13	.19	.25	.30	.30
Innovation score[e]	.49	.50	.33	.43	.49	.46
Competition turnout factor[b]	.28	.37	.30	.33	.34	.29

Industrial relations subenvironment characteristics

Right-to-work law[a]	-.39	-.32	-.29	-.39	-.31	-.36
Average monthly income—all public employees[a]	.34	.45	.33	.49	.45	.35
Total number of workers involved in public sector strikes, 1965-1970[f]	.13	.16	.17	.25	.20	.19
Percent nonagricultural employees unionized, 1968[g]	.33	.27	.25	.32	.36	.29
Percent change in average monthly income of full-time public employees[a]	.32	.26	.24	.19	.30	.27

[a] Source: U.S. Department of Labor (1971b).

[b] Source: These are factor scores based on rankings of the states obtained from a series of factor analyses by Ira Sharkansky and Richard I. Hofferbert. The signs on the correlation coefficients have been reversed to avoid confusion because in these authors' rankings the lower the number the more industrialized, affluent, etc., the state is. For an explanation of the analysis and component variables used to derive the factor scores, see Sharkansky and Hofferbert (1971, pp. 315-53).

[c] Source: Francis (1967).

[d] Source: Schlesinger (1971, pp. 210-37).

[e] Source: Walker (1971, pp. 351-87).

[f] Source: Bureau of Labor Statistics (1969). 1970 data were taken from Bureau of Labor Statistics (1971).

[g] Source: Bureau of Labor Statistics (1970).

firefighters law and population density, percent change in revenue from the federal government, and urbanization are lower than for any other group. This suggests that the firefighters have been more successful than the other groups in obtaining bargaining legislation in the states with a higher percentage of smaller cities and more rural populations. By looking at the correlations for these same three variables in the teachers column, the influence of large cities in the state on the comprehensiveness of the teachers law can be seen. The correlation of .41 for the variable measuring percent change in revenue coming from the federal government and .39 for population density contrast markedly with the .25 correlation for percent population urban. This suggests that the existence of one or several large cities in the state has a stronger influence on the passage of a comprehensive bargaining policy for teachers than does the overall degree of urbanization in the state.

Political System Characteristics

These measures are taken from a number of public policy studies and are variables that are mainly of theoretical interest to political scientists. In addition, they capture a number of characteristics about the structure and process of decision making in state legislatures, and thus provide insight into the conditions within these bodies that affect the actual policy-making process.

The first variable, the centralization of state legislatures, measures the degree to which effective decision-making power in the legislative process is controlled by a few officials or committees in state government or is widely dispersed among the members of the legislative body and was derived from a study by Francis (1967). The consistently negative correlations that appear between this variable and the state law indices indicate that those states with more comprehensive laws have more diffusion of decision-making power institutionalized in their legislative processes. The next two variables are also taken from the Francis study and measure the amount of conflict that characterizes the policy-making process in the states. A strong correlation appears between partisan (interparty) conflict and the comprehensiveness of the laws. This measure is especially interesting because it closely reflects the influence of two-party politics that characterizes most of the northern states—where public sector laws are more evident—as opposed to the essentially one-party domination of the states in the deep South. The influence of conflict among pressure groups seems to be much less important to policy development in this area (only the law for state employees met the criterion of a correlation above .20 to be included in this table).

The length of time that the state has had a merit system for state employees is weakly correlated with the comprehensiveness of the state laws. It is interesting to note that the correlation between this characteristic and the law for state employees is stronger than for the others. This suggests that those states which were quicker to accept the merit system for their own employees are now more willing to accept collective bargaining as a means of decision making in labor relations.

An issue which is widely discussed by political scientists concerns the effect on public policy of having a strong versus weak chief executive. One measure of this is the appointive power of the chief executive, the governor in our case. The correlations presented in table 4 show a positive relationship exists between the governor's appointive power and the comprehensiveness of public sector bargaining policies.

Other political characteristics of the states that have received a good deal of attention are the amount of competition among political parties and the level of voter turnout in state elections. These two political characteristics are generally highly intercorrelated. Thus, we have chosen to use a combined measure of these two variables that was derived by Sharkansky and Hofferbert (1971). Using this measure, strong positive correlations were obtained with our measure of the comprehensiveness of the state laws.

A final political characteristic that shows very strong correlations with the comprehensiveness of the laws is the innovativeness of state legislatures. The measure of this characteristic was derived by Walker (1971, pp. 210-37) by comparing the years in which states adopted eighty-eight different programs between the late 1800s and 1965. The high correlations between this variable and state public sector bargaining policies suggest that industrial relations policy making in the states follows somewhat the same pattern as policy making in other areas of state politics.

Industrial Relations Subenvironment

Finally, it can be seen from table 4 that state policy in the public sector is also closely related to the industrial relations subenvironment of the state. States with a relatively high percentage of unionized workers in the private nonfarm sector, those that do not have right-to-work laws, those with more highly paid public employees, and those in which public employees' incomes are rising most rapidly enacted legislation earlier and have more comprehensive laws.

While analysis of these zero-order correlations points up some interesting associations, sole reliance on them may be somewhat misleading since many of these characteristics are highly intercorrelated. Thus, to get a more precise understanding of the factors which make an independent contribution to the development of public policy in this area, the effects of these intercorrelations need to be taken into account. This problem has been dealt with in public policy research in other areas by using a multiple regression model that enters the economic and social characteristics as independent variables first and then enters the political system variables to see if the latter characteristics add anything to the explained variance of the model. Following this procedure, we would treat the industrial relations subenvironment characteristics as the third set of variables to enter the model in order to see if these characteristics can account for any part of the variance unexplained by the economic and social or the political variables already entered. This is the basic procedure followed in the regression analysis presented below.

Regression Analysis

The results of the multiple regression analysis are presented in table 5. A stepwise regression procedure was used which included representative variables from the factors that emerged in a series of factor analyses.* This procedure for including variables minimizes

---

*Because of the extensive intercorrelations among the independent variables, a series of factor analyses was performed to reduce the number of independent variables that needed to be included in the prediction model. Space does not allow full discussion of this analysis here. Briefly, however, the variables that tended to cluster together on the three factors that explained the most variance were: (1) per capita expenditures, per capita revenues, per capita and public employee income levels, percent unionized, right-to-work laws, decentralization of state legislatures, partisan conflict, and competition-turnout ranking; (2) urbanization, population density, public employee income change, number of public employee strikes, per capita revenue from federal government, innovativeness of state governments, and industrialization rankings; and (3) per capita income change and urbanization change (negative).

redundancy (high intercorrelations) among the independent variables. The data presented in table 5 place great emphasis on the residuals and F statistics of the models. Evaluating the F statistics allows us to assess the significance of the equations as predictive models while the residuals tell us which states deviate from the pattern predicted by the model. The criteria used to build these models were as follows: only those variables were entered that (1) had coefficients significant at the .10 level or better, (2) added a significant amount to R^2, and (3) reduced the standard error of the model. See Draper and Smith (1966). Using these criteria, three independent variables—per capita expenditures of the state government, per capita change in personal income 1960-1970, and the innovation index of state legislatures—consistently combined to form the best model. The proportion of variance explained by these variables included in a linear model varied from a low of 26 percent for firefighters to a high of 38 percent for teachers. All F ratios for the equations were significant well beyond the .01 level. Finally, examination of the residuals showed that the observed values for all except three observations fell within two standard deviations of their predicted values.* ("Overpredicted" states, as listed in table 5, are those whose public bargaining laws are less comprehensive than predicted by the model, while "underpredicted" states are just the opposite.)

These results, although modest in terms of amount of explained variation, clearly show that a significant amount of predictive power can be obtained from a model composed solely of three state characteristics. However, it should be cautioned that the three independent variables included in the regression equations should not be interpreted as the only theoretically important correlates of the types of laws found in the states. We are only concerned here with the predictive power of the environmental characteristics and the amounts of variance that they can collectively account for in the comprehensiveness of public sector bargaining laws. Given the fact that many of the environmental characteristics are highly intercorrelated, future research should continue to sort out these (and other) interrelationships and their linkages with bargaining laws.†

---

*Two standard deviations is a conventional benchmark for judging the significance of the departure of the predicted from the actual values of the dependent variable.

†For example, if we are permitted to speculate about the states in which the bargaining laws are less comprehensive than predicted by our model (see

Table 5
Multiple Regression Results

Independent variable (partial correlation)	Years since passage of legislation	Public employee bargaining law indices				
		Police	Firefighters	Teachers	Local employees	State employees
Per capita state expenditures	.07	.30[b]	.33[b]	.44[c]	.32[a]	.24[a]
Change in per capita income, 1960-1970	.19	.26[a]	.31[b]	.31[b]	.30[a]	.26[a]
Innovation index	.41[b]	.39[c]	.18	.29[a]	.37[c]	.35[c]
R^2	.26	.35	.26	.38	.35	.29
F value (level of significance)	.002	.0001	.0002	.0001	.0001	.001
Standard error of estimate	2.84	6.89	6.96	6.02	6.91	7.05
States underpredicted by greater than one standard deviation						
Connecticut		1.06	1.14			
Delaware		1.25		1.25		1.27
Florida			1.41		1.11	
Georgia			1.25			
Hawaii						
Kansas		1.48	1.15		1.35	1.12
Maine		1.73	1.49	1.90	1.61	1.45
Minnesota	1.07	1.12	1.05	1.22	1.01	1.20
Missouri	1.25					
Nebraska		1.54	1.22		1.41	
Nevada		1.67	1.02	1.32	1.51	
New Jersey		1.14	1.29	1.48	1.07	1.20
New Mexico						1.25
Oklahoma		1.40				
Oregon	1.77					
Pennsylvania				2.04	1.60	1.71
Rhode Island	2.68					1.37
South Dakota					1.01	1.11
Vermont					1.06	1.37
Wisconsin	3.22	1.39	1.37	1.24	1.01	1.17

States overpredicted by greater than one standard deviation

Alaska			−1.12			−1.17
California	−1.77	−1.11	1.49	−1.40	−1.18	1.29
Colorado	−1.34	−1.70	1.66	−1.91	−1.78	−1.54
Connecticut						−1.19
Illinois	−1.24	−1.26				
Kentucky		−1.09				
Louisiana	−1.12	−1.12	−1.33	−1.37	−1.24	−1.19
Maryland		−1.59	−1.74		−1.70	
Montana			−1.36		−1.04	
New Hampshire	−1.24		−1.30	−1.37	−1.28	−1.49
Ohio		−1.31	−1.28	−1.40	−1.38	−1.25
Utah				−1.01		
Vermont		−1.38				
Virginia			−1.34			−1.09
West Virginia				−1.28	−1.05	
Wyoming		−1.08		−1.79	−1.22	

[a] Significant at .10 level.
[b] Significant at .05 level.
[c] Significant at .01 level.

Discussion

The results of the analyses presented in this paper indicate that roughly one-third of the variance in the comprehensiveness of public employee bargaining laws can be explained by a model composed solely of three state environmental characteristics. However, the amount of variance explained varied across different employee groups. The policies for firefighters and state employees showed the weakest relationships to the state environments while the policies covering teachers, police, and local employees showed stronger relationships. Thus, it is clear that a number of additional factors not included in our model also affect the development of policy in this area.

One interesting question that might be usefully addressed in future research concerns the experiences in public employment in those states where the comprehensiveness of public laws deviates from that predicted by the states' environmental characteristics. Do states which have less comprehensive policies than would be predicted by their environmental characteristics experience more conflicts or suppress bargaining among public employees? Or, alternatively, do jurisdictions within states that do not have comprehensive laws establish their own policies and legal frameworks to deal with

---

table 5), we might suggest that in the case of West Virginia, while the degree of unionization is very high and per capita incomes have been growing between 1960 and 1970 because of the resurgence of the coal mining industry, the potential power of the United Mine Workers has not been transformed into an effective political effort on the behalf of public employees. This situation, along with the active opposition of the governor to public employee bargaining, may have ruled out the possibility of legislation. In California, the legal status of public employees has been heavily influenced by pressure on the legislature from the California League of Cities. Their preference for maintaining the meet and confer law, along with the presence of a conservative governor, may have blocked movement toward a more comprehensive law. The lack of a law in Ohio, a highly industrialized and unionized state, might be explained by the high preponderance of blacks in public employment and their lack of political power in the state legislature. Finally, in Illinois, a number of attorney general's opinions have made it possible for unions to be recognized without a law. Perhaps more important, however, as Derber has pointed out, the lack of strong pressure from the powerful trade unions in the Chicago area (presumably because of satisfaction with their political relationship with Mayor Daley) effectively stifled attempts to pass public employee legislation. (See Derber 1968, pp. 541-58.)

public employees who wish to engage in bargaining? There is some evidence to suggest that both phenomena are occurring. For example, Illinois, California, and Ohio were overpredicted states in our model and all have experienced a large number of public employee strikes between 1965 and 1970 (130 in Illinois, 101 in California, and 186 in Ohio). See U.S. Department of Labor (1971b). In addition, a good deal of bargaining goes on in these states even in the absence of comprehensive legislation. Similar questions might be asked about the experiences of states in which the comprehensiveness of public policy is greater than that predicted by state environmental characteristics.

Finally, a number of implications for industrial relations theory and research can be derived from these findings. First, since systematic relationships between environmental characteristics and public policy were found, future studies seeking to evaluate the effects of policy should attempt to control for these interrelationships. Secondly, greater attention should be placed on developing a theoretical framework in which these environment-policy interrelationships are incorporated into the causal sequence leading to dependent variables of interest in industrial relations. And, lastly, future theorizing might especially focus on explaining the interrelationships between various industrial relations subenvironment characteristics and the larger economic, social, and political environment.

References

Barbash, Jack. "Trade Unionism and the General Interest: A Theory of Positive Public Policy Toward Labor." *Wisconsin Law Review* IV (1970): 1135-44.

Bureau of Labor Statistics. *Handbook of Labor Statistics* (Bulletin 1630). Washington, D.C.: The Bureau, 1969.

Bureau of Labor Statistics. *Directory of National and International Labor Unions in the United States, 1969* (Bulletin 1665). Washington, D.C.: The Bureau, 1970.

Bureau of Labor Statistics. *Work Stoppages in 1970, Summary Report*. Washington, D.C.: The Bureau, 1971.

Chamberlain, Neil W. "Collective Bargaining in the Public Sector." Dartmouth: Public Affairs Center, 1968.

Derber, Milton. "Labor Management Commission 1966-1967." *Industrial and Labor Relations Review* XXI (July 1968): 541-58.

Draper, Norman, and Smith, Harry. *Applied Regression Analysis*. New York: John Wiley & Sons, 1966.

Dye, Thomas R. *Politics, Economics and the Public.* Chicago: Rand McNally, 1970.

Francis, Wayne L. *Legislative Issues in the Fifty States.* Chicago: Rand McNally, 1967.

Katz, Daniel, and Kahn, Robert L. *The Social Psycholgy of Organizations.* New York: John Wiley & Sons, 1966.

Nunnally, J. C. *Psychometric Theory.* New York: McGraw-Hill, 1967.

Schlesinger, Joseph A. "The Politics of the Executive." *Politics in the American States* (2d ed.), edited by Herbert Jacob and Kenneth N. Vines. Boston: Little, Brown, 1971.

Sharkansky, Ira. *Spending in the American States.* Chicago: Rand McNally, 1970.

Sharkansky, Ira, and Hofferbert, Richard L. "Dimensions of State Policy." *Politics in the American States* (2d ed.), edited by Herbert Jacob and Kenneth N. Vines. Boston: Little, Brown, 1971.

U.S. Department of Labor. *Summary of State Policy Regulations for Public Sector Relations: Statutes, Attorney General's Opinions and Selected Court Decisions.* Washington, D.C.: The Department, Division of Public Employee Labor Relations, 1971a.

U.S. Department of Labor. *State Profiles: Current Status of Public Sector Labor Relations.* Washington, D.C.: The Department, Division of Public Employee Labor Relations, 1971b.

Walker, Jack L. "Innovation in State Politics." *Politics in the American States* (2d ed.), edited by Herbert Jacob and Kenneth N. Vines. Boston: Little, Brown, 1971.

PART II

The Collective Bargaining Process

Overview

This part introduces the major theoretical perspectives and explanations of bargaining behavior. Bargaining is a pervasive element in our society and is a component in many socially significant processes—from the used car lot to the United Nations. As a result, bargaining behavior is of interest to a variety of scholars and practitioners. Each has a different approach and there is no single dominant school of thought about how to describe or explain bargaining processes.

This diversity of analysis creates a serious problem of selection and synthesis. The diversity springs principally from four sources: different disciplinary frameworks (e.g., economics, sociology), different levels of generality, variations in research methods, and different institutional referents. We have selected works representing a number of distinct theoretical positions. Some of the general theoretical works lack the richness of detail and attention to subphenomena which are so necessary to understanding. Therefore, a number of specific works are included as well. Each was selected because it dealt with one of the key concepts involved in collective bargaining. However, putting those concepts together into a working understanding of something as complex as collective bargaining was not easy. The complexity is reflected in the diversity of the related knowledge base. Therefore, both the practice and the study of labor relations in the schools require some effective intellectual tools. It does not matter whether the individual's interest is scholarship or practice; the need is equally great. Some make a distinction between the "real world" and the interests of research and analysis, as though reality were somehow the private preserve of the practitioner, and of no concern to the theoretician. But practitioner and theoretician alike rely on representations or models of reality to make sense out of the buzzing confusion of the world. Discovering "reality" depends on developing the best models we can and subjecting them to rigorous tests against empirical facts.

Of course, no single collection of articles can provide contact with or understanding of the whole knowledge base pertinent to the bargaining process. We have chosen representative analytical perspectives, theories, and research paradigms, so the reader can encounter different ways in which knowledge can be constructed and organized. Our selections were also made to provide exposure to some of the leading writers in the field. But even careful analysis by the best writers is not sufficient to conquer the problems of understanding bargaining (in the schools or elsewhere). So before examining the works themselves, it is useful to explain why bargaining is so difficult to analyze completely.

The Need for Analytical Models

One of the central difficulties in conducting and understanding the process of bargaining is its multidimensionality. Each bargaining situation contains a number of political, social, economic, and psychological processes. Consequently, the power of the bargainers to enforce their demands or to maintain the support of their constituents is dependent in part on their bargaining prowess, and in part on a number of external circumstances, such as union strength, community interest groups, etc. Dealing with the political context is only one of the critical tasks. Bargaining is an interpersonal process as well. Group dynamics, attitudes, conflicts, and emotional responses are central parts of this process. They all must be confronted in some manner. The economic context of the bargaining also sets constraints on what the opponents can do. Similarly, they must be able to assess the economic consequences of the alternatives before them.

It is not simply the range of complexity which causes problems. None of the political, economic, or psychological concerns can be dealt with independently; they are all part of the same system and interact in many poorly understood ways. For example, the level of interpersonal conflict manifest at the bargaining may seriously influence the rate at which the parties are willing to concede. In some situations the bargaining opponents are on such good personal terms that the process flows very smoothly. Other bargainers may be personally abrasive and create conflict where there are no substantive differences. Bargaining success is more than the product of the interpersonal relationships among the bargaining parties. These relations may in fact be the result of an external political situation which gives great bargaining discretion to the teams. They in turn can use their discretion to make appropriate concessions and maintain a good working relationship. It may not be clear just which causal relationships are involved. Certainly a number of external factors can combine to produce a good (or bad) bargaining relationship. Without the proper conceptual tools one cannot begin to unravel these webs of interrelationships.

Compounding this complexity is the mass of information related to the bargaining process and its environment. Bargaining itself is largely the exchange of information of different types. Participants must receive and process all the signals, cues, and other raw data which flow in great volume during bargaining. Moreover, they must also analyze the information in order to understand the implications of the offers and proposals made by the opponent. Information must also be exchanged with nonparticipants in order to maintain support, inform constituents, and test the validity of opponents' assertions. Complete processing of all the relevant information is clearly not possible within the time and resource constraints which usually apply to the bargaining situation. So bargainers need information-processing strategies to help them decide what information to deal with, in what ways, and at what times. Unless the bargainers are prepared to rely solely on intuition and luck, these strategies must be based on some model of the process itself and the prediction of possible events. The readings included here are building blocks in the construction of these strategies.

The notion of strategies takes into account the dynamic nature of the bargaining process. That is, the process changes in important ways depending on past events or choices. The nature of conflict at any one time depends on previous decisions and outcomes. The passage of time is also an important consideration. Behavior in the earlier sessions is certainly different in significant ways from bargaining under the pressure of an imminent strike. These two types of dynamics combine to increase the problem of planning and prediction.

Strategic planning is further complicated by the high levels of uncertainty in much of the bargaining process. This uncertainty comes from at least three sources: (1) complex, poorly understood interactions, (2) unpredictability of future events, and (3) incomplete information. The last is a basic ingredient of almost any bargaining situation. A car buyer doesn't know the dealer's costs, and so can't know how far to push. A negotiator doesn't know how valuable a concession is to the union since he doesn't know the union's priorities, and so forth. Even if all known information is freely available to the parties, some questions remain, for example, the likelihood of the passage of a tax referendum to support a union salary demand. Things such as tax elections and contract ratification votes have random characteristics and are difficult to predict. Even if the random factors were somehow eliminated, uncertainty would persist. It would result from our inability to analyze all the phenomena which constitute collective bargaining. If we knew how each of the individual components of the system operated and had complete information about the objectives and values of the bargainers, we would still be unable to fully understand the interactions among all these elements.

The Strategic Use of Theories and Concepts

Having outlined the need for certain intellectual tools in the study and conduct of bargaining, we can examine what benefits are to be expected from using the tools. Our focus is on the *conduct* rather than the *study* of bargaining. The broad view we adopt should be of value not only to potential bargainers, but also to those who will have administrative responsibility for the school or the employee organization. This is consistent with our basic view of collective bargaining as an integral part of the administrative and policy-making processes of the schools.

Since bargaining is central to these governance processes, the outcomes of bargaining have serious long-term consequences for the educational program. But the relationships between bargaining decisions and consequences are often subtle and easy to misunderstand. A minor concession at one time may trap one side into an unforeseen but damaging position later. The existence of a sound strategy helps avoid these mistakes, but the development of a sound strategy depends on the ability to accurately predict and project into the future. Predictions and projections require models.

Models and concepts of bargaining assist both bargainers and students of bargaining to understand the wide variety of circumstances they will encounter. The more general their understanding, the more applicable it will be to a variety of situations, and the better equipped they will be to adapt their knowledge to changing conditions. An ability to generalize can also help in avoiding loss of emotional control in face-to-face bargaining situations. The abstraction can help the bargainer handle provocative situations, whether they occur by design or mistake. These bargaining behaviors can be subtle and often misleading. Correct interpretation of such behavior can be extremely difficult, especially under pressure in bargaining sessions. But bargaining actions can be interpreted in terms of some general models of bargaining behavior. These models can provide a basis for understanding the actions of opponents and formulating an effective strategy. Thus, the learning advantages of models apply both to organizing knowledge within a bargaining relationship and to generalizing across situations.

The readings are presented in a sequence which runs essentially from general to specific. The first work, Patchen's overall review of models of cooperation and conflict (reading 8), sets the stage for the remaining readings.* Next is Saraydar's formal model of the basic process of economic bargaining (reading 9), which takes into account some of the dynamics of the process. These general models are followed by the work of Cresswell (reading 10), Hellriegel et al. (reading 11), and Vantine (reading 13). We also include a comment (reading 12) on the work of Hellriegel and his associates. While readings 10, 11, and 13 present fairly general bargaining models, they are cast specifically in reference to public schools. Each provides a different view

---

*Many writers make a distinction between models and theories. In the literature we discuss here, however, the authors tend to use the terms interchangeably. We will follow the same practice.

of teacher-school board bargaining. In reading 14, power perception is examined by Michener et al. This empirical work addresses one of the important but narrower aspects of bargaining behavior. Together, these readings provide an overview of major theoretical aspects of bargaining, as well as an example of how the general models can be applied to one central aspect: power.

General Models of Bargaining

A central issue in the construction of models of bargaining behavior is the question of inclusiveness. Anyone with even a passing familiarity with bargaining (in any of its many manifestations) will acknowledge the large number of important variables involved. When the bargaining is *collective*, the number is even greater. A model or theory which attempts to include all of the variables and events of interest is clearly not now possible. Therefore, a model must contain sufficient components of the process to resemble the real situation in important ways, but not so many as to make analysis impossible. Depending on purpose and style, a different approach and mix of components is chosen by each of the authors included here. Each work can be reviewed in terms of the choices it represents and the corresponding usefulness of the model in understanding collective bargaining in schools.

The problem of how to construct a useful model is treated by Patchen (reading 8) in some detail. His focus on models of decision making is appropriate for our uses, especially the distinction between what he calls *negotiation* models and *influence* models. Influence processes are, of course, an integral part of negotiations, but the concept of influence is broader than that of negotiations. He also distinguishes between models which emphasize learning and models which emphasize reaction processes (such as an international arms race). The most interesting for our purposes are the negotiations models. One basic difference among them is whether they are static or whether they take into account interactions between the bargainers. The static models are oriented toward explaining the outcomes of bargaining rather than the process itself. The interaction models are given more attention, particularly those of Siegel and Fouraker, and Cross. Some of the inherent limitations of each are mentioned, particularly the fact that models of this type ignore all bargaining behaviors other than the making of and reacting to explicit offers. The Cross model is highlighted, although Patchen overlooks some of its more serious problems mentioned by Saraydar and Cresswell. The other three groups of models—cognitive, learning, and reaction—are of somewhat less interest. As Patchen points out, they ignore interactions and more complex forms of bargaining behavior. Those models derived from game theory suffer some of the shortcomings of the restrictive assumptions inherent in that approach. The most important of these are assuming knowledge of opponents' motivations and utilities. By grouping the models into these categories, Patchen highlights their contributions and limitations and prepares the reader for further investigation of any of the particular works mentioned.

Patchen's work is even more useful in its discussion of the relationships among the groups of models. A key point is that understanding the bargaining process comes from the attempt to analyze the interaction and influence processes in *combination*. Clearly, in actual bargaining, no separation exists between the size of any particular offer and the influence it has on an opponent. In fact, the size of an offer, or more particularly the size of a concession from one offer to another, is a significant component of influence. This is a line of research to be pursued and is taken up in some additional detail by Saraydar (reading 9), Cresswell (reading 10), and to a lesser degree by Hellriegel et al. (reading 11). It is also clear that there is no separation in practice between the process of making and reacting to offers and the other aspects of exerting influence, such as threats, persuasion, and bullying. Therefore, models which attempt to take into account the interdependence of these influencing interactions are likely to be more useful in understanding actual bargaining behavior.

Patchen goes on to criticize many authors for not pushing their formulations to more operational definition and empirical testing. This lack is in part caused by the difficulty of creating operational definitions for phenomena as poorly understood as interactions in collective bargaining. There seems to be a definite trade-off between the inclusiveness of a model and its empirical testability. For the time being, it seems, we must be content with models based on simplifying assumptions in order to be analytically manageable.

The model developed by Saraydar offers an example of how simplifying assumptions can be used to good effect. This model of bargaining employs the concept of subjective utility and utility functions. Utility functions as used in this context express the relationship between the dollar size of any wage settlement or concession and the value of that settlement to one of the bargainers. (For a more complete discussion of the concept of utilities, see Cross 1969.) The concept of subjective utility is a way of taking into account the fact that the same dollar amounts may have different values to two persons or two bargaining organizations. A concession of, say, 5 percent by management early in the bargaining may have a substantially different value to management than a concession of the same number of dollars made by labor at a later time in the bargaining. The notion of utility can then be used to construct mathematical models of wage bargaining which can offer fresh insights into bargaining behavior.

For example, some theorists have developed models which yield determinate solutions for concessions, given some basic assumptions about the utility functions of the bargaining partners. This approach may be used to explain, to a limited degree, how bargainers can determine the size of concessions so as to maximize their expected utility, given their opponents' previous offer. The interaction process can be dealt with explicitly since each concession by one party changes the relative bargaining power and requires a reevaluation of position by the opponent. However, most of these models are not dynamic in the sense that they take into account elapsed time or the mutual interactions of concession rates. These are perhaps the most serious shortcomings.

By contrast, Saraydar's model is not intended to yield determinate solutions for concessions, but rather to present a realistic model of bargaining which takes into account some of the dynamics of the situation. The result is a more plausible reflection of the bargaining process, including how the actions of one bargainer affect the actions and expectations of the others. Saraydar's bargainers are future-oriented, in that they view each action in terms of its consequences for the eventual settlement as well as its implications for the next round of bargaining. In his words:

It is proposed that each bargainer's concept of the consequences of concession or no concession is not in terms of the utility of settlement at the wage rate explicitly under deliberation, but rather involves a consideration of the implications, apropos of the *expected outcome* of negotiations, of making a small concession (thereby insuring a continuance of negotiations), or holding for a small concession from the opponent.

Threats and bluffs have a place in this work. The model also explicitly recognizes the role of an offer or concession as a form of communication between bargainers. Saraydar acknowledges the important effect of factors in the environment on the actions of the bargainers. However, he does not delineate all the environmental variables of interest, nor does he go into much detail on the mechanism of the relationship between environmental variables and the outcomes of bargaining. The model is intended to be an analytical approximation of bargaining and not an exact replication of the process. In that sense it does contribute new insights.

By focusing next on models which relate directly to collective bargaining in schools, we acknowledge a point that is implicit in much of the work discussed above. That is, many of the important variables in the analysis of bargaining, both in the process itself as well as the relationship between the process and the environment, are related to the institutional setting. None of the authors discussed above make this point explicitly, but it is suggested in several places and represents the position we will take here. Thus, a more detailed understanding of collective bargaining in schools requires concentrating on the institutional and historical context of public education. By abandoning generalities, we gain in return richer detail and closer application to the problems of bargaining in a school setting.

The three educational collective bargaining models selected are quite different in design and objective. Cresswell's model is much in the same style and design as the general models discussed above and draws heavily on them. Its main contribution is in the attempt to take into account (1) the importance of elapsed time as a variable, and (2) the learning process involved when one bargainer attends to the other's concessions. This approach also gives attention to the question of why bargaining should resume after a period of deadlock or strike. To obtain this level of detail, simplifying assumptions are made about the behavior of the bargainers, e.g., that they use linear extensions of their opponent's current behavior to predict future actions. Also, in obtaining this additional detail, the model becomes analytically unwieldy and does not produce determinate solutions to the outcome of each bargaining session. Similarly, no direct empirical test is possible since many of the variables are not specified in operational terms.

By contrast Hellriegel et al. have presented a model which is much less formal and does not specify relationships in precise ways.

Instead, these authors use general notions of bargaining behavior to lead to data collection and the testing of the validity of the general concepts. The results are somewhat vague analytically, but do contribute data from schools. Hellriegel et al. deal comprehensively with the question of what variables are important, both within the bargaining process and in its environment. Their conceptual scheme groups variables according to (1) the environment, (2) the professional staff, (3) the institutional context, and (4) the bargaining itself. There has been active disagreement on the validity of the model, but it is one of several useful ones. See the exchange between Moore and Hellriegel et al. (reading 12).

With Vantine (reading 13) we find the more general theories of collective bargaining applied to schools, rather than an attempt to generate new theories. Vantine applies the notion of distributive bargaining from Walton and McKersie (1965) to the school situation. In doing so, he highlights the contrast between the demands of distributive bargaining and the cooperative problem-solving required by many school negotiation issues. This raises the question as to what form of bargaining is appropriate for various situations. This reading illustrates the manner in which general theories of bargaining can contribute to the understanding of specific educational bargaining problems.

Bargaining Concepts and Research

In general, the research literature about collective bargaining, particularly in the public sector, has many gaps. There are, however, a number of research reports dealing with some aspect of bargaining behavior. This is not as contradictory as it sounds, since the research literature lacks coherence in the sense of pursuit of major lines of inquiry. The work is based in different disciplines with no single unifying theory. The readings included here were selected to be illustrative of different research methods and at the same time review major concepts of bargaining. For example, an empirical study of bargaining behavior in a laboratory situation is narrow in scope and illuminates only one or two aspects of bargaining behavior. By examining several other laboratory studies, it would be possible to assemble a fairly comprehensive picture of the state of knowledge of bargaining behavior. However, this process would also require a framework within which to organize the research and relate pieces to each other. For understanding the behavior of individual bargainers, the review and synthesis by Rubin and Brown (1975) is cast in an excellent framework and summarizes much of the laboratory literature. For nonlaboratory bargaining, especially collective behavior, no such framework or major collection exists. The articles presented here suggest the outline of one possible framework.

To outline the framework we focus on the situation of the bargainer. He or she is faced with three basic, related problems: (1) how to evaluate information, (2) how to communicate information, and (3) on what to base decisions. The information, from a variety of sources, is input to the decision process. The decision process is affected by this information and the bargainer's experience, perceptions, personality, and analytical skills. The results of the decisions must be communicated to opponents, constituents or clients, and other actors in the environment. How well the bargainer evaluates, decides, and communicates largely determines success.

Several studies have dealt with the role of threats and information in bargaining. Fischer (1969), for example, found that threats per se were not important in determining outcomes, but that threats as part of an information manipulation process, together with the use of lies, did affect bargaining and cooperation. Since both bargainers are dependent on information, the use of threats or punitive behavior interferes with the exchange of information, thus damaging the bargaining relationship. Similarly, risk-taking, presumably governed in part by personality, was found by Harnett et al. (1968) to be affected by the amount of available information. Risk-taking interacted with amount of information to change the bargaining process in an expected way: the less information the greater the effect of risk-taking on outcomes. The importance of information in general is discussed by Harsanyi (1962), particularly in regard to knowledge of the opponent's utility functions. Despite incomplete information, he points out, bargaining does in fact take place and agreements are reached. Bargainers may have implicit assumptions about the propensities and values of the opponent which are modified by information received during the bargaining process, both from the opponent's behavior and elsewhere. The point is: information received during the bargaining itself is only part of the information base and must be combined with other information, assumed and gathered elsewhere, to provide the basis for decisions. How the data are gathered and combined are left as subjects for further work.

The importance of perceptions and roles to decision making and information processing is treated by Michener et al. (reading 14) and elsewhere by Vidmar and McGrath (1970). The Vidmar and McGrath study documents the importance of bargainers' representative role obligations in determining bargaining success. Other studies have dealt with perceptions of fairness and power. Gruder (1971), for example, found that: "bargainers responded in kind to their opponent; they tended to be unyielding with a perceived exploitative opponent and compromising with a fair opponent. . . ." Michener et al. found power perception to be determined by the amount of damage the opponent could inflict and one's ability to avert the damage. In each of these studies, the subjects made decisions on the basis of information received from the laboratory situation and from other sources and filtered that information according to perceptions of various kinds. The filtered information produced different decisions, according to the kind and amount of information and the perceptions.

While this does not constitute a detailed understanding of the process of each case, this approach does assist in organizing our knowledge about bargaining. By focusing on information processing and decision making we can bring some coherence to the available knowledge and relate it more directly to the problem of studying bargaining in the school situation.

References

Cross, John. *The Economics of Bargaining.* New York: Basic Books, 1969.

Fischer, Clause S. "The Effects of Threats in an Incomplete Information Game." *Sociometry* 32, no. 2 (September 1969).

Gruder, Charles L. "Relationships with Opponent and Partner in Mixed Motive Bargaining." *Journal of Conflict Resolution* 15, no. 3 (September 1971).

Harnett, Donald L.; Cummings, Larry L.; and Hughes, David G. "The Influence of Risk-Taking Propensity on Bargaining Behavior." *Behavioral Science* 13, no. 2 (March 1968).

Harsanyi, John C. "Bargaining in Ignorance of the Opponent's Utility Function." *Journal of Conflict Resolution* 6, no. 29 (1962).

Rubin, Jeffrey Z., and Brown, Bert R. *The Social Psychology of Bargaining and Negotiation.* New York: Academic Press, 1975.

Vidmar, Neil, and McGrath, Joseph E. "Forces Affecting Success in Negotiation Groups." *Behavioral Science,* 15, no. 2 (March 1970).

Walton, Richard E., and McKersie, Robert B. *A Behavioral Theory of Labor Negotiations.* New York: McGraw-Hill, 1965.

Reading 8

Models of Cooperation and Conflict

Martin Patchen

A perusal of our social science journals shows that studies of conflictful and cooperative interaction are multiplying at a rapid rate.

A wide variety of variables have been discussed and/or studied as possible determinants of the type of interaction which occurs in a given situation and of the outcome of such interaction. These include various features of the situation (e.g., relative power, conflict of interest, communication channels); various characteristics of the parties (e.g., ideology, motives, group decision-making processes); subjective orientations of the parties during interaction (e.g., perception of the other's intentions); and strategies of interaction (e.g., behaving noncooperatively and then switching to cooperation).

A complete list of all possible relevant features of the objective situation, characteristics of the parties, subjective orientations of the parties, and patterns of interaction would surely be a very long one. This obviously presents a serious scientific problem. On the one hand, there is a temptation—especially in the laboratory—to study

Reprinted by permission from *Journal of Conflict Resolution* 14, no. 3 (September 1970), pp. 389-407. Copyright 1970 by Sage Publications.

one, or a few, isolated variables as they affect conflict and cooperation. Such studies are often useful but it is usually hard to know how
the results are affected by other important but unspecified variables;
nor is it usually easy to see how the results of many studies concerning many apparently disparate variables may be fitted together.

It might seem possible to avoid these problems by "throwing
in" for analysis in a given study a large number of variables which
may conceivably be important or interesting. However, since not all
possible variables can be included in any study (for reasons of time,
cost, etc.), there must be a selection process, explicitly or implicitly
guided by some ideas about which variables are most important.
Moreover, merely having data on many independent variables will
not provide a guide about how to analyze these data. For example,
simply putting all the predictors into a multiple correlation analysis
may be quite inappropriate if their effects are not independent and
linear.

It is clear, then, that in this area of study, as in other areas of
science, we need one or more theoretical models to guide research.
(By theoretical model I mean a formal statement of the key variables
and of their relationships.) In fact, a variety of models concerning
conflictful and cooperative interaction have been presented in recent
years.

These models have been developed by people concerned with
the behavior of a variety of types of actors in a variety of contexts—
including labor and management bargaining about wages, nations
attacking one another, buyer and seller deciding on price, and laboratory subjects choosing cooperative or uncooperative moves. While
there has been some attempt at a comparison of models and a cumulative development of such models within certain circumscribed
fields (especially bargaining models and "Richardson process" models), there has been little attention paid to the wider comparison of
all models falling within the broad field of cooperative and conflictful interaction.

What types of models of cooperation and conflict have been
offered? What contributions to understanding do various types of
models appear to offer and what limitations do they have? What are
the relationships of various types of models to each other and is
there some basis for trying to integrate various types of theoretical
contributions? This paper will suggest some answers to these ques-

tions in the hope that this may help us to see where we now stand and that it may point some fruitful directions for further work.

It would be well to indicate here the boundaries of this review. It is, first, concerned with theories having to do with actions of decision-making entities (e.g., a person, a union board, a national cabinet) and not with theories (see for instance Grimshaw 1969) bearing on the actions of unorganized masses of persons, in such situations as a riot. Second, because of the focus on the action of decision-making entities, theories (e.g., Choucri and North 1969) which attempt to predict the behavior of entire social systems (e.g., nations) as a function of the properties of those systems (e.g., size and wealth) will not be considered. Thirdly, theories (e.g., Galtung 1965; Deutsch et al. 1957; Etzioni 1965) having to do with the development or effectiveness of social mechanisms to regulate interaction will not be considered. Rather the focus is on models dealing with the interaction itself.

Such models of cooperative and conflictful action have been concerned with two basic types of phenomena: the first is the process by which two parties attempt, through a process of *bid and counter-bid*, to reach agreement on the *terms* of their future interaction—i.e., on what the nature of the interaction will be and (perhaps implicitly) what the resulting rewards and costs to each will be. Theoretical models dealing with these phenomena will be discussed under the heading of "negotiation" models.

The second basic type of phenomenon is the series of actions taken by each side which (whether so intended or not) *influences* the other side either (a) to continue present interaction (and the accompanying payoffs to each side); or (b) to change its behavior so that a different type of interaction, and/or different payoffs to each from the interaction, will occur. Some "influence" actions (e.g., coercive acts, cooperative acts) have actual effects on the rewards and punishments experienced by the two sides. Other influence behaviors (e.g., persuasion, threat) affect primarily the perceptions of the other about the presence and magnitude of possible incentives and the probability that they will result from certain actions he may take.

Three major types of theoretical models dealing with "influence" actions may be distinguished in terms of the basic processes which are emphasized in explaining the action of each party in relation to the action of the other. These types are (a) cognitive models;

(b) learning models; and (c) reaction process models. Cognitive models view the action of A as depending on A's perception about the future results of his actions, which, in turn, often depend partly on his expectations about the future actions of B. Learning models view A's actions as depending largely on the previous outcomes of the combination of A's and B's past actions. Reaction process models view each of A's actions as being an almost automatic response to B's last action, based on A's own characteristics and propensities.*

This review of these various types of models will not be exhaustive of all contributions. For each type of model, a number of major contributions will be discussed. The aim will be to assess the strengths and the limitations of each type of model. In addition, we will consider the relationship between negotiation and influence behavior models, the relation between cognitive, learning, and reaction process approaches, and problems of empirical testing of models in this area.

Models of Negotiation

A number of writers have proposed models to explain whether agreement will be reached between two parties to a dispute and/or the terms of the agreement. There is a fairly extensive literature[†] on this topic by economists who have been concerned especially with such questions as (a) when a labor-management dispute over wages will be settled and what the resulting wage rate will be; and (b) when buyer and seller will reach agreement on price and quantity and what

---

*Bernard (1965) has classified approaches to the study of conflict primarily in terms of whether the approach is "rationalistic" or "nonrationalistic." This classification cross-cuts the one used here, since each of the three processes mentioned above may have certain "rational" aspects and certain "irrational" aspects. See Fink (1968, pp. 426-29) for a further discussion of approaches to the study of conflict and Boulding (1962) for a discussion of a number of models of conflict, some of which (the ecological, the epidemiological, the theory of viability) go beyond the bounds of this review.

†See Pen 1952, 1959; Shackle 1964; Zeuthen 1930; Walton and McKersie 1965; Cross 1965, 1969; Bishop 1963; Hicks 1932; Foldes 1964; Harsanyi 1956; Siegel and Fouraker 1960; Fouraker and Siegel 1963; Stevens 1963; Coddington 1968. The work of game theorists (e.g., Nash 1953; Shapley 1953; Raiffa 1953; Howard 1968) is also relevant to the distribution of payoffs to the two sides and to the reaching of agreement.

the terms of such an agreement will be. Despite the anchoring of their analyses in economic issues, many of these theorists have treated bargaining as a more general social process. In addition, somewhat less formal theoretical models to illuminate the success or failure to reach agreements in international disputes have been proposed by several writers (Iklé and Leites 1962; Sawyer and Guetzkow 1965) and at least one model has been proposed to account for settlements in laboratory bargaining situations (Kelley, Beckman, and Fischer 1967).

Each of these models attempts to account for the actions of each bargainer during the course of negotiations—i.e., what bids he will make or is willing to accept. Agreement is seen as occurring when the series of bids or demands by the two sides converges on a common point. For example, in Pen's bargaining theory, "the terminal point of the bargaining process now lies where both equations [describing the decision elements for each party] are satisfied at the same time [i.e., at a common wage rate]" (Pen 1959, p. 137).

At least one bargaining model treats the decisions of each party as entirely independent of the other party's actions. Kelley, Beckman, and Fischer state: "To simplify the problem, we have proceeded from the assumptions that relate R (resistance) for a given party only to his own MNS (minimum necessary share) value and last offer" (1967, p. 383). More commonly, bargaining theorists (e.g., Pen; Walton and McKersie; Stevens; Iklé and Leites) see the action of each party as affected in part by its perception of the other side's likely actions. Thus, for example, Walton and McKersie's formula for the "subjective expected utility" of a given settlement includes the variable "probability that a given demand will be acceptable to the other side." However, most bargaining theorists do not, in their formal models, treat the actions of each side as being in part a reaction to the previous actions of the other. In other words, most theories of bargaining do not give direct and explicit attention to the process of interaction between the parties. And yet it is the interaction process, rather than the separate characteristics of the parties, which may be crucial to the outcomes in a social relationship.

Two notable theories of bargaining which do attempt to handle the phenomenon of interaction between the parties have been proposed by Siegel and Fouraker and by Cross.

Siegel and Fouraker (1960) and Fouraker and Siegel (1963)

have performed a series of experiments on bargaining under conditions of bilateral monopoly (one buyer, one seller).* Their major concern was in predicting the price and the quantity agreed on.

They describe the typical pattern shown by their experimental buyers and sellers as follows (Siegel and Fouraker 1960, p. 90):

(1) The subject would open negotiations at a high level, usually his highest level of expectancy;

(2) The failure experiences represented by the rival's early bids . . . made it apparent that concessions would have to be made . . . ;

(3) As negotiations progressed, in the absence of information, the succession of bids served to (1) give experience to the subject, enabling him to establish a realistic level of aspiration and (2) enable the subject to find means by which concessions could be made to the opponent without making offers below the aspiration level. Aspiration levels were modified as negotiations progressed. . . .

(4) The search for efficient means of making concessions tended to lead the bargainers to solutions on the Paretian optima.[†]

Siegel and Fouraker describe the pattern of bargaining in the following model, which describes the behavior of bargainer 1.

$$\alpha_{i_1} = \text{maximum } E_1 - \frac{\text{max. } E_1 - \text{min. } E_1}{1 + S_1 r_2} \left(1 - \frac{1}{t_i r_1}\right)$$

where

α_{i_1} = the level of aspiration of bargainer 1 at the time of the ith bid;

max. E_1 = bargainer 1's maximum payoff expectancy;

min. E_1 = bargainer 1's minimum payoff expectancy;

r_1 = index of bargainer 1's rate of concession;

r_2 = index of bargainer 2's rate of concession;

S_1 = index of bargainer 1's ability to perceive his opponent's concession rate;

t = duration of negotiations.

---

*These investigators have also studied bargaining under other conditions, such as oligopoly (Fouraker and Siegel 1963). However, it is their work on bilateral monopoly which is of greatest relevance to our consideration of models of conflict and cooperation between two parties.

†The Paretian optima are a set of points from which deviations which increase the utility of one party will decrease the utility of the other party.

A comparable function expresses the behavior of bargainer 2.*
When the negotiations reach a state at which each participant may
satisfy his current level of aspiration[†] and $\alpha_1 + \alpha_2$ = the maximum
joint payoff, the contract will be agreed on at this point.[‡]

The work of Siegel and Fouraker, which has attracted wide attention in several social science disciplines, has made several significant contributions. Unlike the work of most economists on bargaining, which is entirely theoretical, they have subjected important
theoretical predictions—e.g., concerning the tendency of a pair to
maximize joint profit—to empirical test. Moreover, their experimental results concerning the nature of agreements toward which
bargainers tend and the effects on bargaining outcomes of such variables as amount of information and set goals are of considerable
interest.

However, some important limitations of the Siegel-Fouraker
model of bargaining should be noted. First, the experimental situation from which the model derives is almost entirely devoid of costs
during bargaining (e.g., there are no costs, or advantages, of the
status quo which each is suffering or enjoying during the bargaining)
and there are almost no risks (like a war or strike or an economic
hardship) involved if a bargain is not struck. The only risk is that the
advantages of an agreement will not be realized. This "no costs—no
risks" nature of the situation may help to explain why neither costs
nor risks appear in the model which describes the bargaining behavior
of each party. Moreover, the formal model which Siegel and Four-

---

*It should be noted that some of these variables—especially r_1 and r_2—
appear to refer to objective features of the situation, rather than to perceptions
of the bargainers. In this respect the theory differs from most bargaining theories.

[†]It may be noted that the concept of "aspiration" is used differently by
Siegel and Fouraker than by Walton and McKersie. Siegel and Fouraker's "level
of aspiration" is represented by the bargainer's current bid whereas the aspirations discussed by Walton and McKersie—i.e., the "target point" and "resistance
point"—serve to define an area of outcomes within which the bargainer may
make bids. The "maximum expectancy" and "minimum expectancy" concepts
of Siegel and Fouraker appear to be roughly similar to the "target point" and
"resistance point" of Walton and McKersie.

[‡]Johnson and Cohen (1967) have replicated the work of Siegel and Fouraker, noting also the importance of value orientations and of experience in such
bargaining situations.

aker judge to "exhibit close conformity to the observed bargaining patterns" has apparently not actually been tested. In fact, several of the variables of the model—minimum payoff expectancy and bargainer's ability to perceive opponent's concession rate—seem difficult to measure in order to test the model. It may also be questioned whether in many situations each bargainer will actually have a "minimum payoff expectancy" at all times during the course of the negotiation.

Cross (1965, 1969) proposes another bargaining model which takes account of the phenomenon of interaction. Though less well known outside economics, Cross's model may be a better representation of the bargaining process than is that of Siegel and Fouraker. Cross's theory is discussed and extended by Coddington (1968).

Like Siegel and Fouraker, Cross sees the demands of either bargainer at a given time as being in part a function of the concession rate of his opponent. But Cross also emphasizes the costs of non-agreement and analyzes further the factors which affect the concession rates of the parties. He states, "As any economist knows, time has a cost, both in money and in utility terms; it is our position that it is precisely this cost which motivates the bargaining process" (1965, p. 72). In addition to the effects of time on the utility of an agreement (e.g., the cake may get moldy before we agree how to cut it), Cross focuses on the costs of bargaining, which may vary from the inconvenience of spending time at this activity to the loss of profits or wages.

To decide what outcome to demand, player 1 chooses the quantity which maximizes the present value of his utility. The present value of his utility is expressed in a complex equation (not reproduced here) as a function of the particular outcome (quantity) demanded, his cost rate per time-period, and the estimated length of time to agreement.

The expected time necessary to reach agreement (W) is given by the expression:

$$W = \frac{q_1 + q_2 - M}{r_2}$$

where q_1 = a demand by party 1;
       q_2 = the current demand of party 2;

> M = the total fixed quantity of a good which is continuous-
> ly divisible;
>
> r_2 = party 1's estimate of party 2's rate of concession.

Since the concession rate of party 1 depends in part on the estimated length of time to agreement, his concession rate depends in
part, therefore, on his estimate of the concession rate of party 2.
This estimate changes in response to party 2's behavior. Agreement is
reached as the sequence of mutual concessions converges.*

Another feature of Cross's theory is that it links past learning
systematically to present perceptions. Party 1's expectations regarding party 2's concession rate change as a result of a learning process.

In its incisiveness, rigor, and intuitive plausibility (it seems, for
example, to capture much of the dynamics of the Vietnam war situation), Cross's model is quite impressive. However, apparently it has
not yet been subjected to empirical testing.

Nonbid Actions

An important limitation of almost all bargaining models, including the work of Siegel-Fouraker and Cross's earlier work, is that these
theories are limited to a consideration of bargaining in a very narrow
sense—i.e., to the behaviors of making, accepting, or rejecting a given
demand or bid. For example, Walton and McKersie's and Iklé and
Leites' analyses focus on discovering the range of possible agreements
acceptable to both parties.

Most theories of bargaining do not consider, as intrinsic parts of
their models, behavioral choices other than accepting or rejecting
bids. Several of the models (e.g., Walton and McKersie, Pen) consider
the strike occurrence as a possible negative consequence of holding
out for a given settlement and thus as one of the factors affecting the
decisions of the parties to accept or not to accept a given agreement.
But they do not consider at all the action of using coercion (e.g.,
striking) as one of the possible *choices* by the parties. In Pen's model,
the alternative to accepting an agreement is to "go on bargaining"

---

*It may be noted that, although Cross views each party's actions as being
affected by the actions of the other, he does not view the actions of each as
possible attempts to influence the actions of the other. Coddington discusses this
point in some detail.

but there is no behavioral content to this choice. We are given no way of predicting whether "to go on bargaining" is likely to mean simply waiting and doing nothing, or trying to persuade the other side, or taking some coercive action to try to force the other side to accept a favorable agreement. In Siegel and Fouraker's work, the kind of experimental bargaining situations which are created restrict the actions of the bargainers to making, accepting, or rejecting bids. Although there is the time pressure of a deadline for the participants, they do not have the opportunity of exerting direct pressure on their adversaries—e.g., by stopping ongoing trade or by associated threats or promises.

Some of the bargaining theories mentioned (e.g., Walton and McKersie, Stevens, Iklé and Leites) do discuss, sometimes at considerable length, the various coercive and other "tactics" which the parties may perform in order to influence the other side to accept favorable terms. However, the formal, basic theoretical models do not help us to predict the types of "tactics"—for example, the use of coercion—which will be used on the way to agreement.

In short, most of the models of bargaining which have been proposed have been largely restricted to bargaining in a narrow sense— i.e., to the trading of bids until a settlement is reached. They have not described bargaining in the broader sense suggested by Schelling, who writes (1960, p. 5):

To study the strategy of conflict is to take the view that most conflict situations are essentially *bargaining* situations. . . . The bargaining may be explicit, as when one occupies or evacuates strategic territory. It may, as in the ordinary haggling of the market-place, take the status quo as its zero point and seek arrangements that yield positive gains to both sides; or it may involve threats of damage, including mutual damage, as in a strike, boycott, or price war, or in extortion.

We turn next to a consideration of some models of cooperation and conflict which examine some of these other aspects of interaction—i.e., which attempt to explain the occurrence of actions by each side which may influence the other side to accept a certain type of interaction and distribution of rewards.

Models Predicting Influence Behaviors: Cognitive Models

A number of theorists have attempted to explain the "influencing" actions of two interacting parties in terms of cognitive elements in the minds of the decision makers—i.e., the utility which each side places on certain outcomes and its subjective probability that specific outcomes will result from particular actions. This kind of cognitive approach has clear connections to decision theory (see Edwards 1961; Patchen 1965) and to many motivational theories (e.g., Atkinson 1964). It also is similar to the basically cognitive approach taken by most theorists who have been concerned with phenomena of negotiation.*

Cognitive models have been used especially to predict the use or nonuse of coercive action by one party against another. A number of theorists—including Singer (1963), Snyder (1960), Russett (1963, 1967), and Porsholt (1966)—have used what is basically a decision theory approach to account for the use or nonuse of force by one nation against another. (In some contexts, this is the deterrence problem.) The work of Porsholt and of Russett may be examined as particularly interesting examples of this general approach, since both make explicit predictions about the conditions under which coercion will or will not be used.

Review of the Literature

Porsholt (1966) presents a "conflict model" which focuses on the choice by the potential attacker either to attack or not attack and on the choice by the potential defender to resist or not to resist attack.†

The conditions of conflict behavior, Porsholt says, are:

$$(1) \quad - M + pG > 0 \text{ and}$$
$$(2) \quad - \overline{M} + q\overline{G} > 0$$

where M = the utility to the aggressor of using this means (struggle);

---

*For example, it may be noted that the attractiveness of a given policy (say, attack for the aggressor) is predicted in Russett's analysis by a formula which is essentially identical to that proposed by Walton and McKersie for predicting the subjectively expected utility of striving for a given wage settlement. This correspondence is not surprising, since both authors base their analyses on decision theory concepts.

†A more elaborate and advanced model to explain these phenomena is now being developed by Porsholt (1969).

$\overline{M}$ = the utility to the defender of using this means (struggle);

G = the utility to the aggressor of reaching his goal;

$\overline{G}$ = the utility to the defender of reaching his goal;

p = the probability of victory for the aggressor according to his own belief (values from 0 to 1);

q = the probability of victory for the defender according to his own belief.

In verbal terms, these expressions indicate that in order for conflict to occur, the overall value of struggle for both sides must be greater than zero.

Porsholt also considers two components (practical cost and psychological burden) of the utility of a struggle (M) and two components (expansion and security) of the utility of reaching the goal (G).* On the basis of his rather simple formulas, he derives a variety of interesting conclusions about the conditions of conflict or non-conflict and also considers practical steps which may be taken to prevent conflict.

Russett (1963) has also considered the determinants of attack by an aggressor and of a "firm policy" by a defender (i.e., not accepting the demand of a potential aggressor).† In footnotes to his analysis of historical cases, he suggests some general formulas to predict behavior in such situations.

The potential aggressor will attack, Russett says, only if:

$$V_a S + V_w (1 - S) > V_o$$

where V_a = the value of a successful attack (no war);

V_w = the value (usually negative) of an attack which is countered (war);

V_o = the value of doing nothing in this instance (no attack, no war);

S = the probability of a successful attack (no war).

---

*Note that Porsholt's formulas do not include the utility of outcomes other than reaching one's goals of expansion and security—e.g., the utility of the outcome of being defeated or of the status quo. He does discuss this matter somewhat (p. 183).

†See also the critique of Russett's paper by Fink (1965) and Russett's (1967) discussion of deterrence theory and decision theory.

To predict whether the defender will pursue a firm policy, a similar formula is presented, which includes the value of successful firmness (deterrence without war), the value of the failure of firmness (war), the value of retreat, and the probability that firmness will be successful.

It will be noted that the probability factors in the formal analyses of Porsholt and of Russett are different. The decision by Porsholt's actor about whether or not to attack is based in part on the probability of victory in a fight with the other but not on whether the other will resist;* Russett's actor considers whether the other will resist but not the probability of victory if a fight does occur (except as this might be reflected in the value of war). This difference reflects the fact that Porsholt is concerned primarily with the question of when either or both sides are actually willing to fight while Russett is concerned primarily with the question of when each side is willing to take an action (attack, stand firm) which may or may not lead to a fight.

Another difference between the two is that whereas Porsholt considers whether the attractiveness of entering a struggle is less than or equal to zero, Russett more realistically compares the attractiveness of the attack or the "stand firm" decision to the attractiveness of another possible course of action. Thus, for example, Russett compares the expected value of attack to the value of doing nothing. Each of these actions may, of course, be compared also to the expected value of additional actions—like seeking mediation, exerting economic pressures, etc.

A less formal theory of the outbreak of both war and revolution is presented by Timasheff (1965). Timasheff's theory is not directly tied to decision theory but it is heavily cognitive in nature. Concerning war, he asserts (pp. 96-97) that

... two or more states antagonistic to each other are likely to move from the state of peace to that of war if the following conditions are *simultaneously* present:
1. The antagonism must have reached the level of danger as specified, and be further reinforced by aggravating circumstances.

---

*Porsholt does discuss discursively (p. 181), however, the fact that though A may not be willing to enter a fight with B, he may move to acquire his ends if he thinks that B is not willing to fight.

2. None of the parties to the conflict, especially the one likely to play the aggressive role, is dominated by exceptionally strong normative inhibitions to war.

3. One of the parties must have lost hope of achieving its goal short of war, after having tried other procedures or rejected them as inadequate.

4. Subjectively, according to the conclusions of responsible leaders, there is a fair chance of victory for each of the parties, while the problem of cost has not been raised or has resulted in a (subjectively) favorable answer.

The movement from order to violent revolution is explained by Timasheff in terms of a similar pattern of factors.

A cognitive model has also been developed by Wyer (1969) to predict the choice of alternative actions in game situations. Wyer's model is a general one that is applicable to all 2 × 2 situations (i.e., where each party chooses between two possible moves, one of which can sometimes be interpreted as a cooperative one and the other as a competitive one).

The equation used by Wyer to predict the probability with which a subject will choose move 1 (P_1) is as follows:

$$P_1 = W_1 P_{E1} (U_1 - U_3) + W_2 P_{E2} (U_2 - U_4) \\ + W_3 P_{E1} K_2 + W_0$$

where

P_{E1} = the probability with which the subject expects other to choose 1;

U_1 through U_4 = the utilities of each of the four possible outcomes represented by the joint moves of the actors;

K_2 = the amount of fate control which other has over subject (an index computed from the payoffs to subject in each of the four possible outcome states);

P_{E2} = $1 - P_{E1}$; and

W_0 through W_4 = regression parameters.

Wyer reports moderate success in predicting subject actions in a variety of 2 × 2 game situations.

Limitations of Cognitive Models

The theorists who have used a cognitive approach to account for the use of coercion and other "influence" behaviors have pro-

vided a number of potentially useful models to account for such behavior. However, it is important to note a number of limitations of
such models.

First, just as bargaining theorists have focused on the choice between agreement and nonagreement, to the neglect of the choice of
coercion or other influence behaviors, so most analysts of the use of
coercion and related actions have not been concerned with the question of when agreement between disputing parties will be reached.*
(This is not to find fault with either group of theorists for not doing
something that they did not intend to do, but rather to point to the
limited focus of each body of work.)

Secondly, like most models of bargaining, these models do not
handle the phenomenon of interaction between the parties. Porsholt
does mention ways in which the actions of one may change the perceptions and thus the subsequent behavior of the other. However,
such aspects of interaction are not part of the formal model of conflict. Similarly, Russett's formal model is concerned with the decisions of each party at a given point in time and not with interaction
between them over time. Timasheff's set of conditions necessary for
the outbreak of war does not refer to the interaction between the
parties. Nor is Wyer's model concerned with such interaction.

Thirdly, as with most models of bargaining, the theoretical ideas
of cognitive models have usually not been operationalized and tested.
Models concerning coercion and deterrence in international affairs
have served primarily (as in Russett's work) as a conceptual framework within which to interpret data which do not really test the
models. However, in the laboratory, where measurement is easier,
utilities and expectancies of subjects have been measured in a number of studies and Wyer has performed such measurements in testing
his model of action in mixed-motive situations.

Learning Models

Whereas analysts of bargaining and of coercion have usually
focused on the parties' current calculations about possible future

---

*Timasheff is an exception to this generalization. He sees the movement
from war to peace as occurring when the fight removes uncertainty about relative strength and thus at least one party loses hope that it can reach its goal
through fighting. Note the neglect of the time and cost factors affecting willingness to settle, as emphasized by Cross.

outcomes, some analysts have focused on interaction between two parties as a learning process. Several investigators have been able to account for accommodation in some simple social situations by way of basic learning assumptions (Sidowski 1957; Kelley, Thibaut, Radloff, and Mundy 1962). However, the most far-reaching and sophisticated attempt to describe interaction in terms of learning processes has been made by Anatol Rapoport and his associates (Rapoport, Chammah, Dwyer, and Gyr 1962; Rapoport 1963; Rapoport and Chammah 1965; Rapoport and Dale 1966). See also Cohen (1963).

Rapoport and his colleagues have observed the behavior of student subjects in simple Prisoner's Dilemma* experimental situations. On each "round" each of two players can choose either a cooperative (C) or a noncooperative (D) response. Payoffs in money to each of the players depend on the nature of their joint moves, i.e., CC, CD, DC, or DD. The two players go through a large number of such "rounds" and the number of cooperative, noncooperative, and mixed (CD or DC) trials over time is recorded.

The importance of interaction between the parties in accounting for the results is indicated in this comment by Rapoport and Chammah: "Variance among pairs is rather large, even within games. We have strong reason to believe, however, that much of this variance is accounted for not by inherent propensities of the players to cooperate or not to cooperate, but rather by the characteristic instabilities of the dynamic process which governs the interactions in Prisoner's Dilemma" (1965, p. 199).

Rapoport and his associates have proposed a number of possible mathematical models to account for their results and especially for the interactions between the behaviors of the players which their data indicate.

Most of the models they propose involve change in the "propensities" to action (e.g., to cooperate) under various circumstances— i.e., they involve learning during the course of interaction. One set of important "propensities" is as follows:

---

*The Prisoner's Dilemma situation has the characteristic that if both players cooperate they are both better off than if they both don't cooperate. However, the highest possible payoff goes to a player who does not cooperate while his partner does cooperate. The lowest possible payoff goes to a player who cooperates while his partner does not cooperate.

x (trustworthiness): probability of cooperating after having cooperated and having been rewarded;

y (forgiveness): probability of cooperating after having cooperated and having been punished;

z (repentance): probability of cooperating after having not cooperated and having been rewarded;

w (trust): probability of cooperating after having not cooperated and having been punished.

These propensities change as a result of experience. Rapoport (1963) describes "learning parameters" which measure the rate at which trustworthiness is learned when the other is trustworthy, the rate at which trust deteriorates when the other is not trustworthy, and the rate at which forgiveness is learned when the other repents.

In principle, a stochastic model* proposed could predict x, y, z, and w, and the proportion of mutually cooperative responses, as a function of time and of the learning parameters (Rapoport 1963, p. 21). However, this model, as well as other possible mathematical models which Rapoport and his associates discuss, apparently have received only limited empirical testing so far.

The empirical work by the Rapoport group represents a major contribution to our understanding of cooperative and noncooperative behavior in mixed-motive situations. Their mathematical models suggest useful ways of conceptualizing the dynamics of interaction and learning in such situations. However, their work does have a number of important limitations.

First, their models, which are descriptive of a situation where each party faces the same opponents many times in succession and which focus on learning processes, do not seem able to help us to make predictions in new or changed situations. In such novel situations, behavior is usually not based primarily on past learning but on such factors as the present perception of possible outcomes and present perceptions about the other party's likely behavior. In other

---

*Note that whereas most of the models which Rapoport has investigated are based on probability processes, a number of other models examined (e.g., Siegel-Fouraker, Cross, reaction process models) are deterministic. Whereas Rapoport and Chammah have emphasized a probability process that is modified by learning, they and Rausch (1965) have also investigated models based on sheer probability processes. Such models have not proved very successful in accounting for actual interaction sequences.

words, variables representing present calculations about unique situations, so prominent in the economic models of bargaining, are lacking in the learning models.*

Secondly, the possible behaviors which are represented in these models are limited to those representing cooperation and noncooperation. Behaviors of making (verbal) offers and of accepting or rejecting such offers, as well as "influence" behaviors (threat, etc.) are not covered by these models.† Therefore a significant portion of the behavior of the parties in most real conflict situations is not covered by these particular models. One aspect of this limitation on behavior, incidentally, is that all behavior in the game situations which Rapoport studies have consequences in terms of payoffs; there is no room for (verbal) behavior which has no immediate payoff consequences.

A related limitation of the learning models is that the payoffs for particular joint actions (e.g., both sides do not cooperate) are only short-run ones. But in many interaction situations, there is a considerable difference between the short-run payoffs resulting from a given situation and the long-range payoffs resulting from that situation. For example, where both sides do not cooperate and there is a struggle, the immediate payoff to both may be negative. However, the eventual winner of the struggle may gain large positive payoffs and both sides may purposely enter the struggle with this hope in mind. Such distinctions between short-range and long-range results of actions are not handled by these learning models.

Finally, the learning models have been used to describe interaction in situations where the "payoffs" which will occur as a result of a given combination of actions by the two parties are known with certainty to the actors. But in most natural situations, each of the actors is likely to be uncertain about what the payoffs may be. For example, in considering the possibility of a fight between the two

---

*Since there are no appreciable intrinsic costs involved in making moves in the Rapoport-Chammah experimental situations, such costs—which receive prominent attention in Cross's work, for example—are not included in these particular learning models (though they could, in principle, be incorporated into them).

†In their most recent work (e.g., Guyer and Rapoport 1970), Rapoport and his associates have studied the choice between strategies not clearly defined as cooperative and noncooperative. However, behavioral choice is still limited to one of two actions, both of which will bring payoffs to the two sides.

sides, a labor union official or a prime minister will think of several possible outcomes, perhaps assigning each a rough probability. This aspect of the natural situation is not handled by the learning models which have been advanced to account for conflict and cooperation.

Reaction Process Models

Another type of model which has been used to account for the actions of one party in its relationship with another party are those which describe what Boulding (1962) has called "reaction processes." Whereas most cognitive models view the actions of each party as depending (at least in part) upon its expectancies about the future actions of the other side, and learning models view action as a function of a history of past learning, reaction process models see action as an almost automatic reaction of each side to the last action of the other (based on certain of its own characteristics and propensities).

This type of model was originally developed by Richardson (1960) and Rapoport to account for the course of arms races. Richardson developed and applied the following formula to describe change in the level of armament of nation X in competition with nation Y:

$$\frac{dx}{dt} = ky - ax + g$$

where y = the level of strength of the opponent;
     x = one's own level of strength;
     k = the incentive (readiness) to accumulate arms because of the opponent's strength (i.e., a coefficient of reactability);
     a = the inhibiting effect of fatigue and cost consciousness;
     g = the sense of grievance against the opponent.

A similar equation is used to describe the change in Y's level of armament. Note that each nation's behavior at any point in time is at least partially a reaction to the behavior of the other.*

---

*In his later work, Richardson extended his theory to provide for an "intimidation effect" when the discrepancy of strength becomes too great.

On the basis of his approach, Richardson tried to account, with mixed success, for the course of several major arms races. More recently, the study of arms races in terms of reaction processes has been carried forward by others, including Smoker (1964, 1965), Chatterji (1969), and Milstein and Mitchell (1969).

It should be noted that an arms race is not a part of the direct interaction between two parties. An arms race represents an attempt by each side to be in a position to use (or to resist) a certain kind of attempt at influence, or perhaps to serve as a basis for the use of threat as an influence method. An arms race does not in itself represent the use of force or direct threat and it is not, therefore, a direct part of the process of conflict. However, each party's "arming" behavior may have (and may perhaps be intended to have) an influence not only on the other's arming behavior but also on the type of interaction or the terms of a formal settlement which the other party is prepared to accept. (For example, the level of armament of the Arab countries may affect the kind of settlement which Israel is prepared to accept.) For this reason, arms races may be included under the general rubric of "influence" behaviors that we have been considering.

An application of a reaction process model to actions other than arms races has been proposed by Wright (1965). He considers the degree of willingness by each side to either escalate or to stop hostile actions. He proposes the following equation to explain the growth rate of the hostility of nation X (dx/dt) as indicated by willingness to escalate:

$$\frac{dx}{dt} = (N_x + F_y) - (C_x + W_x) + (P_x - P_y) - (V_x - V_y)$$

where N_x = the national interest of the nation X;
$\quad\quad$ F_y = the force available to the opponent nation Y;
$\quad\quad$ C = the costs to X of hostility and preparations;
$\quad\quad$ W = world pressure on nation X for peace;
$\quad\quad$ P = potential military forces;
$\quad\quad$ V = vulnerability to destruction.

Wright sees the latter terms in the equation, reading from left to right, as assuming increasing importance in the decisions of nation X as the dispute progresses through different stages.

Using his own subjective estimates of the values of the variables in the equation, Wright finds his model useful for accounting for the escalation or nonescalation of a variety of international conflicts.

There are a number of problems with Wright's model. One is that the "stages" he discusses are not represented in the basic equation and it is not too clear how much weight each of the predictor variables should be given during each stage. Another is that, unlike models of arms races, Wright's model considers the action of each party (escalation of hostile action in this case) as largely independent of the parallel action of the other side. Wright's equation does take account of increases in armament by the opponent but not of those behaviors by the opponent (i.e., hostile actions) which parallel the actions he is trying to predict.*

In principle, of course, there is no reason why such problems cannot be overcome. The "hostility" of each side toward the other, which Richardson measured by armament expenditures (or armament expenditures minus trade), could be measured by such indicators as the number and magnitude of friendly versus hostile actions (or verbiage) which each side directs toward the other. (For such purposes, a coding system for actions, like that developed by McClelland (1968), might be useful.)

However, it seems doubtful that a reaction process model, where each side reacts fairly mechanically to the actions of the other side, would be adequate to account for the actions of nations (or other social units) during the course of most interactions. Richardson (1960, p. 12) says, "The equations are merely a description of what people would do if they did not stop to think." As Rapoport points out in his discussion of Richardson's work, such concepts as strategy, choice, and decision, which characterize game theory, are foreign to Richardson's thinking, which is based on the mechanical models of classical physics. It may be added that considerations of goals, expectancies, and perceived alternatives are also absent. There are many instances (see, for example, the documents concerning German decisions just prior to the outbreak of World War I (Kautsky 1924)) where it is clear that just such considerations of goals, expectancies, and alternatives—rather than a simple reaction to the other side's previous move—are crucial to understanding the actions taken.

---

*The escalation of hostile action has been discussed by Kahn (1962) in terms of interaction between the parties.

Reaction process models have provided a rigorous approach for studying interaction. And they appear to be quite useful for studying selected phenomena—like certain arms races—where the parties react almost mechanically to each others' moves. But it seems unlikely that the approach of such models will prove to be generally useful for studying most cases of cooperative and conflictful interaction.

Relationships Among Models

Having reviewed a number of different types of models, we may now consider further the relationship among them. In particular, we will consider (a) the relation of models of negotiation behavior to models of influence behavior and (b) the relation of cognitive, learning, and reaction process approaches. In addition, we will consider the problem of operationalizing and testing such models. In the discussion of these issues, we will be concerned especially with directions in which it seems fruitful to develop further and to test models in this area.

This review has suggested that there exists a separation between (a) those theories which are concerned primarily with whether agreement is reached and the terms of agreement; and (b) those theories concerned with actions which influence the other side's willingness to accept various kinds of explicit or tacit agreements.

Yet, as the work of Schelling suggests, it seems highly fruitful to see both the bid-trading process and the influence process as part of a single process of interaction. The demands which each side will make or accept are closely related to the kinds of influence which it can bring to bear on the other to accept its terms. Conversely, the amount and kinds of influence which each side will try to exert depend in part on the pattern of demands and concessions which has taken place. Moreover, the making of a new bid (e.g., a concession) may be seen as an alternative to the making of a new influence attempt aimed at getting the other side to accept a previous offer.

There is a need for the further development of theoretical models which relate these two aspects of the interaction process. Two efforts in this direction have already been made by Nicholson (1967) and by Cross (1969).

Nicholson's model, which derives from the example of tariff wars, is divided into two parts. The first considers the parties in an initial warfare situation. Either party, A, may, at any given moment of time, either (a) immediately concede to the other, B, and take his last best offer, or (b) hang on until B surrenders, meaning that after some delay he will get a larger gain. The longer it is before B makes his concession, the less attractive does hanging on appear to A. The one who first becomes so pessimistic about the expected time of concession of the other that it no longer is worth continuing the fight, gives in and accepts his rival's best offer. When both parties are getting pessimistic about when the rival will concede, a compromise is likely. (This part of the model has strong resemblances to the bargaining model of Cross 1965.) The second part of the model concerns possible escalation of the level of coercion (e.g., punitive tariff levels by one or both sides). Nicholson writes (1967, p. 31):

The basic principle is this: Instead of accepting the current bargaining position, A might feel that another point which involves a lower immediate level of national interest for himself will nevertheless be better for him in the long run, as the opponent will make a concession quicker from this point than he would have done from the higher point. If this concession comes sufficiently quickly, then this will more than compensate for the temporary costs of this worse position.

Nicholson diagrams for each party a set of points, called a satisfaction set, which, if they were attained (probably by escalation), would be held onto by that party as being points where he does better to hold on than to concede to B's offer. A similar satisfaction set exists for the other party. A typical escalation sequence concerning tariffs would go like this: The parties are at some point which is outside A's satisfaction set. A may increase his tariff to a point which is within his satisfaction set. B is now dissatisfied and replies by going to a point within his own satisfaction set, which again makes A increase his tariffs to a point which falls within the overlapping of both satisfaction sets. At this point, both parties think they can "win" the war and they both stay firm; there is a plateau. This will end when one or both of the parties decides that he was mistaken about the other conceding at that point, and that it would be better to concede himself.

Nicholson states that his model appears, in general, to fit the historical cases of tariff wars which he has studied. The model also has a persuasive plausibility; it appears intuitively, for example, to apply to the Vietnam war.

There are, however, several problems with, or limitations to, the model. One problem is that, at a time when either conceding or escalation seems preferable to a present situation, it is not clear how the party decides between concession and escalation. Secondly, the range of decisions covered by the model is a limited one. Most notably, it does not consider the original choice made by one or both of the parties to initiate warfare, nor does it consider the factors which determine that one compromise settlement is acceptable while another compromise is not acceptable.

Cross, in his most recent work (1969), has extended his treatment of bargaining to try to account for the occurrence of certain influencing actions, especially coercion. Coercion ties in to Cross's basic model of bargaining (see above) by affecting the costs of both the party applying the coercion and the party suffering it. By observing B's reaction to his (A's) coercive moves (predicted to be a drop in B's demands), A can see what he is gaining—in terms of reaching his desired settlement sooner—at how much cost to himself. A will increase the costs of the bargaining (to both sides) until the benefits derived from earlier settlement are matched by the increased costs of this "preagreement" period.

Cross acknowledges that his theory makes a number of restrictive assumptions—e.g., that the reaction of the coerced party is to lower his demand in a big drop rather than to increase his concession rate, and that party A does not take into account the psychological reaction of B to A's raising his costs (e.g., B getting stubbornly mad). Most important, A apparently does not consider the probability of B responding to coercion with countercoercion of his own.

Despite limitations in their work, Nicholson and Cross have pointed a direction in which it seems fruitful to go—to try to integrate the analysis of negotiation with the analysis of influence. To move further in this direction, it would seem useful to try to account for each actor's choice among a variety of possible behaviors, including (a) negotiating behaviors (making a bid, accepting or rejecting a bid); (b) standing pat and doing nothing; (c) giving information about possible outcomes or about one's own future actions (threats, promises); (d) doing something which affects the payoffs for the other's present behavior (e.g., coercive actions); and (e) doing something which affects the payoffs which would follow alternative behaviors which the other might choose.

One possibly fruitful approach to explaining the choice among such alternative actions is to use a motivational approach (Atkinson 1964). Such an approach would see the attractiveness of each type of action as a function of (a) each incentive in the situation (including the direct cost of the action); multiplied by (b) the importance of that incentive (i.e., by the strength of the relevant motive); multiplied by (c) the subjective probability that the particular action will lead to that incentive; summed for all relevant incentives. A motivational approach is similar to the cognitive approach of decision theory* but makes no assumptions about the extent to which conscious deliberations are made by the actor at any given time.

Comparison of the attractiveness of alternative actions, which such an approach would entail, would be simplified by two considerations. One is that essentially the same set of outcomes (incentives) and the same motives would be relevant for each potential action. (What is unique for each alternative action is its likelihood of leading to various outcomes and its costs.) A second consideration which would simplify the analysis of most choices is that only a subset of all possible alternative actions would be relevant in the particular situation and salient to the parties involved.

Cognitive, Learning, and Reaction Process Approaches

We have seen that cognitive models which attempt to account for behavior in conflict situations focus on the perceptions of the parties in the present situation and do not consider the residues of previous learning as represented by habits or learned "propensities." On the other hand, those models which are concerned with learning in interaction situations do not usually consider special features of the present situation which may affect the perceptions and actions of each side.

Both of these perspectives appear to have important limitations. An exclusive focus on past learning appears to render a model incapable of accounting for behavior in new or changed circumstances. On the other hand, an exclusive focus on the present situation and on

---

*Incentive multiplied by motive equals "utility," as used in decision theory (Atkinson 1958, pp. 303-05). See also Patchen (1965) for a discussion of a motivational approach to studying national action.

the participants' current perceptions may neglect the very important role of learning processes.

An adequate comprehensive model of conflict and cooperation should include both types of variables. One possible approach is to consider both the present situation and previous learning as variables (or sets of variables) which affect the factors which determine present motivation. From this perspective, both past experience and the present situation influence attention to certain incentives, the value attached to different incentives (i.e., motives), and especially the subjective probability that certain outcomes will follow certain actions. The effects of learning (and even the effects of the present situation) on such factors may or may not be wholly conscious. Thus such a model would be neither strictly cognitive nor strictly noncognitive, but would allow for different levels of awareness and deliberation about incentives, the value of incentives, and subjective probabilities.

To be most useful, an adequate model of cooperation and conflict also would have to incorporate the emphasis of reaction process models (and also of learning models) on social relationships as a dynamic process, wherein A's action affects B's action and so on. However, rather than viewing each party's action as an almost automatic reaction to the other (as reaction process models do), such a model might consider the ways in which certain actions of party A (e.g., a threat, a promise) affect the saliency of certain outcomes, or incentives, for B; the value of various outcomes for B (his motives); and the expectancies of B. If such effects were better understood, the effects of a certain kind of action by A on B's response could be predicted and the dynamic process of interaction between the two parties could be traced.* It should be kept in mind, however, that, at each step of the interaction, the previous action of the other is only one factor which may affect the incentives, motives, and expectancies of the actor. These are also affected by the incentives present in the current situation he faces; his knowledge of the current incentives facing the other; and his previous learning history.

----

*The "interaction model" proposed by Holsti, Brody, and North (1964, p. 175) is in the direction suggested here but the linkage between A's "perception of B's attitude and behavior toward A" and "the expression of A's attitude and behavior toward B" needs to be specified further.

Operationalizing and Testing the Models

In reviewing models of conflict and cooperation, it has been noted that many of them—particularly negotiation models and models to explain the use of coercion—have received little or no operationalization or testing.

One key problem concerns the measurement of subjective variables. In laboratory situations, some measurement has been made of such variables as maximum level of aspiration (Siegel and Fouraker), utility, and expectation of other's action (Wyer) in an effort to test some conflict models. In addition, other techniques for measuring subjective variables like utilities and expectancies have been developed in laboratory studies (see, for example, Ofshe and Ofshe 1968; Siegel, Siegel, and Andrews 1964; Davidson and Suppes 1957).

The problem of measuring subjective variables in natural settings is a more formidable one. Studies of reaction processes in arms races have made rough estimates of subjective variables (e.g., grievance levels, reactability coefficients) on the basis of available objective information. Milstein and Mitchell (1968) have measured the perceptions and preferences of policy makers of nations participating in the Vietnam war. The author and a colleague (Patchen and Hofmann 1970) have developed a method for assessing the incentives, value of incentives, and subjective probabilities of decision makers from their verbal expressions. These measurement efforts and others may prove useful in some natural situations. However, there will be many situations where it will be very difficult or impossible to assess relevant subjective variables of decision makers at a particular time.

Another possible approach is to deal with objective variables, which in some cases (though not all) may be easier to measure than subjective ones. Such an approach is not necessarily inconsistent with the use of a theoretical model which uses subjective variables. Indeed, one of the important uses of such a theoretical model is to permit us to derive predictions about the kind of objective circumstances which are likely to lead to certain kinds of interactions.* For example, if one key variable in a model is the cost incentives of

---

*The author (Patchen 1968) has made a very preliminary effort in this direction.

taking certain actions, this may lead us to consider aspects of the objective situation which would lead to certain actions having important costs. As a specific instance, we might predict that (other things equal) in situations where there is a large amount of mutually beneficial intercourse between two parties to a dispute, neither is likely to use coercion to influence the other because the negative incentive of disrupting the ongoing intercourse is too high. It may also be possible, in some cases, to estimate key subjective variables on the basis of objective information. Subjectively perceived incentives can sometimes be estimated from objective incentives present in the situation. Subjective probabilities can also, in some cases, be estimated from the objective situation. In this connection, Wyer has suggested that we may be able to estimate A's expectations about B's responses on the basis of the objective incentives which A (and the researcher) knows are facing B.

Clearly, there are many unsolved problems and much work to be done before models of conflict and cooperation can be adequately operationalized and tested. Such measurement and testing need to go hand in hand with the further development of theory, much more than they have in many cases in the past. We need to avoid the proliferation of theoretical models which are not tested and which in some cases may be impossible to test. At the same time, we need to avoid putting the bulk of our research effort into a great many narrow studies concerned with isolated variables. We need, instead, to concentrate more of our empirical work on the testing of models of some generality.

References

Atkinson, J. W. "Towards Experimental Analysis of Human Motivation in Terms of Motives, Expectancies, and Incentives." *Motives in Fantasy, Action, and Society,* edited by J. W. Atkinson. Princeton, N.J.: Van Nostrand, 1958.

Atkinson, J. W. *An Introduction to Motivation.* Princeton, N.J.: Van Nostrand, 1964.

Bernard, J. "Some Current Conceptualizations in the Field of Conflict." *American Journal of Sociology* 70, no. 4 (1965): 442-54.

Bishop, R. "Game-Theoretic Analyses of Bargaining." *Quarterly Journal of Economics* 77, no. 4 (November 1963): 559-602.

Boulding, K. *Conflict and Defense.* New York: Harper, 1962.

Chatterji, M. "A Model of Resolution of Conflict Between India and Pakistan." *Peace Research Society Papers* 12 (1969).

Choucri, H., and North, R. "The Determinants of International Violence." *Peace Research Society Papers* 12 (1969).

Coddington, A. *Theories of the Bargaining Process.* Chicago: Aldine, 1968.

Cohen, B. *Conflict and Conformity.* Cambridge, Mass.: MIT Press, 1963.

Cross, J. "A Theory of the Bargaining Process." *American Economic Review* 55, no. 1 (March 1965): 67-94.

Cross, J. *The Economics of Bargaining.* New York: Basic Books, 1969.

Davidson, D., and Suppes, P. *Decision-Making: An Experimental Approach.* Stanford, Calif.: Stanford University Press, 1957.

Deutsch, K., et al. *Political Community and the North Atlantic Area.* Princeton, N.J.: Princeton University Press, 1957.

Edwards, W. "Behavioral Decision Theory." *Annual Review of Psychology* 12 (1961).

Etzioni, A. *Political Unification: A Comparative Study of Leaders and Forces.* New York: Holt, Rinehart & Winston, 1965.

Fink, C. "More Calculations About Deterrence." *Journal of Conflict Resolution* 9, no. 1 (March 1965): 54-65.

Foldes, L. "A Determinant Model of Bilateral Monopoly." *Economica* 31 (May 1964): 117-31.

Fouraker, L., and Siegel, S. *Bargaining Behavior.* New York: McGraw-Hill, 1963.

Galtung, J. "Institutionalized Conflict Resolution." *Journal of Peace Research* 4 (1965): 348-97.

Grimshaw, A. D. *Racial Violence in the United States.* Chicago: Aldine, 1969.

Guyer, M., and Rapoport, A. "Threat in a Two-Person Game." *Journal of Experimental Social Psychology* 6, no. 1 (1970): 11-25.

Harsanyi, J. C. "Approaches to the Bargaining Problem Before and After the Theory of Games: A Critical Discussion of Zeuthen's, Hicks', and Nash's Theories." *Econometrica* 24 (April 1956): 114-57.

Hicks, J. R. *The Theory of Wages.* London: Macmillan, 1932.

Holsti, O.; Brody, R.; and North, R. "Affect and Action in International Reaction Models." *Journal of Peace Research* 3-4 (1964): 170-90.

Howard, N. "Metagame Analysis of Vietnam Policy." *Peace Research Society Papers* 10 (1968): 126-42.

Iklé, F., and Leites, H. "Political Negotiations as a Process of Modifying Utilities." *Journal of Conflict Resolution* 6, no. 1 (March 1962): 19-28.

Johnson, H., and Cohen, A. "Experiments in Behavioral Economics: Siegel and Fouraker Revisited." *Behavioral Science* 12, no. 5 (September 1967).

Kahn, H. *Thinking About the Unthinkable.* New York: Horizon, 1962.

Kautsky, K. *Outbreak of the World War.* New York: Oxford University Press, 1924.

Kelley, H.; Beckman, L.; and Fischer, C. "Negotiating the Division of a Reward Under Incomplete Information." *Journal of Experimental Social Psychology* 3, no. 3 (July 1967): 361-98.

Kelley, H.; Thibaut, J.; Radloff, R.; and Mundy, D. "The Development of Cooperation in the 'Minimal Social Situation.'" *Psychology Monographs* 76 (1962): 1-19.

McClelland, C. "International Interaction Analysis: Basic Research and Some Practical Applications" (Technical Report no. 2, World Event Interaction Survey). Los Angeles: Department of International Relations, University of Southern California, 1968.

Milstein, J., and Mitchell, W. "Computer Simulation of International Processes: The Vietnam War and the Pre-World War I Naval Race." *Peace Research Society Papers* 12 (1969).

Milstein, J., and Mitchell, W. "Dynamics of the Vietnam Conflict: A Quantitative Analysis and Predictive Computer Simulation." *Peace Research Society (International) Papers* 10 (1968).

Nash, J. F. "Two Cooperative Games." *Econometrica* 21 (1953): 128-40.

Nicholson, M. "Tariff Wars and a Model of Conflict." *Journal of Peace Research* 6 (1967): 26-38.

Ofshe, R., and Ofshe, L. *A General Utility-Based Theory of Decision-Making.* Berkeley, Calif.: Center for Research in Management Science, University of California, 1968.

Patchen, M. "Decision Theory in the Study of National Action: Problems and a Proposal." *Journal of Conflict Resolution* 9, no. 2 (June 1965): 164-76.

Patchen, M. "A Model of Interaction in Conflict of Interest Situations." Lafayette, Ind.: Sociology Department, Purdue University, 1968 (mimeo).

Patchen, M., and Hofmann, G. "A Technique for the Assessment of Incentives, the Value of Incentives, and Expectancies from the Verbal Outputs of Decision-Makers." Lafayette, Ind.: Sociology Department, Purdue University, 1970 (draft).

Pen, J. "A General Theory of Bargaining." *American Economic Review* 42 (March 1952): 24-42.

Pen, J. *The Wage Rate Under Collective Bargaining.* Cambridge, Mass.: Harvard University Press, 1959.

Porsholt, L. "On Methods of Conflict Prevention." *Journal of Peace Research* 2 (1966): 178-93.

Porsholt, L. "A Quantitative Conflict Model." Oslo: International Peace Research Institute, 1969 (draft).

Raiffa, H. "Arbitration Schemes for Generalized Two-Person Games." *Contributions to the Theory of Games* (vol. II), edited by H. Kuhn and A. Tucker. Princeton, N.J.: Princeton University Press, 1953.

Rapoport, A. *A Stochastic Model for Prisoner's Dilemma.* Ann Arbor: Mental Health Research Institute, University of Michigan, 1963.

Rapoport, A., and Chammah, A. *Prisoner's Dilemma: A Study in Conflict and Cooperation.* Ann Arbor: University of Michigan Press, 1965.

Rapoport, A.; Chammah, A.; Dwyer, J.; and Gyr, J. "Three-Person, Non-Zero-Sum Nonnegotiable Games." *Behavioral Science* 7, no. 1 (January 1962): 38-58.

Rapoport, A., and Dale, P. "The Models for Prisoner's Dilemma." *Journal of Mathematical Psychology* 3, no. 2 (July 1966).

Rausch, H. "Interaction Sequences." *Journal of Personality and Social Psychology* 2 (1965): 487-506.

Richardson, L. *Arms and Insecurity.* Chicago: Quadrangle Books, 1960.

Russett, B. "The Calculus of Deterrence." *Journal of Conflict Resolution* 7, no. 2 (June 1963): 97-109.

Russett, B. "Pearl Harbor Deterrence Theory and Decision Theory." *Journal of Peace Research* 6, no. 2 (1967): 89-106.

Sawyer, J., and Guetskow, H. "Bargaining and Negotiation in International Relations." *International Behavior,* edited by H. Kelman. New York: Holt, Rinehart & Winston, 1965.

Schelling, T. *The Strategy of Conflict.* Cambridge, Mass.: Harvard University Press, 1960.

Shackle, G. L. S. "The Nature of the Bargaining Process." *The Theory of Wage Determination,* edited by J. Dunlop. London: Macmillan, 1964.

Shapley, L. S. "A Value for N-Person Games." *Contributions to the Theory of Games* (vol. II), edited by H. Kuhn and A. Tucker. Princeton, N.J.: Princeton University Press, 1953.

Sidowski, J. "Reward and Punishment in a Minimal Social Situation." *Journal of Experimental Psychology* 54 (1957): 318-26.

Siegel, S., and Fouraker, L. *Bargaining and Group Decision-Making: Experiments in Bilateral Monopoly.* New York: McGraw-Hill, 1960.

Siegel, S.; Siegel, A. E.; and Andrews, J. M. *Choice, Strategy, and Utility.* New York: McGraw-Hill, 1964.

Singer, J. D. "Inter-Nation Influence: A Formal Model." *American Political Science Review* 57 (1963): 420-30.

Smoker, P. "Fear in the Arms Race: A Mathematical Study." *Journal of Peace Research* 1 (1964): 55-64.

Smoker, P. "Trade, Defense, and the Richardson Theory of Arms Races: A Seven Nation Study." *Journal of Peace Research* 2 (1965): 161-76.

Snyder, G. H. "Deterrence and Power." *Journal of Conflict Resolution* 4, no. 2 (June 1960): 163-78.

Stevens, C. *Strategy and Collective Bargaining Negotiation.* New York: McGraw-Hill, 1963.

Timasheff, N. *War and Revolution.* New York: Sheed & Ward, 1965.

Walton, R., and McKersie, R. *A Behavioral Theory of Labor Negotiations.* New York: McGraw-Hill, 1965.

Wright, Q. "The Escalation of International Conflicts." *Journal of Conflict Resolution* 9, no. 4 (December 1965): 434-49.

Wyer, R. "Prediction of Behavior in Two-Person Games." *Journal of Personality and Social Psychology* 13, no. 3 (1969): 222-38.

Zeuthen, F. *Problems of Monopoly and Economic Warfare.* London: Routledge & Sons, 1930.

Reading 9

A Certainty-Equivalent Model
of Bargaining

Edward Saraydar

In economic theory, there have been in essence two broad approaches to the question of how agreement is reached when each participant in the market has at least some control over the terms of exchange. The first, which places major emphasis on the economic determinants of the outcome, is best exemplified by Zeuthen's theory of bargaining (1930, 1957), which assumes away "purely personal elements, the skill of the negotiators, misunderstandings, bluff, etc."—all of the "recognized technique and psychology of negotiations" (1930, p. 104).* The second approach to the bargaining prob-

Reprinted by permission from *Journal of Conflict Resolution* 15, no. 3 (September 1971), pp. 281-97. Copyright 1971 by Sage Publications.

*Harsanyi (1956) has demonstrated that Zeuthen's solution—which maximizes the bargainers' utility product—is mathematically equivalent to the Nash solution to the bargaining problem (1950, 1953). Further, Harsanyi (1961) has shown that a few rationality postulates added to those used by von Neumann and Morgenstern are sufficient to yield a decision rule identical to Zeuthen's, i.e., that the party who is willing to face the smaller risk of conflict will concede. Harsanyi's claims (1965) for the Zeuthen-Nash theory have been challenged by Bishop, who takes the position that "Harsanyi's approach [is] based on a pre-

lem has tended to emphasize those very aspects of the bargaining process excluded by Zeuthen, e.g., uncertainty, bluff, deception, threat tactics; a prime exponent of this approach has been Pen (1952, 1959).* Pen's theory has been called "one of the most brilliant and most beautiful pieces of theoretical analysis that has been produced in many years past" (Shackle, 1957, p. 309) and, as Pen himself acknowledges (1959, p. ix), his model is constructed on a foundation provided by Zeuthen. However, Pen's position is that Zeuthen, by abstracting from omnipresent bargaining tactics, eliminated the warp and woof of the bargaining process itself. According to Pen (1952, pp. 24, 39), a determinate solution to the bilateral monopoly problem requires a theory such as his own—one which encompasses those tactical elements that comprise what Dunlop has called "pure" bargaining power.†

In the first part of this paper Zeuthen's and Pen's theories—both developed in terms of union-management contract negotiations—are summarized and compared, so as to bring into focus the extent to which the two theories essentially differ, as well as the extent to which they parallel each other. In particular it is shown that while Pen's model does provide a framework for the tactical maneuvering excluded by Zeuthen, it nevertheless shares a mutual behavioral assumption which, in effect, limits its relevance to negotiations that are restricted to only a single round of bargaining.

Of course the normal pattern of collective bargaining is for negotiations to proceed over a number of rounds, with bargaining

---

conception . . . that any game has a unique solution" (1965, p. 467). Nevertheless, Bishop (1964) has himself utilized the Zeuthen concession criterion—while concomitantly borrowing from another "economic" bargaining theory, that of Hicks (1932) to construct a model the solution of which maximizes a time-discounted utility product.

*Shackle (1949; 1957, pp. 311-13) has used his own concept of uncertainty to focus on the process through which a bargainer might make a prenegotiation decision choice as to a bargaining plan. For a good discussion of the general role of tactics in bargaining see Stevens (1963), and Walton and McKersie (1965).

†Dunlop (1950, p. 77) has defined "pure" bargaining power as the "ability to get favorable bargains, apart from market conditions." Pen seems to accept this definition, although he has some general reservations about Dunlop's three-part classification of the determinants of bargaining power (Pen 1952, pp. 40-41; 1959, pp. 154-56).

characterized by a series of concessions by both sides. Hence a much more fruitful approach would be one that envisages negotiators—at any particular round i—as thinking in terms of whether to hold out for a concession by the opponent at the risk of a strike or lockout, or make a minimal concession and thereby keep the bargaining game alive.

In the second section of the paper a Zeuthen-type bargaining model is developed within this minimal-concession context, in which concession decisions at each round are based on a comparison of "propensity to fight" indices that reflect the certainty-equivalent value of continued bargaining. Further, as in Pen, the model embodies those elements of "pure" bargaining power which are normally a part of the collective bargaining process, and it provides the framework for an analysis of their impact on the concession decision.

In the third part the implications of certainty-equivalent bargaining suggest an "optimal" bargaining strategy characterized by an appropriate mixture of tactics of conflict and conciliation and designed to "favorably" affect the opponent's expectations. Finally it is shown that, unlike the Zeuthen model, the certainty-equivalent paradigm encompasses the possibility of meaningful bargaining outside of the range of feasible outcomes; i.e., when at least one side holds to a manifestly "unrealistic" demand.

The Zeuthen-Pen Bargaining Models

Both Zeuthen and Pen begin by noting that at any particular point in negotiations between labor and management over the wage rate, each side has two options: (a) accept a current offer (Zeuthen), be willing to accept a current wage rate under discussion (Pen); or (b) stand firm—at the risk of a strike or lockout—in the expectation that the opponent will, in the end, make a settlement at the bargainer's preferred wage outcome. At the ith round of negotiations, the expected gain from no-concession for labor (and there is a comparable computation for management) would be:*

---

*Although this exposition is in terms of von Neumann-Morgenstern cardinal utility, Zeuthen conceptualized expected gain and maximum risk in terms of money, i.e., the wage bill. The modification does not represent a major departure, especially since Zeuthen refers explicitly to "the estimated gains and

$$[(1 - r_i^l)L_i^l + r_i^l S_i^l] - L_i^m; \text{ or} \tag{1}$$
$$(L_i^l - L_i^m) - r_i^l(L_i^l - S^l),$$

where L_i^l = utility to the union of a settlement at its preferred wage outcome w_i^l;

L_i^m = utility to the union of a settlement at management's current offer w_i^m (Zeuthen), or the wage rate under discussion w (Pen);

S^l = utility to the union of a strike;

r_i^l = union's subjective estimate of the probability of a breakdown in negotiations if it holds out for a settlement at wage rate w_i^l; and

$(1 - r_i^l)$ = union's subjective estimate of the probability that management will settle at wage rate w_i^l.

The utility function may be constructed so as to leave $S^l = 0$. Then, setting (1) equal to zero and solving for r_i^l, an index is derived which reflects the union's determination to stand firm:

$$r_{max_i}^l = 1 - \frac{L_i^m}{L_i^l}; \tag{2}$$

and similarly for management,

$$r_{max_i}^m = 1 - \frac{M_i^l}{M_i^m} \tag{3}$$

where M_i^m = utility to management of a settlement at its preferred wage outcome w_i^m; and

M_i^l = utility to management of a settlement at labor's current offer w_i^l (Zeuthen), or the wage rate under discussion w (Pen).

This index is equal to the maximum risk of a strike that labor (man-

---

costs of the parties in terms of money or utility" (1930, p. 135). The utility functions for labor and management may be conceived of as concave downward, increasing with the wage rate for labor, and decreasing with the wage rate for management. Pen calls the utility functions "ophelimity functions" (1959, p. 14).

agement) is willing to face rather than concede at the ith round of bargaining.*

Zeuthen—who stresses the economically rational aspects of bargaining—would view the utility functions as data, and both the utility functions and estimates of the probability of breakdown as invariant with respect to "pure" bargaining power. What, then, would compel one side rather than the other to make a concession if the expected gain from no-concession is positive for both bargainers? Zeuthen's position is that it is essentially relative bargaining power. Bargaining power in turn is economically determined by such elements as the tastes, institutional factors, and market conditions which underlie each side's utility function; it is therefore reflected in the maximum risk of conflict which each side is willing to take rather than concede. A comparison of the two non-zero propensity-to-fight indices would determine which side (i.e., that side willing to face the smaller maximum risk of conflict) is to make a concession at the ith round of negotiations.

For Zeuthen, $r^l_{\max_i} > r^m_{\max_i}$, for example, would imply that management will concede. But management need not concede all the way to w^l_i. Since $L(w)$ is an increasing function of the wage rate, L^m/L^l increases with management's concession; therefore management only has to make a concession of a size sufficient to leave $r^l_{\max_{i+1}} < r^m_{\max_{i+1}}$ in order to elicit a concession from labor at round $i + 1$. Bargaining thus assumes a multiround character, with alternate concession and movement toward an equilibrium wage rate and settlement, at which point $w^l = w^m$, $L^m = L^l$, $M^l = M^m$, and $r^l_{\max} = r^m_{\max} = 0$.

Pen's approach to reaching the equilibrium wage rate differs from that of Zeuthen. Pen proposes the following situation at round i:

A certain wage rate comes under discussion. The way in which this happens does not matter; let us assume that one of the parties makes a tentative proposal. Let us call the wage rate under discussion w. (1959, p. 128)

Consider the implications of the above for the expected-gain com-

---

*$L^m_i > 0$, $M^l_i > 0$ is a sufficient condition for the existence of a range of practicable bargains, i.e., a set of feasible wage settlements which both bargainers prefer to a strike.

ponents of each party's maximum risk index at the ith round. For the union, L_i^l equals the utility to labor of a settlement at its preferred wage outcome w_i^l; the concept here is identical to that of Zeuthen. However, Pen and Zeuthen each have a different conception of wage rate w and utility L_i^m. For Zeuthen, w is precisely defined as management's preferred wage outcome w_i^m, and L_i^m therefore equals the utility to labor of a settlement at management's current offer and preferred wage outcome. For Pen, on the other hand, L_i^m equals the utility to labor of a settlement at some loosely defined wage rate w which just happens to come under discussion. Wage rate w is not necessarily management's preferred wage outcome; indeed, w is not even necessarily management's offer at round i. (Analogous to L_i^l and L_i^m, the utility to management of a settlement at management's preferred wage rate is equal to M_i^m, and the utility of a settlement at the discussion wage rate w is equal to M_i^l.)

The maximum risk that each party is willing to face rather than concede at the ith round of bargaining—i.e., each party's propensity-to-fight index—is computed as in (1) through (3) above. But, unlike Zeuthen, Pen does not have concession depend upon a comparison of maximum risk indices. Instead, Pen postulates that labor's willingness to accept wage rate w depends upon whether $r_{max_i}^l \leqslant r_i^l$. Similarly, management is prepared to accept wage rate w only if $r_{max_i}^m \leqslant r_i^m$.* In general, the discussion wage rate will leave at least one bargainer with $r_{max} > r$, and therefore unwilling to conclude a contract at w. Equilibrium of bargaining and consequent agreement requires a discussion wage rate which simultaneously satisfies both equations:

---

*Pen modifies the propensity-to-fight index by what he calls a "risk valuation function," which enhances or attenuates the index, depending upon whether the bargainer is attracted to, or has an aversion for, risk as such (1959, pp. 131-32). Zeuthen anticipated Pen when he observed that the maximum-risk indices, and therefore the wage outcome, may be affected by "the unpleasantness or maybe, the attractiveness, of the element of uncertainty, i.e., the cost of risk-taking" (1930, p. 111). As above, r_i^l and r_i^m refer to subjective estimates of the probability of a breakdown in negotiations if the bargainer does not accept, in this case, wage rate w. Pen makes this estimate a function of the degree of certainty with which each bargainer perceives the limits of the contract zone; i.e., he introduces a "correspection function" (1959, pp. 130-31). For simplicity, we have omitted the risk valuation and correspection functions from this abbreviated version of Pen's theory.

$$r^l_{max} = r^l \tag{4}$$

$$r^m_{max} = r^m \tag{5}$$

"The function of the bargaining process is to transform the relevant magnitudes and relations in such a way that the equilibrium conditions are no longer in conflict" (1959, p. 137). In other words, given a discussion wage rate at which, for example, $r^l_{max_i} = r^l_i$, but $r^m_{max_i} > r^m_i$, labor would try to bring management to agreement by attempting to (a) reduce management's propensity-to-fight, and/or (b) increase management's estimate of the probability that further disagreement would result in conflict. Efforts directed at achieving (a) would involve attempts to influence management's utility function $M(w)$ so as to decrease M^m_i and increase M^l_i, while (b) would require tactics designed to convince management that it had underestimated labor's willingness to fight.

Thus, in contrast to Zeuthen, Pen envisages the utility functions as volatile and subject to shifts and changes in shape, with both the utility functions and probability estimates of breakdown quite sensitive to "pure" bargaining power. For Pen, there are a multitude of psychological factors, with and without economic basis, underlying each side's utility function. At the ith round of negotiations, each side is guided in its concession decision by an implicit comparison of the maximum risk of conflict which it is willing to face rather than accept the discussion wage rate, with its estimate of the probability of a breakdown in negotiations if it does not accept that wage rate. Since, typically, the expected gain from no-concession is positive for at least one bargainer, it is precisely because Pen assumes that utility functions and probability estimates *are* subject to alteration by bargaining tactics, that equilibrium and settlement become possible without maximum risk comparisons.

If Pen's theory is to determine (as the title of his book suggests) the wage rate under collective bargaining, it should be consistent with the negotiatory rules of collective bargaining. It could be argued that Pen seems to conceive the bargaining process as a kind of *tâtonnement,* with wage proposals—capable of being withdrawn at will and without prejudice—being interjected at various points either by the participants themselves or by some third party.* But this is

---

*Recall his reference—quoted above—to a discussion wage rate of unspecific origin, perhaps a tentative proposal. Pen nowhere states clearly that each

surely an unrealistic view of collective bargaining procedure. Typically, at any particular stage in the proceedings, both sides have made "on the table" offers, and it is these two wage rates which are "under discussion." An offer once made cannot normally be withdrawn; if it was, the negotiator would be subject to the serious charge of "bad faith."

The implications for Pen's model may be noted by considering labor's position at the ith round of bargaining (the reasoning is analogous for management). Labor's only feasible preferred wage settlement is its announced demand w_i^l (since it would not expect to reach a better, higher, wage settlement via bargaining once it has made the offer w_i^l). The wage rate which is open to labor to accept is management's current offer (demand) and preferred wage settlement w_i^m. There are, then, two wage rates which alternately come under discussion at the ith round. If labor's offer is being discussed, $w = w_i^l$, and labor's propensity-to-fight is, of course, equal to zero, while the index for management is equal to $r_{max_i}^m > 0$. If management's offer is being discussed, the situation is reversed: $w = w_i^m$, $r_{max_i}^m = 0$, and $r_{max_i}^l > 0$.*

While Pen's model does represent a positive contribution to bargaining theory, in that it embraces the contingency that bargaining tactics are significant for the wage outcome, it nevertheless contains a methodological flaw which raises serious doubts as to its general applicability to collective bargaining. Assume that at the ith round neither side is prepared to concede from its announced (and preferred) wage offer. Coincident to a consideration of management's offer, management utilizes its bargaining skills (as noted above) in an attempt to influence labor's utility function so as to reduce $r_{max_i}^l$; management also tries to increase r_i^l. Its purpose is to bring the two quantities to equality, and thereby reach an agreement at wage rate w_i^m. Suppose that management successfully brings $r_{max_i}^l$ into equality with r_i^l. According to Pen's criterion, the union would be "imme-

---

bargainer explicitly proposes his preferred wage settlement in the form of a demand or offer. Instead, he refers somewhat opaquely to bargainers "achieving a more favorable result" (1959, p. 127), getting "a better wage rate" (p. 128), hoping "to arrive at the most favorable wage rate possible" (p. 128), and continuing "to aim at a higher wage" (p. 129).

*Although, unlike Zeuthen, Pen does not have concession depend upon their relative size, the two *non-zero* propensity-to-fight indices are nevertheless conceptually identical to $r_{max_i}^m$ and $r_{max_i}^l$ as computed in Zeuthen's theory.

diately ready to accept a contract" and, in fact, would "hasten to conclude a contract" at this wage rate (w_i^m)—and bargaining is terminated (1959, pp. 128, 133, 136-37).

But it then follows that Pen's theory implies and is most relevant to a form of "collective bargaining" that is limited to a single round of negotiations, i.e., the ith round is the last round. For while it is true that one side or the other *could* conceivably make a modified offer, each bargainer *in fact* restricts himself to the alternatives: (a) accept the opponent's offer, or (b) reject the opponent's offer and hold out for his concession to the bargainer's preferred wage rate.* The possibility that the opponent may make a less-than-total concession is ruled out by inference, since the expected utility of such an outcome at the ith round is not included in either side's expected gain function, and is therefore not reflected in its propensity-to-fight index.

This deficiency—the implied exclusion of the commonly observed multiround pattern of collective bargaining—is also to be found in Zeuthen's theory of bargaining, since the alternatives embodied in his propensity-to-fight indices are also limited to total

---

*If modified offers were permitted within the context of Pen's construction, the wage outcome, curiously enough, might very well depend upon the degree to which each side is successful in keeping its particular wage demand under discussion. In the example cited, management's bargaining tactics were successful in yielding the situation: $1 - (L_i^m/L_i^l) < r^l$, and $1 - (M_i^m/M_i^m) = 0 < r^m$, relative to a consideration of management's offer. The situation relative to a consideration of labor's demand is: $1 - (M_i^l/M_i^m) > r^m$, and $1 - (L_i^l/L_i^l) = 0 < r^l$. Therefore management remains adamant, but labor is prepared to concede with the discussion of management's offer. If labor is allowed to make its concession in increments, we then have the Zeuthenian phenomenon in operation, whereby management's propensity-to-fight relative to labor's demand continuously decreases with labor's incremental concessions—i.e., $1 - (M^l/M^m)$ diminishes as M^l increases with labor's concessions. It is quite possible, then, for *labor's concessions alone* to yield $1 - (M^l/M^m) \leq r^m$ well before labor concedes as far as management's offer w_i^m. At that point, *both* sides would be willing to concede, and a sufficient condition for eliciting concessions from the opponent is for the bargainer to keep his own wage offer under discussion. This could result in an anomalous situation wherein each side is willing to accept the other side's wage offer, but neither side is willing to discuss the very wage offer that he is willing to accept.

concession (see (2) and (3) above).* In short, both models are most relevant as single-round bargaining models.

In the following section we shall develop a Zeuthen-type bargaining model that preserves the multiround aspect of bargaining, and also incorporates those elements of "pure" bargaining power upon which Pen has placed so much emphasis.

The Certainty-Equivalent Bargaining Model

Again, implicit in what has preceded is the assumption that negotiators view each step in the bargaining process as final, in the sense that the utilities and expected utilities involved presume, at each round, outright acceptance or rejection of their underlying wage rates. Since, in fact, bargaining is typically not restricted to a single round, it is proposed that each bargainer's concept of the consequences of concession or no-concession is not in terms of the utility of settlement at the wage rates explicitly under deliberation, but rather involves a consideration of the implications, apropos of the *expected outcome* of negotiations, of making a small concession (thereby ensuring a continuance of negotiations), or holding for a small concession from the opponent.

Accordingly, we can postulate that—in conjunction with a utility function L(w) (or M(w))—at the ith round each side constructs a distribution function $l(w)_i$ (or $m(w)_i$), which yields a subjective estimate of the probability that the *outcome* of negotiations will be greater than or equal to (less than or equal to) wage rate w. ($w_i^m \leqslant w \leqslant w_i^l$; where w_i^m = management's offer, or demand, at round i, and w_i^l = labor's offer, or demand, at round i.)†

It is at least theoretically valid to assume that a bargainer, say labor, can utilize $l(w)_i$ and utility function L(w) to estimate the *certainty equivalent* of bargaining negotiation, i.e., what the bargaining game is worth *in toto*—in terms of expected utility—from the ith

---

*For further implications of "full concession" apropos of Zeuthen's model, see Saraydar (1965).

†Following Zeuthen, we assume that the utility functions are "rationally" determined and invariant with respect to "pure" bargaining tactics; however, the distribution functions are not independent of, and may be affected by, such tactics (see below).

round to its conclusion. The computation of expected gain from no-concession at the ith round may then be made on the basis of a comparison of certainty equivalents incorporating the alternatives: (a) hold out for a small concession from the opponent; or (b) make a small concession, and thereby ensure a continuance of bargaining into round $i + 1$. (Small concession here means the smallest unit of negotiation.)

Figure 1 illustrates hypothetical distribution and utility functions for the union which underlie its certainty equivalents at the ith round of bargaining. There are n possible wage settlements, bounded by and inclusive of management's offer w_i^m and labor's demand w_i^l. $l(w)_i$ is the union's distribution function of wage outcomes given a concession by management to $w_i^{(2)}$, while $l(w)_i^*$ is its distribution function constructed on the alternative assumption that the union itself concedes to $w_i^{(n-1)}$.

The calculation of certainty equivalents for labor at the ith round is as follows (management makes a similar calculation):

Figure 1
Hypothetical Distribution and Utility Functions for the Union
at Round i

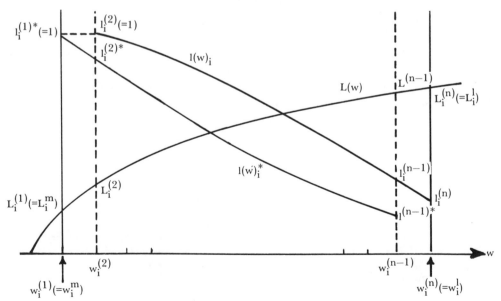

$$C_i^{l*} = L_i^{(1)} + l_i^{(2)}*(L_i^{(2)} - L_i^{(1)}) + l_i^{(3)}*(L_i^{(3)} - L_i^{(2)})$$
$$+ \ldots + l_i^{(n-1)}*(L_i^{(n-1)} - L_i^{(n-2)})$$

$$C_i^{l*} = L_i^{(1)} + \sum_{j=2}^{n} l_i^{(j)}*(L_i^{(j)} - L_i^{(j-1)}) \tag{6}$$

and

$$C_i^l = L_i^{(2)} + l_i^{(3)}(L_i^{(3)} - L_i^{(2)}) + l_i^{(4)}(L_i^{(4)} - L_i^{(3)})$$
$$+ \ldots + l_i^{(n)}(L_i^{(n)} - L_i^{(n-1)})$$

$$C_i^l = L_i^{(1)} + \sum_{j=2}^{n} l_i^{(j)}(L_i^{(j)} - L_i^{(j-1)}) \tag{7}$$

where C_i^{l*} = certainty equivalent of bargaining on the assumption that the union concedes to $w_i^{(n-1)}$;

C_i^l = certainty equivalent of bargaining on the assumption that management concedes to $w_i^{(2)}$;

$L_i^{(k)}$ = utility to the union of a settlement at wage rate $w_i^{(k)}$, when $w_i^m = w_i^{(1)} \leqslant w_i^{(k)} \leqslant w_i^{(n)} = w_i^l$;

$l_i^{(k)}*$ = subjective estimate of the probability of ultimate settlement at a wage rate greater than or equal to $w_i^{(k)}$, on the assumption that the union concedes to $w_i^{(n-1)}$;

$l_i^{(k)}$ = subjective estimate of the probability of ultimate settlement at a wage rate greater than or equal to $w_i^{(k)}$, on the assumption that management concedes to $w_i^{(2)}$;

$l_i^{(1)}* = l_i^{(2)} = 1$; and
$l_i^{(n)}* = 0$.

It seems reasonable to assume that $l_i^{(j)} \geqslant l_i^{(j)}*$, and therefore that $C_i^l \geqslant C_i^{l*}$. In words, labor's estimate of the probability of a settlement greater than or equal to any wage rate $w_i^{(j)}$—and therefore its certainty equivalent—is at least as large when based on the prospect of a hypothesized concession by management as it is when labor considers the alternative prospect of its own concession. (The same reasoning applies to management.)

After making an estimate of C_i^l and C_i^l*, the union may compute the expected gain from no-concession as:

$$[(1 - p_i^l)C_i^l + p_i^l S^l] - C_i^l*; \text{ or} \qquad (8)$$
$$(C_i^l - C_i^l*) - p_i^l(C_i^l - S^l)$$

where $\quad p_i^l =$ union's estimate of the probability of a breakdown in negotiations at round i if it holds out for a concession from management to $w_i^{(2)}$; and

$\quad 1 - p_i^l =$ union's estimate of the probability that management will concede.

If, for simplicity, we assume $L(w)$ to be constructed so that $S^l = 0$, set (8) equal to zero, and solve for p_i^l, we get:

$$p_{max_i}^l = 1 - \frac{C_i^l*}{C_i^l}. \qquad (9)$$

Similarly, for management:

$$p_{max_i}^{m=} = 1 - \frac{C_i^m*}{C_i^m}. \qquad (10)$$

p_{max_i}, then, is the maximum risk of a strike that the union (or management) would be willing to face rather than make a small concession to $w_i^{(n-1)}$ (or $w_i^{(2)}$). Following Zeuthen, we adopt the rule: $p_{max_i}^l > p_{max_i}^m$ implies management concedes; $p_{max_i}^l < p_{max_i}^m$ implies labor concedes.

At the round at which agreement is reached—say round i—certainty-equivalent bargaining reduces to Zeuthen's solution, since $p_{max_i}^l = 1 - L_i^m/L_i^l$, and $p_{max_i}^m = 1 - M_i^l/M_i^m$. This is clear when we note that at "agreement-minus-one," $j = n$, since $l_i^{(n)}* = 0$, (6) reduces to $C_i^l* = L_i^m$. Further, since $l_i^{(j)} = l_i^{(2)} = 1$, (7) assumes a value of $C_i^l = L_i^m + L_i^l - L_i^m = L_i^l$. (Similar calculations could be made for management.) Therefore, when the ith round is the last round, the Zeuthen solution is applicable.

Each side employs bargaining tactics designed to modify the other side's distribution functions, so that certainty equivalents are thereby altered in such a way as to reduce the opposition's maximum risk.* Important for forcing concession and movement toward agreement is the strike deadline. Concession will take place when that side with the smaller maximum risk is convinced that further attempts to "favorably" influence the other side's distribution functions at round i would be fruitless, and that—with the approaching deadline—a breakdown in negotiations is imminent. If, at the deadline, $p_{max}^l = p_{max}^m$, breakdown does in fact occur, with consequent strike or lock-out.†

An Optimal Bargaining Strategy

It is argued in what follows that there is an optimal strategy which each side should adopt in utilizing its negotiatory skills to reduce the opponent's maximum risk. Since one side's bargaining aims are essentially an analogue of the other's, the analysis shall be restricted, for the sake of brevity, to a consideration of management's efforts to gain a concession from labor.

Substituting (6) and (7) into (9), the maximum risk of a strike that labor would be willing to face at the ith round is:

$$p_{max_i}^l = 1 - \frac{L_i^{(1)} + \sum_{j=2}^{n} l_i^{(j)} * (L_i^{(j)} - L_i^{(j-1)})}{L_i^{(1)} + \sum_{j=2}^{n} l_i^{(j)} (L_i^{(j)} - L_i^{(j-1)})} . \tag{11}$$

From (11) we note that labor's maximum risk is *minimized* when its distribution functions at round i are "consistent" with each other, in the sense that $l(w)_i$ approaches $l(w)_i^*$. That is, certainty-equivalent bargaining implies that labor is most likely to concede

---

*With $1 > l_i^{(j)} > l_i^{(j)}* > 0$, the Zeuthenian phenomenon whereby management's concession, for example, is in itself a sufficient condition to reduce labor's maximum risk is lost, since $\Delta C_i^l > 0$ with management's concession. In order for management's concession to lower labor's maximum risk, it is necessary that $\Delta C_i^l*/\Delta C_i^l > C_i^l*/C_i^l$.

†Note that this permits the possibility of breakdown even though both sides may prefer wage offers $w_i^{(1)}$ and $w_i^{(n)}$ to a strike.

when the expected consequences of neither its concession or management's concession make a significant impact on its estimates of the probability of wage outcomes within the bargaining range. This is tantamount to the not unreasonable proposition that to the extent that the bargaining game would be worth significantly more with management's concession than it would be with labor's concession, labor is less willing to concede at round i.

We further discern from (11) that—given $L(w)$, w_i^l, and w_i^m—*maximization* of $p_{max_i}^l$ would occur under the conditions: $l_i^{(j)}* = 0$, and $l_i^{(j)} = 1$ $(2 \leqslant j \leqslant n)$. This situation is illustrated in figure 2, where $l(w)_i^* = ACD$, and $l(w)_i = FEG$. In this case, wherein labor's maximum risk at any round i is maximized, $p_{max_i}^l = 1 - L_i^m/L_i^l.*$ This implies that labor holds the following extreme, twofold view of the implications of concession:

Figure 2
Labor's Distribution Functions Which Reflect Its Maximum Resistance to Concession

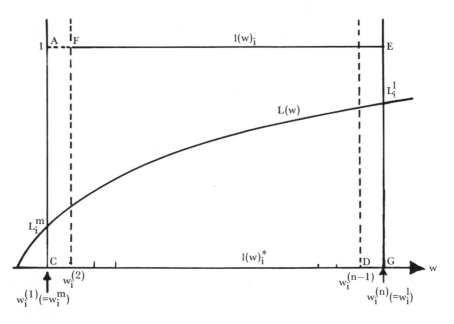

---

*Recall that, for Zeuthen and Pen, this is the maximum risk of conflict that labor would be willing to face rather than accept management's offer, at round i.

1. A small concession by labor will do nothing to elicit a subsequent concession from management; on the contrary, management would interpret such a concession as absolute confirmation that it need only adopt a completely rigid position in order to gain labor's ultimate acceptance of its (management's) round i offer.

2. If management makes a small concession, labor considers this to be a harbinger of complete collapse; i.e., with a small concession by management at round i, labor is certain that an uncompromising stand will lead to management's eventual accession to its (labor's) current demand.*

We may therefore postulate a set of distribution functions for labor which is undesirable from management's viewpoint, in that, given $L(w)$, such a set tends to minimize the prospect of labor's concession at round i. The situation is as illustrated in figure 3. For any feasible wage outcome $w_i^{(j)}$, $l_i^{(j)}$ is relatively large, $l_i^{(j)}*$ relatively small; from (11), the maximum risk of conflict that labor would be willing to face rather than make a concession at round i is therefore relatively large. The shape of $l(w)_i$, then, reflects labor's view that a concession by management, if one is made, is warrant for enhanced optimism as to ultimate settlement at one of the more desirable (higher) wage rates. On the other hand, should labor itself be forced to concede, $l(w)_i*$ reflects labor's pessimistic view that the consequences of its own concession have extremely adverse implications for the likelihood of a favorable wage outcome.

What bargaining posture would be most likely to produce the unpromising set of distribution functions depicted in figure 3? Suppose that management, in an effort to extract a concession from labor, should take a strongly adamant stand exemplified by the ultimatum "concede or else." From the very nature of the challenge, labor knows that if it makes a concession management will take this as a significant sign of weakness, thus diminishing labor's chances for a favorable settlement. C_i^l* may approach $L_i^{(1)}$ as labor downgrades its aspirations, with the consequences of its own concession at round

---

*Thus, Zeuthen's bargaining model is a special case of the certainty-equivalent bargaining model, where *each* bargainer holds the extreme view implied by (1) and (2) *at every round*. Maximum-risk calculations are made on this basis, and their comparison determines which side is to concede. But there is a strong presumption, then, that the ith round is the last round, and the bargaining process reduces to a single round of negotiations.

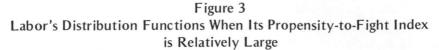

Figure 3
Labor's Distribution Functions When Its Propensity-to-Fight Index is Relatively Large

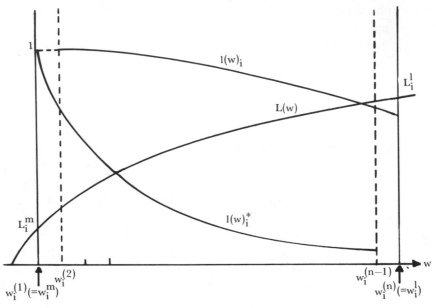

i now "built into" a revised distribution function $l(w)_i^*$ which is more positively skewed toward the higher wage outcomes. To this extent, labor's maximum risk is increased.

It is conceivable that management's uncompromising negotiatory stance will have little or no impact on C_i^l. Labor may well remain uncommitted in its assessment of the weight which it should give to the apparently rigid position indicated by the alleged "finality" of management's offer. This would tend to leave $l(w)_i$, and therefore C_i^l, invariant with respect to this particular tactic.

However, to the degree that management's threat gambit is effective, it could have the unintended result of actually *increasing* $l(w)_i$, and therefore C_i^l. If labor does itself stand firm in this situation, management's subsequent concession, if it is made, would likely have a significance for labor which increases in direct proportion to the intensity with which management expounds its raw no-concession dictum. That is, management would stand to incur considerable loss of face with its concession, in the sense that labor would view its previous adamant posture as mere bluff. Thus, labor's expectations contingent upon management's concession at round i could be strongly enhanced, as management's hypothetical concession would perhaps condition labor to heavily discount subsequent expressions of firmness by management. It would therefore be to labor's interest to determine whether management is bluffing by itself standing firm at round i. C_i^l, then, may be relatively large as compared with C_i^l*; this would leave C_i^l*/C_i^l relatively small, and to that degree labor's maximum risk would be enhanced.

The above suggests a rationale for employing bargaining tactics designed to simultaneously decrease the opposition's C_i *and* hold his C_i^* to a rate of decrease less than that of C_i in order to effect distribution functions as in figure 4 (for labor). Thus, in our present example, at round i management could assure labor that it is confident that if it held out labor would be sure to concede, since a concession

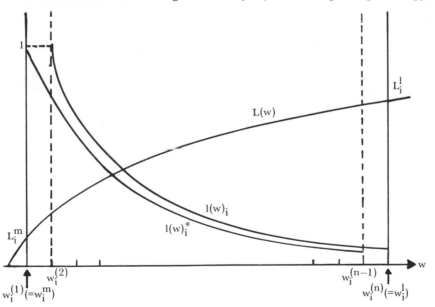

Figure 4

Labor's Distribution Functions When Its Resistance to Concession is Attenuated—A Set Engendered by Optimal Bargaining Strategy

would in fact be consistent with existing bargaining realities. At the same time, however, management would seek to restrain the rate of decrease of C_i^1*, by minimizing the significance of labor's concession for management's own aspirations. In this respect, management could perhaps establish the impression that a concession by labor would not be interpreted as a sign of imminent collapse, but rather as a positive indication that labor is willing to continue meaningful negotiations.

Of course, this emphasis on meaningful negotiations would implicitly retain the possibility of a subsequent concession by management. As noted above, this is generally desirable, for it is to management's advantage to preserve its credibility. Unless it does in fact view the ith round as the last round, it should refrain from ultimatum bargaining, for this would tend to maximize labor's resistance to making a concession. Consistent with its efforts to decrease C_i^1, management should ideally maintain a difficult and delicate balance between firmness and flexibility, conflict and conciliation.* While not explicitly shutting the door on the *possibility* of a subsequent concession, management would seek to persuade labor that it should give less weight to the probabilities of settlement at the higher wage rates, and that it should not construe the prospect of a hypothetical concession by management so as to greatly enhance its expectations vis-à-vis the wage outcome. The contingency of management's concession should itself be broached within the context of a "generous" gesture made to affirm management's good faith in the negotiation process, with the strong suggestion that labor would be expected to reciprocate.

At first blush, the certainty-equivalent maximum risk construct makes it equally rational for management to attempt to increase C_i^1* while holding C_i^1 to a slower rate of increase. Management would thus place major emphasis on its willingness to make a subsequent concession if labor would but concede at round i. This would tend to encourage a general enhancement of labor's expectations as to the wage outcome, shift labor's $l(w)_i^*$ function upward and to the right, and

---

*Relevant here is an observation by Peters, an experienced labor mediator: "To be effective, a negotiator must have the skill and ability to combine [a readiness to make war with the willingness to explore the possibilities for peace] and pursue a balanced course in negotiations, so that one aspect does not undermine the other" (1966, p. 28).

increase C_i^l*. But within this environment it would be very difficult for management to restrain a concomitant upward shift in labor's $l(w)_i$ function. Further, this type of negotiation is likely to disadvantage management in later rounds. Even if management is successful in reducing labor's maximum risk enough to elicit a concession at round i by inducing distribution functions as in figure 5, it will find itself at

Figure 5
Labor's Distribution Functions When Its Propensity-to-Fight is Relatively Small—Nevertheless a Suboptimal Set from Management's Point of View

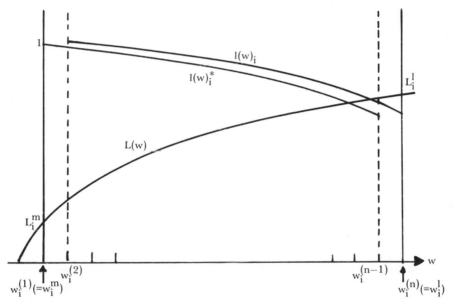

round $i + 1$ under pressure to redeem its earlier explicit or implicit promise to concede; concession is required in order to keep $l(w)*$ from sagging. Its earlier tactics may thus lead management into an undesirable situation wherein it is open to the charge of bad faith. Accurately or not, labor may interpret management's reluctance to concede at round $i + 1$ as confirmation that it should view further negotiatory efforts by management with a more jaundiced eye. This could cause a significant divergence between $l(w)*$ and $l(w)$, and an increase in labor's maximum risk in rounds subsequent to round i. Having demonstrated bad faith, it would be difficult for management to subsequently alter labor's distribution function favorably.

In sum, certainty-equivalent bargaining involves an attempt to decrease the maximum risk of a strike that the opponent would be willing to face rather than concede, by utilizing negotiation tactics in an effort to minimize the impact of both the bargainer's *and* the opponent's hypothetical concessions on the opponent's expectations as to the wage outcome—i.e., management attempts to minimize $l(w)_i - l(w)_i^*$, and labor attempts to minimize $m(w)_i - m(w)_i^*$. Since $1 \geqslant l_i^{(j)} \geqslant l_i^{(j)} * \geqslant 0$, minimization of $l(w)_i - l(w)_i^*$ by management, for example, could theoretically be accomplished within the environment of either a general buoyancy in labor's expectations or a general diminution of its expectations as to the wage outcome. However, the latter milieu of modest expectations for labor should normally be preferred by management, since high expectations engendered in earlier rounds can only continue to be supported in later rounds by its own concessions. On the other hand, management's continual resistance to concession *is* consistent with minimizing $l(w)_i - l(w)_i^*$ while maintaining low to moderate expectations for labor. If we assume that management wants the best wage outcome possible, tactics intended to impose upward concavity (as in figure 4) are to be preferred to those that tend to impose upward convexity (as in figure 5) on labor's distribution functions.

Bargaining Outside of the Practicable Range

A property which distinguishes Zeuthen's theory of bargaining is that it is restricted to bargaining *within* the range of practicable bargains (the set bounded by those wage rates at which $L(w) = 0$ and $M(w) = 0$). Bargaining as such is ruled out as long as one side or the other holds to an offer outside of the practicable range. If both positions are outside this range, all that is needed for one side to induce the other to concede to a point within the range is to concede itself to a wage rate just within the range. This is so because the utility of the opponent's offer is an integral part of the bargainer's maximum risk function, so that any offer outside the practicable range leaves the bargainer with a maximum risk of unity.

One difficulty with this conception of bargaining is that it implies that both bargainers enter the practicable range symmetrically; that is, at some round of offer-counteroffer both bargainers will be positioned simultaneously at the extremities of the bargaining range. The possibility that through superior bargaining ability one bargainer may gain an advantage over the other by holding to an offer still outside the range while his opponent's offer is well within the range is excluded by the assumptions of the model.

Nevertheless, in actual bargaining situations negotiators often *do* make initial offers which are "unrealistic" in the sense that they seem to be so obviously far above (below) any possible maximum (minimum) wage settlement; such extreme offers are made in the belief that they perform some real function in the bargaining game. The initial offer here is essentially a bargaining tactic, made with no serious expectation that it will be accepted, but designed instead to communicate to the opponent that he should revise his own conception of a reasonable wage settlement so as to be consistent with the "facts" as the bargainer has presented and interpreted them.*

In other words, each side by making an unrealistic initial demand seeks to communicate, at an early stage in the negotiation process, that the other would do well to assign greater weight to the less-favorable wage rates as potential outcomes. In terms of our model, each side seeks to impose incipient distribution functions on the other that are concave from above.

---

*In light of the paucity of empirical data available that could be used to reveal the record of strategy and tactics utilized in actual bargaining processes, the study by Douglas (1962) is significant, in that she was able to get the agreement and cooperation necessary to allow her to observe and tape record the negotiations in four collective bargaining cases. Relevant to our consideration of the initial offer, Douglas concludes that there is an initial phase in the negotiating process, at the outset of which bargainers typically take "firm positions which everyone knows will eventually give way, though the principals continue stoutly to deny this" (p. 14). Typically, according to Douglas, "there are vehement demands and counter-demands, arguments and counter-arguments. . . . This is the phase which is the most universally standardized in its trappings. Seasoned negotiators understand perfectly well the strategy of the opponent, and they profess to relish the opportunity for parrying verbal thrusts" (pp. 14-15). In our estimation, if the "extreme" demand is knowingly unrealistic and not taken seriously *per se,* then the carefully prepared sequence of initial demand, subsequent vehement justification and counter-justification of each bargainer's position is best viewed as an attempt to alter the opponent's expectations in a favorable direction.

As noted above, certainty-equivalent bargaining reduces to Zeuthen's solution at the agreement round. If the ith round is the round at which agreement is reached, $p^1_{\max i} = 1 - L^m_i/L^1_i$, and $p^m_{\max i} = 1 - M^1_i/M^m_i$. A necessary condition for agreement, then, is that at least one offer at the *final* round must lie within the range of practicable bargains—i.e., $L^m_i > 0$, or $M^1_i > 0$. But note from (9) and (10) above, that it is not necessary for this final-round condition to hold at *preceding* rounds of negotiation; that is, in the general case, "bargaining" as such remains meaningful as long as $C^1_i* > L^m_i$, and $C^m_i* > M^1_i$.

Thus, certainty-equivalent bargaining embraces the possibility of a sequence of concessions which leaves one side significantly inside the practicable range, even though the other side's offer is still outside that range. Bargaining in terms of certainty equivalents does encompass this possibility because (unlike Zeuthen's construct) it postulates that negotiators, in making their risk calculations, do not confine themselves to a consideration of the utility of settlement at wage rates which are on the table. Even though the utility of an offer open for acceptance may not exceed the utility of a strike, the bargainer may still evaluate the opportunity to participate in further negotiations, as embodied in the certainty equivalent, to be worth more than a strike. The calculation of expected gain and comparison of maximum risk may thus be meaningful even though wage rates under discussion lie outside the range of practicable bargains.

Conclusion

As enunciated by Harsanyi (1961, p. 193), a bargaining model should serve at least one of three main analytical purposes: (1) predict or explain the outcome; (2) conceptually clarify rational behavior in bargaining situations; and/or (3) define a theoretical bargaining equilibrium point. One condition that enables Zeuthen's model to generate a unique equilibrium point is that concession decisions are a function of indices that are themselves invariant to bargaining tactics. In this paper, we have developed a model that retains a Zeuthen-like concession criterion, but because the maximum risk indices *are* subject to revision as a result of bargaining tactics, the theory does not identify a unique equilibrium point *per se.** However, it does purport

---

*Of course, behavioral assumptions may be made sufficiently restrictive to yield a determinate solution for any theoretical model, and it is worth taking

to explain the outcome, in the sense of analytically isolating those factors, especially uncertainty, which should be among its more significant determinants, and hypothesizing the implicit structure through which the outcome is effected. Further, our paradigm provides a useful vehicle for conceptualizing an optimum route through which bargaining tactics can affect the concession decision, and thus the outcome of bargaining.

Finally, although the problem of how to directly measure shifting expectations is such as to preclude at this point a test of the outcome-predicting power of the certainty-equivalent model, it should be possible to test its tactical implications. In regard to tactics, the model predicts that ultimatum bargaining is likely to increase rather than diminish the opponent's resistance to concession, and that a more favorable sequence of concession is likely to follow bargaining tactics that stress both the conflictive and conciliatory elements in the bargaining situation, rather than either one alone. It would be preferable to test the hypothesis within a natural milieu; however, there are formidable obstacles to rigorously confirming generalizations about the bargaining process via the actual observation of, for example, labor-management negotiation sessions (although Douglas

---

note of the implicit as well as explicit behavioral assumptions that underlie determinacy. For example, we have shown elsewhere (Saraydar 1971), that, from the point of view of the bargaining process, a necessary condition for a determinate solution to Hicks' "theory of industrial disputes" (1932) is behavioral asymmetry, requiring one bargainer to take an aggressive, the other a passive, stance. Again, in his recent review of Cross' important and stimulating work, *The Economics of Bargaining*, Coddington (1970) has pointed out that determinacy in the Cross bargaining model is achieved via the assumption that while each bargainer believes the other will concede at a rate independent of his own behavior, the concession rate of each in fact depends on the other's concession behavior—an interdependence that necessarily must remain recognized by both. Apropos of the Cross model, we noted in our own review (Saraydar 1970), that participants at each juncture in the bargaining process optimistically behave as if each was *certain* of the feasibility of his own demand and the other's concession rate ("pure intransigence")—an optimism which, of course, turns out to be continuously unjustified. Thus, unlike our own model, there is no subjective uncertainty to attenuate the determination with which each stands fast. For each bargainer, the subjective probability of the other's concession behavior is implicitly either unity or, when the bargainer's estimate proves to be incorrect, zero. (A further point of difference is related to the relative emphasis on costs: an anonymous referee has suggested that the Cross model may be best suited to an overt-conflict, and ours to a pre-conflict stage of negotiations.)

has made a first step). The alternative, then, is simulated bargaining under laboratory conditions, although this procedure is disadvantaged by the need to utilize novice bargainers under conditions wherein bargaining interests cannot approach those that affect institutionalized relationships.* Nevertheless, attempts at empirical verification of bargaining hypotheses need to be made. With the increasing complexity and interdependence of our economic and political institutions, the impact of bargaining can be significant and widely diffused, and theoretical and empirical efforts can be useful for shedding some light on the forces that determine agreement or failure in particular negotiations.

References

Bishop, Robert L. "A Zeuthen-Hicks Theory of Bargaining." *Econometrica* 32 (1964): 410-17.

Bishop, Robert L. "Discussion." *American Economic Review* 55 (1965): 467-69.

Coddington, Alan. "Review of *The Economics of Bargaining* by John G. Cross." *Journal of Economic Literature* 8 (1970): 1211-12.

Douglas, Ann. *Industrial Peacemaking.* New York: Columbia University Press, 1962.

Dunlop, John T. *Wage Determination Under Trade Unions.* New York: Augustus M. Kelley, 1950.

Harsanyi, John C. "Approaches to the Bargaining Problem Before and After the Theory of Games: A Critical Discussion of Zeuthen's, Hicks' and Nash's Theories." *Econometrica* 24 (1956): 144-57.

Harsanyi, John C. "On the Rationality Postulates Underlying the Theory of Co-operative Games." *Journal of Conflict Resolution* 5, no. 2 (June 1961): 179-96.

Harsanyi, John C. "Bargaining and Conflict Situations in the Light of a New Approach to Game Theory." *American Economic Review* 55 (1965): 447-57.

Hicks, John R. *The Theory of Wages.* London: Macmillan, 1932.

Nash, John F. "The Bargaining Problem." *Econometrica* 18 (1950): 155-62.

Nash, John F. "Two-Person Cooperative Games." *Econometrica* 21 (1953): 128-40.

Pen, Jan. "A General Theory of Bargaining." *American Economic Review* 42 (1952): 24-42.

---

*Patchen (see reading 8) provides a useful overview of interactive models of conflict and cooperation, and cites some of the approaches made to measuring the subjective variables associated with models of this type.

Pen, Jan. *The Wage Rate Under Collective Bargaining.* Cambridge, Mass.: Harvard University Press, 1959.

Peters, Edward. "Strategy and Tactics in Labor Negotiations." *Personnel Journal* (1966).

Saraydar, Edward. "Zeuthen's Theory of Bargaining: A Note." *Econometrica* 33 (1965): 802-13.

Saraydar, Edward. "Review of *The Economics of Bargaining* by John G. Cross." *Industrial and Labor Relations Review* 23 (1970): 591-93.

Saraydar, Edward. "Hicks' Bargaining Theory as a Positive and as a Normative Model of Wage Determination." *Zeitschrift für die gesamte Staatswissenschaft* 127 (1971): 476-85.

Shackle, G. L. S. *Expectations in Economics.* London: Cambridge University Press, 1949.

Shackle, G. L. S. "The Nature of the Bargaining Process." *The Theory of Wage Determination,* edited by J. T. Dunlop. London: Macmillan, 1957.

Stevens, Carl M. *Strategy and Collective Bargaining Negotiation.* New York: McGraw-Hill, 1963.

Walton, Richard E., and McKersie, Robert B. *A Behavioral Theory of Labor Negotiations.* New York: McGraw-Hill, 1965.

Zeuthen, Frederik. *Problems of Monopoly and Economic Warfare.* London: G. Routledge, 1930.

Zeuthen, Frederik. *Economic Theory and Method.* London: Longmans, Green, 1957.

Reading 10

An Interactive Model of Collective Bargaining in Public Education

Anthony M. Cresswell

Background

In recent years two phenomena have combined to increase the labor costs in public sector: (1) the total size of the public sector (as a percent of GNP) has risen, and (2) wages of public employees have grown at a greater rate than wages in the private sector. Unionization of public employees and widespread collective bargaining are important aspects of the rising costs.

This trend has been particularly evident in public education. Widespread teacher strikes and defeats of local tax referenda indicate resistance to rising tax burdens. However, as table 1 shows, these costs are likely to continue to increase.

Higher labor costs have large effects on public education. Typical school budgets will allocate as much as 70 percent of the total to salaries, and instructional costs average about 68 percent of total expenditures. Rising labor costs are not offset elsewhere in the budget, as shown in table 1. Thus, the resources devoted to salaries remain stable and total costs rise. Along with the rising tax burden of providing educational services go levels of conflict and frequency of work stoppages and their related costs. Controlling these costs and structuring the bargaining in more effective ways require under-

Table 1
Expenditures in Regular Public Elementary and Secondary Schools, in 1974-75 Dollars (Billions)

	1964-65	1969-70	1974-75	1975-80[b]
Total current expenditure[a]	31.8	47.9	54.3	56.3
Salary for instructional staff	19.2	27.3	29.2	30.7

[a]excludes capital expenditures
[b]projections

Source: National Center for Educational Statistics, *Projections of Educational Statistics to 1984-85* (Washington, D.C.: U.S. Government Printing Office, 1976).

standing of the process. This paper presents a model which is intended to be useful in that respect.

Review of the Literature

Existing studies of the bargaining process fall into three rough categories:

1. Descriptive studies which deal with much of the richness of detail of the bargaining process and may include general theories of bargaining behavior but not explicit models or analytical structures to account for outcomes or aspects of the bargaining process;

(2) Analytical models often based directly or indirectly on game theory, which include assumptions of complete information, known utility functions and a single bargaining session;

(3) Interactive models which may or may not include the assumptions from the second group but do take into account the tactical interaction between bargainers and time dependent characteristics of the bargaining process.

The work of Walton and McKersie (1965) is an example of the first category. They attempt to deal with the full range of behaviors in collective bargaining, describing the substantive basis for more analytical theories. Works such as Vantine's (see reading 13) deal in more detail, but still descriptively, with some subsection of the total process and also belong in this first group.

Game theoretic and related models fall into the second group.

They depend on the concept of strategy as the basis for analysis. Coddington's (1968) comments on this approach illustrate a basic problem: "The whole series of interactions leading to some outcome are collapsed inside the strategies and they remain there as long as the strategy concept is the basis of the framework" (p. 75). Simon's (1955) arguments regarding the limited information access and processing capacity of the bargainer apply as well. See also Von Neumann and Morgenstern (1964), Zeuthen (1930), Harsanyi (1962), and Nash (1950).

The majority of the works surveyed are based on the Zeuthen-Nash model of a two-person bargaining situation, in which the objective of the model is to arrive at a determinate solution to the bargaining process based upon specified prior assumptions and restricted to the limitations of classical game theory; i.e., it is assumed that the two parties know each other's utility functions, as well as each other's preferences for risk.

Pen's (1952) model does not depend on the game theoretic assumptions. Although this theory does not include the dynamic aspects of the model presented in this paper, Pen's work does provide one basis for our model. That is, to determine his decision, the bargainer employs two functions: (1) the cost of accepting his opponent's offer, and (2) the expected costs of strike if the offer is not accepted (or in Pen's theory the risk of strike incurred by not accepting any given offer). It does not yield a determinate solution, however, nor does it account for the dynamics of the bargaining process and the affects of those dynamics on the bargainer's risk and cost functions.

But the bargaining process is more accurately described as a series of offers and counter-offers, than as a series of accept-or-reject decisions. Bishop (1964), Cross (1965), and Saraydar (reading 9) address the problem of accounting for sequential concessions. Bishop's model deals with the question of sequential bargaining and exchange of concessions over time, but does not describe the effect of one bargainer's behavior on the other. A much richer characterization of the bargaining process is found in Cross's work. In his theory the bargainers learn—that is, modify their expectations—as a result of their opponent's behavior. His focus on the concession process led to the formulation of this model. However, the structure of the theory leads to an unreasonable convergence: namely, that the change in one bargainer's concession rate influences the other in a strictly inverse manner. That is, as bargainer 1 offers less than bargainer 2 expects, bargainer 2 *increases* his concession rate. This is plausible only if bargainer 2 is desperate for a rapid agreement. It is much more plausible to expect bargainer 2's behavior to either converge or diverge, depending on more than just bargainer 1's concession rate. It is reasonable to expect many situations in which bargainer 1 would "toughen" his position (reduce concession rate) in order to cause bargainer 2 to "soften" his position (increase concession rate). This is not allowed by Cross's assumptions. See Coddington (1970) and Saraydar (reading 9). Saraydar deals directly with the problem of convergence but depends on unspecified bargaining tactics (other than concession rate changes) to account for divergent or convergent bargaining at any point in the process.

A Preliminary Model

If one is to improve the structure of the bargaining process it is necessary to distinguish the effects of structural and environmental factors from those of bargaining tactics. This is a critical point in any bargaining model; it is of special significance for our purposes. A model which does not allow the relationships among these variables to be explored is of little use for policy purposes. We turn our attention, therefore, to our preliminary model. It is intended to afford insight into the general nature of bargaining as well as to serve as the foundation of empirical examination of collective bargaining between school boards and teachers. Therefore, where we refer to labor and management, the immediate reference is to teacher organizations and public school boards.

This modeling effort is part of a larger research strategy. Only the preliminary model is presented in detail in this paper, but we will discuss its place in the overall effort in order to provide some perspective on its eventual use. As noted earlier, the purpose of the work is to improve the collective bargaining process in the public sector, particularly the public schools. This will come through developing and testing models of the process which suggest new structures for the legal and organizational framework. We are therefore interested in a model which will illuminate the relationships among structural, procedural, and environmental variables. The preliminary model is designed to allow these three groups of variables to be included. The portion of the work described here concentrates on the formal or analytical aspects of the model rather than the examination of environmental variables. When the relationship among the fundamental processes of bargaining variables have been explored, the model will be discussed in terms of the role of environmental variables. That is, when we have analyzed the role of process variables in bargaining, we will proceed to explore the interactions among environment, process, and outcomes. When these interactions are better understood it will be possible to suggest procedural and structural modifications which improve the efficiency and reduce the conflict of the bargaining.

Because the emphasis at this stage is not on the environmental and structural variables, we present a highly generalized model dealing only with distributive bargaining (zero-sum) and ignoring the effects of most bargaining tactics and skills. We concentrate instead on the environmental parameters of the situation and the basic tactic of bargaining: choosing the size of the offer.

A multisession bargaining process is assumed. It is sequential in nature, an offer by one party followed by a counter-offer from the other, until a settlement is reached. The process, as characterized by Coddington (1968), is shown in figure 1. The interaction proceeds

Figure 1
The Multisession Bargaining Process

until a settlement is reached. Our interest in collective bargaining for public education allows no provision for a permanent break-off in bargaining. A settlement must be reached; only temporary break-offs are possible. We assume further that bargaining proceeds in light of a deadline, known to both parties, after which a strike ensues.

The decision in question is, of course, the size of the offer to be made at the next step in sequence. For purposes of simplification we ignore any symbolic behavior of the bargainer associated with making an offer; it is the magnitude which is of interest. We assume further that no back-tracking is permitted. Each offer may be no smaller a concession than the previous one. That is:

$$C_i^l \geqslant 0,$$

$$C_i^m \geqslant 0,$$

where C_i^l is labor's concession rate at bargaining session i; C_i^m is management's concession rate at session i. The choice of an offer at any stage is, therefore, a choice of a concession rate. This model is based on an examination of the concession rate and adjustments therein as the fundamental bargaining tactics. The model must have these basic properties: (1) it must describe converging offers and (2) it must explain the bargaining process in terms of both structural (environmental) variables and bargaining tactics.

To build such a model we begin with attention to behavior of bargainers. Real bargainers have limited information access and processing capability. As Simon (1955) and others have noted, assumptions about complete knowledge or complex calculations by decision makers are much less appealing as behavioral models than ones which emphasize simple decision processes and limited information. This effort is aimed at these latter criteria.

We assume, therefore, that the bargainer proceeds on the basis of a simple model of expectations of the other bargainer's behavior. As new information, in the form of a new offer in each session, becomes available, the bargainer adjusts his model and reaches a new decision based on the modified expectations. The datum at each new session is the new offer. It in turn implies a current concession rate and a rate of change in concession rate (both overall and with respect to the previous bargaining session). The concession rate inferences become the input to the first bargainer's adjustment, resulting in a similar set of data becoming input to the second bargainer's adjustments, and so forth. The adjustments apply to an assumed overall concession rate for one bargainer which is held by the other. This assumed concession rate implies an expected outcome at the deadline for the bargaining. That is:

$$\overline{C}_i^l = \frac{q_o^l - q_i^l}{t_i - t_o} \, ,$$

where $\overline{C}_i^l$ is management's assumed overall (or average) concession rate for labor at round i; q_o^l is labor's opening offer; q_i^l is labor's offer at round i; t_i is the time at round i; t_o is the time at the opening of the bargaining process. The corresponding argument for management is symmetrical and is omitted in the interest of brevity.

It is assumed that each bargainer begins the negotiations with an expectation about a best possible outcome, $\overset{*}{q}$. This is the benchmark against which all expected outcomes, $\bar{q}$, are assessed. The cost of any expected outcome is therefore simply $\overset{*}{q} - \bar{q}$. Each bargainer also begins with an expectation about the other's concession rate, C, as well as subjective estimates of the costs of a strike. There are two cost determinants, one based on a projected outcome, the other on the probability of a strike. (In this respect, this model is similar to the others discussed above.) In its simplest terms, therefore, this model describes the choice of a new offer at time t_i which minimizes the total cost. Generally speaking, if one concedes too fast, the cost of the settlement in terms of difference from the "best" outcome increases. If one concedes too slowly, the expected cost of a strike increases. The key question is: how fast is just fast enough? This model suggests that there is no determinate answer, only a dynamic one, and in this sense the implications are similar to those of Cross (1965) or Saraydar (reading 9).

The new concession rate for labor at t_i, C_i^l, is based on the projected cost of settlement, x_i^l, and the expected strike cost, y_i^l:

$$C_i^l = f(x_i^l, y_i^l). \tag{1}$$

Labor's calculation of the cost of settlement, x_i^l for time t_i, is based on an extrapolation of management's behavior to the deadline t_d. The extrapolation is the explicit form of labor's behavioral model for management. The cost is:

$$x_i^l = \overset{*l}{q} - \bar{q}_i^m \, , \tag{2}$$

where x_i^l is labor's expected cost of the settlement implied by management's offer at t_i, and $\bar{q}_i^m$ is the expected final position of management as projected by labor at t_i. If management's actions are independent of labor's, that final position would be taken as a function of management's offer, q_i^m at t_i, and labor's extrapolation on q_i^m such that:

$$\bar{q}_i^m = q_i^m + \overline{C}_i^m(t_d - t_i) + \dot{C}_i^m(t_d - t_i)^2 , \qquad (3)$$

where $\overline{C}_i^m = (q_i^m - q_o^m)/(t_i - t_o)$, the overall concession rate to t_i; $\dot{C}_i^m = (\overline{C}_i^m - \overline{C}_j^m)/(t_i - t_j)$; and $j = i - 1$. This states that the bargainer operates on the basis of an exponential extrapolation of opponent's behavior. The use of the overall concession rate for labor's extrapolation makes the model of expectations a cumulative learning function where the overall expectation of labor for management's future behavior is adjusted to take into account the latest offer along with past actions.

But management's future behavior also depends on labor's actions. In the above cost function, labor adopts a concession rate which will converge with management's position at the deadline (see figure 2). But that assumed concession rate, C'^l_i may differ from C_i^l. Labor assumes management will be sensitive to that difference. Thus, if C'^l_i is greater than C_i^l, management might be expected to further adjust downward, further increasing the cost to labor. Expression (2) must then be expanded to include this interaction term. The interaction is based on the assumption that the past interaction between concession rates will continue. Therefore, expression (2) is adjusted for the mean rate of change in management's concession rate, $\overline{C}^m$ at t_i, with respect to the mean rate of change in labor's concession rate, $\overline{C}^l$ at t_i. Equation (2) becomes

$$x_i^l = \bar{q}^l - \alpha \left[\bar{q}_i^m - \frac{\dot{C}^m}{\dot{C}^l}(C_i^l - C'^l_i)(t_d - t_i)^2 \right]. \qquad (4)$$

Thus, there is a learning component in this aspect of the model since the mean rate of change is adjusted to account for the new rate at each bargaining period. The parameter α represents an adjustment sensitivity.

This result is, in its effect, similar to Cross's (1965) and other models which predict convergence via an analogous adjustment process.

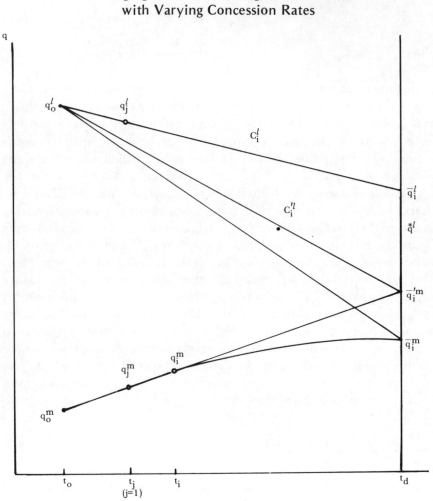

Figure 2
Converging Labor and Management Positions
with Varying Concession Rates

Note: For simplicity we have chosen the special case for management when

$$\frac{d^2 q^m}{dt^2} = 0 .$$

But C_i^l depends on y_i^l as well, the expected strike cost, which is determined by the probability of a strike, $p(s)$, and the perceived fixed cost of a strike for labor, σ. The strike probability is taken as a function of the distance between the offers at t_i, $q_i^l - q_i^m$, the elapsed time, $t_i - t_o$, and labor's "propensity to strike" or militancy parameter, k. Thus:

$$p(s) = 1 - e^{-k} \left[(t_i - t_o) \; \frac{q_i^l - q_i^m}{q_o^l - q_o^m} \right]. \tag{5}$$

Then the expected strike cost becomes:

$$y_i^l = \sigma \left[1 - e^{-k} \; (t_i - t_o) \; \frac{q_i^l - q_i^m}{q_o^l - q_o^m} \right]. \tag{6}$$

The basis of probability of a strike in this function is the same for both parties and varies with their concession rates and parameter, k. We see that y_i^l decreases with increasing rates of concession for labor, and x_i^l increases with increasing rates of concession for labor. For C_i^l to be at a minimum, y_i^l and x_i^l must be evaluated together. Therefore at any t_i convergence or divergence depends on initial conditions. Under suitable conditions, q^l and q^m will converge and there will be a settlement point. With the assumption of $C_i^l \geqslant 0$, $C_i^m \geqslant 0$, there can be no divergence, only intransigence. But since y_i^l is time dependent, intransigence implies a shift in concession rate, and therefore a new concession rate at each new bargaining session leading to a reevaluation of costs. Implicit bargaining goes on whether the parties meet or not. And so in a situation of mutual intransigence, the one with the larger expected strike cost will begin concession first (values of the parameters being equal).

If there is no settlement at the strike deadline, the value of σ is reevaluated by the bargainers, along with the sensitivity and learning parameters, α and k. Bargaining then proceeds as before the deadline with the exception that the previously agreed upon deadline, t_d in the equations, is replaced with t_d^l, labor's subjective estimate of the deadline, and t_d^m for management. The primary effect of allowing for different deadlines is the removal of one of the stabilizing influences in the model. This would lead, supposedly, to faster learning, exaggerated reactions, and possible greater concession rates than prior to the deadline.

The following transformations would be made in (6):

$$k \rightarrow k',$$

$$t_o \rightarrow t_d,$$

$$q_o^l \rightarrow q_d^l,$$

$$q_o^m \rightarrow q_d^m.$$

Discussion

We have described a simultaneous equation model of bargaining in which the equations are cost functions according to which a bargainer chooses the size of a concession at any point in the bargaining process. It appears that a cost minimum is implied at the point when the two cost functions are equal, providing for the possibility of an analytical solution. At this stage of the work no extensive effort at such a solution has been made.

At a fairly general level of specification, this model is successful in dealing with two central aspects of formal bargaining models: (1) why the parties eventually do settle, that is, concede to a mutually acceptable point, and (2) how the dynamic (time-dependent) characteristics of the process integrate with the static characteristics of the parties and the bargaining context. Thus, each bargainer "learns" from the other's behavior and can adjust to changing patterns and expectations. But that learning and adjustment is conditioned and constrained by the bargainer's own preferences and objectives.

For example, the model predicts that one party's pattern of high early concessions will cause the other to project better outcomes, and hold out for more than originally expected. Thus, the early conceder will face a tough response in attempting to reduce concessions late in the process. This is consistent with some laboratory research on individual bargainers. The model also suggests that the concession rates should be quite sensitive to perceived strike costs. These are in turn determined in large part by exogenous (with respect to the bargaining) variables. For example, a teacher union could be forced to abandon a tough bargaining position and make large concessions by a loss of community support. The loss of community support for teachers would suggest both the reduced ability to pressure the board of education to concede and the enhanced ability of the board to take a strike. Both these factors indicate higher strike costs to the teachers.

By using time-to-deadline as a key variable, strikes and impasses can be easily accommodated in the model and lead to plausible predictions. An impasse is not really a cessation of the bargaining dynamic, either in the model or in practice. The parties are in fact manipulating the overall concession rate and the perceived strike costs. As an impasse persists, the time-to-deadline inexorably diminishes, driving up the probability of a strike. If both parties have the same expected strike costs, the higher probability will affect them alike. But more likely, one side will perceive a strike as somewhat more costly than the other. Thus, the approach of the deadline may force that side to concede first. By contrast, however, if one side is much closer to its objective at the point of impasse, it will be more sensitive to the strike costs, since the costs of settlement may be small compared to the costs of not agreeing—i.e., allowing a strike to occur.

The key to accounting for agreement is the dependence of strike costs on time-to-deadline and on distance between the parties. This is another way of expressing the "pressure" on bargainers to settle as the deadline approaches. Without the pressure there is little reason to incur the costs of conceding. As the pressure increases, it forces both parties to concede, and perhaps to reassess their objectives. The ability to withstand pressure is not seen as a consequence of the bargaining itself, but depends on outside factors usually referred to as *bargaining power*. (See, for example, Chamberlain and Cullen 1971, pp. 227-37.) These affect both the strike cost (cost of disagreeing) and distance from objectives (cost of agreeing). Power depends on such factors as organizational solidarity, political influence, etc. But the amount of pressure is a consequence of the bargaining itself. Therefore, in this view, bargaining effectiveness is a combination of power, determined by outside factors and reflected in strike costs and objectives, and bargaining behavior. The critical behavior is adjusting the concession rate to keep pressure on the opponent, and interpreting the opponent's concessions correctly.

Another element of bargaining is purposely omitted: threats, bluffs, and interpersonal actions between the persons at the bargaining table. These elements are, of course, recognized as important parts of the total process. Their role in affecting bargaining outcomes and behaviors has been extensively studied in the laboratory and comprehensively reviewed by Rubin and Brown (1975). But comparatively little is known about the effects of economic and contextual variables in actual collective bargaining situations. A model formulated in this manner provides a basis for the statistical study of bargaining in a number of schools (or other organizations). The data required to test the hypotheses suggested here are much more accessible than the direct observation of minute-by-minute negotiation required for the study of bargaining tactics. By statistical studies of the economic and contextual variables suggested here, it may be possible to estimate their importance in the conduct and results of bargaining relative to interpersonal table tactics. It may be, for example, that interpersonal tactics are only important when the gross economic and contextual factors suggest a balanced bargaining process or comparable strike costs and objectives. Or it may be that table behavior is more a consequence of the bargainers' personalities, and does not vary systematically with the other elements of the process. The value of a model of this type is that it suggests these (and other) questions, and provides a framework for further expanding general understanding of bargaining—both by empirical studies and further formal modeling.

References

Bishop, R. L. "A Zeuthen-Hicks Theory of Bargaining." *Econometrics* 32 (1964).

Chamberlain, Neil W., and Cullen, Donald E. *The Labor Sector* (2nd ed.). New York: McGraw-Hill, 1971.

Coddington, Alan. *Theories of the Bargaining Process.* Chicago: Aldine, 1968.

Coddington, Alan. "Review of *The Economics of Bargaining* by John G. Cross." *Journal of Economic Literature* 8 (1970).

Cross, John. "A Theory of the Bargaining Process." *American Economic Review* 55, no. 1 (March 1965): 67-94.

Harsanyi, John C. "Bargaining in Ignorance of the Opponent's Utility Function." *Journal of Conflict Resolution* 6, no. 1 (1962).

Nash, J. F. "The Bargaining Problem." *Econometrica* 18 (1950).

Pen, J. "A General Theory of Bargaining." *American Economic Review* 42 (1952).

Rubin, Jeffrey Z., and Brown, Bert R. *The Social Psychology of Bargaining and Negotiation.* New York: Academic Press, 1975.

Simon, Herbert A. "A Behavioral Model of Rational Choice." *Quarterly Journal of Economics* 69 (February 1955).

Von Neumann, J., and Morgenstern, O. *Theory of Games and Economic Behavior.* New York: John Wiley & Sons, 1964.

Walton, R., and McKersie, R. *A Behavioral Theory of Labor Negotiations.* New York: McGraw-Hill, 1965.

Zeuthen, F. *Problems of Monopoly and Economic Warfare.* London: G. Routledge, 1930.

Reading 11

Collective Negotiations and Teachers: A Behavioral Analysis

Donald Hellriegel, Wendell French, and Richard B. Peterson

Since the mid-1950s so much has happened in public school employer-employee relations that it should really be considered an entirely new field.

... Prior to 1960, not a single state authorized collective, or any other form of, negotiations between teacher organizations and boards of education. There were, at that time, in the educational literature, only vague references to some sort of teacher negotiations and the improvement of staff relations. (Allen 1967, pp. 6-7)

Although a body of literature is developing in this new field, there appears to be a lack of conceptualizing and of empirical evidence regarding classroom teachers' satisfactions and dissatisfactions with their organizational environment, attitudes toward teaching as a profession, perceptions of collective negotiations, and the interrelations among these variables. For a discussion of the need for more research and theorizing in public employment, see Smith and McLaughlin (1962).

One manifestation of the strains which are occurring in the teacher-employer role relationships and of the growing willingness

Reprinted by permission from *Industrial and Labor Relations Review* 23, no. 3 (April 1970), pp. 380-96. Copyright 1970 by Cornell University.

among teachers to take direct action is the upswing in teachers' strikes commencing with 1966. Prior to 1966, teachers' strikes were infrequent. "During the 26 years beginning in 1940, a total of 129 such stoppages occurred but only 35 of these were recorded in the decade immediately preceding 1966" (Glass 1967). An official of the National Education Association (NEA) estimated 140 teacher strikes occurred during the 1968-69 school year, an increase of 23 percent from the 114 strikes in the 1967-68 school year.* The growing militancy of teachers during the 1968-69 period of this study has been reported widely and discussed in the popular news media. However, Stieber (1967, p. 80) has noted that "too often the strike in public employment has been treated as an unmitigated evil to be exorcized rather than the symptoms of a malady which needs treatment."

This study provides a conceptual framework and empirical insights into such "symptoms" of one group of public employees—school teachers. The conceptual model presented is a means of identifying and portraying the assumed relationships among the key variables considered to provide the behavioral framework of teachers vis-à-vis collective negotiations. The research design and statistical findings which follow partially test the utility of the model.

The Model

The underlying assumptions of the conceptual model and the research design are (1) attitudes affect the direction of the perceptual process, (2) this process may be related to particular motivational dispositions, and (3) these dispositions may be reflected in overt acts such as a strike or a vote against a strike.

The conceptual model (see figure 1) of factors related to teachers' attitudes toward collective negotiations was developed on the basis of an extensive review of the literature from which the component variables and their assumed relationships were abstracted. Much of the available literature regarding teacher behavior and collective negotiations in education has not considered the form or degree of

---

*Data obtained from Howard Carroll, National Education Association, Washington, D.C., October 29, 1969. Mr. Carroll estimates 40 teacher strikes had occurred as of October 29. These figures include both NEA and American Federation of Teachers (AFT) affiliates.

Figure 1
Conceptual Model of Factors Related to Teachers' Attitudes
Toward Collective Negotiations

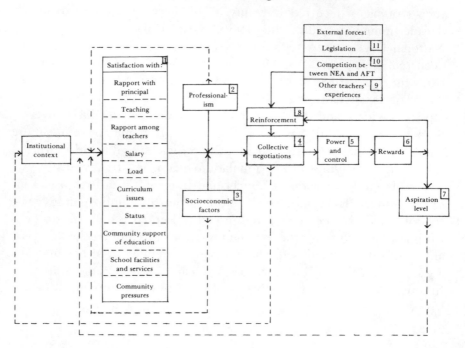

their interrelationships. The writings which have attempted such a synthesis typically are more limited in scope, i.e., they consider a few "behavioral" variables in relation to a few "negotiation" variables. Thus, the model is affected by some a priori reasoning. For a synthesis and discussion of related literature see Hellriegel (1969).

The model is assumed also to be a means of explaining and integrating the findings from the empirical investigation. Additional research may indicate that other variables need to be included or that the hypothesized relationships among the variables need to be altered. Thus, there is no attempt to conclude that this model provides a complete explanation of the relationships being investigated or that the sequence of relationships are as posited.

The Model: Internal Forces

Variable 1 in the conceptual model refers to the perceived satisfactions or dissatisfactions by the teachers with ten different dimensions of the institutional and environmental context within which they function. These dimensions of satisfaction include: rapport with principal, satisfaction with teaching, rapport among teachers, salary, load, curriculum issues, status, community support of education, school facilities and services, and community pressures. Thus, teacher satisfaction is analyzed as a multidimensional phenomenon. The model assumes varying satisfaction levels will have differential relationships with attitudes toward collective negotiations.

Variable 2 refers to the extent teachers support professional norms of behavior. Like satisfaction, professionalism is considered to be a multidimensional concept, consisting of the following elements: client orientation, colleague orientation, monopoly of knowledge, and decision making. It is assumed the nature of the professional role concept will have an interacting effect on the level of satisfaction as well as influence attitudes toward collective negotiations.

Corwin explains the process of professionalism for teachers as follows:

For decades teachers have subscribed to the idea that they have professional obligations (such as staying late to work with students); now they are demanding professional rights as well (such as rights to select their own teaching materials and methods). . . . Militant professionalism, then is intended to compromise both the control that administrators have over public education and the control traditionally exercised by the lay public. (Corwin 1965b)

This model, which attempts to conceptualize the frame of reference of teachers, infers the intervening variables to be both professional role conception and the socioeconomic characteristics of the teachers. These "interacting" relationships are portrayed by "feedback" loops to the satisfaction dimensions.

Variable 3 denotes socioeconomic factors which characterize the sample population: sex, marital status, teaching experience, educational level, and income. These characteristics are not of a particular explanatory value in themselves but rather serve as operational criteria for evaluating the relevance of other behavioral dimensions. For instance, one might hypothesize that perceived low income on the part of a female teacher may result in dissatisfaction with respect to salary. But if the female in society has been conditioned to assume a more passive and nonaggressive role than the male, there may be a lower propensity for females to support strikes.

Variable 4 in the model refers to classroom teacher attitudes toward collective negotiations in terms of the following scales: (a) support of negotiations, (b) support of strikes, (c) support of penalties for striking, (d) support of arbitration, (e) support of broad scope to negotiations, (f) perceived similarity between NEA and AFT in terms of goals of the two organizations, and (g) teachers' perceptions of school boards' support of collective negotiations.

Relation of Variables to Collective Negotiations

The model connotes variables 1, 2, and 3 (i.e., satisfaction, professionalization, and socioeconomic factors) have differential and patterned relationships with variable 4 (collective negotiations). However, caution must be exercised in not assuming that this model or the research methodology proves causation because "correlational studies can sometimes disprove but never prove that a causal relationship exists" (Porter and Lawler 1968, p. 41).

The feedback loop from variable 4 (collective negotiations) to the "institutional context" implies that this process may affect other parties in the total educational system in terms of the decision, communication, planning, control, and organization processes. For instance, the administrations in the three systems included in this study have created institutional positions to deal with negotiations.

Variable 5 (power* and control) connotes collective negotiations provide the means and serve the function of increasing the amount of power and control one subsystem (teachers) has within the total educational system. The state of mind of the leadership of NEA, with respect to the uses of power, is partially demonstrated in some of their statements. For instance, Elizabeth D. Koontz, president of NEA, stated at the 1968 convention:

---

*In this study, "the *power* of an individual [or organization] in a social situation consists of the sanctions others in the situation perceive that he [or the organization] has available to employ in ways that will affect them." See Hill and French (1967).

We will use our power. In too many communities teachers have been handed a bill of goods. We intend to hand right back a bill of rights. . . . For too long teachers have worked under the theory, you educators do the teaching and leave the decisions to us. ("NEA Briefs Teachers" 1968; see also Cole 1969)

In summary, teachers may have an influence through collective negotiations on the amount and forms of control they can exercise. This ability to "control" may be facilitated through the use of various power tactics. For as Horvat (1968) puts it,

Negotiation is a rapidly growing force in American education because it is a method by which teachers can gain some real control over decision-making in the schools. No longer can administrators and board members choose to, or afford to, reject out of hand or ignore the requests and demands of teacher groups. Collective negotiation processes create political, psychological, and in some cases legal pressures which force boards and administrators to listen to and respond to the demands of teachers of their districts. (see also Belasco and Alutto 1969)

If such an increase in power actually occurs, the model posits that a means for increasing the rewards (variable 6) has been created. Generically, rewards may be thought of as desirable outcomes or returns. This is not to infer rewards are not, or would not, be available to teachers without the power and control which they may be able to create through collective negotiations. However, it is assumed one motivation for teachers engaging in collective negotiations is that it is perceived as a means to obtain increments of power and control. Concurrently, such increments of power and control may provide the means of gaining rewards which may be both intrinsic and extrinsic in nature. For, Blau (1964, p. 37) has noted,

. . . workers participate in unions not only to improve their employment conditions but also because they intrinsically enjoy the fellowship in the union and derive satisfaction from helping to realize its objectives.

Thus, the model indicates increases in rewards obtained from negotiations serve to reinforce (variable 8) the perceived legitimacy of this process by teachers.

Aspiration level (variable 7) refers to the concept that as a consequence of obtaining rewards through collective negotiations a potentially higher level of attainment for present goals, or a different set of goals, may be established. This propensity is indicated by the feedback loop from aspiration level to satisfaction (variable 1). Hypothetically, teachers initially may utilize collective negotiations primarily as a means to increase extrinsic rewards such as salary. Eventually, their span of attention may focus on the satisfaction of other perceived needs such as greater autonomy or participation in decision making (Taffel 1968). The recognition of such possible changes in aspiration levels enables the model to be considered as "open" rather than "closed." However, it is not necessary to assume the changes in aspirations follow in a simple incremental pattern with changes in rewards (variable 6). The fundamental characteristics of open models are described by Alexis and Wilson (1967, p. 161) as follows:

(a) Predetermined goals are replaced by some unidentified structure that is approximated by an aspiration level.

(b) All alternatives and outcomes are not predetermined, nor are the relations between specific alternatives and outcomes always defined.

(c) The ordering of all alternatives is replaced by a search routine that considers a relatively small number of alternatives.

(d) The individual does not maximize but seeks to find a solution to satisfy an aspiration level.

Reinforcement (variable 8) refers to the primary "internal" and "external" forces which may be serving to shape the nature of and attitudes toward collective negotiations. The "reinforcement" concept may be thought of as having "positive" or "negative" valences. For instance, legislation could reduce or enhance the ability of teachers to engage in collective negotiations.

The Model: External Forces

The model posits three major external forces as generally having a reinforcing effect on collective negotiations: the perception of other teachers' experiences with collective negotiations in other school systems across the country (variable 9), competition between the NEA and AFT (variable 10), and legislation (variable 11).

The first external force hypothesized as having a reinforcing effect is the success teachers in other school systems across the country are having with this process. More importantly, it appears teachers *not* utilizing collective negotiations generally have not been able to make gains comparable to those made by teachers who *have* used the process. This may result in the perception of relative deprivation. For several examples which tend to document this claim, see Shils and Whittier (1968). This reasoning assumes that one of the most important reference or comparison groups of teachers is their peers in other systems. For discussion of the import of reference group theory, see Jackson (1962).

From a psychological perspective, it is known that behavior which is rewarded or perceived to be rewarding is reinforced and thus repeated. Zaleznik and Moment (1964, p. 378), in reviewing the work of Skinner, state

... any behavior followed by a reward which satisfies an active want is "learned" as an appropriate way in which to satisfy wants henceforth. Similarly, behaviors that are followed by deprivation of wants will tend to be avoided.

In sum, teachers may have learned rewards can be obtained through collective negotiations, thereby reinforcing this process for those already engaged in it and increasing the likelihood of other teachers desiring to utilize negotiations.

Competition between NEA and AFT (variable 10) is assumed as having a reinforcing effect on collective negotiations and teachers' attitudes toward this process. Although such a causal relationship must be inferred, the reasoning does appear convincing. The successes of AFT in winning the right to represent teachers in several large metropolitan areas, commencing with New York City, may have stimulated NEA to aspirations for greater organizational growth.

Competition probably was initially created by AFT. For, as Muir (1968) states,

The AFT has acted as the spark to ignite the lethargic engine of the NEA in its drive to improve the economic welfare of the teaching profession. In this regard the impact of the AFT on the NEA can be compared to the impact of the CIO upon the AFL during the 1930's. ... In much the same way the activities of the AFT have forced the NEA to change its position on bargaining, sanctions, and strikes and has caused them to seek protective legislation, exclusive bargaining rights and also to embark upon a campaign to organize the unorganized workers.

Further, the current competition between NEA and AFT may partially explain the present militancy among some teachers

(Neirynck 1968). The rationale for this assertion is developed by Brown (1964).

The present teacher militancy, though rooted in economic conditions, is fed and fertilized by competition between the NEA and AFT. In the search for membership and support, each is attempting to demonstrate to prospective members that it can and does win greater benefits for teachers than the others. (see also Elam 1964)

Dashiell (1967) and Schmidt (1968) provide case studies on the realities of this conflict in Michigan. It appears some evidence exists for inferring that the competition between NEA and AFT is having a reinforcing impact on the process of and attitudes toward collective negotiations.

Legislation Reflects Lobbying Efforts

The last major external force in the model is legislation (variable 11). Much of the legislation concerning collective negotiations passed in recent years appears to reflect the lobbying efforts of both school boards and teacher associations. Moskow (1966) notes that the Washington act (1965) was sponsored by the Washington Education Association and opposed by the AFT. For the most part, legislation regarding collective negotiations has been enacted since 1962 and is, at a minimum, supportive of the concept of negotiations. Beyond this, there are wide differences among states. The states with legislation permitting or requiring school boards to engage in collective negotiations totaled sixteen as of 1968: Alaska, California, Connecticut, Florida, Maryland, Massachusetts, Michigan, Nebraska, New Hampshire, New Jersey, New York, Oregon, Rhode Island, Texas, Washington, and Wisconsin (National Education Association 1968). Lieberman (1967) anticipates

By 1972, 80 percent of the teachers will probably be in states which statutorily provide for some form of negotiations. . . . Statutes which have not resulted in meaningful negotiations are likely to be amended to result in more significant negotiations.

Since the teacher attitudes reported were obtained in the state of Washington, it might be helpful to review some of the basic dimensions of the Washington act.

Representatives of an employee organization, which organization shall by secret ballot have won a majority in an election to represent the certificated employees within its school district, shall have the right, after using established administrative channels, to meet, confer and negotiate with the board of directors of the school district or a committee thereof to communicate the considered professional judgment of the certificated staff prior to the final adoption by the board of proposed school policies relating to, but not limited to, curriculum, textbook selection, in-service training, student teaching program, personnel hiring and assignment practices, leaves of absence, salaries and salary schedules and non-instructional duties. (Laws of Washington, rev. Code (1965), ch. 28, §72.030, p. 23)

The model purports this legislation probably affects (even though indirectly) and has been affected by teacher attitudes toward collective negotiations. Figure 2 attempts to conceptualize the interactional "tensions" between the legal context and the social-psychological context with respect to collective negotiations.

Figure 2
Simplified System of Relations between the Legal Context and Social-Psychological Context

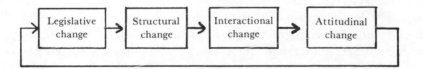

Thus, the generality of the findings to other states may be affected somewhat by the specific nature of the legislation in the State of Washington. The degree of such impact is a moot question. A priori, it is hypothesized that in the major industrialized sections of the country there may be more similarities in the "social" contexts analyzed in empirical portions of this study than in the "legal" contexts of the various states.

The analytical basis for this discussion has been that the conceptual model represents a particular "system" functioning within a given "environment." For an elaboration of the concepts of "system" and "environment," see Hall and Fagen (1968). It is felt the model assists in the cognitive process of identifying and tracing the nature of the relationships among the variables abstracted from this subsystem of the total educational system. Further, the use of a systems approach and an "open" rather than "closed" model is considered to have more utility to the researcher and practitioner than a simplified static approach.

The remaining discussion will be concerned with the empirical dimensions of the study.

Research Design

The universe for this study comprised all counselors and classroom teachers at eight secondary public schools in three school systems within the Seattle metropolitan area. The eight schools represented a spectrum from lower to upper socioeconomic student backgrounds. The sample population specifically excluded full-time administrative personnel.

After approval of the study was obtained from the administrative cores in the three school systems, copies of the research proposal were distributed to the leaders of each of the four organizations representing the teachers. The teachers in one school system were represented by affiliates of both NEA and AFT. Teachers in the other two systems were represented exclusively by affiliates of NEA.

The leaders were told they had the right and power to veto the study since their members were directly involved and the subject being studied concerned their relationships to the administrative cores. Open and full support was sought from these leaders, since they could informally destroy the relevance of the study by simply requesting their members not to cooperate or, at a minimum, by creating hostility among some teachers toward the study. The positive support of these leaders was considered critical since teacher participation in completing the instruments was anonymous and voluntary. The leadership of all four teacher organizations approved the study. They also were willing to have the researcher express their support of the study to the teachers when he appeared at faculty meetings to explain the study and distribute the research instruments. The instruments were returned at the teachers' convenience in self-addressed stamped envelopes.

The rationale for limiting the study to secondary schools, and thereby eliminating representation of elementary and junior-high teachers, represents a subjective balancing of goals. A male and female balance in the sample population was desired to facilitate testing the differences in the behavioral variables vis-à-vis sex. Some of these differences will be reported under the findings. The sex dimension is considered to have relevance because of the possibilities that males may experience more "relative deprivation" than females and may be an influence on female teachers' changing attitudes with respect to negotiations. Limiting the study to secondary teachers was also based on the following factors:

1. There is less turnover with secondary teachers than junior-high or elementary teachers. There are two possible implications to this finding.

In a macro sense, there may be a stronger identification of secondary teachers with their roles and the concern with the long-run impact of possible changes in their role relationships. Second, it was desired to minimize the proportion of newer teachers among respondents since there was a stronger likelihood that they may be undergoing a process of attitude formation with respect to the variables being investigated.

2. Secondary teachers, as a whole, tend to have a higher level of formal education than elementary teachers. The assumption is that the level of formal education is a significant criterion in the development of professionalism, which is one of the intervening variables in the model. Thus, the level and diversity of professional role conceptions was assumed, a priori, to be greater with secondary teachers than with other groups.

3. Secondary teachers tend to be somewhat more diverse by virtue of their greater specialization, relative to elementary teachers (Clark 1964).

Several limitations with respect to the sample design need to be made. The findings of this study cannot be assumed to be representative of all secondary teachers in the United States or even in the Seattle area. For, as Chein (1959, p. 514) has stated:

In nonprobability sampling, there is no way of estimating the probability that each element has of being included in the sample, and no assurance that every element has some chance of being included.

Also, the exclusion of elementary and junior-high teachers from the sample population may limit the applicability of the findings. But the research questions being investigated were of particular relevance to those segments of the teaching profession which may be "pattern setters." Thus, the exclusion of elementary teachers is not judged to be especially damaging; whereas the exclusion of junior-high teachers, who may experience the greatest amount of frustration in teaching, suggests the need for replication with this segment of teachers.*

In evaluating the choices and consequences with respect to the alternative samples, the researchers opted for in-depth study of eight schools at the secondary level among three school systems.

The research instruments provided measurements on the following four variables in the conceptual model: satisfaction (variable 1), professionalism (variable 2), socioeconomic factors (variable 3), and collective negotiations (variable 4). The research instruments were distributed at faculty meetings at the schools during October and November 1968.†

The Purdue Teacher Opinionnaire (Bentley and Rempel 1967) was utilized to determine the general level of satisfaction, as well as provide scores on ten dimensions to satisfaction. The professional role concept perceived by the respondents was measured by the Teacher Orientation Survey.‡ The four role segments which comprise the professional scale are (a) orientation to students, (b) orientation to the profession and professional colleagues, (c) belief that competence is based on knowledge, and (d) belief that teachers should have

---

*This point was suggested to the authors by a reader of an earlier draft of this article, who stated "This [frustration] is in part due to the fact that the particular age level is most difficult to teach and handle, and secondly, because junior-high teachers who are nearly all certified to teach in the senior-high school are very often resentful of the fact that they have not been 'promoted' to their proper social and intellectual station." Of course, this reasoning lends further credibility to the model and research design, while noting the limitation in the sample.

†The teachers who were not at the faculty meetings were given the instruments in self-addressed return envelopes by their principals. In no instance did the number of absent teachers exceed 12; the most typical figure was about 6.

‡This instrument is a slight modification of a scale developed by Corwin. See Corwin (1966, pp. 466-69).

decision-making authority. The General Information Questionnaire was utilized to identify the socioeconomic characteristics of the respondents such as sex, income, marital status, age, teaching experience, formal education, organizational affiliation, discipline taught, etc.

The Collective Negotiations Survey was developed to determine the respondents' attitudes with respect to several dimensions of collective negotiations. The scales in this instrument included (a) support of broad scope to negotiations, (b) support of arbitration of disputes, (c) support of teacher strikes, (d) perceived similarity between NEA and AFT organizational goals, (e) teachers' perceptions of school boards' support of collective negotiations, (f) support of teacher penalties for striking, and (g) other items. The instrument was developed by recording on cards normative statements regarding collective negotiations made in articles, speeches, and books by academicians, school board members, superintendents, leaders of various teacher associations, and other public officials. The three hundred statements obtained were then classified according to their apparent content or meaning. The statements included within each of these classifications were compared, rewritten, and reduced in number. The criteria for revising or eliminating statements were redundancy between statements, the assessed degree of ambiguity in a statement, the extent to which statements about a phenomenon might be widely interpreted as a question of fact, and the extent of conflict between groups over ideas expressed in the statements. A number of other criteria, generally considered acceptable in the construction of attitude scales, were used in the development of the scales (Edwards 1957, pp. 13-14).

Findings: Descriptive Dimensions

The findings are based on usable returns from 335 secondary teachers, including 193 males and 142 females. The 335 returns represent about 55 percent of the 612 research instruments distributed. The most responsive school had a return rate of 67 percent, while the least responsive school had a return rate of 44 percent.

An analysis of the data from the thirteen socioeconomic characteristics warrants the conclusion that the respondents were a highly diverse group. This diversity tends to remain even when the respondents are classified by school. The major difference in the socio-economic characteristics among schools appears to be that 42 of the 47 responding AFT members are found in only two schools.

The first set of attitudinal clusters to be reviewed are the ten satisfaction subscales plus the general satisfaction rating. The mean levels and standard deviations for the 335 respondents are presented for each subscale in descending order in table 1. Satisfaction with

Table 1
Mean Levels of Satisfaction for All Respondent Teachers in Descending Order by Satisfaction Factor

Satisfaction factor	All respondents N = 335	
	$\overline{X}$	s
Satisfaction with teaching	3.4433	.4033
Community pressures	3.4184	.4308
Rapport among teachers	3.0976	.5254
Overall satisfaction	3.0375	.3739
Teacher load	3.0254	.5267
Teacher rapport with principal	2.9833	.6791
Community support of education	2.8887	.7047
Curriculum issues	2.7833	.7703
School facilities and services	2.7393	.7784
Teacher status	2.6860	.6682
Teacher salary	2.5042	.6704

Note: The categories are weighted in the following manner: a score of 4.0 indicates "agree" with satisfaction statements, a score of 3.0 indicates "probably agree," a score of 2.0 indicates "probably disagree," a score of 1.0 indicates "disagree." Thus, the higher the mean score the higher the mean level of satisfaction and vice versa.

teaching ($\overline{X}$ = 3.44) is the factor with the favorable and "high" satisfaction rating. By school, the rating on this factor is consistently favorable, varying between a mean of 3.62 and 3.29. Thus, the respondents at all eight schools like to teach, feel competent, and enjoy students. Another major finding is the relative dissatisfaction with both teacher status ($\overline{X}$ = 2.686) and teacher salary ($\overline{X}$ = 2.5042). These factors are defined as follows:

"Teacher Status" samples feelings about the prestige, security, and benefits afforded by teaching. Several of the items refer to the extent to which the teacher feels he is an accepted member of the community.

"Teacher Salary" pertains primarily to the teacher's feelings about salaries and salary policies. Are salaries based on teacher competency? Do they compare favorably with salaries in other school systems? Are salary policies administered fairly and justly, and do teachers participate in the development of these policies? (Bentley and Rempel 1967, p. 4)

The satisfaction with status factor varies by school from mildly negative ($\overline{X}$ = 2.8845) to negative ($\overline{X}$ = 2.3967). The mean level of satisfaction with teacher salary ($\overline{X}$ = 2.5042) was negative and the lowest compared to the other ten factors. This low and negative mean level was found in all eight schools, with variations in means by school between 2.6872 and 2.1135. Summarizing, the respondent teachers are relatively satisfied with the role of teaching, while they are somewhat dissatisfied with the status and economic rewards available in the role. The literature is generally consistent with this finding.

The third major finding is that one school ranked as highest on six of the satisfaction factors, whereas another school ranked lowest on eight of the factors.* This may represent, to some degree, an operational manifestation of the concept of an organization as a system wherein the parts or dimensions of the system are continuously reinforcing one another. For example, in the "high" ranking school, the writers found a high income and educational level of parents of the students, whereas in the lowest ranking school just the opposite—with further problems of racial integration—was found.

Least Variation on Professionalism

Of the three attitudinal scales administered, professionalism provided the least amount of variation by school in terms of mean levels (and standard deviations). This is not a particularly surprising finding, since the respondents are relatively comparable to one another in terms of age, sex, formal education level, income, etc. The mean response for all respondents on the professionalism scale† was

---

*The "low" satisfaction school was located in the central area of Seattle, serving a sizeable minority group of students from the lower socioeconomic strata.

†The categories are weighted in the following manner: a score of 5.0 indicates "strongly agree" with the statements used to measure "professional role orientation," a score of 4.0 indicates "probably agree," a score of 3.0 indicates

3.64 (s = .4216), which is in the "positive" direction of the scale toward professional role orientation. Although the mean levels tend to indicate an orientation toward professional values, they do not warrant the conclusion that respondents articulate overwhelmingly strong sentiments toward these values.

Data on teachers' attitudes toward various dimensions of collective negotiations are provided in table 2.

Table 2
Mean Levels of Attitudes Toward Collective Negotiations in Descending Order of Negotiation Factors for All Respondent Teachers

	All respondents N = 335	
Negotiation factor	$\overline{X}$	s
Support of broad scope to negotiations	4.3149	.6690
Support of arbitration of disputes	3.6786	.5904
Support of teacher strikes	3.3512	.9538
Perceived similarity between NEA and AFT	2.9167	.9022
Teacher perceptions of school boards' support of collective negotiations	2.7374	.8678
Support of teacher penalties for striking	1.8584	.7925

Note: The response categories are weighted in the following manner: a score of 5.0 indicates "strongly agree," a score of 4.0 indicates "agree," a score of 3.0 indicates "undecided," a score of 2.0 indicates "disagree," and a score of 1.0 indicates "strongly disagree." Thus, the higher the score the greater mean "agreement" with the subscale.

With a mean of 4.31 for support of a broad scope for collective negotiations, it is evident most teachers are desirous of including within the negotiation process many of the dimensions of their relationships with the administrations. This subscale is constructed from statements which attempt to determine the extent to which the respondents felt the following areas should be included in the negotiation process: wages, working conditions, teacher responsibilities, procedures of appeal, and curriculum issues. At present, many adminis-

"undecided," a score of 2.0 indicates "disagree," and a score of 1.0 indicates "strongly disagree." Thus, the higher the mean score the higher the mean level of professional role orientation of the teachers.

trations and/or school boards are concerned with limiting the scope of negotiations. Thus, a source of conflict between the parties may be the types of issues subject to negotiation in addition to conflicts over the issues per se.

There are generally supportive sentiments for use of neutral third-party arbitrators in disputes which do not appear to be subject to solution by other processes. A mean level of support for arbitration of 3.62 indicates the intensity of feeling is not quite as great as with the desired scope for negotiations. At a minimum, teachers are accepting the idea of introducing an alternate decision mechanism which might be used on a limited basis. The difference in means between the "high" school and the "low" school on this factor is minor.

The mean support of teacher strikes of 3.35 is greater than expected considering the traditional antipathy most teachers have expressed toward the strike. However, the standard deviation of 0.90 for the mean indicates the dispersion or spread of attitudes on this factor is greater than for any other negotiation factor. The "high" school on this factor has a mean of 3.76 versus 3.11 for the "low" school, revealing a considerable difference by respondents between schools. The data tends to support the conclusion that a considerable range of attitudes exists among teachers with respect to the strike issue. The possible relationship of the socioeconomic characteristics of respondent teachers in relation to their attitudes toward the strike issue will be explored later.

Ironically, the mean level of perceived similarity between NEA and AFT was greatest in the school which had twenty-three respondents with membership in the AFT and thirty respondents with membership in NEA. In contrast, the school which had the lowest mean level of perceived similarity ($\overline{X} = 2.58$) between NEA and AFT had no respondents from AFT; thus, a stereotype situation may have developed. Conversely, the respondents from the school with members in both organizations perceived fewer differences in one another —this may be the result of daily interaction which leads to more "valid" data about each other.

The factor with the greatest variation in mean attitudes between schools is the teachers' perceptions of the degree to which they think their school board accepts the process of collective negotiations. The mean attitudes range from the evaluation of the school board as being mildly acceptant of the negotiation process at the "high" school ($\overline{X}$ = 3.26) to one of definite disagreement with the process at the "low" school ($\overline{X}$ = 1.99).

As expected, the respondents generally disagreed with penalizing teachers for engaging in strikes. For all respondents, a low mean of 1.86 was obtained, with a variation among schools from 2.26 to 1.62.

Findings: Analytical Dimensions

This section will discuss some of the significant relationships found among the previously described variables.

A dimension to the data which might be worth exploring is the relationship between support of teacher strikes and various satisfaction factors. It is assumed that the strike question continues to be a highly emotional issue; it is also assumed the ideology of the strike is more likely to be accepted by teachers under conditions of perceived dissatisfaction or frustration.

The results of testing this relationship through all the satisfaction factors for the 335 respondents are reported in table 3.

Table 3
Degree of Correlation in Descending Order between Satisfaction Factors and Support of Teacher Strikes by Respondent Teachers

Satisfaction factors	Correlation between satisfaction factors and support of teacher strikes
Teacher salary	−.3639
Teacher status	−.3073*
Overall satisfaction	−.2702*
Community support of education	−.1903*
Curriculum issues	−.1898*
Teacher load	−.1661*
School facilities and services	−.1643*
Teacher rapport with principal	−.1614*
Satisfaction with teaching	−.1052†
Community pressures	−.1005†
Rapport among teachers	−.0689†

Note: No star indicates correlation significant at .001 level or better. *Indicates correlation significant at .01 level or better. †Indicates correlation is *not* significant at .05 level or better.

There is a statistically significant relationship between eight of the satisfaction factors and support of teacher strikes. As expected, the direction of relationship between the variables is negative. The degree of negative correlation, at the .001 level of significance, is greatest (−.3639) between satisfaction with teacher salary and support of teacher strikes. By school, the power of this negative relationship tends to remain, and in one school increases to −.5145 (with a .001 level of significance). The second most powerful relationship is between satisfaction with status and support of teacher strikes. The correlation for all respondents is −.3073 (with a significance level of .01). Two schools have high negative correlation coefficients of −.4952 (.001 level) followed by −.4147 (.05 level). The coefficients for the remaining six sets of statistically significant relationships decline fairly rapidly to a low of −.1614 (.01 level).

In brief, the strongest negative relationships are found between salary and status and support of teachers strikes. The power of the relationships, although statistically significant, is weaker between overall satisfaction, teacher rapport with principal, teacher load curriculum issues, community support of education, and school facilities and services *and* teacher support of strikes.

Corwin (1965a) and others (see Kleingartner 1967) claim the drive to professionalism is a militant process. If this assumption is valid, those with a greater professional role orientation may express stronger and more favorable sentiments toward various dimensions of collective negotiations. On the other hand, the traditional ideology in the education field has been that professionalism and collective negotiations, particularly the strike, are inconsistent with one another.

A test of the data reveals a significant (.01 level) but low correlation (.2073) between professional role conception and support of teacher strikes by males (N = 192), while there is virtually no correlation for females (N = 143). Although this correlation indicates only a small amount of the variation in professional role conception is associated with variations in the support of teacher strikes, it is considered a relevant finding on the basis of three factors. First, the proposition in the literature, with few exceptions, is that those who are professionally oriented would not and/or should not support strikes. Second, there is a slight differential pattern between these two variables when evaluated on the basis of sex. Third, the general assumption that professional role conception and support of teacher strikes are incompatible is not confirmed. There is no evidence indicating professional role conception is antithetical to support of teacher strikes. In turn, there are no data indicating they are strongly and positively associated.

Statistically significant (.01 level) results were also obtained between professionalism and the negotiation subscales of support of binding arbitration (.2176) and support of broad scope for negotiations (.1700). Again, the correlations are quite low, thereby explaining a little of the variation, but the positive direction of the correlations is as posited.

In sum, the correlations between professionalism and the negotiation subscales provide mixed results. The negotiation factors and professional role conception are associated by low correlations, but it is considered significant that the general proposition which assumes support of strikes and professionalism as being incompatible is not confirmed. Further, the associations between these variables vary somewhat by sex. For males there is a statistically significant and positive association between the two variables.

Relationship Between Support of Strike
and Age, Sex, and Affiliation

The last major domain to be investigated concerns the relationship between the support of teacher strike scale* and selected socioeconomic factors (variable 3 in the conceptual model). The three sets of comparisons presented in table 4 were all significant at the .001 level.

The data confirms the assumption that males might be somewhat more predisposed toward strikes than females. Unfortunately, the findings do not provide their own explanation; several reasons may be given. For instance, this may be the result of different cultural socialization, wherein certain forms of aggressiveness by males tend to be more acceptable than for females. Or this finding may be a consequence of males experiencing greater frustration with respect to the available rewards, particularly economic ones. Another possibility is that males may perceive themselves as being more deprived in social status than are females, with the current manifestation being

---

*This is the most "controversial" of the negotiation scales.

Table 4
Support of Teacher Strikes by Sets of Socioeconomic Factors

Socioeconomic factors	Support of teacher strikes		
	N	X̄	s
Males	193	3.5322	0.8591
Females	142	3.1087	1.0251
"Younger" teachers (40 or under)	183	3.5183	0.9048
"Older" teachers (50 or over)	75	3.0553	0.9663
NEA members	255	3.2762	0.9585
AFT members	47	3.7933	0.7469

Note: Differences are significant at the .001 level or better. The significance levels are based on the F value.

increased militancy. Of course, these "explanations" are only illustrative of others to which one might appeal. The younger teachers (under forty) had a mean level of support of teacher strikes of about 3.52, whereas this figure declined to approximately 3.06 for the older teachers (over fifty). This finding is of the form anticipated, because it is assumed, for the most part, the older teachers have worked many years in a social milieu in which the strike was anathema. Further, older teachers may be more adjusted or adapted to their environment and therefore may be less favorably responsive to the strike issue. However, these explanations are only generalities and may be quite irrelevant in specific situations and when combinations of variables are considered. For instance, the support of teacher strikes by the only four older male respondents from one school was a high mean of about 4.29.

The last set of relationships to be tested in this section concerns possible variations in support of teacher strikes on the basis of organizational affiliation. The AFT traditionally has represented a more militant or aggressive posture in its relations to various school administrations than has NEA. One manifestation of this militancy is assumed to be the ideological support of teacher strikes. Recently, the position of NEA (or at least some of its organizational units) on this tactic has altered, but AFT continues to be viewed as being more acceptant of the strike than NEA. Thus, it is assumed that teachers who are members of AFT will be supportive of teacher strikes. The further assumption is that teachers opposed to teacher strikes would tend not to join AFT because of the conflict it might create between personal and organizational values. The findings reveal a statistically significant difference (at the .001 level) in support of teacher strikes between the respondents based on their organizational affiliation. The mean level of support of teacher strikes is 3.28 for the 225 NEA respondents versus 3.79 for the 47 AFT respondents. But at two schools, the support of teacher strikes by NEA respondents is virtually as high as for AFT respondents.

Conclusion

For the most part, the model has been useful for conceptualizing and providing an understanding of the "internal" and "external" factors related to the various dimensions of collective negotiations. Some confirmation of this conclusion is provided by the insights acquired through the literature and by the knowledge generated through the empirical dimensions of this study. Some of the variables included in the empirical study revealed more substantial degrees of association with the negotiation factors than other variables. In brief, the model met its purpose of providing a framework of understanding, which was partially tested on an empirical plane.

A degree of speculation can be made with respect to the relationships between the theoretical assumptions and the empirical findings. First, the finding that lower levels of satisfaction with salary and status are significantly associated with several of the negotiation factors may indicate that some teachers perceive this process as a means of increasing their rewards, thereby leading to a reduction in their frustrations. Of course, these findings may contain necessary but not sufficient conditions for negotiations to be incorporated as a strategy of decision making by teachers. This is suggested through some deductive reasoning. Studies have shown that for years teachers were expressing dissatisfaction with their salary and social status, among other factors. But nothing happened! It is interesting to hypothesize that two shifts in the elements of the system were necessary for the emergence of negotiations. First, teachers had to reconcile themselves to the idea that collective negotiations were both a legitimate process and a potentially effective one for reducing their sources of dissatisfaction. Second, the officials of teacher organizations had to generate leadership and the philosophical conviction that this process could be functional for themselves, their members, and the educational system. Thus, with respect to the emergence of collective negotiations, other important variables may be shifts in leadership styles and in the goals of teacher organizations.

The positive, although mild, degree of association between support of teacher strikes and other negotiation factors with higher levels of professional role conception indicates a possible related effect with the sources of dissatisfaction. Thus, collective negotiations may be perceived by some respondents as a means of attaining professional goals such as participation in decision making and some control over task accomplishment. Support for this possibility also has been revealed in the literature which indicates that the drive toward professionalism for occupational groups may involve a degree of militancy as members attempt to change their traditional role relationships.

The third major conclusion is the possibility that some of the militancy expressed by certain respondents is a consequence of their perception of school board members as being hostile toward the process of negotiations per se. Therefore, the ability to resolve specific issues may be compounded by the distrust or lack of acceptance which one or both parties have toward the other.

References

Alexis, Marcus, and Wilson, Charles Z. *Organizational Decision Making.* Englewood Cliffs, N.J.: Prentice-Hall, 1967.

Allen, James E., Jr. "Interest and Role of the State Education Department (of New York) with Respect to Employer and Employee Relations." *Employer-Employee Relations in the Public Schools,* edited by Robert E. Doherty. Ithaca, N.Y.: New York State School of Industrial and Labor Relations, Cornell University, 1967.

Belasco, James A., and Alutto, Joseph A. "Organizational Impacts of Teacher Negotiations." *Industrial Relations* 9, no. 1 (October 1969): 67-79.

Bentley, Ralph R., and Rempel, Averno M. *The Purdue Teacher Opinionnaire.* West Lafayette, Ind.: Purdue Research Foundation, 1967.

Blau, Peter M. *Exchange and Power in Social Life.* New York: John Wiley & Sons, 1964.

Brown, George A. "Teacher Power Techniques." *American School Board Journal* 152, no. 2 (February 1966): 12.

Chein, Isidor. "An Introduction to Sampling." *Research Methods in Social Rela-*

tions, edited by Claire Sellitz et al. New York: Holt, Rinehart & Winston, 1959.

Clark, Burton R. "Sociology of Education." *Handbook of Modern Sociology,* edited by Robert E. L. Faris. Chicago: Rand McNally, 1964.

Cole, S. "Teachers' Strike: A Study of the Conversion of Predisposition into Action." *American Journal of Sociology* 14, no. 5 (March 1969): 506-20.

Corwin, Ronald G. "Militant Professionalism, Initiative and Compliance in Public Education." *Sociology of Education* 28, no. 4 (Summer 1965a): 310-31.

Corwin, Ronald G. "Professional Persons in Public Organizations." *Educational Administration Quarterly* 1, no. 3 (Autumn 1965b): 4-5.

Corwin, Ronald G. *Staff Conflicts in the Public Schools.* Columbus, Ohio: Department of Sociology and Anthropology, Ohio State University, 1966.

Dashiell, Dick. "Teachers Revolt in Michigan." *Phi Delta Kappan* 49, no. 1 (September 1967): 20-26.

Edwards, Alan L. *Techniques of Attitude Scale Construction.* New York: Appleton-Century-Crofts, 1957.

Elam, Stanley. "The NEA-AFT Rivalry." *Phi Delta Kappan* 46, no. 1 (September 1964): 12-15.

Glass, Ronald W. "Work Stoppages and Teachers: History and Prospect." *Monthly Labor Review* 90, no. 8 (April 1967): 43.

Hall, A. D., and Fagen, R. E. "Definition of System." *Modern Systems Research for the Behavioral Scientist,* edited by Walter Buckley. Chicago: Aldine, 1968.

Hellriegel, Don. "Collective Negotiations and Teachers: A Behavioral Analysis." D.B.A. dissertation, University of Washington, 1969.

Hill, Winston W., and French, Wendell L. "Perception of the Power of Department Chairmen by Professors." *Administrative Science Quarterly* 11, no. 4 (March 1967): 552.

Horvat, John J. "The Nature of Teacher Power and Teacher Attitudes Toward Certain Aspects of This Power." *Theory into Practice* 7, no. 2 (April 1968): 53-54.

Jackson, E. F. "Status Consistency and Symptoms of Stress." *American Sociological Review* 27, no. 4 (August 1962): 469-80.

Kleingartner, Archie. *Professionalism and Salaried Worker Organization.* Madison, Wis.: Industrial Relations Institute, University of Wisconsin, 1967.

Lieberman, Myron. "Collective Negotiations: Status and Trends." *American School Board Journal* 155, no. 4 (October 1967): 8-9.

Moskow, Michael H. *Teachers and Unions.* Philadelphia: Wharton School of Finance and Commerce, University of Pennsylvania, 1966.

Muir, Douglas. "The Strike as a Professional Sanction: The Changing Attitude of the National Education Association." *Labor Law Journal* 19, no. 10 (October 1968): 627.

National Education Association. "Comparison of 1966-67 and 1967-68 Negotiation Survey Data." *Negotiation Research Digest* (June 1968).

"NEA Briefs Teachers for War on School Boards; Administrators Get a Reprieve." *American School Board Journal* 156, no. 2 (August 1968): 26.

Neirynck, Robert W. "Teachers' Strikes: A New Militancy." *Labor Law Journal* 19, no. 5 (May 1968): 293.

Porter, Lyman W., and Lawler, Edward E. *Managerial Attitudes and Performance.* Homewood, Ill.: Richard D. Irwin, 1968.

Schmidt, Charles T., Jr. "Representation of Classroom Teachers." *Monthly Labor Review* 91, no. 7 (July 1968): 27-36.

Shils, Edward B., and Whittier, C. Taylor. *Teachers, Administrators, and Collective Bargaining.* New York: Thomas Y. Crowell, 1968.

Smith, Russell A., and McLaughlin, Davis. "Public Employment: A Neglected Area of Research and Training in Labor Relations." *Industrial and Labor Relations Review* 16, no. 1 (October 1962): 30-44.

Stieber, Jack. "Collective Bargaining in the Public Sector." *Challenges to Collective Bargaining,* edited by Lloyd Ulman. Englewood Cliffs, N.J.: Prentice-Hall, 1967.

Taffel, Alexander. "The Principal and Teacher—School Board Negotiations." *The Bulletin of the National Association of Secondary Principals* 52, no. 329 (September 1968): 72.

Zaleznik, Abraham, and Moment, David. *The Dynamics of Interpersonal Behavior.* New York: John Wiley & Sons, 1964.

Reading 12

Comment on "Collective Negotiations and Teachers"

William J. Moore

In reading 11, Don Hellriegel, Wendell French, and Richard B. Peterson presented a conceptual model for the purpose "of identifying and portraying the assumed relationships among the key variables considered to provide the behavioral framework of teachers vis-à-vis collective negotiations." Furthermore, the authors claimed to have partially tested their model on an empirical plane. In this writer's opinion, however, their model is deficient in a number of respects and their empirical analysis simply confirmed what everybody in the field of industrial relations already knows, "that worker dissatisfaction is a necessary, but not sufficient condition for collective action." See Husaini and Geschwender (1968); Stagner (1956); Seidman, London, Karsh, and Tagliacozzo (1958); Mills (1956); and Bakke (1945).

Although the authors' model has added to our understanding of the form or degree of the interrelationships among a number of factors related to teachers' attitudes toward collective negotiations, several important variables were omitted which influence teachers'

Reprinted by permission from *Industrial and Labor Relations Review* 24, no. 2 (January 1971), pp. 249-64. Copyright 1971 by Cornell University.

willingness to engage in collective negotiations. Specifically, in their discussion of "socioeconomic factors" the authors limited themselves to the following five variables: sex, marital status, teaching experience, educational level, and income. Conspicuously omitted from their analysis was the social and economic background of teachers, especially information as to whether the teachers' fathers were blue-collar or union workers. This should have been included in the model, since this factor has long been cited as an important element influencing a worker's decision to join a union or engage in collective action. In this regard see Seidman, London, and Karsh (1951); Husaini and Geschwender (1968); Bakke (1945); and Mills (1956). Moreover, this factor already has been shown to play an important role in teachers' decisions to affiliate with organized labor. Browder reported in 1965 that 64.3 percent of the fathers of members of American Federation of Teachers (AFT) had not completed high school and that only 10.9 percent had completed college. In addition, 58.2 percent of the members had fathers who were blue-collar workers.

Another factor missing in the model was whether the teacher was raised in a rural or urban area. Browder (1965) noted that 52.7 percent of AFT members had been raised in the city, 20.5 percent in small towns, 14.4 percent in the country, and 12.3 percent in the suburbs. This is not too surprising when one remembers that farmers and rural residents are known to share a strong antilabor bias which they impart to their children. See Gallup Poll (1946); Doherty and Oberer (1967); and Zeigler (1967).

In addition to omitting these two important variables, it appears that Hellriegel, French, and Peterson erred when they stated "these characteristics [socioeconomic factors] are not of a particular explanatory value in themselves but rather serve as operational criteria for evaluating the relevance of other behavioral dimensions." Available evidence suggests that at least three of the "socioeconomic factors"—sex, teaching experience, and educational level—discussed by the authors have influenced teachers' decisions to join unions or other organizations which engage in collective bargaining. According to Browder (1965) and Lowe (1965), the typical AFT member in the mid-1960s was a male secondary teacher who had been teaching longer and had more formal education than most of his colleagues.

In 1965, almost half of the AFT membership consisted of men, whereas only 31 percent of the total teaching force was male. Even Hellriegel, French, and Peterson's empirical data suggest that "males might be somewhat more predisposed toward strikes than females." Whereas they suggest several reasons for this finding, they are hesitant to suggest any causal relationship between sex of teacher and attitude toward collective bargaining. They note the relationship could be due to either economic or social-cultural causes. In this writer's opinion, however, the factors causing men to join teacher unions and participate in militant collective action more frequently than women are primarily economic in nature. To begin with, the salaries of most women teachers represent second incomes for their families, while those of men are usually the only source of family income (Moskow 1966). Second, because of the widespread adoption of the single salary schedule since 1920, the sex differential in men and women teachers' salaries has been all but eliminated over the years. As a result, the teaching profession has become a far more attractive occupation for women than for men. In 1966, the median earnings of a male full-time civilian worker classified as a professional, technical, and kindred worker was $9,205; the figure for females classified in the same category was $5,779 (U.S. Bureau of the Census 1967). That same year the median income for public school teachers was $7,629 for men and $5,910 for women. These figures go a long way toward explaining the higher level of job dissatisfaction among men teachers.

The reasons why secondary teachers and teachers with higher educational attainment levels and more experience join the AFT and participate in collective action more frequently than other groups of teachers are less obvious and more complex. For one thing, secondary teachers usually are trained in specific subject areas which provides them with more marketable skills than elementary teachers, thus lessening their fear of reprisal from hostile school authorities and frequently increasing the inequity of their relative economic status. Available evidence indicates that although teachers are rewarded under the single salary schedule for advanced education and teaching experience, they are not as well compensated for these assets as are similar workers in other professions. In this regard see Kershaw and McKean (1962) and Wells (1967). Finally, the higher levels of education and teaching experience reported by AFT members, particularly secondary teachers, suggests a strong attachment to the profession, which is generally conducive to the development of collective action. As Dunlop (1948) has explained, one

necessary condition in the emergence of organization is the view of the employees that they should look forward to spending a substantial proportion of their lifetime as workmen. . . . It is also necessary that a substantial proportion in any given community look forward to remaining in the same or similar work community.

Thus, it is not surprising that unionization and collective action have greatest appeal today among those teachers most firmly committed to their occupation, that is, those teachers with the highest level of education and teaching experience.

For whatever reasons, recent studies conducted by the National Education Association (NEA Research Division 1961, 1967) clearly indicate that secondary teachers and teachers with advanced academic training and longer teaching experience are less satisfied with their jobs than are other groups of teachers. Although the evidence is by no means conclusive, there appear to be sufficient grounds for disputing Hellriegel, French, and Peterson's statement that teacher characteristics [socioeconomic factors] are not of a particular explanatory value in influencing teachers' interest in collective negotiations. On the basis of the findings cited above, one would expect for a given community the larger the proportion of male teachers and the more experienced and better trained the teaching force the greater the interest in collective action and negotiations is apt to be, other things equal. Significant changes in the composition of the nation's teaching force also could be expected to influence the growth and development of collective negotiations in the public schools.

Within their model the authors set forth three major external forces as generally having a reinforcing effect on collective negotiations: (1) the perception of other teachers' experiences with collective negotiations in other school systems across the country, (2) competition between the NEA and AFT, and (3) legislation. That these three factors have influenced teachers' propensity for collective negotiations cannot be doubted. However, my own study of the growth and development of teacher unions revealed there are several other community institutions which have stimulated or retarded the development of collective bargaining in the public schools (Moore 1969).

The support of organized labor in the community appears to

have been a strategic factor in the origin, growth, and development of teacher unions and collective bargaining in our nation's schools. From the beginning, teacher union membership and collective negotiations between teachers and school boards have tended to be concentrated in those cities and regions where organized labor has been particularly powerful and active (Moore 1969). In 1964, six states (New York, California, Pennsylvania, Illinois, Ohio, and Michigan) accounted for 55 percent of the nation's total union membership (U.S. Bureau of Labor Statistics 1965). These same six states accounted for roughly 80 percent of the total number of teachers covered by AFT affiliates in successful collective bargaining elections as of October 1967 (*American Teacher* 1967). Finally, it should be noted that AFT strength has been concentrated within these states in the large urban areas where organized labor traditionally has been strong. The cities of New York, Chicago, Philadelphia, Cleveland, Washington, Detroit, Baltimore, Pittsburgh, and others where teacher unions and collective bargaining have been most active and teacher work stoppages have occurred most frequently have long been recognized as centers of organized labor power.

There appear to be four major reasons for the close relationship between the strength of organized labor and the location of AFT membership. First, the ability of organized labor "to obtain concessions greatly enhances the potentialities of unionism [and collective negotiations] in the eyes of the unorganized" (Shister 1953). Second, close proximity to unions and union leaders tends to reduce teachers' antiunion attitude (Mills 1956). Third, fear of retaliation from school authorities who are opposed to teacher unions and collective negotiations usually is reduced if the teachers have the active support of a strong labor movement. A heavily unionized community generally represents a powerful political ally to developing teacher organizations. School board members are, by and large, elected officials who rarely can afford to incur the wrath of a strong labor movement. Teachers usually lack a sufficiently broad base for political success and do not have the leverage necessary to force recognition and bargaining demands from reluctant school boards. It is no accident that most of the favorable collective bargaining legislation affecting teachers has been passed in states which have relatively strong labor movements.

Although Hellriegel, French, and Peterson argue that "much of the legislation concerning collective negotiations passed in recent years appears to reflect the lobbying efforts of both school boards and teacher associations," the need for wider political support seems obvious. Whereas it is true that some sixteen states had passed laws dealing with collective negotiations and teachers as of 1968, most bargaining activity is concentrated in the ten states, listed in table 1,

Table 1
Union Membership for Selected States in 1964

State	Total (thousands)	Rank	Union membership As percent of employees in nonagricultural establishments	Rank
California	1,888	2	33.8	13
Connecticut	244	16	24.6	22
Massachusetts	572	8	29.1	19
Michigan	962	6	38.9	4
Minnesota	339	15	33.0	14
New York	2,507	1	39.4	3
Oregon	198	18	34.8	11
Rhode Island	89	30	29.6	18
Washington	367	13	43.1	1
Wisconsin	400	11	31.5	17

Source: U.S. Bureau of Labor Statistics, *Directory of National and International Labor Unions in the United States, 1965,* Bulletin no. 1493 (Washington, D.C.: U.S. Government Printing Office, 1965), p. 58.

which require school boards to engage in some form of negotiation, consultation, or discussion with their employees. The figures in the table indicate the relative and absolute strength of organized labor in each of the ten states in 1964. Each of the states having positive collective negotiation laws for public school teachers ranked among the twenty top states either in terms of total union membership and/or in terms of the percent of the nonagricultural work force organized. The fact that their study was based on an examination of secondary teachers in Seattle, Washington, a large urban area where labor has considerable strength,* may have caused Hellriegel, French, and Peterson to implicitly assume such conditions in their model. These

---

*As indicated in table 1, the state of Washington had the highest proportion of organized nonagricultural workers (43.1 percent) in 1964.

factors, however, should have been explicitly included in the external forces which influence teachers' perceptions of collective negotiations.

Finally, organized labor, desiring to use teachers as a breakthrough into mass organization of white-collar, professional, and public employee groups, has provided the AFT with the financial and organizational aid necessary to combat the more firmly established and powerful professional associations. This, in turn, has caused the education associations to take an increased interest in the economic welfare of teachers, thus greatly stimulating the drive for collective negotiation rights for teachers across the country.

For the above reasons, one would expect teacher unions and collective bargaining between teachers and school boards to flourish primarily in those communities where organized labor is strong. The pattern of the development of teacher unions, comprehensive collective bargaining legislation, and of collective bargaining activity among teachers adds credence to this thesis.

One other variable which needs to be added to the Hellriegel, French, and Peterson model as an external force is the significance of social movements as a conditioning agent for collective action. A number of writers have noted that organized labor in the United States has experienced rapid rates of growth in periods of fundamental unrest. See, for example, Dunlop (1948); Bernstein (1954); and Blum (1968). Teacher unions, originating relatively late in history, have been influenced by only three periods of social upheaval—women's rights movement of the early 1900s, the New Deal, and the recent civil rights movement.* The close correlation in time between the rise of the civil rights movement, the rapid increase in AFT membership, and the rapid expansion of collective bargaining and teacher militancy in the public schools appears to have been more than just a coincidence. The AFT, which had strong ties with this movement, including a substantial black minority within its membership, was greatly influenced by developments in the civil rights area. Furthermore, the wide acceptance of civil disobedience as an appropriate means for challenging social wrongs created a major change in na-

---

*For a discussion of the impact of these movements on the growth and development of teacher unions and collective bargaining in the schools see Moore (1969).

tional views which was reflected in teacher attitudes. Having considered some factors omitted in the author's model, it is time to examine their findings.

Hellriegel, French, and Peterson claim their "model met its purpose of providing a framework of understanding, which was partially tested on an empirical plane." In this writer's opinion, the authors set forth a model which partially explains teachers' perceptions toward collective negotiations but one which they failed to test empirically. The authors' finding that significant negative correlations exist between levels of satisfaction, particularly with regard to salary and teacher status, and several negotiation factors is not conclusive proof of the validity of their model. The consensus in the literature has long regarded favorable attitudes toward unionism and collective action as a function of job dissatisfaction, which may be with the job as a whole, specific job factors, and/or various sociocultural conditions. See Husaini and Geschwender (1968); Stagner (1956); Seidman, London, Karsh, and Tagliacozzo (1958); Mills (1956); and Bakke (1945). Hellriegel, French, and Peterson conceded that low levels of satisfaction "may contain necessary but not sufficient conditions for negotiations to be incorporated as a strategy of decision making by teachers." They went on to note "studies have shown that for years teachers were expressing dissatisfaction with their salary and social status, among other factors. But nothing happened." At this stage the authors hypothesized that two shifts in the elements of the system were necessary for the recent emergence of negotiations.

First, teachers had to reconcile themselves to the idea that collective negotiations were both a legitimate process and a potentially effective one for reducing their sources of dissatisfaction. Second, the officials of teacher organizations had to generate leadership and the philosophical conviction that this process could be functional for themselves, their members, and the educational system.

Without attempting to explain how or why these two necessary shifts came about, the authors lamely conclude, "Thus, with respect to the emergence of collective negotiations, other important variables may be shifts in leadership styles and in the goals of teacher organizations." Neither of these two variables is explicitly included in their model.

It appears other variables need to be added to their model before a reasonable explanation can be given for the recent growth in teacher collective negotiations; many of these have been suggested above. In this writer's opinion, there were four major causes of recent growth of teacher unions and collective negotiations in the public schools.

1. *Economic forces.* Between 1960 and 1967 the average annual income of teachers rose from $5,275 to $7,296 or 4.5 percent per year. The deflated "real" income of teachers increased from $5,116 to $6,283 during this same period. This represents a 3.1 percent average annual increase. Although this sounds favorable, the truth of the matter is that the average annual gains in teachers' real and money incomes were considerably smaller in the 1960s than in the period from 1947 to 1960.* Also, perhaps more important, the average real income paid teachers in eighteen of the nation's largest cities (including Seattle, by the way) declined between 1958 and 1966.† It was in these same cities that the AFT reported the greatest gains in membership during the period and the greatest number of teachers were involved in collective negotiations. These findings suggest that certain groups of teachers were operating under increasing economic hardships during the period—thus explaining at least part of the recent interest in collective negotiations.

2. *Favorable governmental policy.* In the 1960s the federal government and a number of state governments adopted policies favorable to the expansion of public employee unions. In 1962, President Kennedy issued Executive Order 10988, which directed agencies of the federal government to recognize and meet and confer with employee organizations. Following the issuance of this order, there occurred a sharp increase in public union membership and interest in collective bargaining at all levels of government. Meanwhile, the state of Wisconsin passed a law in 1959, amended in 1962, which permitted public employees—including teachers—to bargain collectively with their employers. As noted earlier, some sixteen states by the end of 1968 had passed permissive legislation concern-

---

*Conclusions based on data presented in the following sources: National Education Association (1967); Comer (1965); and Sackley (1966).

†This finding was arrived at by deflating the average salaries paid teachers in these cities by city workers budget data published by the Bureau of Labor Statistics. For a complete discussion of this analysis and its limitations, see Moore (1969).

ing teachers and collective negotiations, and most other state legislatures are currently under pressure from teacher organizations to enact similar legislation. The passage of such legislation has led to an expansion of teacher union membership and the level of collective negotiations.

3. *Support of organized labor.* Although total union membership in the United States has been declining both in absolute numbers and as a percentage of the labor force, organized labor has been increasing its level of aid to the AFT. From 1961 to 1968, labor gave the AFT and its affiliates more than $1.2 million in gifts and loans to help organize teachers (Moore 1969). The reason for the increased interest of organized labor in the development of teacher unions was summed up by Nicholas Zonarich, organizing director of the Industrial Union Department, at the 1964 AFT convention as follows:

... technology is seriously eroding the blue-collar manufacturing base of the labor movement. To survive, the movement must change its direction. It needs white-collar and professional unions, such as teachers, just as much as the AFT needs the labor movements' resources and organizing experience. (Lunden 1964)

With the financial aid of organized labor, the AFT has been able to compete effectively with the NEA in organizing teachers, at least in the large urban centers of the country. The widely publicized successes of these organizations in collective bargaining have greatly stimulated the interest of teachers across the country in collective negotiation.

4. *Social forces.* The civil rights movement has brought a number of community values and institutions under attack. The fairness of many of the protestors' demands led to a widespread acceptance of civil disobedience as an appropriate means for challenging social injustice. Teacher unions and teachers in general were greatly influenced by developments within this movement. Under the leadership of Charles Cogen, the AFT adopted increasingly militant tactics which were highly successful. In the absence of the civil rights movement, it is unlikely the AFT tactics would have been as successful and as widely accepted. Available evidence indicates that contrary to earlier periods a majority of the nation's teachers now believe it is proper for them to strike for economic gain (Teacher Opinion Poll 1966).

In summary, the addition of several important variables to Hell-riegel, French, and Peterson's model in the areas of "socioeconomic factors" and "external factors" is required for that model to provide an adequate explanation for the pattern of the growth and develop-ment of collective bargaining in the public schools in recent years. The rapidly deteriorating economic status of teachers, particularly in our large urban areas; widespread enactment and agitation for favor-able collective bargaining legislation; increased financial and organiza-tional support from organized labor; the impact of the civil rights movement on the attitudes of teachers and the public toward civil disobedience; and a change in the composition of the nation's teach-ing force in the direction of increasing percentages of men, secondary teachers, and number of teachers concentrated in large urban areas all have had a significant influence on the drive to obtain collective bargaining rights for teachers in the 1960s.

Hellriegel, French, and Peterson suggested "additional research may indicate that other variables need to be included or that the hypothesized relationships among the variables need to be altered." Such is the purpose of this comment.

Reply by Hellriegel and Peterson

To minimize the burden on the reader, we will structure our reply in terms of the sequence of comments presented by William J. Moore. However, our reply seems to fall into three analytical cate-gories: methodological, conceptual, and "factual" items.

Our discussion of the types of socioeconomic factors was con-sidered to be illustrative rather than exhaustive in nature. The assumption was that the socioeconomic variables investigated might vary with the particular purposes of the research and the nature of the population at hand. In contrast to Moore, we were more inter-ested in the attitudes of individual teachers than individual teachers as union members. Further, the overwhelming number of people in our sample belonged to the National Education Association (NEA) or its affiliates; not the American Federation of Teachers (AFT) which seems to be the population of concern to Moore. Our article was condensed from a study reported in greater detail elsewhere (Hellriegel 1969). In this larger study, we did investigate the "socio-economic factors" Moore is concerned about as well as several other characteristics. In table 2 we report on those characteristics that Moore says were "conspicuously omitted."

Table 2
Selected Personal Characteristics of Respondent Teachers

Characteristic	Number of males	Number of females	Total	Percent of total
Distribution by organizational affiliation				
AFT and/or local affiliate	26	21	47	14.03
NEA and/or local affiliate	150	105	256	76.42
Neither	17	16	32	9.55
Total	193	142	335	100.00
Distribution by membership of parent in union				
Union member	74	42	116	34.63
Not a union member	118	100	219	65.37
Total	193	142	335	100.00
Distribution by parent's occupation				
Business, managerial	40	47	87	25.97
Clerical, white-collar	17	13	30	8.96
Farm	33	16	49	14.62
Professional	41	40	81	24.18
Skilled craft	35	15	50	14.93
Unskilled, semiskilled	27	11	38	11.34
Total	193	142	335	100.00

We do not feel we erred in the statement "These characteristics (socioeconomic factors) are not of a particular explanatory value in themselves but rather serve as operational criteria for evaluating the relevance of other behavioral dimensions." The fact that participation in collective action might differ according to sex, income, and other characteristics is not proof that these factors, as Moore states, "have influenced teachers' decisions to join a union . . . ."

Moore uses data regarding the characteristics of AFT members, but they represented only 14 percent of our 335 respondents. In addition, teachers in the three school systems included in our sample were represented by affiliates of the NEA, not the AFT. Second, there is evidence that socioeconomic characteristics do not, per se, cause or influence a particular pattern of behavior as much as the types of socialization, role pressures, or learning experiences which may vary with different socioeconomic classifications. Numerous examples of this point are provided by Berelson and Steiner (1964). Our difference with Moore here may be more a matter of degree than kind. However, we are quite concerned that the emphasis by Moore is too conducive to stereotyping. This is especially inappropriate since teacher attitudes and behavioral styles have undergone and are undergoing a state of change with respect to collective negotiations.

We will not quibble with Moore on the relative importance of economic factors as one of the primary explanations for men engaging in militant collective action. The data we reported in other sections of the article clearly indicate this.

Unfortunately, Moore fails to make an important distinction. Here, as elsewhere in his commentary, he seems to imply that participation in or support of collective negotiations and of militant action (such as strikes) are synonymous. This was not demonstrated by one of our other unreported findings. We found that male teachers were *not* more supportive of the process of collective negotiations as a means of establishing terms of employment than female teachers ($x = 3.4359$, $s = 0.5666$ versus 3.4648, $s = 0.5561$). Of course, males were more willing to use the strike tactic as a means of obtaining their ends.

We will attempt to demonstrate the subtleties and importance of not presenting the "either-or" alternatives with respect to collective negotiations in the educational sector. First, the process can be considered as resulting in three kinds of agreement on the basis of scope and procedures (Stinnett, Kleinmann, and Ware 1966, pp. 17-18). Second, collective negotiations can be considered as following one of three "avenues of thought and action" (Frymier 1968), that is, the legal model, the labor model, or the professional model. Our impression is that Moore implicitly assumes that collective negotiations exist only if the "labor model" is operational. This is partially demonstrated in his continuous use of the AFT as the basis for many of his conclusions.

The scope and procedures of agreements have been described by Stinnett, Kleinmann, and Ware (1966) in terms of the following three levels:

1. Level I—This is simply a recognition type agreement. It recognizes teaching as a profession and a local education association as the representative of the professional staff. It expresses the intent of the board to hear proposals of the recognized association. . . . It is not a commitment to negotiate issues. . . .

2. Level II—This includes the features of Level I, and, in addition, contains an outline of the procedures to be followed in the negotiation process. . . .

3. Level III—This agreement contains the ingredients of Levels I and II plus a written appeals procedure providing for impartial, third party mediation, or fact-finding in the event of impasse or persistent disagreement. . . . (pp. 17-18)

It has also been suggested that there "are [three] different avenues of thought and action—each presumes a different authority base and different motivation and serves a different party" (Frymier 1968). These three models have been described (pp. 103-04) as follows:

1. *Legal Model*—The legal model is the traditional way. The basic source of authority is the constitutional or statutory power of the state to demand compliance with the law, and, the primary group served under this arrangement is the body politic of a particular state. Thus, in the legal model, schools exist to serve the people of the state, and the motivations inherent stem directly from a consideration and concern for satisfying the taxpayers and voters of the state.

2. *Labor Model*—In the labor model, the basic source of authority is rooted in the collective power of the practitioner to demand action or inaction along a particular line. In banding together, advocates of its adoption ask: "What's in it for me?" Emphasis is given to the attention and concerns of the members of the group, and group activity is dedicated to the proposition of enhancing or furthering the members' objectives and aims. The motivation behind this model arises from a primary concern for what the group members want and need to satisfy themselves.

3. *Professional Model*—The professional model is aimed at serving the needs of students and youth and derives its authority from the competence of the members of the group. Decisions of practitioners who adopt the professional model, in other words, do not presume a primary consideration for the people of the state, or for themselves, but for the students to be served. Furthermore, such persons work in ways which are predicated upon their technical abilities and conceptual understandings to help students, rather than the people of the state or the self-serving efforts of the group.

It is conceivable each of these "ideal" types may be combined to varying degrees to obtain a variety of "mixed" models. The assumed consequences of each of these "ideal" models has been summarized as follows:

The legal model fosters subservient relationships and the labor model generates interpersonal conflict. The professional model requires cooperation and interdependence. (Frymier 1968, p. 104)

By combining the three *levels* of relations and the three *forms* of relations, it is possible to construct a three-by-three matrix of the generic types of collective negotiations relations. Table 3 provides a typology of the principal kinds of possible relations. It is speculated

Table 3
Principal Types of Possible Collective Negotiation Relations for Teachers

Levels	Negotiation models		
	Legal	Labor	Professional
I	1	2	3
II	4	5	6
III	7	8	9

tentatively that the "tension" will be to move eventually toward a type 9 relationship. This type may best serve to integrate the needs of the teachers with the needs of their clientele, the students. Subjective support for this position is provided by Garbarino (1968) in his analysis of alternative approaches to professional relationships. He anticipates that

organizations of professional employees—both those which call themselves unions and those which do not—will increasingly take their ideology and rhetoric from the general employed professional model, their goals and status aspirations from the academic model, and their tactics from the union model.

Moore's discussion of the reasons why secondary teachers and teachers with more education and experience join the AFT more frequently than other groups is interesting but simply does not relate to the scope or purpose of our discussion. Moreover, Moore seems to have underplayed two historical watersheds. The first concerns the changed role of the NEA and the second concerns the diminishing validity of predicting interest in collective negotiations on the basis of certain demographic characteristics. For instance, new teachers have come from four years or more of turmoil on the campus. Having read about and discussed at length the development of collective negotiations, they actually may be much more militant than teachers with greater experience. Also, the assumption that women will be tranquil with their salaries because they represent second incomes rests on shaky grounds. This has been demonstrated by the pressures from women and allied groups, including the Women's Liberation Front, for the establishment of equal rights and benefits through a variety of strategies. However, in the latter part of his commentary, Moore does invoke the importance of "social forces" as means of explaining general teacher militancy.

Since 1959 the membership of the AFT has increased to approximately 200,000 (*Educator's Negotiating Service*, July 1, 1970), having won negotiating rights in such cities as New York, Philadelphia, Boston, Detroit, and Cleveland (Collins 1967). However, with the successes of the AFT and the growing dissatisfaction of teachers since 1961, "there has been a complete about-face of the NEA's position on collective bargaining and the use of strikes and sanctions" (Muir 1968). Thus, the NEA, with its 1,100,000 members (Goldberg 1970) representing 52 percent of the teachers, has moved from a position of opposition, to indifference, to passive acceptance, to its present state of enthusiastic and financial support of collective negotiations (Muir 1968).

We would like to turn now to Moore' discussion of the major external forces we identify as generally having a reinforcing effect on collective negotiations. The rationale for our choice of the external forces was in terms of the variables which may be having the greatest impact "here and now" rather than the "forces" which may have created the conditions to permit the "here-and-now" variables to become operational. We feel the current support of the labor community is probably a better direct explanation for the growth of the AFT than for the growth in use of collective negotiations by affiliates of the NEA, where the bulk of recent expansion has taken place. A survey by the NEA comparing the 1967-1968 period with the 1966-1967 period serves to illustrate this point. A few of the salient statistics follow.

1. The number of school systems with some form of agreement increased to 2,212, up from 1,531 in the 1966-67 period for a 44.5 percent increase.

2. Instruction personnel employed in school systems with agreements increased to 910,000 in the 1967-68 period from 648,000 in the 1966-67 period. This was a 40.4 percent increase.

3. In the 1967-68 period, 34.8 percent of the responding school systems had agreements, compared to 25 percent in the 1966-67 period. (*Negotiation Research Digest*, June 1968, p. B-1)

Of course, the scope of the issues covered and the role of the teacher organizations in affecting the nature of the agreements varies widely, but as a minimum, the above statistics give some indication of the thrust to collective negotiations within the NEA.

In their introduction into a school system, Taffel (1968) contends negotiations are concerned primarily with improvements in salaries, class size, and other working conditions. After this initial phase, teachers become concerned with areas traditionally the prerogatives of administrators, particularly principals. The expanding areas of concern include matters of school policy such as: "Planning of reforms in school organization, in disciplinary procedures, and in supervision and administration." However, Gittel's and Hollander's (1968) study of six large school systems suggests that, up to 1967, teacher organizations played a relatively limited role in the broader areas of school policy making.

Our final point with respect to the view that the labor community "mechanically" supports negotiations in the public sector is the danger of overgeneralization. For example, Derber (1968) and Weber (1969), in their analyses of collective action by social workers and other public servants in the state of Illinois, suggest that the broader labor movement may find it more to its liking to use the political process rather than to support further collective bargaining agents in the public and professional sectors.

Our intended meaning in the statement that "much of the legislation concerning collective negotiations passed in recent years appears to reflect the lobbying efforts of both school boards and teacher associations" was not presented clearly. Contrary to Moore's implications, we were *not* attempting to explain the form and nature of the intergroup cooperation and competition which take place in the *process* of getting bills enacted. Rather, we were suggesting both of these groups have been the primary sources of "expertise" for the drafting of legislation. The process of lobbying for any type of legislation or position is probably much more complex and variable than suggested by Moore, who seems to imply that "the" political ally of teachers with respect to legislation dealing with negotiations is the labor movement. It has been noted that

Few organizations have everything their own way: any proposed statute or regulation may arouse opposition from one or more other associations, and the programs of some other groups have constantly to be fought. It is natural, therefore, that coalitions and alliances should form and form again in the never-ending struggle of interest group politics. Working out the terms of the coalitions is, in the nature of the process, as secret as the participants can make it; for the mere revelation that certain unpopular associations are involved might cause an alliance to fail. (Hall 1969, p. vii)

In his table, Moore shows California as one of the top states with respect to the strength of organized labor. However, strength is apparently relative to the power of the countervailing forces. This is illustrated in the recent comment by Robert H. Chanen, NEA general counsel, that "there's a lot of grumbling in California" due to the state law which presumably prohibits union teacher contracts (*Boulder Daily Camera* 1970).

Moore's comment about the role of the AFT in stimulating action by the educational associations is explicitly presented by us under variable 10, competition between the NEA and AFT.

Again, as a macro and indirect external force, we would agree with Moore that our "age of turmoil" has acted as a precondition for collective action.

We never claimed to provide "conclusive proofs of the validity" of the model as asserted by Moore. We stated:

However, caution must be exercised in not assuming that this model or the research methodology proves causation because "correlational studies can sometimes disprove but never prove that a causal relationship exists."

We would like to comment on the "four major causes of recent growth of teacher unions and collective negotiations in the public schools," identified by Moore. While our findings did demonstrate the importance of economic forces as a likely influence on the growth of negotiations, other important explanations have been advanced as well. We feel the evidence simply does not permit an ordering of these forces as presented by Moore. The rationale for negotiations seems to be much deeper than simply representing a means to increase compensation. In sum, the rationale for this process has been advanced from a number of perspectives, including (1) it provides a means to increase compensation (Rees 1962); (2) it introduces democratic processes into the school system for teachers (Taylor 1966; Weisenfeld 1965); (3) it provides a means of countervailing power vis-à-vis other power groups concerned with the school system (Brooks 1964; Zeigler 1967); and (4) it provides a means to reduce the frustrations and conflicts (other than economic) of teachers (Blanke 1965).

Moore's second point is highly questionable. He states, "Following the issuance of this order [Executive Order 10988], there occurred a sharp increase in public union membership and interest in collective bargaining at all levels of government." Separate analyses by Vosloo (1966) and Hart (1966) present substantially different conclusions from Moore on the impact of Executive Order 10988. They have concluded that overall union membership in the federal sector has increased at a relatively modest pace with little or no change in the overall rate of union growth as a result of the order. Under his second point, Moore states that the passage of legislation has influenced the expansion of collective negotiation. It is obvious that we tend to agree with this position, since we included "legislation," or variable 11, as one of the "here-and-now" external forces.

The third point presented by Moore regarding the support of organized labor is basically a repetition of an earlier point to which we have responded. The same case holds for his fourth point regarding the impact of social forces, but we want to add two qualifications. Moore's interpretation of a teacher poll that "a majority of the nation's teachers now believe it is proper for them to strike for economic gain" may be misleading. For, the findings actually showed (1) 3 percent thought teachers should have the same right to strike as any other groups; (2) 50 percent thought strikes were permissible *under extreme circumstances,* such as perceived low salaries; (3) 38 percent thought teachers should never strike; (4) 9 percent were undecided (Teacher Opinion Poll 1966).

Finally, Moore seems to imply that teacher groups and those in the civil rights movement have perceived fairness or equity through the same set of glasses. It seems that some teacher militancy has been in reaction to the activities of those in the civil rights movement. In some instances, it appears that threats to teachers' prerogatives and the personal insecurity generated by the civil rights movement have created greater collaboration and militancy by teachers. This may also be an explanation of one connection between the civil rights movement and teachers. The New York teacher strikes by the AFT in 1968 seem to be a case in point. Here, the AFT fought decentralization policies and legislation within New York City and at the state capitol (Mayer 1968) while this was a goal of many in the civil rights movement.

In sum, we were not attempting to present the macro or historical forces which may have created the conditions to make the "here-and-now" variables we discuss operational. Thus, we feel Moore provides important background factors in his discussion of the role of organized labor and the role of the civil rights movement. However, our emphasis and interpretation of these two forces might vary slightly from his. Our study was concerned primarily with determining individual teachers' perceptions with regard to professionalism, job satisfaction, and collective negotiations rather than why teachers belong to unions. Why a teacher might or might not belong to the American Federation of Teachers or the National Education Association was, at best, secondary to the thrust of the article.

References

American Teacher 52, no. 2 (October 1967): 8.

Bakke, E. Wight. "Why Workers Join Unions." *Personnel* 22, no. 1 (July 1945): 3-5.

Berelson, Bernard, and Steiner, Gary A. *Human Behavior: An Inventory of Scientific Findings.* New York: Harcourt, Brace & World, 1964.

Bernstein, Irving. "The Growth of American Unions." *American Economic Review* 44, no. 3 (June 1954): 315-17.

Blanke, Virgil E. "Teachers in Search of Power." *American School Board Journal* 151, no. 5 (November 1965): 7-9.

Blum, Albert A. "Why Unions Grow." *Labor History* 9, no. 1 (Winter 1968): 39-72.

Boulder Daily Camera. "Teacher Labor Leaders Predict Greater Union Activity" (August 5, 1970): 11.

Brooks, George. "A Case for Teachers' Unions." *Monthly Labor Review* 87, no. 3 (March 1964): 292.

Browder, Lesley Hughes, Jr. "Teacher Unionism in America: A Descriptive Analysis of the Structure, Force, and Membership of the American Federation of Teachers." Ph.D. dissertation, Cornell University, 1965.

Collins, Daniel G. "Labor Relations Under Boards of Education and in Other Municipal Employment." *Proceedings of New York University Nineteenth Annual Conference on Labor,* edited by Thomas G. Christensen. Washington, D.C.: Bureau of National Affairs, 1967.

Comer, Roger A. "City Public School Teachers' Salaries, 1961-63." *Monthly Labor Review* 58, no. 4 (April 1965): 396-400.

Derber, Milton. "Labor-Management Policy for Public Employees in Illinois: The Experience of the Governor's Commission, 1966-1967." *Industrial and Labor Relations Review* 21, no. 4 (July 1968): 541-58.

Doherty, Robert E., and Oberer, Walter. *Teachers, School Boards, and Collective Bargaining: A Changing of the Guard.* Ithaca, N.Y.: New York State School of Industrial and Labor Relations, Cornell University, 1967.

Dunlop, John T. "The Development of Labor Organization: A Theoretical Framework." *Insights into Labor Issues,* edited by Richard A. Lester and Joseph A. Shister. New York: Macmillan, 1948.

Frymier, Jack R. "Teacher Power, Negotiations, and the Roads Ahead." *Theory into Practice* 7, no. 2 (April 1968): 103.

Gallup Poll. "Do You Think Teachers Should Form Unions?" Princeton, N.J.: American Institute of Public Opinion, 1946.

Garbarino, Joseph W. "Professional Negotiations in Education." *Industrial Relations* 1, no. 2 (February 1968): 106.

Gittel, Marilyn, and Hollander, Edward T. *School Systems: A Comparative Study of Institutional Response.* New York: Frederick A. Praeger, 1968.

Goldberg, Joseph P. "Changing Policies in Public Employee Labor Relations." *Monthly Labor Review* 93, no. 7 (July 1970): 6.

Hall, Donald R. *Cooperative Lobbying—The Power of Pressure.* Tucson: The University of Arizona Press, 1969.

Hart, Wilson R. "The Impasse in Labor Relations in the Federal Civil Service." *Industrial and Labor Relations Review* 19, no. 2 (January 1966): 175.

Hellriegel, Don. "Collective Negotiations and Teachers: A Behavioral Analysis." D.B.A. dissertation, University of Washington, 1969.

Husaini, Bagar A., and Geschwender, James A. "Some Correlates of Attitudes Toward and Membership in White-Collar Unions." *Southwestern Social Science Quarterly* 48, no. 4 (March 1968): 595.

Kershaw, Joseph A., and McKean, Roland N. *Teacher Shortages and Salary Schedules.* New York: McGraw-Hill, 1962.

Lowe, William T. "Who Joins Which Teachers' Groups?" *Teachers College Record* 66, no. 7 (April 1965): 614-19.

Lunden, Leon E. "The 1964 Convention of the Teachers' Union." *Monthly Labor Review* 87, no. 10 (October 1964): 1140.

Mayer, Martin. *The Teachers Strike: New York 1968.* New York: Harper & Row, 1968.

Mills, C. Wright. *White Collar.* New York: Oxford University Press, 1956.

Moore, William J. "The Growth and Development of Teacher Unions in the Public Schools: A Theoretical Interpretation." Ph.D. dissertation, University of Texas, 1969.

Moskow, Michael. *Teachers and Unions.* Philadelphia: Industrial Research Unit, Wharton School of Finance and Commerce, University of Pennsylvania, 1966.

Muir, J. Douglas. "The Strike as a Professional Sanction: The Changing Attitude of the National Education Association." *Labor Law Journal* 19, no. 10 (October 1968): 625.

National Education Association. *Estimate of School Statistics, 1967-68* (Research Report 1967 R-19). Washington, D.C.: The Association, 1967.

National Education Association, Research Division. *The American Public School Teacher, 1960-61* (Research Report 1961 R-1). Washington, D.C.: The Association, 1961.

National Education Association, Research Division. *The American Public School*

Teacher, 1965-66 (Research Report 1967 R-4). Washington, D.C.: The Association, 1967.

Rees, Albert. *The Economics of Trade Unions.* Chicago: University of Chicago Press, 1962.

Sackley, Arthur. "Long Term Trend in Urban Teachers Compensation." *Monthly Labor Review* 89, no. 11 (November 1966): 1223-29.

Seidman, Joel; London, Jack; and Karsh, Bernard. "Why Workers Join Unions." *Annals of the American Academy of Political and Social Science* 274 (March 1951): 75-83.

Seidman, Joel; London, Jack; Karsh, Bernard; and Tagliacozzo, L. Daisey. *The Worker Views His Union.* Chicago: University of Chicago Press, 1958.

Shister, Joseph A. "The Logic of Union Growth." *Journal of Political Economy* 41, no. 5 (October 1953): 423.

Stagner, Ross. *Psychology of Industrial Conflict.* New York: John Wiley & Sons, 1956.

Stinnett, T. M.; Kleinmann, Jack H.; and Ware, Martha L. *Professional Negotiation in Public Education.* New York: Macmillan, 1966.

Taffel, Alexander. "The Principal and Teacher School Board Negotiations." *The Bulletin of the National Association of Secondary Principals* 42, no. 329 (September 1968): 72.

Taylor, George W. "The Public Interest in Collective Negotiations in Education." *Phi Delta Kappan* 47, no. 1 (September 1966): 16-22.

"Teacher Opinion Poll: Should Teachers Strike?" *NEA Journal* 55, no. 5 (May 1966): 54.

U.S. Bureau of the Census. "Income of Families and Persons in the United States." *Current Population Reports: Consumer Income* (Series P-60, no. 53). Washington, D.C.: U.S. Government Printing Office, 1967.

U.S. Bureau of Labor Statistics. *Directory of National and International Labor Unions in the United States, 1965* (Bulletin no. 1493). Washington, D.C.: U.S. Government Printing Office, 1965.

Vosloo, William B. *Collective Bargaining in the United States Federal Service.* Chicago: Public Personnel Administration, 1966.

Weber, Arnold. "Paradise Lost; Or Whatever Happened to the Chicago Social Workers." *Industrial and Labor Relations Review* 22, no. 3 (April 1969): 323-38.

Weisenfeld, Allan. "Public Employees—First or Second Class Citizens." *Labor Law Journal* 16, no. 11 (November 1965): 685-704.

Wells, Jean A. "Women College Graduates Seven Years Later." *Monthly Labor Review* 90, no. 7 (July 1967): 31-32.

Zeigler, Harmon. *The Political Life of American Teachers.* Englewood Cliffs, N.J.: Prentice-Hall, 1967.

Reading 13

Toward a Theory of Collective Negotiations

A. William Vantine

In the past few years the literature in education has been inundated with articles dealing either with the effects of negotiations on school officials and/or teachers or cookbook recipes designed to help practitioners develop the art of one-upsmanship. Few articles have appeared in educational journals that have attempted to analyze the bargaining process. The following article is designed to help the reader make sense out of teacher-school board negotiations. To accomplish this end the writer has developed a formulation that may be used to understand methods of bargaining that occur in collective negotiations and might be used as a basis to build a more sophisticated theory. The formulation is based on concepts drawn from game theory, labor negotiations, and theories of conflict resolution.

Bargaining Methods

Two distinctly different methods of reaching agreement are apparent in collective negotiations. Pure bargaining is a highly con-

Reprinted by permission from *Educational Administration Quarterly* 8 (Winter 1972), pp. 27-43.

flictual experience in which one party demonstrates and uses its bargaining power to coerce the other party into granting concessions. Mutual accommodation is a low conflict process by which each party makes concessions to the extent that the other party demonstrates a need for assistance (Pruitt 1968a). It is primarily joint problem solving in which each party gains benefits from the solution to a problem.

These two methods of reaching agreement can be thought of as polar positions on a continuum. Mixed bargaining is the fusion of the tactics ascribed to pure bargaining and elements inherent in mutual accommodation applied to the resolution of differences over items or sets of items. The concepts of pure bargaining and mutual accommodation were used by Schelling (1960) in his development of a framework for the expansion of game theory. Walton and McKersie (1965) referred to the major methods of reaching agreement in an industrial setting as distributive and integrative bargaining. Pruitt (1968a) uses the terms pure bargaining and mutual responsiveness to develop a conceptualization of negotiations as a form of social behavior.

Bargaining Power

Bargaining power is a significant factor in each method of reaching agreement. Bargaining power may be defined as the ability to obtain concessions and satisfy or refrain from satisfying an opponent's needs. Bargaining power is a two dimensional concept. It increases or decreases with the quantity and quality of the human components that comprise an organization and with the topics that are brought to the negotiating table. Bargaining power does not remain constant during the negotiation process but changes as the human inputs that affect the state of an organization vary and fluctuates with the items and/or set of items that are being negotiated. Items are issues or problems that are topics of negotiations but are not identified by the method of negotiations used to resolve them. Issues are demands that generate conflict between the parties. They describe topics acted upon in pure bargaining situations. Problems are cooperative undertakings used to describe topics acted upon in mutual accommodating situations.

A tactic is a maneuver used in collective negotiations to gain an advantage. Stevens (1958) states that "changes of tactics should be

viewed as the use of existing bargaining power to gain objectives rather than changes in the magnitude of bargaining power." Paradoxically, in bargaining some forms of weakness may constitute bargaining strength. For, to place an opponent in an apparently
untenable position to his constituency on an issue or set of issues
that is extremely important to obtain or reject will tend to increase
the opponent's bargaining power on the issue or issues in question.
Bargaining power is effective only if it can be perceived or sensed by
the negotiators and can convince the weaker party to make concession or the stronger party to satisfy needs.

   Bargaining power can be decreased by those acts which lower
the cost of agreement to an opponent or raise the relative cost of
disagreement. Yet, it is dependent as much upon what each party is
seeking to obtain as it is upon each party's coercive ability (Chamberlain and Kuhn 1965, p. 172). In essence, bargaining power may be
used by one negotiator or negotiating team to influence the behavior
of the other so as to change the probabilities that the other will respond to certain stimuli. The amount of influence one has over the
other is the weight or degree of power (Kaplan 1964). Since bargaining power can be operationally defined, it may lend itself to rough
empiricism on selected issues in a true bargaining situation. True bargaining occurs between employees and employers over salary and
terms and conditions of employment.

Origins of Bargaining Power

   An employee organization's degree of bargaining power is affected by the size of the unit, its cohesiveness, the type of personnel
represented, the quality of leadership, character and choice of a
negotiating team, and the objectives of the organization. Bargaining
power enables a negotiator to grant rewards or coerce his opponent,
hold a legitimate position which enables him to wield his influence,
and exercise the expertise that he has as a negotiator.

   A study by Goe (1968) lends support to the premise that neither negotiator will prevail in his knowledge of all the items on the
table but it also lends credibility to the statement that a negotiator
who is well schooled in the topics and tactics of negotiation will have
a tendency to increase his bargaining power. This point receives some
support from limited laboratory studies conducted by Bartos

(1964a). He found that experience and learning alone account for much of the behavior displayed in negotiations.

Pure Bargaining

Pure bargaining is a method by which opposing parties reduce their demands by granting concessions until a level is reached where each side can accept agreement. Three motives of pure bargaining are applicable to this formulation. Each motive constitutes a different phase of the bargaining process.

Motive One—Moving the Opponent Toward One's Own Position

Motive One consists of "moving" the opposing party toward the negotiator's own position. A move is defined as a change in position from one alternative to another. The structural elements that a move depends on are threats, enforcement, and the capacity to communicate or destroy communications (Pruitt 1968a). A move requires the opponent to make concessions based on the negotiator's ability to persuade his opponent that it is in his own best interest to concede by using pressure tactics such as threats and commitments, and persuasive tactics or appeals to reason to alter specific positions (Pruitt 1968a). Moves communicate a negotiator's value system or can be used to disguise it (Schelling 1958).

Pressure Tactics

Threats. Bautsch and Knauss (1962) define a threat as the expression of an intention to do something which is detrimental to the interest of another. The motive behind a threat is to coerce, deter, or constrain the other negotiator's choice of action (Schelling 1958). There are two types of threats: overt threats are direct and explicitly stated, covert threats are disguised and require interpretation by the threatened party regarding their meanings and implications.

A threat works if it changes the other negotiator's expectation of how the threatener will react. It is an attempt to alter the threatener's own incentives as they are perceived by the threatened party. Schelling (1958, pp. 223-24) states:

the threatener risks having to retaliate in the hope that, by the sheer act of creating the risk, he will deter the act that reaction is made contingent on. There is consequently a motive to make the threat but not to carry it out. More correctly, there is a motive to bind one's self so that fulfilling the threat is obligatory; but if the threat fails so that it has to be carried out, the only motive for carrying it out is the obligation that was deliberately incurred earlier plus any motive arising from the likelihood that fulfillment in this case increases the potency of some further threat.

A threat is meaningful only if the consequences would cause worse damage to the threatened party than to the threatener (Schelling 1958). Rapoport (1964) emphasizes that each threat, if carried out, involves a cost to the threatener as well as his opponent. The trick then, is to use the most effective threat to minimize potential costs.

Commitments. Schelling refers to a commitment as a strategic move, a move that requires the other negotiator to choose in one's favor. It limits the other negotiator's choice by changing his expectations about one's behavior (Iklé and Leites 1962). It involves communicating inflexibility to another thereby making it clear to him that no more further concessions are possible and that he will have to make a concession if the parties are to reach closure (Pruitt 1968a). This tactic can be successful in obtaining concessions from the other party if, and only if, the commitment is above the opponent's clearly understood and defined minimal disposition. The least favorable terms at which a negotiator would prefer agreement to no agreement is called the negotiator's minimal disposition (Iklé and Leites 1962). The successful use of a commitment involves discovering the other negotiator's minimal disposition and making a commitment to grant him just that much and no more (Pruitt 1968a). Schelling (1958, p. 224) states that:

The threat is related to the commitment in two ways. First like the commitment, it is a surrender of choice, a renunciation of alternatives, that makes one worse off than he need be in the event that the tactic fails; the threat and the commitment are both motivated by the possibility that a rational second player (negotiator) can be constrained by his knowledge that the first player (negotiator) has altered his own incentive structure. Both tactics are intended to rig one's own incentive structure so that the other player (negotiator) is left the initiative and will be induced to choose in the first player's (negotiator's) favor.

Second, the threat is related to the commitment in that it depends on it; the threat can constrain the other player (negotiator) only insofar as it carries to the other player (negotiator) at least some appearance of obligation. If one is not committed to the threat in any way and cannot even seem to be committed, it is ineffectual.

Threats differ from commitments, in that in the former one's courses of action are conditioned on the other negotiator's response, while in the latter a negotiator fixes his course of action.

Appeals to Reason

A negotiator's attempt to persuade his opponent that it is in his own best interest to concede based on logical arguments is called appeals to reason. It is assumed that the stronger the appealing party feels his bargaining power to be on specific issues, the more reasonable and convincing his argument and the lower the cost (in terms of money and administrative flexibility to the board and its advisors and in terms of support from the faculty for the teachers' organization) of submission on the issue.

To move an opponent toward one's position requires a negotiator to obtain information about his opponent's concession points.

Techniques of Obtaining Information

A negotiator's disposition or attitude toward a move may reveal the point at which he will make a concession. Techniques of obtaining information or clues about an opponent's concession points during negotiations include assessing the direct content clues dropped in negotiations and forcing the opponent to tip his hand. The former can be obtained from keen observation and accurate record keeping. The latter includes some specific techniques, some of which are: directing questions to a less-coached member of the opponent's team; personally abusing the opposing negotiator, showing signs of exaggerated impatience over an opponent's failure to move, implying overt threats without using them, and displaying emotional reactions over an opponent's position.

It is reasonable to assume that the more reluctant an opposing negotiator is to concede on issues that are important to his adversary the more likely the adversary will be to resort to these kinds of techniques.

Off the record comments made away from the table, remarks dropped by naive parties, insights of team members concerning issues and personalities, and general feedback regarding the attitudes of personnel in both organizations can serve to provide a negotiator with valuable information needed to identify his opponent's attitude toward making a concession.

Motive Two—Impressing One's Own Reference Group

The second motive of pure bargaining requires one to impress his own reference group. Pruitt (1968a) states that most negotiators act as agents and, hence, must impress a constituency in order to retain their offices and keep their autonomy.

In collective negotiations two types of negotiators may be used: those internal or external to the system. An external or "professional" negotiator may have a distinct advantage over a teacher or board negotiator in performing pure bargaining tasks for he is not forced to live with a contract or with the personnel who faced him across the table.

Motive Three—Reaching Agreement

Pruitt (1968a) states that, "both parties are motivated to reach agreement because the cost of no agreement is seen as larger than what may possibly be gained from agreement." This statement takes on a particular twist when applied to public education. The costs to a board of education are significantly different from those experienced in the private sector. A school system deals in services rather than consumable items, therefore, costs to management tend to be basically political rather than economic.

Statute law in most states does not force either party to sign an agreement; even a fact-finder's recommendation is in no way binding in the absence of mutual agreement. In some instances a school board or teachers' organization may be willing to take risks to defeat its opponent or satisfy economic or political objectives. It is also conceivable that agreements may not be reached because the minimal dispositions of both parties are too far apart for the parties to reach agreement. However, the preceding statement does not imply minimal dispositions have remained stable during all stages of negotiations.

Often, the granting of concessions can cause the negotiator to face a conflict of interest, for in spite of the fact that a concession must be made if agreement is to be reached, the contents of the concession will serve to betray the negotiator's minimal disposition. Faced with this dilemma the negotiator may refrain from making concessions unless he is forced to or he may resort to pressure tactics in an attempt to cover his own weakness and force the other party to submit to his demands (Pruitt 1968a).

It is apparent that reaching agreement is in opposition to "moving the other party toward one's own position," and "impressing one's own reference group." For agreement to be reached a shift in attitudes of one or both of the parties must occur. This motive embodies a willingness of the negotiator to make concessions if concessions by the opponent are forthcoming. Yet, it is conceivable that the party who perceives that he has the least bargaining power will concede on issues that are more valuable to his team than the stronger party. Trading of concessions then are actually tactical commitments or bilateral promises that will benefit both parties to some degree. The practice of getting something for what is given is called a tradeoff.

For a negotiator to make a concession he must legitimize the move in some respect to his own team but especially to his opponent. Failure to clothe a concession with reason will leave the negotiator in a vulnerable position, for his opponent is apt to view such a move as a weakness in bargaining power rather than a move toward agreement (Walton and McKersie 1965). The misinterpretation of the motive for a move could convey the message to one's opponent that the negotiator would be willing to make additional concessions. One might speculate then that if both parties know the "rules of the game" they will try to provide their opponent with additional information, or shift the line of reasoning, so as to provide the opponent with a face saving rationale for retreat. Such retreats can be enhanced by indirect communications.

Indirect communications consist of informal discussions between the parties; "off the record" remarks and sign language, i.e., indirect verbal signals concerning a negotiator's willingness to concede or remain firm; and nonverbal signs (Pruitt 1968b). Nonverbal signs are physical movements that convey an intended message. This writer's experiences in negotiations suggest that nonverbal signs increase in the agreement stage of negotiations. They serve as subtle indicators of a negotiating team's disposition to move or hold firm on specific issues.

If the parties are unable to agree on the terms of an agreement, in states where statute law governs public employee bargaining, then mediation and in some instances fact-finding may occur. It is the mediator's role to facilitate agreement and the fact-finder's job to propose solutions that will enable the parties to reach an agreement.

The fact-finder who understands his role knows that his function is not to "find facts" in the judicial sense of the word but to interpret the facts in such a manner as to bring the parties closer to an agreement. Inexperienced negotiators have a tendency to believe that equity is inherent in the third party's role; this writer contends that agreement and not equity is the third party's primary motive. This statement is supported by Bartos (1964b), who found in a limited laboratory study that a mediator will tend to have a bias towards endorsing the proposal that was last endorsed by the parties. Mediation and fact-finding then can be thought of as extensions of the negotiation process.

Summary of Pure Bargaining

Three motives of pure bargaining, techniques of obtaining information, methods of identifying content clues, and breakdown procedures have been discussed. The complexities of pure bargaining are apparent from this formulation. To attempt a thorough analysis of the collective negotiation process in any one school district on all issues placed on the table would be a nearly impossible task. However, selected bargaining issues might be examined. A model adapted from international negotiations can be used for this purpose.

An Adapted Pure Bargaining Model

Schelling (1960), Iklé and Leites (1962), and Walton and McKersie (1965) do not recognize stable utilities in negotiations. They contend that negotiations are psychological in nature. This concept entails changes in preference, in distinction to the act of preference which occurs at the time a choice is made and which can be used operationally to define utility at that time. A disposition to prefer is defined as the negotiator's estimate that he will prefer one alternative over another if and when he has to make a choice. The most important choice is that between "agreement at given terms" and "an impasse and/or no agreement." The least favorable terms at which a negotiator would prefer agreement to no agreement is called a negotiator's minimum disposition (at time t) (Iklé and Leites 1962).

To construct a changing utility model for selected issues in pure bargaining it is necessary to assume that pure bargaining deals with issues where the two sides have a conflict of interest on one set of mutually exclusive alternates for each issue (issue a, b, c, . . . N), and one side always prefers a to b, b to c . . . (N − 1) to N, while preferences of the other side are in reverse order (Iklé and Leites 1962).

An estimated bargaining range for both sides extends along the continuum of alternatives from each team's minimal disposition to its estimate of the opponent's minimal disposition. A sham bargaining position constitutes any alternative on the continuum either above for the demanding party's or below for the responding party's estimate of its minimal disposition. A negotiator's change in bargaining position from one he prefers more to one he prefers less is called a sham concession if the two positions lie in his sham bargaining range and a genuine concession if they fall within his genuine bargaining range. A payoff is the settlement obtained in negotiations (Iklé and Leites 1962).

The model can be used in the following manner. During the course of negotiations in one school district the writer found that the teacher negotiator's minimal disposition at the outset of negotiations was $94,000 in total salary demands for their constituents, i.e., the teacher negotiating team estimated that they would prefer no agreement to an agreement that allowed for less than $94,000 in total salary increases. (The range of alternatives varies with the issue and is clarified by the negotiation process.) The teachers estimated that the board's minimal disposition was about $163,000. Thus, the teachers' estimated bargaining range extended from $94,000 to $163,000. This range, however, did not keep them from asking for more. They originally demanded a salary package that cost $450,000. Consequently the teachers pretended that they thought this demand was within their expectations rather than a sham. The teachers actually believed they would obtain a payoff of about $100,000 in salary increases.

The school board's estimates were in opposition to the teachers' but both perceived (even though neither was aware of the disposition of the other in the early stages of bargaining) that they would settle for a total salary payoff of about $100,000. As the reader can see, the board exceeded its originally perceived minimal disposition by granting an increase that exceeded its own and the teachers' original estimates by about $35,000. The board's move beyond its predetermined minimal disposition was attributed to the teacher organization's rejection of a fact-finder's report, a hardening of the teacher team's negotiating posture, and the board's collective belief that failure to move would bring about a teacher strike. (See figure 1.)

Figure 1 can be used to demonstrate that some selected, numerically-based pure bargaining issues (salary, leave days, etc.) will remain on the table throughout negotiations and will be modified by the interaction process. Consequently, changes in dispositions and outcomes can be recorded.

The principal objective of pure bargaining is to modify the opponent's estimate of one's probable outcomes and minimum dispositions. However, danger lies in the fact that inexperienced mediators, fact-finders, and arbitrators that seek to resolve impasses may mistake the differences between the prominent demands of the parties and the initial position of the parties as the parties' actual bargaining range and may make the mistake of estimating that the probable outcome should occur between the two extremes rather than within an actual bargaining range.

The model for selected numerically based pure bargaining issues may help the reader more accurately map the changes that occur in the bargaining process.

Mutual Accommodation

Mutual accommodation is a significant cooperative venture directly in opposition to the wanton aspect of pure bargaining. In pure bargaining situations opponents attempt to modify each other's positions to the extent that a settlement may reflect a compromise or even a win-lose solution. Mutual accommodation results in joint problem solving and provides a method by which both parties make gains. Yet, cooperation does not necessarily include the principle of equity for both parties. "One party may even suffer minimal inconveniences in order to provide substantial gains for the other" (Walton and McKersie 1965, p. 127). The negotiator who gives up the most to submit to the other usually expects to receive reciprocal treatment from the other in another problem area that will yield him substantial benefits. Mutual accommodation requires trust between the parties in order for them to honestly present their needs and discuss their aspirations without regard to the effort needed to solve problems and without forming preconceived solutions (Walton and

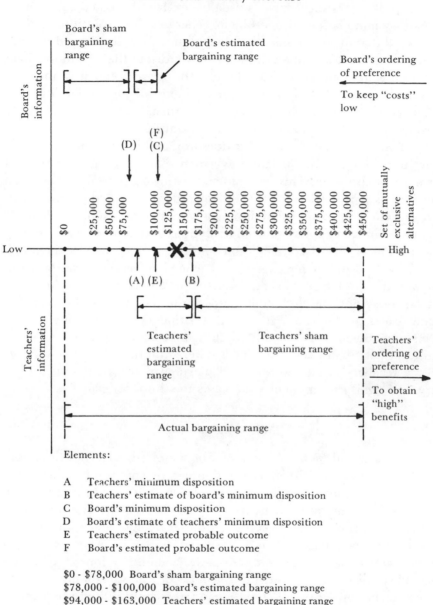

Figure 1
Changing Utility Model for a School District's Total Dollar Salary Increase

Board's sham bargaining range

Board's estimated bargaining range

Board's ordering of preference

To keep "costs" low

Board's information

Teachers' information

(D)   (F) (C)

$0 $25,000 $50,000 $75,000 $100,000 $125,000 $150,000 $175,000 $200,000 $225,000 $250,000 $275,000 $300,000 $325,000 $350,000 $375,000 $400,000 $425,000 $450,000

Low ———— X ———— High

Set of mutually exclusive alternatives

(A) (E)   (B)

Teachers' estimated bargaining range

Teachers' sham bargaining range

Teachers' ordering of preference

To obtain "high" benefits

Actual bargaining range

Elements:

A   Teachers' minimum disposition
B   Teachers' estimate of board's minimum disposition
C   Board's minimum disposition
D   Board's estimate of teachers' minimum disposition
E   Teachers' estimated probable outcome
F   Board's estimated probable outcome

$0 - $78,000   Board's sham bargaining range
$78,000 - $100,000   Board's estimated bargaining range
$94,000 - $163,000   Teachers' estimated bargaining range
$163,000 - $460,000   Teachers' sham bargaining range
X   Payoff—about $135,000

McKersie 1965, p. 139). Yet, even in a problem solving situation the party who perceives itself as being weaker will have a tendency to patronize the stronger party.

Unlike an issue which is usually resolved by compromise, mutual accommodation of a problem generates new solutions and requires different communication techniques than those used in pure bargaining. Walton and McKersie (1965) indicate that the more channels of communication available and the more frequently they are used, the more likely it will be for problem solving to develop. The absence of record keeping, pressure of time, and the use of study groups are apt to stimulate cooperative solutions.

Every negotiation situation does not lend itself to problem solving, but there may be instances when the parties see an advantage in using this approach. This phenomenon is most likely to occur when an item is perceived as a real problem and the troubled party appeals to the other for help in developing a workable solution, or when the troubled party expresses a need and requests the other team for help in meeting it. Pruitt contends that pure bargaining will be the dominant method of reaching agreement when bargaining power between opponents is changing. Therefore, the fact that in most school districts today both teachers and boards are in the process of developing new "rules of the game" it is doubtful that they will be able to successfully use mutual accommodation in reaching agreement on significant cost items. Costs are defined here in terms of faculty support for a teachers' team and loss of managerial prerogative and flexibility, and significant monetary increases to school officials.

Mixed Bargaining

Walton and McKersie in their theory of labor negotiations conceptualize a mix of distributive and integrative bargaining. These two opposite methods of reaching agreement in collective bargaining contain some of the same elements that were used to develop the major concepts in this article. They contend that by applying a soft or hard strategy to each basic method, a combination of four basic strategies in collective bargaining is developed. A modification of these selected strategies consists of: (1) a negotiator using accommodation to increase his own gains, (2) the negotiator choosing pure bargaining and a hard attitude toward his opponent, (3) the negotiator choosing pure bargaining and adopting a soft attitude toward his opponent which would enable the opponent to obtain larger payoffs, and (4) the negotiator selecting accommodation methods to enhance joint gains and then developing harder attitudes toward his opponent so as to obtain a higher payoff. This combination of negotiating methods serves to shed light on some of the ways in which the basic methods can be combined. However, these combinations do not take into account the attitudes of one's opponent. The opponent may alter his strategy in such manner so as to use the same or different combinations of the heretofore discussed strategies to obtain higher or lower, short or long term, payoffs for himself.

In true bargaining negotiators may change strategies depending on the demands of the situation. Collective negotiation does not depend on a specific set of rules of play. It is a dynamic process between two parties in which the strategies being used are not always clear. Therefore, the following simplifying assumptions are necessary to develop a sound basis for understanding mixed bargaining. It is assumed that mixed bargaining can be observed as the parties practice pure bargaining and/or accommodation methods. It is also assumed that a shift from an attitude that mirrors pure bargaining towards one that embodies elements of accommodation and one that shifts from mutual accommodation toward pure bargaining can be observed in a true bargaining situation.

Writings by Harbison and Coleman (1951), Lasswell and Kaplan (1963), Boulding (1963), and others give rise to the premise that in viable organizations where parties bargain collectively over terms and conditions of employment, relationship patterns, regardless of how amiable they may be, will contain an element of conflict. However, in such relationships an element of cooperation may also be present in inverse proportion to the degree of conflict.

The relationship that exists between parties who negotiate collectively differs from most legal arrangements for, while most contractual relationships terminate after a period of time, as a result of natural processes, or are severed in a court of law, the parties to a collective agreement participate in a continual relationship for as long as the institution remains operable and the parties continue to represent opposing factions. Similar to a marriage contract, the parties must live with one another and develop procedures that will facilitate their relationship. However, the nature of the relationship between the parties will depend on the degree of cooperation and conflict that exists between them and their ability to live with these phenomena. Therefore, it is reasonable to assume that, as in the private sector, teacher-school board—employee-employer relationship patterns will fall at points on a continuum between total conflict or complete cooperation.

Walton and McKersie and Harbison and Coleman advanced the notion that such a range could be used in the private sector to identify the differences in union management relationships. These relationships were not used to explain the ends sought by the parties but the means employed to achieve these ends. They contended that union-management accommodation relationships were rare but when they were identified they tended to occur in small companies where working conditions and wage levels were equal to, or above, employee's benefits in other firms that were used as a reference group by employees, and where decision making was relatively simple and both union and management shared an informal relationship in which mutual respect was evident and problems were handled jointly by the parties.

It was also contended that economic conditions, changes in personnel, and other factors could affect shifts toward either extreme. Various writers contend that when the power dimensions have not been tested and the relationship between the parties is in the developmental stages both parties tend to be insecure and suspicious of each other. There are obvious dangers in applying private sector notions literally to public education, yet these notions lend support to the premise that teacher-board relationships, as they are forged by the collective negotiations process, will develop patterns according to a set of meaningful criteria along a continuum of relationships that range from predominantly "antagonistic" to basically "cooperative." The absence of an experience factor necessary for the formulation of such a continuum is evident. Nevertheless, this writer postulates the existence of such a continuum. Consequently, a school district in which the perceived level of conflict between the organizations is high is referred to as a conflict centered environment whereas a district in which a low level of conflict between the parties exists is called a cooperative environment.

Based on the aforementioned statements, and on the fact that collective negotiations are relatively new in public education, one can assume that there is a high probability that antagonistic relationships exist between a majority of the boards of education and teacher organizations in the United States. If this assumption is valid it would appear that pure bargaining will continue to be the dominant method used to forge contractual agreements in the majority of our public schools in the 1970s.

Accommodation will most likely evolve in the resolution of low cost items in negotiation dyads where the parties have developed a significant degree of mutual trust and have fully tested and assessed their bargaining power.

It is this writer's contention that true mutual accommodation will seldom be achieved by well-meaning idealists intent on unilaterally initiating collaborative problem solving. If this higher order of problem resolution is used with high cost negotiable items in public education, and it is doubtful if it will be in most school districts, it will be instituted by realists on both sides of the negotiating table who are willing to take risks to gradually abandon the secrecy and controls inherent in pure bargaining in a genuine attempt to satisfy the needs of the other party and to seek creative solutions to perceived problems.

To paraphrase John Gardner, we need men on both sides of the negotiating table who are sufficiently honest and open-minded to recognize problems, sufficiently creative to conceive new solutions, and sufficiently purposeful to put those solutions into effect. Negotiations never are a series of easy victories. We cannot win every round or arrive at a neat solution to every problem. But driving, creative effort to solve problems should be the breath of life.

References

Bartos, Otmar J. *Predictive Model for Intergroup Negotiations* (Report to the United States Air Force Office of Social Research, no. 62-314). Honolulu: University of Hawaii, 1964a.

Bartos, Otmar J. "A Model of Negotiations and Regency Effect." *Sociometry* XXVII (September 1964b): 6.

Bautsch, Morton, and Knauss, Robert M. "Studies of Interpersonal Bargaining." *Journal of Conflict Resolution* 4 (March 1962): 53.

Boulding, Kenneth. *Conflict and Defense.* New York: Harper & Row, 1963.

Chamberlain, Neil W., and Kuhn, James W. *Collective Bargaining.* New York: McGraw-Hill, 1965.

Goe, Donald K. "A Comparison of Behaviors in Teacher Negotiations and the Character of Teacher-Administrator Relationships." *Dissertation Abstracts* XXVIII (February 1968): 2940A.

Harbison, Frederick H., and Coleman, John R. *Goals and Strategy in Collective Bargaining.* New York: Harper & Brothers, 1951.

Iklé, Fred C., and Leites, Nathan. "Political Negotiations as a Process of Modifying Utilities." *Journal of Conflict Resolution* 6 (March 1962): 3-22.

Kaplan, Abraham. "Power in Perspectives." *Power and Conflict in Organizations,* edited by Robert L. Kahn and Elise Boulding. New York: Basic Books, 1964.

Lasswell, Harold, and Kaplan, Abraham. *Power and Society.* New Haven: Yale University Press, 1963.

Pruitt, Dean G. *Negotiations as a Form of Social Behavior* (Report to the Office of Naval Research, no. 6). Buffalo: Department of Psychology, State University of New York, 1968a.

Pruitt, Dean G. "Indirect Communications in Negotiations." Buffalo: Department of Psychology, State University of New York, 1968b.

Rapoport, A. *Strategy and Conscience.* New York: Harper & Row, 1964.

Schelling, Thomas C. "The Strategy of Conflict: Prospectus for a Reorientation of Game Theory." *Journal of Conflict Resolution* 3 (September 1958): 220-28.

Schelling, Thomas C. *The Strategy of Conflict.* Cambridge, Mass.: Harvard University Press, 1960.

Stevens, Carl. "On the Theory of Negotiations." *The Quarterly Journal of Economics* LXXII (February 1958): 93.

Walton, Richard E., and McKersie, Robert B. *A Behavioral Theory of Labor Negotiations.* New York: McGraw-Hill, 1965.

Reading 14
Perception of Power in Conflict Situations

H. Andrew Michener, Edward J. Lawler, and Samuel B. Bacharach

General Erwin Rommel arrived in North Africa in February, 1941, to assume command of the German panzer forces. At that time, the Afrika Korps had few tanks, and Rommel, concerned with this deficiency, quickly ordered his workshops to fabricate dummy tank frames suitable for mounting on a Volkswagen chassis. These vehicles, which included devices to churn up trailing clouds of dust, created the impression of enormous armored strength when viewed at a distance across the arid desert terrain (Lewin 1968). The astute German commander understood the tactical importance of power perception. In adversary situations involving confrontations of force, the mere appearance of strength can rival the real thing.

What information does an individual use in assessing the strength of an adversary? Are certain data more central than others in shaping such impressions? These are important questions because judgments about power are crucial in situations of conflict. Tactical decisions often hinge on judgments about relative power, and the outcome of a clash may depend on the accuracy of these judgments.

Reprinted by permission from *Journal of Personality and Social Psychology* 28, no. 2 (November 1973), pp. 155-62.

Any misjudgment of an opponent's true capabilities—either an under-estimate or an overestimate—may create untoward consequences. Thus, if an opponent can manipulate a target's impression of their relative power capabilities, he can probably affect the target's reaction.

The research reported in this article treats power perceptions in conflictual encounters where coercion and force are used. Focusing on confrontations between antagonists who can obstruct one another's valued outcomes, this research investigates factors that determine impressions of power.

Previous Research on Power Perception

Previous research on the perception of power has been narrow in scope, and there apparently exists no broad-based theory of attributed power. In approaching the available literature, however, it is useful to think in terms of a conflictual situation involving a sequence of attack and counterattack. As Swingle (1970) noted, persons in severe discord may define the interaction in terms of the offensive and defensive capabilities of the opposing parties. Offensive potential refers to the capacity of one opponent to initiate attacks against the interests of another. Existing literature on power perception distinguishes between the *magnitude of damage* that an attacker can potentially inflict on the target and his *probability* of actually exercising control over the target. In contrast, defensive potential denotes the target's ability to *block* the attacker's efforts and to *retaliate* after the aggressor has struck an initial blow. All of these variables—damage, probability, blockage, and retaliation—characterize situations of conflict and consequently may affect perceptions of power.

Previous research offers no more than limited evidence regarding the effects of the four variables (damage, probability, blockage, and retaliation) on attributed power. The clearest evidence concerns damage, which indexes the extent to which an adversary can exercise control over the outcomes valuable to the target. Several studies have found that the greater the damage an antagonist can inflict, the more powerful he is judged to be. Employing diverse measures of attributed power, studies by Teger (1970), Johnson and Ewens (1971), and Michener, Griffith, and Palmer (1971) have demonstrated this effect for individual opponents. The same effect holds for conflictual situations in which the stimulus objects are coalitions rather than lone individuals (Michener and Zeller 1972). And Chu (1966) reported similar results for nonhuman adversaries capable of damaging the target person.

Other research shows that a second factor, the probability that the antagonist will actually lambast the target, also affects ascribed power. Schelling (1960) has argued that the manipulation of perceived probability (as by intentionally committing oneself to an apparently irrevocable line of action) constitutes an important tactic in bargaining. Moreover, various empirical studies (Benton, Gelber, Kelley, and Liebling 1969; Chu 1966; Faley and Tedeschi 1971; Horai, Haber, Tedeschi, and Smith 1970) indicate that persons impute more potency to opponents having a high likelihood of using their offensive capabilities than to those manifesting a lower likelihood.

But these two factors, damage and probability, characterize only the aggressor's abilities, not the target's. Assessments of an adversary's power (and of the target's own power) may reflect not only what the adversary can and/or will do but also the defensive ripostes possible in the situation. Surprisingly, the capacity to block attacks has apparently received little attention as a factor affecting ascribed power. Nevertheless, the present conceptualization of conflictual encounters as involving both offense and defense implies that blockage should affect imputed power. Blockage indicates the extent to which the target can neutralize an attack and retain control of outcomes he values. The target is likely to view an easily neutralized adversary as less powerful than one who cannot be checked.

A final factor, the target's ability to retaliate, may also color judgments of power, although one might speculate that it influences impressions of the target's power more than impressions of the adversary's. Research by Tedeschi, Bonoma, and Novinson (1970), which used the potency dimension of the semantic differential scale as a measure of attributed power, found that subjects ascribed greater potency to targets who wielded retaliatory capacity than to those who did not, although inconclusive results for the control group render these findings provisional. One may nevertheless hypothesize that in general the capacity to retaliate affects perceived power. Because retaliation refers to the target's ability to exert control over outcomes valuable to the adversary, more power may be ascribed to the adversary under low retaliation than under high; similarly, the target of the attack should be adjudged stronger under high retaliation than under low.

The present study extends previous work on the perception of power. Limited to situations involving an attacker and a target, it investigates how persons syncretize information relevant to power. That is, it inquires how persons combine diverse information in arriving at judgments of power. Specifically, it broaches the following questions: (a) Do each of the four independent variables—damage, probability, blockage, and retaliation—affect the amount of power ascribed to the adversary? (b) Do they also affect assessments of the target's power? (c) Do the independent variables affect each of these judgments in the same way? That is, are the predictive equations for the target's power and the adversary's power similar? (d) Are there some underlying commonalities in the judgments of the adversary's and the target's power that provide a basis for a general theory of power perception?

Method

Subjects

This study employed a 2 × 2 × 2 × 2 factorial design (i.e., Damage × Probability × Blockage × Retaliation). The sample consisted of 288 undergraduates at the University of Wisconsin. Half of the subjects were male and half were female, and they represented the four undergraduate levels (freshman, sophomore, junior, senior) approximately in proportion to enrollment. As a group, the subjects possessed no special knowledge about social power or about perceptions of power. Data collection occurred in five group-administered sessions of varying size. Subjects were randomly assigned to the 16 experimental treatments with the constraint that equal numbers of males and females (i.e., 9 of each) appear in each cell of the design.

Materials

Each subject read a set of four situations; these incorporated the manipulations of the independent variables. Each situation portrayed a conflictual relationship between two parties—that is, an adversary on the attack and a target on the defense. Subjects viewed the situation from the standpoint of the target in the confrontation. Each situation conformed to a standard format, as follows: The adversary had the capability either to destroy 90% of some valued outcome (high damage) or to destroy 10% of that outcome (low damage). Simultaneously, there was either a 90% chance that the adversary would actually attempt to carry out the destruction (high probability) or a 10% chance (low probability). In turn, the target had either a 90% chance of blocking the attack (high blockage) or a 10% chance (low blockage). Moreover, he could retaliate against the adversary by destroying either 90% of an outcome valued by the adversary (high retaliation) or 10% of that outcome (low retaliation).

While morphologically identical, the four stimulus situations differed in their specific content. One depicted a confrontation between a salesman and his regional manager, where the manager could reduce the salesman's commission-based income by either 10% or 90% (depending on experimental treatment) and where there was either a 10% or a 90% probability that he would actually do so. On the other hand, the salesman had either a 10% or a 90% chance of blocking the manager's onslaught by appealing to a higher official in the organization, and he could retaliate by moving to another company and taking either 10% or 90% of his customers with him, thereby hurting the manager's sales record.

A second situation described an altercation between a newspaper editor and a local judge. The judge could obstruct newspaper coverage of an important trial, and the editor could block the judge's action by a lawsuit and retaliate by publishing articles that would diminish the judge's chances of reelection. Similarly, a third situation delineated a conflict between two countries with military capabilities, while the fourth treated a dispute between two congressmen where passage of a bill and campaign support were at stake.

Dependent Measures

Each subject was assigned to only one experimental treatment in the 16-cell factorial design for all four stimulus situations. The sequential ordering in which subjects read the four situations was randomized. The subjects in the role of the target responded by recording their impressions of the adversary's power and the target's power (i.e., their own power) in each situation. Specifically, they provided separate ratings for the adversary and the target on various semantic differential items, each with 9-point scales. These items, selected on the basis of face validity and usage in previous studies of power perception (Heise 1970; Johnson and Ewens 1971; Pruitt and Johnson 1970), included: powerful-powerless, threatening-not threatening, potent-not potent, dominant-submissive, tenacious-yielding, aggressive-nonaggressive, and attacking-not attacking. Besides completing the semantic differentials, subjects concurrently indicated (on 9-point scales) their level of confidence in their ratings for the adversary and the target.

For each of the four stimulus situations, the seven semantic differential scores for the adversary were added (i.e., unit weighted) to yield an adversary power score, while those for the target were summed to obtain a target power score. Using these summative scales as dependent variables, a repeated measures analysis of variance showed that there were negligible differences between the four situations and no significant interactions between situations and the four independent variables (i.e., damage, probability, blockage, and retaliation); this is not surprising, of course, because the four situations were designed to be structurally isomorphic.

Next, since any given subject was in the same experimental treatment for all four situations, the four scores for the adversary's power (i.e., one score for each situation) were summed to create a single score, and the four scores for the target's power were summed to create a single score. Thus, for purposes of data analysis, this study includes two major dependent variables, termed adversary power and target power.

Data from the present sample indicated that each of these dependent variables achieved a high level of reliability (internal consistency). Cronbach's alpha for adversary power was .941, while that for target power was .912.

Results

Adversary Power

Table 1 presents the mean values for adversary power as a function of the four orthogonally manipulated independent variables (i.e., damage, probability, blockage, and retaliation). An analysis of variance indicates significant main effects for each of the independent variables. Adversary power is greater under high damage

Table 1
Mean Scores for Adversary Power

Treatment	Low damage		High damage	
	Low probability	High probability	Low probability	High probability
High blockage				
High retaliation	111.2	142.8	116.8	152.3
Low retaliation	122.4	148.8	135.9	166.4
Low blockage				
High retaliation	103.2	162.6	136.7	173.3
Low retaliation	123.8	190.7	160.2	194.7

than under low ($F = 26.35$, $df = 1/272$, $p < .001$), greater under high probability than under low ($F = 158.93$, $df = 1/272$, $p < .001$), greater under low blockage than under high ($F = 33.88$, $df = 1/272$, $p < .001$), and greater under low retaliation than under high ($F = 31.84$, $df = 1/272$, $p < .001$). Stated simply, power ascribed to an adversary is higher when the adversary can and does wreak severe damage and when the target cannot intercept the assault or do much in response.

Some of these findings correspond to those of earlier studies. The damage main effect corroborates that found by Michener and Zeller (1972) as well as that reported by Johnson and Ewens (1971). Moreover, the probability main effect replicates the finding reported by Benton et al. (1969), where probability was manipulated by varying the actual frequency of power usage. Similar probability effects emerged in the study by Horai et al. (1970).

This correspondence between the present findings and earlier findings deserves notice for two reasons. First, the present findings replicate previous discoveries, which is important for the accumulation of reliable scientific information. Second, this correspondence strengthens confidence in the methodology used here. Further evidence for the adequacy of the present procedures comes from the subjects' reports of their own confidence in their ratings. Although the four independent variables had no impact on the confidence scores, the subjects expressed considerable confidence in their ratings of both the adversary and the target. On a 9-point scale the mean confidence for the target's ratings was 6.0 ("moderately confident"), while that for the adversary's ratings was 6.4.

Considered jointly, the four independent variables are important determinants of the power attributed to the adversary. The coefficient of determination (R^2) is .458. Especially noteworthy is the effect of probability, which alone accounts for 29.1% of the variance in adversary power. The surprising magnitude of this effect imparts an important lesson regarding the tactical use of power: The probable deployment of a power base, regardless of the magnitude of damage implied, affects judgments of power in a pivotal fashion.

Raven and Kruglanski (1970) advanced a useful distinction between possessing a power base, threatening to use the power base, and actually using the base. The present findings suggest that the threatened likelihood of using a coercive power base—rather than mere possession of the resource—exerts a great impact on attributed power. Even persons who are outgunned or trapped in low-power positions can manipulate the power attributed to them by vigorously activating (or pretending to activate) their limited resources. The consequences for impression management seem obvious, given that one can frequently fake the probability of initiating action with relative ease.

Target Power

The four independent variables not only affect judgments regarding the adversary's power, but they also determine the power ascribed to the target. Table 2 presents the mean values for target power as a function of the independent variables. Interestingly, the pattern of effects differs from that for adversary power.

Table 2
Mean Scores for Target Power

Treatment	Low damage		High damage	
	Low probability	High probability	Low probability	High probability
High blockage				
High retaliation	187.1	187.1	178.4	171.9
Low retaliation	182.3	168.6	163.6	176.9
Low blockage				
High retaliation	179.8	173.6	163.8	165.1
Low retaliation	149.4	159.6	137.6	146.0

The analysis of variance for the target power scores reveals a significant damage main effect ($F = 13.02$, $df = 1/272$, $p < .001$), a significant blockage main effect ($F = 36.71$, $df = 1/272$, $p < .001$), and a significant retaliation main effect ($F = 27.70$, $df = 1/272$, $p < .001$). No significant effect emerges for probability ($F < 1$). Target power is greater under low damage than under high, greater under high blockage than under low, and greater under high retaliation than under low. These independent variables are moderate determinants of target power, as indicated by the coefficient of determination ($R^2 = .212$).

Notice that the various independent variables affect both adversary power and target power, but the *pattern* of effects is different. This difference emerges clearly in a comparison of the regression equations for the two dependent variables. The equation for adversary power (AP) is:

$$AP = + .22D + .54P - .25B - .24R + e_1 , \qquad (1)$$

while that for target power (TP) is:

$$TP = - .19D + .02P + .32B + .28R + e_2 . \qquad (2)$$

In these equations the independent variables are D (damage), P (probability), B (blockage), and R (retaliation). The symbols e_1 and e_2 designate stochastic disturbance terms. Since all of the variables in these equations are standardized and the independent variables are uncorrelated, the coefficients in each equation (commonly called "path coefficients") indicate the relative contributions of the various independent variables.

Equations 1 and 2 assume an underlying causal model in which adversary power is not a cause of target power and target power is not a cause of adversary power. Although the data show a significant zero-order correlation between adversary power and target power ($\gamma_{AT} = -.193$), this correlation should not be construed as evidence that adversary power causes target power, or vice versa. In fact, nearly all of the covariation between the two dependent variables is produced by the independent variables, as indicated by the fact that the *partial* correlation between adversary power and target power, holding constant the four independent variables, is virtually zero

$(\gamma_{\text{AT.DPBR}} = -.023, ns)$. Thus, this test supports a model in which the direct causal paths between the two dependent variables are essentially zero.

Although the independent variables affect both adversary power and target power, they affect these outcomes differently. This is shown by the pattern of algebraic signs, which is different in equation 1 and equation 2. Thus, blockage and retaliation increase target power but reduce adversary power. Damage augments adversary power but diminishes target power. Some of these empirical findings are intuitively obvious, but others are not. Damage, for instance, might be expected to increase adversary power, but why should it have any effect on target power? And while retaliation plausibly determines the power ascribed to the target (who actually wields the retaliatory capacity), why does it affect adversary power?

Discussion

To explain the pattern of findings in equations 1 and 2, a *theoretical-construct* model is needed. The remainder of this article, therefore, formulates a generalized model of power perception in conflict situations. Although advanced post-factum, this theory not only subsumes the equations for the two dependent variables but also generates predictions transcending the present data.

A Theory of Power Perception

The conflictual situations in the present study had several elements in common. In all cases there were two participants, an adversary and a target. And in all cases, various outcomes were at stake. Some of these outcomes were valuable to the target, while others were valuable to the adversary. For purposes of understanding equations 1 and 2, it is useful to construe the four independent variables (damage, probability, blockage, and retaliation) as *indexes of control* over these valued outcomes.

Figure 1 represents the structure common to the four situations. It depicts the two participants (target and adversary) and an outcome valuable to each. The valuable outcomes, of course, differed from situation to situation. In one situation, a salesman valued his commission-based income, while the salesman's manager wanted to retain the company's customers; in another situation, a newspaper

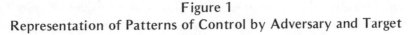

Figure 1
Representation of Patterns of Control by Adversary and Target

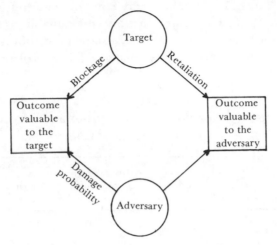

editor wanted the opportunity to cover a trial, while the opposing judge valued his chances of reelection to office. Figure 1 delineates a situation where *both* participants exercise some control over *both* outcomes. This structure accords with the four stimulus situations viewed by the experimental subjects. In essence, the damage and probability variables indicate the extent of the adversary's control over the outcome valued by the target; the blockage variable specifies the extent of the target's control over the outcome valuable to himself; and the retaliation variable indexes the target's control over the outcome valued by the adversary.

Interestingly, figure 1 also reveals that as a logical possibility, the adversary could exercise control over the outcome valuable to himself. Although the stimulus situations in the present study provided no information about this linkage, the patterns of control in figure 1 convey what it might involve (one possibility, for instance, being "counterblockage," or the extent to which the adversary can obstruct the retaliatory efforts of the target).

Given the patterns of control depicted in figure 1, a theory to explain the causal pattern in equations 1 and 2 requires only one postulate: If a participant in a conflictual situation increases his control over any valued outcome (i.e., either an outcome that he values or an outcome that his antagonist values), the power attributed to the other person decreases. Note that control and power are not the same thing. A man, for instance, may control many outcomes, but he remains powerless if these outcomes are not valuable to someone.

Predictions derived from this postulate are elaborated in table 3. These derivations indicate how changes in control over outcomes

Table 3
Predictions Regarding Adversary's Power and Target's Power from the Patterns of Control

	Indexed in present study by:	Predictions	
Patterns of control		Target's power	Adversary's power
(1) Target's control over outcome valued by target	Blockage	Increase (+)	Decrease (−)
(2) Target's control over outcome valued by adversary	Retaliation	Increase (+)	Decrease (−)
(3) Adversary's control over outcome valued by target	Damage, probability	Decrease (−)	Increase (+)
(4) Adversary's control over outcome valued by adversary	(None)	Decrease (−)	Increase (+)

affect attributed power. For example, an increase (from .1 to .9) in the target's control over the outcome valued by the target would result in an increase (+) in the power ascribed to the target and in a decrease (−) in the power ascribed to the adversary; analogously, an increase in the adversary's control over the outcome valued by the target would result in a decrease (−) in the power ascribed to the target and in an increase (+) in the power ascribed to the adversary; and so on.

In essence, the predictions summarized in table 3 specify the form of the equations for adversary power and target power. Using the independent variables of D (damage), P (probability), B (blockage), and R (retaliation), the equation for adversary power (AP) becomes:

$$AP = +D + P - B - R, \tag{3}$$

while that for target power (TP) becomes:

$$TP = -D - P + B + R. \tag{4}$$

Since the theory predicts only the direction (not the magnitude) of the effects for the independent variables, no numerical coefficients are included in these equations.

Keeping in mind that the theory is post-factum (and therefore cannot be "proved" by the present data), compare the theoretical equation 3 with the empirical equation 1 (for adversary power), and compare the theoretical equation 4 with the empirical equation 2 (for target power). The concordance of signs is striking, and the only disparity occurs for the effect of probability on target power, where the predicted relationship is negative but the empirical data show a nonsignificant positive relationship. All other signs are consistent.

Further Issues in Power Perception

The theory has been advanced to explain why equations 1 and 2 assume the form they do. Since one cannot test a theory on the same data used to formulate it, future research should attempt a direct assessment. Ideally, a test of the theory would include data on all four patterns of control represented by the theory (see figure 1). As indicated earlier, the present study includes no empirical data on one of these linkages (i.e., the adversary's control over outcomes valuable to him), and one of the theory's virtues is to point to this gap.

Although cast at a high level of generality, the theory is narrow in scope because it applies only to power perceptions in *conflictual* situations. But a parallel theory of power perception, stressing control over valued outcomes, might apply to cooperative, nonadversary relationships. Expansion in this direction seems possible.

The theory might also be extended to incorporate variations in *value*. Recent research by Rothbart (1970) showed that the value of the outcomes in an interaction may affect the perception of threat and power. And the formulation of power tactics derived from social exchange theory (Michener and Schwertfeger 1972; Michener and Suchner 1972) similarly stresses the value of outcomes. If the target of an attack, for instance, suddenly stopped caring about an outcome jeopardized by the adversary (i.e., used the tactic of "withdrawal"), then the adversary would effectively exercise less control over those outcomes valued in the interaction, and consequently he would be viewed as less powerful. The present study did not experimentally manipulate the values of the outcomes at stake, and the theory implicitly assumes that these values are fixed and unchanging. Future elaborations of the theory, however, might explicitly incorporate differences in outcome values.

Finally, the role of probability in the perception of power requires further clarification. Probability should be treated as conceptually distinct from damage capability because as earlier research has shown, the fact that someone possesses a coercive power base does not necessarily imply he will actually deploy it (Michener and Cohen 1973; Michener and Lawler 1971). The present empirical results indicate that although the adversary's probability of attacking is an important determinant of adversary power, it has virtually no impact on target power. This may have occurred because the subjects viewed the situations from the target's role. Nevertheless, this is the only point where the theory cannot reproduce the empirical findings, and it therefore poses an interesting question for future research.

References

Benton, A.; Gelber, E.; Kelley, H.; and Liebling, B. "Reactions to Various Degrees of Deceit in a Mixed-Motive Relationship." *Journal of Personality and Social Psychology* 12 (1969): 170-80.

Chu, G. C. "Fear Arousal, Efficacy, and Imminency." *Journal of Personality and Social Psychology* 4 (1966): 517-24.

Faley, T., and Tedeschi, J. T. "Status and Reactions to Threats." *Journal of Personality and Social Psychology* 17 (1971): 192-99.

Heise, D. R. "Potency Dynamics in Simple Sentences." *Journal of Personality and Social Psychology* 16 (1970): 48-54.

Horai, J.; Haber, I.; Tedeschi, J. T.; and Smith, R. B., III. "It's Not What You Say, It's How You Do It: A Study of Threats and Promises." *Proceedings of the 78th Annual Convention of the American Psychological Association* 5 (1970): 393-94.

Johnson, M. P., and Ewens, W. "Power Relations and Affective Style as Determinants of Confidence in Impression Formation in a Game Situation." *Journal of Experimental Social Psychology* 7 (1971): 98-110.

Lewin, R. *Rommel as Military Commander.* New York: Ballantine, 1968.

Michener, H. A., and Cohen, E. D. "Effects of Punishment Magnitude in the Bilateral Threat Situation: Evidence for the Deterrence Hypothesis." *Journal of Personality and Social Psychology* 26 (1973): 427-38.

Michener, H. A.; Griffith, J.; and Palmer, R. L. "Threat Potential and Rule Enforceability as Sources of Normative Emergence in a Bargaining Situation." *Journal of Personality and Social Psychology* 20 (1971): 230-39.

Michener, H. A., and Lawler, E. J. "Revolutionary Coalition Strength and Collective Failure as Determinants of Status Reallocation." *Journal of Experimental Social Psychology* 7 (1971): 448-60.

Michener, H. A., and Schwertfeger, M. "Liking as a Determinant of Power Tactic Preference." *Sociometry* 35 (1972): 190-202.

Michener, H. A., and Suchner, R. W. "The Tactical Use of Social Power." *The Social Influence Processes,* edited by J. T. Tedeschi. Chicago: AldineAtherton, 1972.

Michener, H. A., and Zeller, R. A. "The Effects of Coalition Strength on the Formation of Contractual Norms." *Sociometry* 35 (1972): 290-304.

Pruitt, D. G., and Johnson, D. F. "Mediation as an Aid to Face-Saving in Negotiations." *Journal of Personality and Social Psychology* 14 (1970): 239-46.

Raven, B. H., and Kruglanski, A. W. "Conflict and Power." *The Structure of Conflict,* edited by P. G. Swingle. New York: Academic Press, 1970.

Rothbart, M. "Assessing the Likelihood of a Threatening Event: English Canadians' Evaluation of the Quebec Separatist Movement." *Journal of Personality and Social Psychology* 15 (1970): 109-17.

Schelling, T. C. *The Strategy of Conflict.* Cambridge, Mass.: Harvard University Press, 1960.

Swingle, P. G. "Dangerous Games." *The Structure of Conflict,* edited by P. G. Swingle. New York: Academic Press, 1970.

Tedeschi, J. T.; Bonoma, T.; and Novinson, N. "Behavior of a Threatener: Retaliation versus Fixed Opportunity Costs." *Journal of Conflict Resolution* 14 (1970): 69-76.

Teger, A. I. "The Effect of Early Cooperation on the Escalation of Conflict." *Journal of Experimental Social Psychology* 6 (1970): 187-203.

PART III

Impasse Resolution and Strikes

Overview

Probably no collective bargaining issue in education has stirred as much interest as impasse. Impasse management has been traumatic for public sector bargaining generally and for the education sector particularly. The problems generally revolve around how to have free and meaningful collective bargaining without service-disrupting strikes against government. Though most states have been willing to embrace collective bargaining for public employees, they have been noticeably unwilling to accept strikes, or acknowledge them as an essential cost of bargaining. The short history of public sector bargaining is repleat with experiments in strike prevention and impasse management. Strike substitutes (mostly third-party neutrals) and negative incentives have been tried as methods of preventing or resolving impasse without work stoppage trauma.

It follows that primary issues in the analysis of public sector collective bargaining are the strike and alternative impasse mechanisms. The special significance of these issues is reinforced by the observation that, although strikes by teachers are prohibited in all but four jurisdictions,* they have nonetheless occurred in growing numbers.

*Hawaii, Oregon, Pennsylvania, and Vermont. The Michigan legislature recently passed a bill which would allow strikes under specified conditions, but the act was vetoed by the governor.

Readings in this category have been collected for several reasons:

1. The literature on strikes and impasse resolutions is extensive, and positions are well developed and documented. This is probably the result of the long and active strike—no-strike debate in public employment and the fact that impasses are highly visible indicators of an emerging phenomenon.

2. The importance of strikes and impasse resolution to collective bargaining systems results in a topical literature rich in insights into public bargaining generally. Debates over the merits of strikes and third-party impasse mechanisms often include revealing discussions of power in bargaining, legal issues, the political and economic context, and the relationship between private and public sector bargaining.

3. Although agreement is the objective of collective bargaining, impasse does and always will occur. Bargainers need to be able to examine it in a proper perspective.

What is the best avenue to take when parties in the public sector cannot agree on contract terms? Three options present themselves: allow the parties to escalate their conflict via the strike or lockout, seek resolution through third-party intervention, and empower the employer to make a unilateral determination of terms. Because the latter method undermines bargaining, two directions for analysis remain:

1. The causes of strikes in the public sector and the function of the right to strike in traditional collective bargaining systems; and

2. Third-party mechanisms for impasse resolution and their effectiveness, both in cases where the strike is legal and where it is illegal.

The Strike Case

Although it is illegal in most jurisdictions, teachers have repeatedly struck in the pursuit of collective goals. Recent events have fueled the debate on whether teachers should be allowed at least limited rights to strike. The debate turns on three questions:

1. If teachers were given the strike, would collective bargaining be well served? Would settlements be better and more frequent, for instance?

2. What are the likely political, organizational, and economic consequences of teacher strike rights (and presumably the boards' right to lock out)?

3. Are satisfactory substitute mechanisms available, such as a controlled strike or a third-party intervention?

Two models are generally available, each with its own advocates: the legal strike model and the illegal strike model, in which the strike is replaced by some third-party dispute mechanism. Now that the first flurry of organizing has subsided and collective bargaining has had ten years to become the operating norm in education, debate on the relative merits of the two models is somewhat more analytic than in the early years of educational bargaining. It is certainly less bound by tradition or myth (e.g., the strike is unprofessional). There is still little agreement, however, about the relative merits of the two models. Rather than referee, we seek to reflect the mainstreams of the debate.

Function of the Strike

To evaluate the utility of the models to public employee bargaining, we first return to the traditional function of the strike in the private sector. Here the strike serves as a power equalizing mechanism. Its use and threat of use enables the union to put economic pressure on the employer. The threat or actual loss of revenue due to stopped production and lost markets, which occur when the employer's product is removed from the market and customers shift to competitive merchandise, encourage concession from stubborn employers. To a lesser degree, political pressure may also be employed, e.g., protest actions directed toward the product. (This weapon has been used effectively by the United Farm Workers.)

In the private sector, resistance to such mechanisms is generated by competitive market restraints. Consumers can and usually will seek a substitute if a product is eliminated or priced above its competition. Excessive wage rate demands are tempered by the reality of the employment demand function, that is, higher wage rates in a competitive market usually result in higher product prices and less employment through lower product demand or capital substitution. Defenders of the strike (and that includes most labor economists) argue that without the power generated by the union's ability to impose direct costs on the employer, collective bargaining becomes a much less effective means for democratically resolving conflict.

Although strikes in traditional private sector bargaining systems impose economic and to a lesser degree political costs on employers, they also impose economic costs on employees. During a period of striking, employees are substantially without income. Unions provide strike funds, but in most cases the strike wage is considerably less than the worker would earn were the industry at work. Strike funds are not common in public employment.

Strikes, although functional in the collective bargaining context, have serious consequences. They disrupt the economic marketplace, the delivery of essential goods and services, and the productive relationship between employer and employee. Possibilities of extended strikes by the United Auto Workers or the Steelworkers send economic shudders throughout the country. When regional industries are struck, within a short time many small shopkeepers are forced to the brink of economic disaster. Although the strike is a painful process, there is yet no alternative which clearly is superior. Australia and some European countries have experimented with compulsory binding arbitration systems as alternatives to the strike. Analysis of the effectiveness of these systems suggests that they have not been successful in reducing labor strife.

Strikes in the Public Sector—Condition of Market Constraints

Strikes by public employees, including teachers, are generally prohibited by law. The argument for prohibition of teacher strikes first turned on the issue of public health and safety. Most experts now agree that teacher strikes represent no real threat to public health and safety. A public emergency does not exist when schools are closed in the same sense that it exists when police or fire service or health care is interrupted. School days can be made up; if this were not the case there would be fewer holidays in the school calendar.

A second strike issue revolves around the sovereignty of the state. Opponents of the public employee strike often base their argument on the notion that a strike represents an attack on the sovereign state and hence must be considered an illegal act.

They also point out that some of the conditions necessary for containing the strike in the private sector are not operative in the public sector. For instance, there is no competitive market pricing structure for public services. The effect of strikes on employment is much more difficult to estimate because services provided by governmental agencies are essential ones with an assumed inelastic demand. In education, for example, compulsory attendance laws and the absence of a well-developed system of alternative education (e.g., private schools) makes it more difficult for teachers to price themselves out of a job in the same way that a factory worker can under more elastic demand conditions. In the same way, education's labor intensive character makes it almost impossible for school boards to reduce rising labor costs through capital investment. No one has yet developed a mechanism for automating the teaching process.

Wellington and Winter (reading 15) use the absent market constraint argument in taking their position against public sector strikes. Burton and Krider (reading 16) and Shanker (reading 17) take the view that there are active "market constraints" sufficient to make the strike safe. They suggest the market advantage really lies with the employer. Public employees can bring no real economic pressure on their employer. Closing schools through a strike does not impose direct costs on the public employer (although it may impose indirect costs on parents who must make provisions for babysitters). In fact, Shanker suggests that a strike by public employees may represent a saving to their employer, because tax derived income continues uninterrupted while costs are greatly reduced. (Teacher salaries count for roughly two-thirds of school district operating costs.)

Burton and Krider further develop their market restraint argument by substituting taxpayer resistance for market demand elasticity and labor replacement (e.g., contracting out for services) for capital substitution. Inasmuch as local governmental services are financed by public revenue, generated primarily by local taxation, it is wrong to assume an unlimited public purse. As taxes rise to pay for salary increases, taxpayer resistance also increases. This resistance is carried to the bargaining table by public boards and representative officials.

When labor costs rise to an unacceptable level, local governments are free to seek alternative ways of performing a service. In Burton and Krider's example, if sanitation men do not exercise reasonable constraints in their wage demands, a city can and will contract out garbage collection to a private firm (whose employees, ironically, can legally strike). Many school custodial and maintenance functions can be contracted in the same way if contracted services are less expensive or performance is less problematic. Direct contract services are not presently an alternative for teaching functions, but there are ways of reducing teacher demand. Class size can be increased. Paraprofessionals can be worked in with teachers in ways which "extend" a teacher's contact to a larger number of students.

The Public Employee Strike as a Political Weapon

All of the authors represented here seem to agree that the political dimension is of much more importance in the analysis of public sector strikes than in traditional private industry analyses. Pressure on public employers to settle is politically rather than economically derived. When teachers strike, angry parents put pressure on school board members and other elected officials to resolve the strike so their children can get back to school. Elected officials are generally very sensitive to this kind of political pressure for it affects their job security; they are eager to reduce conflict and bring about a settlement. Although public sector bargaining and strikes require political interpretation, analysts do not agree on that interpretation.

Shanker (reading 17) and Burton and Krider (reading 16) hold that public decisions are political decisions, and that the balance of power required for effective collective bargaining dictates that employees must be able to inflict political "costs" on public managers. Wellington and Winter (reading 15) oppose strikes in the public sector precisely because they fear these political costs. They argue that, because of organization and control peculiarities, public managers are in a comparatively weak position to counter political pressure, and thus unnecessarily vulnerable to union pressure. Employing a pluralistic view of local political processes, Wellington and Winter hold that the increment of political power added by strike rights might seriously distort the political process, in that public employees could avail themselves of force not available to competing interest groups. Teachers salaries, they contend, may not be a function of the economic marketplace, but rather an expression of community value preferences. To allow teachers mechanisms which permit them disproportionate influence in the distribution of scarce public resources is to distort the political system.

However, the strike's political dimension is a double-edged sword. In choosing to strike, teachers risk angering the public, and anger can easily turn against them and result in increased resistance to their demands.

Debate over the economic and political merits of public employee strike rights, although instructive, are somewhat paled by reality. Legal opinion notwithstanding, teachers and other public employees have struck with increasing frequency. In some ways public strike prohibition is not unlike our experience with the Volstead Act. It is questionable whether a legislative action can end an otherwise common practice. It may be an exercise in futility. Acknowledging this problem, the prestigious American Assembly has said:

The Assembly does not support the total prohibition of strikes for several reasons: such a ban gives rise to unequal treatment of public and private doing similar tasks. It relies on the mistaken view that every strike by governmental workers effects public health and safety. It does not recognize the realities of public employment labor relations in that a strike may often result in loss of wages and no real discomfort for public employers whose revenues continue unimpaired. Therefore if all public workers are prohibited from striking, disrespect for law is encouraged and the feeling of lesser status is unnecessarily fostered. Finally, a ban on strikes does not guarantee there will be no strikes. (Report of the Fortieth American Assembly, October 28-31, 1971)

Third-Party Neutrals in the Bargaining System

Third-party impasse resolution mechanisms must be considered in the context of the total bargaining system. Of particular importance is their interaction with strike provisions. If employees have strike rights, third-party intervention is of a different order than when it is offered as a strike substitute. In the former case, mediation and arbitration are not expected to resolve all impasses. In the latter, however, the third-party mechanism is expected to supply motivational substitutes for the strike as well as resolve impasses.

Third-party neutrals have a long history in labor relations. They have been utilized both as mediators who assist the parties toward agreement and as factfinders or arbitrators who render a decision and function in an adjudicative capacity. Mediators generally function only in disputes over contract terms, whereas arbitrators are used both in contract disputes and in disputes arising during contract administration, e.g., grievances. In the private sector, mediators are employed extensively in contract impasses, arbitrators to a lesser degree.

Four forms of arbitration are frequently employed:

1. Advisory, noncompulsory arbitration. In this system, arbitrators (or factfinders) render decisions which are not binding on the parties to the dispute. Submission of issues to arbitration is voluntary.

2. Advisory, compulsory arbitration. In this instance arbitrators again issue recommendations that are not binding, but the parties to a dispute are required to submit their unresolved issues to advisory arbitration. (Some purists contend that advisory arbitration is a contradiction in terms. By some definitions, "arbitration" implies a binding decision.)

3. Binding, noncompulsory arbitration. In this instance, the parties to the dispute have the option of whether or not to submit the issue to arbitration, but once it is submitted, the parties agree to abide by the decision of the arbitrator.

4. Binding, compulsory arbitration. In this instance, the parties must submit an impasse to arbitration and they must abide by the ruling of the arbitrator. This last form most closely approximates a judicial model.

In the private sector, noncompulsory binding arbitration is the most utilized form, except in instances where the strike threatens the public interest and provisions of the Taft-Hartley or the National Railway Labor Act are employed. Employers and employees in the private sector are under no compulsion to submit their disputes to third-party ruling. When they choose to do so they usually agree in advance to abide by the ruling of the arbitrator or arbitration panel. Arbitration is not widely employed in contract disputes in the private sector, but has been favored in the settlement of grievances or disputes arising out of contract interpretation. Most union contracts contain provision for arbitration to be used in the event of grievance impasse.

In the public sector, the legal issue of sovereignty has mitigated against the use of binding arbitration. Most public employee bargaining statutes instead require that disputes be submitted to factfinding or advisory arbitration. These are now offered in lieu of the right to strike in most states, though there is growing interest in binding forms of arbitration. Maine and several other states now require educational contract disputes not having economic consequences to be submitted to binding arbitration. The public sector has begun to actively employ binding arbitration in grievances.

The literature on third-party intervention generally falls into one of three categories:

1. Discussions of the possible forms of third-party intervention and descriptions of their uses.

2. Analyses of the functional utility of third-party mechanisms in a collective bargaining system. These discussions generally turn on the question of (a) whether some form of third-party intervention represents an effective and equitable impasse resolution mechanism, or (b) the impasse prevention effects of these mechanisms.

3. Studies which treat mediation or arbitration as a variable and consider behavioral characteristics of mediators and arbitrators and role performance.

Included here are readings by Doering (reading 18) and Johnson and Pruitt (reading 19) which address the issue of third-party intervention. Doering describes the use and effects of factfinding in one state, New York, which has had a period of experience with that mechanism. She provides insight into both the extent of need for third-party intervention and the behavior of neutrals. Suggested perhaps by her analysis is the failure of advisory systems (e.g., mediation and factfinding) to supply anti-impasse motivation in the bargaining. Unlike the strike, the cost to parties of advisory third-party intervention may be insufficient to spur negotiations toward settlement. Doering's work also provides an excellent discussion of the types of issues likely to come to impasse and of the methods and criteria used by neutrals in search of a workable solution.

Johnson and Pruitt provide research evidence that anticipation of third-party consequences may influence bargaining behavior. It is an excellent companion piece to the Doering work in that the findings of Johnson and Pruitt suggest that the number and types of impasses requiring third-party intervention may be a function of the impasse mechanism itself. In their research it was found that bargainers (in the laboratory at least) were more conciliatory under the threat of binding arbitration, and were therefore more likely to settle differences without need of the threatened intervention. This work also suggests that binding arbitration may function more like a strike threat in producing movement at the table, and hence be a more likely candidate for strike substitute than advisory arbitration.

In public education generally, the procedure has been for declaration of impasse by either party, submission of the matter to mediation and, in the event that mediation fails, use of factfinding or advisory arbitration. Serious bargaining is frequently postponed until after mediation and advisory arbitration have taken place. Hence, mediation and arbitration do not foster collective bargaining, but indeed retard it. Inasmuch as public sector bargaining is much less dependent upon economic sanctions and much more dependent upon the use of political power, the arbitrator or factfinder's report becomes one of the elements in the political arsenal. Both school boards and teachers' unions, it has been argued, make only minimal concessions before third-party bargaining, in hopes that their position at the time of impasse will influence the arbitrator's decision and can be used as public justification for granting fewer concessions.

Grievances

For impasses arising out of the interpretation or administration of a contract the most common resolution mechanism is a formal grievance procedure. The procedure commonly employs a series of administrative review steps in which the dispute can be settled by mutual consent of the worker and employer. If these fail, binding or advisory arbitration is the final step. Long an accepted process in the private sector, binding arbitration of grievances in public schools is still a troublesome issue, specifically because it involves the sovereignty of the school board to settle disputes. Some states require negotiation of grievance procedures, others prohibit it, while others leave it to the bargaining parties. Even though this variation exists, the trend is clearly to include grievance procedures in public school contracts. Once in place the procedure can have important effects on the operation of the school as described by Glassman and Belasco (reading 20). This article not only describes a central element of labor relations in schools, but also points out that grievances may be part of a strategy to elicit fundamental changes as well as a response to immediate circumstances.

Conclusion

Taken as a whole, the readings in Part III offer no easy or sure answer to the question of what to do about impasses in public sector bargaining. What does seem to be clearly illustrated is the systemic nature of bargaining, and the difficulty of trying to respond with public policy conceived sectionally. Bargaining behavior cannot be analyzed without recognizing that bargainers look ahead to the consequences of impasse and structure their action accordingly. Impasse policy deliberations are incomplete to the extent that they derive only from consideration of impasse resolution, and not impasse prevention or the relative consequences on power of the various alternatives.

Reading 15

The Limits of Collective Bargaining in Public Employment

Harry H. Wellington and Ralph K. Winter, Jr.

Good lawyers are good critics. The nature of their discipline makes this skill necessary, and the content of their work brings it inevitably to bear upon doctrines and concepts laboriously constructed by their predecessors. In approaching questions involving collective bargaining and public employment, union lawyers and academic commentators have for some years been criticizing the concept of the sovereignty of the public employer, and its offspring, the doctrine of the illegal delegation of power. These two lawyer-made constructs once had imposed formidable obstacles to collective bargaining in the public sector of our economy.* But this criticism,

Reprinted by permission of The Yale Law Journal Company and Fred B. Rothman & Company from *The Yale Law Journal* 78, no. 7 (June 1969), pp. 1107-27.

*For the flavor of the rhetoric, see *Railway Mail Ass'n v. Murphy*, 180 Misc. 868, 875, 44 NYS2d 601, 607 (Super Ct 1943). rev'd on other grounds sub nom. *Railway Mail Ass'n v. Corsi*, 267 App. Div. 470, aff'd, 293 NY 315, 56 NE2d 721, aff'd 326 US 88 (1945):

To tolerate or recognize any combination of civil service employees of the government as a labor organization or union is not only incompati-

vastly strengthened by the changing nature of government employment and the ever visible example of collective bargaining in the private sector, has led to a liberalized common law and a growing body
of enacted law and has reduced to a whisper the counsel of restraint
voiced by these constructs.*

Consider sovereignty, that concept so elusive as an analytical
tool, yet so fundamental to all notions of government. *Black's Law
Dictionary* (1933) advises that it is the "supreme, absolute, and un-
controllable power by which any independent state is governed . . . ." Since collective bargaining in the private sector is believed by many to be a system of countervailing power—a means,
that is, by which the power of employees is increased to offset that
of employers—one might easily see its establishment in the public
sector as an infringement on governmental power and the sovereignty
of the state itself. Viewing the "supreme, absolute, and uncon-
trollable" sovereign in its role as an employer, therefore, Franklin
Roosevelt (1937) understandably said, "A strike of public employees
manifests nothing less than an intent on their part to obstruct the
operations of government until their demands are satisfied. Such
action looking toward the paralysis of government by those who
have sworn to support it is unthinkable and intolerable."

But, to the lawyer-critics, sovereignty seems a weak reed when
the private analogy is pressed. It was 1836 when a judge observed
that if collective bargaining in the private sector were "tolerated, the
constitutional control over our affairs would pass away from the

---

ble with the spirit of democracy, but inconsistent with every principle
upon which our government is founded. Nothing is more dangerous to
public welfare than to admit that hired servants of the State can dictate to
the government the hours, the wages and conditions under which they will
carry on essential services vital to the welfare, safety and security of the
citizen. To admit as true that government employees have power to halt or
check the functions of government, unless their demands are satisfied, is to
transfer to them all legislative, executive and judicial power. Nothing
would be more ridiculous. (180 Misc. at 875)

*The most important of the "liberal" common law decisions is the early
Connecticut case of *Norwalk Teachers Ass'n v. Board of Education*, 138 Conn
269, 83 A2d 482 (1951). Among the states recently enacting comprehensive
public employee relations acts are Massachusetts, Mass. Ann. Laws ch. 149
§§423.201-216 (1967); and New York, N.Y. Civil Serv. Law §§200-12
(McKinney Supp. 1967).

people at large, and become vested in the hands of conspirators. We should have a new system of government, and our rights [would] be placed at the disposal of a voluntary and self-constituted association" (*People v. Faulkner,* NY (1836), reproduced in Commons et al. (1958)). Such sovereignty-related assertions are no longer thought to have applicability to the private sector, for private collective bargaining has served as the nation's labor policy for more than a generation —not without criticism, but surely without any sign of the apocalypse. And so, conclude the critics, the notion of sovereignty as a bar to collective bargaining is not a concept peculiar to the public employer, but is merely an anti-union make-weight left over from an earlier day when the law was hostile to all collective bargaining.

Sovereignty must also seem to the critics too elusive and too remote a concept to be of practical significance in the fashioning of labor policy. The issue is not, they say, whether government's power is "supreme," but how government as an employer ought to exercise that power. And the concept of sovereignty, while it locates the source of ultimate authority, does not seem to speak to that issue.

The doctrine of the illegal delegation of power, however, does address itself to that question, for it is a constitutional doctrine which sometimes forbids government from sharing its powers with others (*Muford v. Mayor and City Council of Baltimore,* aff'd, 185 Md 266, 44 A2d 745 (1946)). The doctrine of illegal delegation commands that certain discretionary decisions be made solely on the basis of the judgment of a designated official. And because a great deal of shared control is implicit in any scheme of collective bargaining, the delegation doctrine has been employed in the past to prevent all bargaining between government and its employees. Even today it serves as a basis for establishing limits on the scope of collective bargaining in public employment. Often subjects of vital interest to employees are subjects that cannot be resolved through the collective bargaining process, because they are by law nondelegable (see, e.g., Executive Order 10988, Employee-Management Cooperation in Federal Service, 27 Fed Reg 551 (1962); *In re Farmingdale Classroom Teachers,* 68 LRRM 2761 (NY Super Ct 1968)). In some jurisdictions, moreover, the delegation doctrine places in doubt the binding force of bargains struck (see *Transit Union v. Public Transit Board,* 430 SW2d 107 (Texas Ct Civ. App. 1968)); and in others it is employed as an excuse for not bargaining even though such bargaining is legally permissible (compare *Regents v. Packing House Workers*, 68 LRRM 2677 (Iowa Dist Ct 1968), with *Fort Smith v. Council no. 38, AFSCME,* 433 SW2d 153 (Ark 1968)).

Again, however, the lawyer-critics press the analogy of the private sector and again find the limiting doctrine an inadequate basis for a distinction. Private employers from the beginning of American labor history have insisted upon management prerogatives. Certain decisions—their rhetoric claims—must be made by management alone and cannot be subject to shared control.* While the decisions at issue have changed over the years—from wage rates to subcontracting, from hours of work to automation—the assertion of management prerogatives has been the private sector's analogue to the illegal delegation of power (see, e.g., *Inland Steel Co. v. NLRB,* 170 F2d 247 (7th Cir 1948), cert. denied, 336 US 960 (1949); *Fibreboard Paper Products Corp. v. NLRB,* 379 US 203 (1964)): management is charged with the lawful responsibility for making management decisions; the decision in question is a management decision; it cannot be shared, for to share would be to give control to those without legal responsibility. The earliest American labor cases sometimes contained rhetoric of this sort. Compare *State v. Glidden,* 55 Conn 46, 72, 8 A 890, 894 (1887), with *Commonwealth v. Pullis* (1806), reproduced in Commons et al. (1958).

In the private sector the establishment of collective bargaining is itself a rejection of these arguments. Based on a belief that bargaining

---

*Consider the following statement of Charles E. Wilson made in 1948 when he was President of General Motors:

If we consider the ultimate result of this tendency to stretch collective bargaining to comprehend any subject that a union leader may desire to bargain on, we come out with the union leaders really running the economy of the country; but with no legal or public responsibility and with no private employment except as they may permit.

Under these conditions, the freedom of management to function properly without interference in making its every-day decisions will be gradually restricted. The union leaders—particularly where they have industry-wide power—will have the deciding vote in all managerial decisions, or at least, will exercise a veto power that will stop progress.

Only by defining and restricting collective bargaining to its proper sphere can we hope to save what we have come to know as our American system and keep it from evolving into an alien form, imported from East of the Rhine . . . . (Chamberlain and Cullen 1965)

is likely to be unfair when the individual employee is ranged against the employer, and that "industrial democracy" is necessary to rescue the employee from the psychological emasculation of modern industry, collective bargaining inevitably entails shared control of "wages, hours, and other terms and conditions of employment" (Labor-Management Relations Act §8(d), 29 USC §158(d) (1964)). And there is nothing in any realistic description of the management function to require that the quoted language be given anything other than an expansive reading (Wellington 1968). Given the conservative ideology of the American labor movement, we need not fear that the unions will intrude on matters which in fact are "solely of interest to management." They are hardly likely to expend their limited power in disputes over issues having no impact on the worker. Nor are there lines to be drawn on grounds of economic efficiency. Since the efficiency of an employer is reflected in the cost of his product, whether that cost is imposed through high wages or a restriction on the introduction of machinery, is a matter of indifference to society. Thus, in our system of private collective bargaining, economic power and the parties' desires are the only rational determinants of what matters should be subjects of bargaining (see Cox and Dunlop 1950; Kerr et al. 1961).

Therefore, ask the lawyer-critics, is not the doctrine of illegal delegation in the public sector to be treated in the same way as the management prerogatives question in the private?* And are not the reasons for collective bargaining in the public sector the same as those in the private?

While there seems to be considerable justification for viewing the public employee as the functional equivalent of the private employee, we believe collective bargaining cannot be fully transplanted from the private sector to the public. The reasons why this is so are reasons, moreover, that should lead lawyers to a rather more sympathetic treatment of delegation and sovereignty. Our argument begins with the rationale for collective bargaining in the private sector.

----

*In the private area, many subjects, in fact, have been held not to be mandatory subjects of bargaining. As to nonmandatory subjects, neither employer nor union has a duty to bargain. Indeed, to press bargaining about such a subject is itself an unfair labor practice. See *NLRB v. Wooster Division of Borg-Warner Corp.*, 356 US 342 (1958).

The Claims for Collective Bargaining in the Private Sector

Those who deny the validity of the claims for collective bargaining in the private sector will surely not find those claims to have merit in the public. We do not intend to debate the merits of these claims. We must, however, if we are fully to test our thesis that a full transplant of collective bargaining to the public sector is inappropriate, assume a minimal validity of the claims that are made for it in the private.

Four claims then, are made for private-sector collective bargaining. First, it is a way to achieve industrial peace. The point was put as early as 1902 by the Industrial Commission:

The chief advantage which comes from the practice of periodically determining the conditions of labor by collective bargaining directly between employers and employees is that thereby each side obtains a better understanding of the actual state of the industry, of the conditions which confront the other side, and of the motives which influence it. Most strikes and lockouts would not occur if each party understood exactly the position of the other.

Second, collective bargaining is a way of achieving industrial democracy—that is, participation by workers in their own governance. It is the industrial counterpart of the contemporary demand for community participation (see, e.g., testimony of Louis D. Brandeis before the Commission on Industrial Relations, January 23, 1915, S. Doc. no. 415, 64th Cong., 1st sess. 8, 7657-81 (1916)).

Third, unions that bargain collectively with employers represent workers in the political arena as well. And political representation through interest groups is one of the most important types of political representation that the individual can have. Government at all levels acts in large part in response to the demands made upon it by the groups to which its citizens belong (Wellington 1968).

Fourth, and most important, as a result of a belief in the unequal bargaining power of employers and employees, collective bargaining is claimed to be a needed substitute for individual bargaining.*

----

*See, e.g., *Final Report of the Industrial Commission* (1902):
    It is quite generally recognized that the growth of great aggregations of capital under the control of single groups of men, which is so prominent a feature of the economic development of recent years, necessitates a cor-

Monopsony—a buyer's monopoly,* in this case a buyer of labor—is alleged to exist in many situations and to create unfair contracts of labor as a result of individual bargaining. While this, in turn, may not mean that workers as a class and over time get significantly less than they should—because monopsony is surely not a general condition but is alleged to exist only in a number of particular circumstances†—it may mean that the terms and conditions of employment for an individual or group of workers at a given period of time and in given circumstances may be unfair. What tends to ensure fairness in the aggregate and over the long run is the discipline of the market.‡ But monopsony, if it exists, can work substantial injustice to individuals. Governmental support of collective bargaining represents the nation's response to a belief that such injustice occurs. Fairness between employee and employer in wages, hours, and terms and conditions of employment is thought more likely to be ensured where private ordering takes the collective form (see, e.g., Labor-Management Relations Act § 1, 29 USC § 151 (1964)).

---

responding aggregation of workingmen into unions, which may be able also to act as units. It is readily perceived that the position of the single workman, face to face with one of our great modern combinations, such as the United States Steel Corporation, is a position of very great weakness. The workman has one thing to sell—his labor. He has perhaps devoted years to the acquirement of a skill which gives his labor power a relatively high value, so long as he is able to put it to use in combination with certain materials and machinery. A single legal person has, to a very great extent, the control of such machinery, and in particular of such materials. Under such conditions there is little competition for the workman's labor. Control of the means of production gives power to dictate to the workingman upon what terms he shall make use of them.

*Our use of the term monopsony is not intended to suggest a labor market with a single employer. Rather we mean any market condition in which the terms and conditions of employment are generally below that which would have existed if the employers behaved competitively.

†There is by no means agreement that monopsony is a significant factor. For a theoretical discussion, see Machlup (1952); for an empirical study, see Bunting (1962).

‡See, e.g., Reynolds (1961). To the extent that monopsonistic conditions exist at any particular time one would expect them to be transitory. For even if we assume a high degree of labor immobility, a low wage level in a labor market will attract outside employers. Over time, therefore, the benefits of monopsony seem to carry with them the seeds of its destruction. But the time may seem a very long time in the life of any individual worker.

There are, however, generally recognized social costs resulting from this resort to collectivism.* In the private sector these costs are primarily economic, and the question is, given the benefits of collective bargaining as an institution, what is the nature of the economic costs? Economists who have turned their attention to this question are legion, and disagreement among them monumental (compare, e.g., Simons 1944 with Lester 1947). The principal concerns are of two intertwined sorts. One is summarized by Rees (1962, pp. 194-95):

If the union is viewed solely in terms of its effect on the economy, it must in my opinion be considered an obstacle to the optimum performance of our economic system. It alters the wage structure in a way that impedes the growth of employment in sectors of the economy where productivity and income are naturally high and that leaves too much labor in low-income sectors of the economy like southern agriculture and the least skilled trades. It benefits most those workers who would in any case be relatively well off, and while some of this gain may be at the expense of the owners of capital, most of it must be at the expense of consumers and the lower-paid workers. Unions interfere blatantly with the use of the most productive techniques in some industries, and this effect is probably not offset by the stimulus to higher productivity furnished by some other unions.

The other concern is stated in the 1967 Annual Report of the Council of Economic Advisors:

Vigorous competition is essential to price stability in a high employment economy. But competitive forces do not and cannot operate with equal strength in every sector of the economy. In industries where the number of competitors is limited, business firms have a substantial measure of discretion in setting prices. In many sectors of the labor market, unions and managements together have a

---

*The monopsony justification views collective bargaining as a system of countervailing power—that is, the collective power of the workers countervails the bargaining power of employers. See Galbraith (1956). Accepting the entire line of argument up to this point, however, collective bargaining nevertheless seems a crude device for meeting the monopsony problem, since there is no particular reason to think that collective bargaining will be instituted where there is monopsony (or that it is more likely to be instituted there). In some circumstances collective bargaining may even raise wages above a "competitive" level. On the other hand, the collective bargaining approach is no cruder than the law's general response to perceived unfairness in the application of the freedom of contract doctrine. See Wellington (1968).

substantial measure of discretion in setting wages. The responsible exercise of discretionary power over wages and prices can help to maintain general price stability. Its irresponsible use can make full employment and price stability incompatible. (p. 119)

And the claim is that this "discretionary power" too often is exercised "irresponsibly" (see generally Sheahan 1967).

Disagreement among economists extends to the quantity as well as to the fact of economic malfunctioning that properly is attributable to collective bargaining (see, e.g., Lewis 1963 and earlier studies discussed therein). But there is no disagreement that at some point the market disciplines or delimits union power. As we shall see in more detail below, union power is frequently constrained by the fact that consumers react to a relative increase in the price of a product by purchasing less of it. As a result any significant real financial benefit, beyond that justified by an increase in productivity, which accrues to workers through collective bargaining, may well cause significant unemployment among union members. Because of this employment-benefit relationship, the economic costs imposed by collective bargaining as it presently exists in the private sector seem inherently limited (see generally Dunlop 1944; Friedman 1957).

The Claims for Collective Bargaining in the Public Sector

In the area of public employment the claims upon public policy made by the need for industrial peace, industrial democracy, and effective political representation point toward collective bargaining. This is to say that three of the four arguments that support bargaining in the private sector—to some extent, at least—press for similar arrangements in the public sector.

Government is a growth industry, particularly state and municipal government. While federal employment between 1963 and 1968 has increased from 2.36 million to 2.73 million, state and local employment has risen from 6.87 to 9.42 million (*Labor Relations Yearbook—1968,* p. 451), and the increase continues apace. With size comes bureaucracy, and with bureaucracy comes the isolation and alienation of the individual worker. His manhood, like that of his industrial counterpart, is threatened. Lengthening chains of command necessarily depersonalize the employment relationship and contribute to a sense of powerlessness on the part of the worker. If he is to share in the governance of his employment relationship as he does in the private sector, it must be through the device of representation, which means unionization (see *Final Report of the Industrial Commission* 1902; Summers 1962). Accordingly, just as the increase in the size of economic units in private industry fostered unionism, so that the enlarging of governmental bureaucracy has encouraged public employees to look to collective action for a sense of control over their employment destiny. The number of government employees, moreover, makes it plain that those employees are members of an interest group which can organize for political representation as well as for job participation. (For the "early" history, see Spero 1970.)

The pressures thus generated by size and bureaucracy lead inescapably to disruption—to labor unrest—unless these pressures are recognized and unless existing decision-making procedures are accommodated to them. Peace in government employment too, the argument runs, can best be established by making union recognition and collective bargaining accepted public policy (see, e.g., Governor's Committee on Public Employee Relations 1966).

Much less clearly analogous to the private model, however, is the unequal bargaining power argument. In the private sector that argument really has two aspects. The first, which we have just adumbrated, is affirmative in nature. Monopsony is believed sometimes to result in unfair individual contracts of employment. The unfairness may be reflected in wages, which are less than they would be if the market were more nearly perfect, or in working arrangements which may lodge arbitrary power in a foreman, i.e., power to hire, fire, promote, assign, or discipline without respect to substantive or procedural rules. A persistent assertion, generating much heat, relates to the arbitrary exercise of managerial power in individual cases. This assertion goes far to explain the insistence of unions on the establishment in the labor contract of rules, with an accompanying adjudicatory procedure, to govern industrial life (see, e.g., Chamberlain 1967).

Judgments about the fairness of the financial terms of the public employee's individual contract of employment are even harder to make than for private sector workers. The case for the existence of private employer monopsony, disputed as it is, asserts only that some private sector employers in some circumstances have too much bargaining power. In the public sector, the case to be proven is that the governmental employer ever has such power. But even if this case could be proven, market norms are at best attenuated guides to questions of fairness. In employment as in all other areas, governmental decisions are properly political decisions, and economic considerations are but one criterion among many. Questions of fairness do not centrally relate to how much imperfection one sees in the market, but more to how much imperfection one sees in the political process. "Low" pay for teachers may be merely a decision—right or wrong, resulting from the pressure of special interests or from a desire to promote the general welfare—to exchange a reduction in the quality or quantity of teachers for higher welfare payments, a domed stadium, etc. And we are limited in our ability to make informed judgments about such political decisions because of the understandable but unfortunate fact that the science of politics has failed to supply us with either as elegant or as reliable a theoretical model as has its sister discipline.

Nevertheless, employment benefits in the public sector may have improved relatively more slowly than in the private sector during the last three decades. An economy with a persistent inflationary bias probably works to the disadvantage of those who must rely on legislation for wage adjustments.* Moreover, while public employment was once attractive for the greater job security and retirement benefits it provided, quite similar protection is now available in many areas of the private sector (see Taylor 1967). On the other hand, to the extent that civil service, or merit, systems exist in public employment and these laws are obeyed, the arbitrary exercise of managerial power is substantially reduced. Where it is reduced, a labor policy that relies on the individual employment contract must seem less unacceptable.

The second, or negative aspect of the unequal bargaining power argument, relates to the social costs of collective bargaining. As we have seen, the social costs of collective bargaining in the private sector are principally economic, and seem inherently limited by market

---

*This is surely one reason which might explain the widely assumed fact that public employees have fallen behind their private sector counterparts. See Stieber (1967).

forces. In the public sector, however, the costs seem to us economic only in a very narrow sense and are on the whole political. It further seems to us that, to the extent union power is delimited by market or other forces in the public sector, these constraints do not come into play nearly as quickly as in the private. An understanding of why this is so requires further comparison between collective bargaining in the two sectors.

The Private Sector Model

While the private sector is, of course, extraordinarily diverse, the paradigm case is an industry which produces a product that is not particularly essential to those who buy it and for which dissimilar products can be substituted. Within the market or markets for this product, most—but not all—of the producers must bargain with a union representing their employees, and this union is generally the same through the industry. A price rise of this product relative to others will result in a decrease in the number of units of the product sold. This in turn will result in a cutback in employment. And an increase in price would be dictated by an increase in labor cost relative to output, at least in most situations.* Thus, the union is faced with some sort of rough trade-off between, on the one hand, larger benefits for some employees and unemployment for others, and on the other hand, smaller benefits and more employment. Because unions are political organizations, with a legal duty to represent *all* employees fairly (*Steele v. Louisville & N.R.R.*, 323 US 192 (1944)), and with a treasury that comes from per capita dues, there is pressure on the union to avoid the road that leads to unemployment.[†]

This picture of the restraints that the market imposes on collective bargaining settlements undergoes change as the variables change. On the one hand, to the extent that there are nonunion firms within a product market, the impact of union pressure will be diminished by the ability of consumers to purchase identical products from

---

*The cost increase may, of course, take some time to work through and appear as a price increase. See Rees (1962). In some oligopolistic situations the firm may be able to raise prices after a wage increase without suffering a significant decrease in sales.

[†]The pressure is sometimes resisted. Indeed, the United Mine Workers has chosen more benefits for less employment. See generally Baratz (1955).

nonunion and, presumably, less expensive sources. On the other hand, to the extent that union organization of competitors within the product market is complete, there will be no such restraint and the principal barriers to union bargaining goals will be the ability of a number of consumers to react to a price change by turning to dissimilar but nevertheless substitutable products.

Two additional variables must be noted. First, where the demand for an industry's product is rather insensitive to price—i.e., relatively inelastic—and where all the firms in a product market are organized, the union need fear less the employment-benefit trade-off, for the employer is less concerned about raising prices in response to increased costs. By hypothesis, a price rise affects unit sales of such an employer only minimally. Second, in an expanding industry, wage settlements which exceed increases in productivity may not reduce union employment. They will reduce expansion, hence the employment effect will be experienced only by workers who do not belong to the union. This means that in the short run the politics of the employment-benefit trade-off do not restrain the union in its bargaining demands.

In both of these cases, however, there are at least two restraints on the union. One is the employer's increased incentive to substitute machines for labor, a factor present in the paradigm case and all other cases as well. The other restraint stems from the fact that large sections of the nation are unorganized and highly resistant to unionization ("Trends and Changes in Union Membership" 1966; Bernstein 1961). Accordingly, capital will seek nonunion labor, and in this way the market will discipline the organized sector.

The employer, in the paradigm case and in all variations of it, is motivated primarily by the necessity to maximize profits (and this is so no matter how political a corporation may seem to be). He therefore is not inclined (absent an increase in demand for his product) to raise prices and thereby suffer a loss in profits, and he is organized to transmit and represent the market pressures described above. Generally he will resist, and resist hard, union demands that exceed increases in productivity, for if he accepts such demands he may be forced to raise prices. Should he be unsuccessful in his resistance too often, and should it cost him too much, he can be expected to put his money and energy elsewhere.*

---

*And the law would protect him in this. Indeed, it would protect him if he were moved by an anti-union animus as well as by valid economic considera-

What all this means is that the social costs imposed by collective bargaining are economic costs; that usually they are limited by powerful market restraints; and that these restraints are visible to anyone who is able to see the forest for the trees.*

The Public Sector Model

The paradigm case in the public sector is a municipality with an elected board of aldermen, and an elected mayor who bargains (through others) with unions representing the employees of the city. He bargains also, of course, with other permanent and ad hoc interest groups making claims upon government (business groups, save-the-park committees, neighborhood groups, etc.). Indeed, the decisions that are made may be thought of roughly as a result of interactions and accommodations among these interest groups, as influenced by perceptions about the attitudes of the electorate, and by the goals and programs of the mayor and his aldermanic board (see generally Dahl 1961; on interest theory, see Truman 1951).

Decisions that cost the city money are generally paid for from taxes and, less often, by borrowing. Not only are there many types of taxes, but also there are several layers of government which may make tax revenue available to the city; federal and state as well as local funds may be employed for some purposes. Formal allocation of money for particular uses is made through the city's budget, which may have within it considerable room for adjustments (see, e.g., Sayre and Kaufman 1960). Thus, a union will bargain hard for as large a share of the budget as it thinks it possibly can obtain, and beyond this to force a tax increase if it deems that possible.

In the public sector too, the market operates. In the long run, the supply of labor is a function of the price paid for labor by the public employer relative to what workers earn elsewhere (Moskow 1966). This is some assurance that public employees in the aggregate —with or without collective bargaining—are not paid too little. The

---

tions. See *Textile Workers Union v. Darlington Manufacturing Co.*, 380 US 263 (1965).

Of course, where fixed costs are large relative to variable costs, it may be difficult for an employer to extricate himself.

*This does not mean, of course, that collective bargaining in the private sector is free of social costs. It means only that the costs are necessarily limited by the discipline of the market.

case for employer monopsony, moreover, may be much weaker in the public sector than it is in the private. First, to the extent that most public employees work in urban areas, as they probably do, there may often be a number of substitutable and competing private and public employers in the labor market. When that is the case, there can be little monopsony power.* Second, even if public employers occasionally have monopsony power, governmental policy is determined only in part by economic criteria, and there is no assurance, as there is in the private sector where the profit motive prevails, that the power will be exploited.

As we have seen, market-imposed unemployment is an important restraint on unions in the private sector. In the public sector, the trade-off between benefits and employment seems much less important. Government does not generally sell a product the demand for which is closely related to price. There usually are not close substitutes for the products and services provided by government and the demand for them is inelastic. Such market conditions are, as we have seen, favorable to unions in the private sector because they permit the acquisition of benefits without the penalty of unemployment, subject to the restraint of nonunion competitors, actual or potential. But no such restraint limits the demands of public employee unions. Because much government activity is, and must be, a monopoly, product competition, nonunion or otherwise, does not exert a downward pressure on prices and wages. Nor will the existence of a pool of labor ready to work for a wage below union scale attract new capital and create a new, and competitively less expensive, governmental enterprise. The fear of unemployment, however, can serve as something of a restraining force in two situations. First, if the cost of labor increases, the city may reduce the quality of the service it furnishes by reducing employment. For example, if teachers' salaries are increased, it may decrease the number of teachers and increase class size. However, the ability of city government to accomplish such a change is limited not only by union pressure, but also by the pressure

---

*This is based on the reasonable but not unchallengeable assumption that the number of significant employers in a labor market is related to the existence of monopsony. See Bunting (1962). The greater the number of such employers in a labor market, the greater the departure from the classic case of the monopsony of the single employer. The number of employers would clearly seem to affect their ability to make and enforce a collusive wage agreement.

of other affected interest groups in the community (organized parent groups, for example). Political considerations, therefore, may cause either no reduction in employment or services, or a reduction in an area other than that in which the union members work. Both the political power exerted by the beneficiaries of the services, who are also voters, and the power of the public employee union as a labor organization, then, combine to create great pressure on political leaders either to seek new funds or to reduce municipal services of another kind. Second, if labor costs increase, the city may, even as a private employer would, seek to replace labor with machines. The absence of a profit motive, and a political concern for unemployment, however, may be a deterrent in addition to the deterrent of union resistance. The public employer which decides it must limit employment because of unit labor costs will likely find that the politically easiest decision is to restrict new hires, rather than to lay off current employees.

Even if we are right that a close relationship between increased economic benefits and unemployment does not exist as a significant deterrent to unions in the public sector, might not the argument be made that in some sense the taxpayer is the public sector's functional equivalent of the consumer? If taxes become too high, the taxpayer can move to another community. While it is generally much easier for a consumer to substitute products than for a taxpayer to substitute communities, is it not fair to say that, at the point at which a tax increase will cause so many taxpayers to move that it will produce less total revenue, the market disciplines or restrains union and public employer in the same way and for the same reasons that the market disciplines parties in the private sector? Moreover, does not the analogy to the private sector suggest that it is legitimate in an economic sense for unions to push government to the point of substitutability?

Several factors suggest that the answer to this latter question is at best indeterminate, and that the question of legitimacy must be judged not by economic, but by political criteria.

In the first place, there is no theoretical reason—economic or political—to suppose that it is desirable for a governmental entity to liquidate its taxing power, to tax up to the point where another tax increase will produce less revenue because of the number of people it drives to different communities. In the private area, profit maximization is a complex concept, but its approximation generally is both a legal requirement and socially useful as a means of allocating resources (see generally Dorfman 1972). The liquidation of taxing power seems neither imperative nor useful.

Second, consider the complexity of the tax structure and the way in which different kinds of taxes (property, sales, income) fall differently upon a given population. Consider, moreover, that the taxing authority of a particular governmental entity may be limited (a municipality may not have the power to impose an income tax). What is necessarily involved, then, is principally the redistribution of income by government rather than resource allocation,* and questions of income redistribution surely are essentially political questions.†

For his part, the mayor in our paradigm case will be disciplined not by a desire to maximize profits, but by a desire—in some cases at least—to do a good job (to effectuate his programs), and in virtually all cases either to be reelected or to move to a better elective office. What he gives to the union must be taken from some other interest group or from taxpayers. His is the job of coordinating these competing claims while remaining politically viable. And that coordination will be governed by the relative power of the competing interest groups. Our inquiry, therefore, must turn to the question of how much power public employee unions will exercise if the full private model of collective bargaining is adopted in the public sector.

Public Employee Strikes and the Political Process

Although the market does not discipline the union in the public sector to the extent that it does in the private, the paradigm case,

---

*In the private sector what is involved is principally resource allocation rather than income redistribution. Income redistribution occurs to the extent that unions are able to increase wages at the expense of profits, but the extent to which this actually happens would seem to be limited. It also occurs to the extent that unions, by limiting employment in the union sector through maintenance of wages above a competitive level, increase the supply of labor in the nonunion sector and thereby depress wages there.

†In the private sector the political question was answered when the National Labor Relations Act was passed: the benefits of collective bargaining (with the strike) outweigh the social costs.

nevertheless, would seem to be consistent with what Robert A. Dahl (1956) has called the " 'normal' American political process," which is "one in which there is a high probability that an active and legitimate group in the population can make itself heard effectively at some crucial stage in the process of decision," for the union may be seen as little more than an "active and legitimate group in the population." With elections in the background to perform, as Mr. Dahl tells us, "the critical role . . . in maximizing political equality and popular sovereignty," all seems well, at least theoretically, with collective bargaining and public employment.

But there is trouble even in the house of theory if collective bargaining in the public sector means what it does in the private. The trouble is that if unions are able to withhold labor—to strike—as well as to employ the usual methods of political pressure, they may possess a disproportionate share of effective power in the process of decision. Collective bargaining would then be so effective a pressure as to skew the results of the " 'normal' American political process."

One should straightway make plain that the strike issue is not *simply* the essentiality of public services as contrasted with services or products produced in the private sector. This is only half of the issue, and in the past the half truth has beclouded analysis (see, e.g., Spero 1970). The services performed by a private transit authority are neither less nor more essential to the public than those that would be performed if the transit authority were owned by a municipality. A railroad or a dock strike may be much more damaging to a community than "job action" by teachers. This is not to say that governmental services are not essential. They are, both because the demand for them is inelastic and because their disruption may seriously injure a city's economy and occasionally the physical welfare of its citizens. Nevertheless, essentiality of governmental services is only a necessary part of, rather than a complete answer to, the question: What is wrong with strikes in public employment?

What is wrong with strikes in public employment is that because they disrupt essential services, a large part of a mayor's political constituency will press for a quick end to the strike with little concern for the cost of settlement. The problem is that because market restraints are attenuated and because public employee strikes cause inconvenience to voters, such strikes too often succeed. Since other interest groups with conflicting claims on municipal government do not, as a general proposition, have anything approaching the effectiveness of this union technique—or at least cannot maintain this relative degree of power over the long run—they are put at a significant competitive disadvantage in the political process. Where this is the case, it must be said that the political process has been radically altered. And because of the deceptive simplicity of the analogy to collective bargaining in the private sector, the alteration may take place without anyone realizing what has happened.

Therefore, while the purpose and effect of strikes by public employees may seem in the beginning merely designed to establish collective bargaining or to "catch up" with wages and fringe benefits in the private sector, in the long run strikes must be seen as a means to redistribute income, or, put another way, to gain a subsidy for union members,* not through the employment of the usual types of political pressure, but through the employment of what might appropriately be called political force.

As is often the case when one generalizes, this picture may be thought to be overdrawn. In order to refine analysis, it will be helpful to distinguish between strikes that occur over monetary issues and strikes involving nonmonetary issues. The generalized picture sketched above is essentially valid as to the former. Because there is usually no substitute for governmental services, the citizen-consumer faced with a strike of teachers, or garbage men, or social workers is likely to be seriously inconvenienced. This in turn places enormous pressure on the mayor, who is apt to find it difficult to look to the long-run balance sheet of the municipality. Most citizens are directly affected by a strike of sanitation workers. Few, however, can decipher a municipal budget or trace the relationship between today's labor settlement and next year's increase in the mill rate. Thus, in the typical case the impact of a settlement is less visible—or can more often be concealed—than the impact of a disruption of services. Moreover, the cost of settlement may be borne by a constituency

---

*Strikes in some areas of the private sector may have this effect, too. The difference in the impact of collective bargaining in the two sectors should be seen as a continuum. Thus, for example, it may be that market restraints do not sufficiently discipline strike settlements in some regulated industries, or in industries that rely mainly on government contracts. If this is so—and we do not know that it is—perhaps there should be tighter restraints on the use of the strike in those areas.

much larger—the whole state or nation—than that represented by the mayor. It follows that the mayor usually will look to the electorate which is clamoring for a settlement, and in these circumstances, the union's fear of a long strike, a major check on its power in the private sector, is not a consideration.* In the face of all of these factors other interest groups with priorities different from the union's are apt to be much less successful in their pursuit of scarce tax dollars than is the union with power to withhold services.†

With respect to strikes over some nonmonetary issues—decentralization of the governance of schools might be an example—the intensity of concern on the part of well-organized interest groups opposed to the union's position would support the mayor in his resistance to union demands. But even here, if union rank-and-file back their leadership, the pressures for settlement from the general public, which may be largely indifferent as to the underlying issue, would in time become irresistible.‡

Sovereignty and Delegation Revisited

As applied to public employment, there is a concept of sovereignty entitled to count as a reason for making strikes by public employees illegal. For what sovereignty should mean in this field is not the location of ultimate authority—on that the critics are dead right—

---

*Contrast the situation in the private sector:
Management cannot normally win the short strike. Management can only win the long strike. Also management frequently tends in fact to win the long strike. As a strike lengthens, it commonly bears more heavily on the union and the employees than on management. Strike relief is no substitute for a job. Even regular strike benefits, which few unions can afford, and which usually exhaust the union treasury quite rapidly (with some exceptions), are no substitute for a job. (Livernash 1963)

†A vivid example would seem to be provided by recent experience in New Jersey. After a twelve hour strike by Newark firefighters on July 11, 1969, state urban aid funds, originally authorized for helping the poor, were diverted to salary increases for firemen and police. See *N.Y. Times*, August 7, 1969, p. 25. Moreover, government decision makers other than the mayor (e.g., the governor) may have interests different from the mayor, interests which manifest themselves in pressures for settlement.

‡Consider also the effect of such strikes on the fabric of society. See, e.g., Mayer (1969).

but the right of government, through its laws, to ensure the survival
of the " 'normal' American political process." As hard as it may be
for some to accept, strikes by public employees may, as a long run
proposition, threaten that process.*

Moreover, it is our view—although this would seem to be much
less clear—that the public stake in some issues makes it appropriate
for government either not to have to bargain with its employees on
these issues at all (compare Executive Order 10988, 27 Fed Reg 551
(1962)) or to follow bargaining procedures radically different from
those of the private sector. It is in this respect that the judicial doctrine of illegal delegation of power should have relevance.

Consider, for example, the question of a public review board for
police; or, for that matter, the question of school decentralization.
These issues, viewed by the unions involved primarily as questions of
job security, engage the interest of so many disparate groups in a
relevant population, that it may be thought unfair to allow one
group—the police, the teachers—to exert pressure through collective
bargaining (quite apart from the strike) in which competing groups
do not directly participate as well as through the channels (e.g.,
lobbying) open to other interest groups.

Our hesitation in this area is caused by two factors. First, models of the political process have trouble with fine-grained distinctions
about too much power. Given the vulnerability of most municipal
employers, one can say with some confidence that the strike imparts
too much power to an interest group only because the distinction
addressed there is not fine-grained at all. Second, it is difficult indeed
for any governmental institution to make judgments about the issues
that should be included in the nonbargainable class. The courts are
badly suited to this task; and the legislature is not well constituted to
come in after the fact and effect a change. Nevertheless, limits will
have to be set or bargaining procedures radically changed, and this
will in a sense be giving content to the doctrine of delegation as it
bears upon the subject of public employment.

---

*It should be understood that this claim is with respect to the employ-
ment of the strike once collective bargaining is established. In our opinion the
opportunity for public employees to organize and bargain through a union is
compelled by the private sector analogy and is consistent with the survival of the
"normal American political process."

While there is increasing advocacy for expanding the scope of bargaining in public employment and in favor of giving public employees the right to strike—advocacy not just by unionists but by disinterested experts as well—the law generally limits the scope of bargaining and forbids strikes. This is often done with little attention to supporting reasons. Ours has been an attempt to supply these reasons and thereby to give some legitimate content to sovereignty and delegation.

We do not, however, mean to suggest that legislatures should abdicate to the courts the task of constructing a new system of collective bargaining for the public sector through the elaboration of sovereignty and delegation. Legislation is needed, for the problems we have explored require solutions beyond the power of the courts to fashion. In the future, if strikes are to be barred, sophisticated impasse procedures must be established. If, on the other hand, some strikes are to be tolerated, changes in the political structure which will make the municipal employer less vulnerable to work stoppages must be developed. And, in any event, legislative action will be necessary either to separate out those nonmonetary issues which might not be decided solely through collective bargaining, or to change bargaining procedures so that all interested groups may participate in the resolution of such issues.

References

Baratz, M. *The Union and the Coal Industry*. Port Washington, N.Y.: Kennikat Press, 1955.

Bernstein, I. "The Growth of American Unions 1945-1960." *Labor History* 2 (1961): 131.

Black's Law Dictionary (3rd ed.). St. Paul, Minn.: West Publishing, 1933.

Bunting, R. *Employer Concentration in Local Markets*. Chapel Hill: University of North Carolina Press, 1962.

Chamberlain, N. *The Union Challenge to Management Control*. Hamden, Conn.: Shoe String, 1967.

Chamberlain, N., and Cullen, D. E. *The Labor Sector*. New York: McGraw-Hill, 1965.

Commons, J. R., et al. *A Documentary History of American Industrial Society* (vols. 3-4). New York: Russell & Russell, 1958. Reproduction of 1910 edition.

Cox, A., and Dunlop, J. "Regulation of Collective Bargaining by the National Labor Relations Board." *Harvard Law Review* 63 (1950): 389.

Dahl, R. *A Preface to Democratic Theory.* Chicago: University of Chicago Press, 1956.

Dahl, R. *Who Governs: Democracy and Power in an American City.* New Haven: Yale University Press, 1961.

Dorfman, R. *Prices and Markets.* Englewood Cliffs, N.J.: Prentice-Hall, 1972.

Dunlop, J. *Wage Determination Under Trade Unions.* Clifton, N.J.: Kelley, 1944.

Friedman, M. "Some Comments on the Significance of Labor Unions for Economic Policy." *The Impact of the Unions,* edited by D. Wright. Plainview, N.Y.: Books for Libraries, 1957.

Galbraith, J. K. *American Capitalism.* Boston: Houghton Mifflin, 1956.

Governor's Committee on Public Employee Relations. *Final Report.* Albany: State of New York, 1966.

Kerr, C., et al. *Public Interest in National Labor Policy.* New York: Committee for Economic Development, 1961.

Lester, R. "Reflections on the 'Labor Monopoly' Issue." *Journal of Political Economics* 55 (1947): 313.

Lewis, H. G. *Unionism and Relative Wages in the United States.* Chicago: University of Chicago Press, 1963.

Livernash, R. "The Relation of Power to the Structure and Process of Collective Bargaining." *Journal of Law and Economics* 6 (1963): 10-15.

Machlup, F. *The Political Economy of Monopoly.* Baltimore: Johns Hopkins, 1952.

Mayor, M. *The Teacher Strike: New York, 1968.* New York: Harper & Row: 1969.

Moskow, M. H. *Teachers and Unions.* Philadelphia: University of Pennsylvania Press, 1966.

Rees, A. *The Economics of Trade Unions.* Chicago: University of Chicago Press, 1962.

Reynolds, L. *Labor Economics and Labor Relations* (3rd ed.). Englewood Cliffs, N.J.: Prentice-Hall, 1961.

Roosevelt, F. D. Letter to L. C. Stewart (President, National Federation of Federal Employees), August 16, 1937. Cited in S. Vogel, "What About the Rights of the Public Employee?" *Labor Law Journal* 1: 604, 612.

Sayre, W., and Kaufman, H. *Governing New York City.* New York: Russell Sage, 1960.

Sheahan, J. *The Wage-Price Guideposts.* Washington, D.C.: Brookings Institution, 1967.

Simons, K. "Some Reflections on Syndicalism." *Journal of Political Economics* 52 (1944): 1.

Spero, S. *Government as Employer.* Carbondale: Southern Illinois University Press, 1970.

Stieber, J. "Collective Bargaining in the Public Sector." *Challenges to Collective Bargaining,* edited by L. Ulman. Englewood Cliffs, N.J.: Prentice-Hall, 1967.

Summers, N. "American Legislation for Union Democracy." *Modern Law Review* 25 (1962): 273-75.

Taylor, G. "Public Employment: Strike or Procedures." *Industrial and Labor Relations Review* 20 (1967): 623-25.

Truman, D. *The Governmental Process*. New York: Knopf, 1951.

Wellington, H. H. *Labor and the Legal Process*. New Haven: Yale University Press, 1968.

Reading 16

The Role and Consequences of Strikes by Public Employees

John F. Burton, Jr. and Charles Krider

Reason is the life of the law.

—Sir Edward Coke

The life of the law has not been logic: it has been experience.

—Oliver Wendell Holmes

The vexing problem of strikes by public employees has generated a number of assertions based largely on logical analysis. One common theme is that strikes fulfill a useful function in the private sector, but are inappropriate in the public sector, because they distort the political decision-making process. Another is that strikes in nonessential government services should not be permitted because it is administratively infeasible to distinguish among the various government services on the basis of their essentiality. The present article attempts to evaluate these assertions in terms of labor relations experience at the local level of government.

The assertions concerning strikes by public employees which we

Reprinted by permission of The Yale Law Journal Company and Fred B. Rothman & Company from *The Yale Law Journal* 79, no. 3 (January 1970), pp. 418-43.

shall discuss have been drawn mainly from Governor's Committee on Public Employee Relations (1966), hereinafter cited as the Taylor Report, and "The Limits of Collective Bargaining in Public Employment" (reading 15). Most of the evidence used to evaluate these assertions has been gathered in connection with the Brookings Institution *Study of Unionism and Collective Bargaining in the Public Sector*.* Statistical information on all local public employee strikes which have occurred between 1965 and 1968 has been provided by the Bureau of Labor Statistics. Because education is outside the scope of our portion of the Brookings study, the data used in this article primarily relate to strikes by groups other than teachers.

The Role of Strikes in the Private Sector

Wellington and Winter (reading 15) have catalogued four claims which are made to justify collective bargaining in the private sector. First, collective bargaining is a way to achieve industrial peace. Second, it is a way of achieving industrial democracy. Third, unions that bargain collectively with employers also represent workers in the political arena. Fourth, and in their view the most important reason, collective bargaining compensates for the unequal bargaining power which is believed to result from individual bargaining. Wellington and Winter recognize that the gains to employees from collective bargaining, such as protection from monopsony power, are to be balanced against the social costs resulting from the resort to collectivism, such as distortion of the wage structure. While noting that considerable disagreement exists among economists concerning the extent of the benefits and costs, they stress the fact that costs are limited by economic constraints. Unions can displace their members from jobs by ignoring the discipline of the market. These four justifications for private sector collective bargaining are presumably relevant to some degree whether or not strikes are permitted. Nonetheless, one can conceptualize two models of collective bargaining—the strike model, which would normally treat strikes as legal, and the no-strike model,

---

*Some fifty cities, counties, and special districts were visited during 1968-69, and numerous interviews were conducted. Specific references to these interviews are not included because of our guaranty of anonymity to those we interviewed.

which would make all strikes illegal—and evaluate whether, in terms of the above justifications, society benefits from permitting strikes.

Most scholars of industrial relations accept the view that the right to strike is desirable in the private sector. Chamberlain and Kuhn (1965) assert, "The possibility or ultimate threat of strikes is a necessary condition for collective bargaining." The distinguished scholars who comprised the Taylor Committee asserted similarly (p. 15), "The right to strike remains an integral part of the collective bargaining process in the private enterprise sector and this will unquestionably continue to be the case." One reason for this endorsement of the strike is that its availability is often essential to the union in its bid for recognition by the employer.* In addition, once the bargaining relationship is established, the possibility that work may be interrupted forces the parties to bargain seriously.† The possibility of a strike thus increases the likelihood that the parties will reach an agreement without third-party intervention. More important, the ability to strike increases the bargaining power of employees and their union so that, unlike the no-strike model, the employer cannot dominate the employer-employee relationship.

Use of the strike model instead of the no-strike model appears to enhance all but the third of the four claims for private sector collective bargaining offered by Wellington and Winter.‡ While they do

---

*Private sector unions subject to the Labor Management Relations Act (Taft-Hartley Act), 29 USC §§141-97 (1947), have little need for recognition strikes because the right of self-organization is protected by statute.

†"Since a strike hurts management by stopping production and workers by cutting of their wages, neither party is apt to reject terms proposed by the other without serious consideration. . . . Without such a threat they may continue to disagree indefinitely and never bargain seriously, each simply refusing to give ground in an effort to reach a settlement acceptable to both" (Chamberlain and Kuhn 1965).

‡The first reason offered—it is a way to achieve industrial peace—appears to be inconsistent with the notion of permitting strikes as a method of increasing the employees' bargaining power. One possible resolution of this apparent contradiction is that the enhanced bargaining power of the employees will enable them to work out mutually satisfactory terms with their employer without having to resort to the strike, while workers with limited bargaining power will often engage in strikes as an expression of their futility. This explanation is not totally compelling, however, and one may therefore have to justify collective bargaining among parties with equal power on grounds other than the diminution of strikes. The favorable consequences of the last three claims offered by

not provide a claim by claim analysis of the consequences of permitting strikes, their endorsement of strikes in the private sector must indicate that they believe the strike model preferable to the no-strike model.

The Role of Strikes in the Public Sector

What are the virtues of collective bargaining in the public sector, and what are the consequences of permitting strikes by public employees?

The advocates of one view presumably assume that the four reasons offered by Wellington and Winter to justify collective bargaining in the private sector have equal relevance in the public sector. They also assert that strikes play the same role in the public and private sectors, and that our private sector strike policy should be replicated in the public sector. Strikes would not be banned *ab initio* in any function, but could be dealt with *ex post facto* by injunction if an emergency occurred.

This approach has been argued by Theodore W. Kheel (1969), a noted labor arbitrator. He asserts that it is now "evident that collective bargaining is the best way of composing differences between workers and their employers in a democratic society. . . ." The only alternatives to collective bargaining are two: "either the employer makes the final determination or it is made by a third party, an arbitrator." While collective bargaining is the superior type of industrial relations, "collective bargaining cannot exist if employees may not withdraw their services or employers discontinue them."

[However, this does not mean] that the right to strike is sacrosanct. On the contrary, it is a right like all other rights that must be weighed against the larger public interest, and it must be subordinated where necessary to the superior right of the public to protection against injury to health or safety. . . .

These principles, in my judgment, apply to the private sector as well as to the public sector. Moreover, their application cannot be determined in advance.

Instead, Kheel believes, a procedure should be developed which

---

Wellington and Winter for private sector collective bargaining presumably offset any possible increase in strikes.

would halt a strike only after it could be demonstrated that the public health and safety were endangered.

Proponents of the opposing view of public sector strikes argue that such strikes are invariably inappropriate. The Taylor Report (p. 16) concluded that in the public services, "the strike cannot be a part of the negotiating process." And Wellington and Winter clearly believe that overall the four claims for collective bargaining are valid in the public sector only if strikes are illegal. Their primary concern is the fourth reason offered for collective bargaining—collective activity is needed as a substitute for individual activity because individuals are weak.* This reason is always troublesome because increased bargaining power involves costs as well as benefits. They do not endorse the strike model in the public sector because the costs which result from increasing employee bargaining power by permitting strikes are higher and the benefits are less in the public sector than in the private sector.

The benefits of collective action are less in the public sector for several reasons. The problem of employer monopsony is not as consequential, not only because employer monopsony is less likely to occur, but also because existing monopsony power is less likely to be utilized. In addition, the low pay given to certain groups in the public sector, such as teachers, may reflect society's view about the best uses of its resources, while low pay in the private sector for a particular occupation presumably reflects a misallocation of resources.

The costs of substituting collective for individual bargaining are also likely to be higher in the public sector. According to Wellington and Winter, the market restraints on trade union activity are weak, reflecting the inelastic demand for public services, a lack of substitutes for these services, and the fact that many public services are essential. Second, strikes in the public sector lead to public pressure on officials which compels quick settlements. Further, there are no other pressure groups competing for public resources which have weapons comparable to the strike, and, thus, unions have a more advantageous arsenal of weapons. The net result of the lack of mar-

---

*"In the area of public employment the claims upon public policy made by the need for industrial peace, industrial democracy, and effective political representation point toward collective bargaining. . . . Much less clearly analogous to the private model, however, is the unequal bargaining power argument" (reading 15).

ket restraints, the pressure on public officials to settle strikes quickly, and the absence of comparable weaponry by other pressure groups is that strikes in the public sector impose high costs by distorting the normal political process.

Because the cost-benefit ratio which results from the substitution of collective action, including strikes, for individual action is so high in the public sector, Wellington and Winter argue that public employee strikes should be illegal. Their argument is based on their notion of sovereignty. This is not the traditional doctrine of sovereignty, which they specifically reject, but a new version of sovereignty which asserts that the government has the right, through its laws, "to ensure the survival of the 'normal' American political process." This rationale for sovereignty, fully articulated in Wellington and Winter and implicit in the Taylor Report analysis, deserves a careful scrutiny in terms of empirical evidence.

Consequences of Strikes in the Public Sector

The best procedure for evaluating public sector strikes would be to investigate the respective impacts of the strike model and the no-strike model on each of the claims made for collective bargaining. Such an analysis should consider the economic, political, and social effects produced. An inquiry into these effects is particularly important since several authors who have implicitly endorsed the strike model in the private sector have done so more on the basis of non-economic reasons than economic reasons (Rees 1962). Nonetheless, the attack on the strike model in the *public* sector has been based largely on the evaluation of the fourth claim for collective bargaining, that relating to unequal bargaining power. We will attempt to meet this attack by confining our discussion to the economic consequences of collective bargaining with and without strikes.

Even an examination confined to economic consequences is difficult. The most desirable economic data, which would measure the impact of unions on wages and other benefits, is unavailable. A major examination of the relative wage impact of public sector unions is now being conducted by Paul Hartman,* but pending the outcome

---

*Paul Hartman of the University of Illinois is examining the impact of public sector unions on wages as part of the Brookings Institution's *Study of Unionism and Collective Bargaining in the Public Sector*.

of his study we have to base our evaluation on less direct evidence. Our approach will be to review carefully the various steps in the analytical model developed by Wellington and Winter by which they arrive at the notion of sovereignty. If we find that the evidence available on public sector strikes contradicts this model, we shall conclude that the differential assessment they provide for public and private strikes is unwarranted.

Benefits of Collective Bargaining

Wellington and Winter believe the benefits of collective action, including strikes, are less in the public sector than in the private sector since (1) the problem of employer monopsony is less serious, and (2) any use of monopsony power in the public sector which results in certain groups, such as teachers, receiving low pay may reflect, not a misallocation of resources, but rather a political determination of the desired use of resources.

Wellington and Winter assert that employer monopsony is less likely to exist or be used in the public than in the private sector. But as they concede, referring to Bunting, monopsony is not widespread in the private sector and, except in a few instances, cannot be used as a rationale for trade unions. They provide no evidence that monopsony is less prevalent in the public than in the private sector. Moreover, other labor market inefficiencies, common to the public and private sectors, are probably more important than monopsony in providing an economic justification for unions. For example, the deficiencies of labor market information are to some extent overcome by union activities,* and there is no reason to assume that this benefit differs between the public and private sectors.

Assuming there is monopsony power, Wellington and Winter believe that collective bargaining in the private sector can eliminate unfair wages "which are less than they would be if the market were

---

*"Under purely competitive conditions, it is assumed that perfect knowledge of existing wage rates in other firms, regions, and occupations, and mobility of both labor and capital would tend to eradicate unnecessary wage differentials (i.e., differentials which did not truly reflect the marginal productivity of labor). Both knowledge and mobility, however, are very imperfect in the real market. The existence of trade unions to a large extent compensates for the lack of knowledge and represents a force tending toward wage standardization for similar work" (Cartter and Marshall 1972, pp. 324-25).

more nearly perfect." They assert, however, that low pay for an occupation in the public sector may reflect a political judgment which ought not to be countered by pressures resulting from a strike. To say, however, that the pay for an occupation would be higher if the employees had the right to strike than if they did not is not independent proof that strikes are inappropriate. The same criticism could be made of any activity by a public employee group which affects its pay. An independent rationale must be provided to explain why some means which are effective in raising wages (strikes) are inappropriate while other means which are also effective (lobbying) are appropriate. Whether the Wellington and Winter discussion of the politically based decision-making model for the public sector provides this rationale will be discussed in more detail subsequently.

Costs of Collective Bargaining

Wellington and Winter's discussion of the cost of substituting collective for individual bargaining in the public sector includes a chain of causation which runs from (1) an allegation that market restraints are weak in the public sector, largely because the services are essential; to (2) an assertion that the public puts pressure on civic officials to arrive at a quick settlement; to (3) a statement that other pressure groups have no weapons comparable to a strike; to (4) a conclusion that the strike thus imposes a high cost since the political process is distorted.

Let us discuss these steps in order:

1. *Market restraints:* A key argument in the case for the inappropriateness of public sector strikes is that economic constraints are not present to any meaningful degree in the public sector.* This argument is not entirely convincing. First, wages lost due to strikes are as important to public employees as they are to employees in the private sector. Second, the public's concern over increasing tax rates may prevent the decision-making process from being dominated by political instead of economic considerations. The development of multilateral bargaining in the public sector is an example of how the

---

*"It further seems to us that, to the extent union power is delimited by market or other forces in the public sector, these constraints do not come into play nearly as quickly as in the private" (reading 15).

concern over taxes may result in a close substitute for market con-straints (McLennan and Moskow 1968). In San Francisco, for exam-ple, the chamber of commerce has participated in negotiations be-tween the city and public employee unions and has had some success in limiting the economic gains of the unions. A third and related eco-nomic constraint arises for such services as water, sewage and, in some instances, sanitation, where explicit prices are charged. Even if representatives of groups other than employees and the employer do not enter the bargaining process, both union and local government are aware of the economic implications of bargaining which leads to higher prices which are clearly visible to the public. A fourth eco-nomic constraint on employees exists in those services where sub-contracting to the private sector is a realistic alternative.* Warren, Michigan, resolved a bargaining impasse with an American Federation of State, County and Municipal Employees (AFSCME) local by sub-contracting its entire sanitation service; Santa Monica, California, ended a strike of city employees by threatening to subcontract its sanitation operations. If the subcontracting option is preserved, wages in the public sector need not exceed the rate at which sub-contracting becomes a realistic alternative.

An aspect of the lack-of-market-restraints argument is that public services are essential. Even at the analytical level, Wellington and Winter's case for essentiality is not convincing. They argue:

The services performed by a private transit authority are neither less nor more essential to the public than those that would be performed if the transit author-ity were owned by a municipality. A railroad or a dock strike may be much more damaging to a community than "job action" by teachers. This is not to say that government services are not essential. They are both because they may seri-ously injure a city's economy and occasionally the physical welfare of its citi-zens.

This is a troublesome passage. It ends with the implicit conclu-sion that all government services are essential. This conclusion is

---

*The subcontracting option is realistic in functions such as sanitation and street or highway repairs, and some white collar occupations. Several other func-tions, including hospitals and education, may be transferred entirely to the pri-vate sector. The ultimate response by government is to terminate the service, at least temporarily. In late 1968, Youngstown, Ohio, closed its schools for five weeks due to a taxpayers' revolt. In late 1969, ten Ohio school districts ran out of money and were closed down. Wall Street Journal, December 19, 1969, p. 1.

important in Wellington and Winter's analysis because it is a step in their demonstration that strikes are inappropriate in all governmental services. But the beginning of the passage, with its example of "job action" by teachers, suggests that essentiality is not an *inherent* characteristic of government services but depends on the specific service being evaluated. Furthermore the transit authority example suggests that many services are interchangeable between the public and private sectors. The view that various government services are not of equal essentiality and that there is considerable overlap between the kinds of services provided in the public and private sectors is reinforced by our field work and strike data from the Bureau of Labor Statistics. Examples include:

a. Where sanitation services are provided by a municipality, such as Cleveland, sanitationmen are prohibited from striking. Yet, sanitationmen in Philadelphia, Portland, and San Francisco are presumably free to strike since they are employed by private contractors rather than by the cities.

b. There were 25 local government strikes by the Teamsters in 1965-68, most involving truck drivers and all presumably illegal. Yet the Teamsters' strike involving fuel oil truck drivers in New York City last winter was legal even though the interruption of fuel oil service was believed to have caused the death of several people (*New York Times,* December 26, 1968, p. 1, and December 27, 1968, p. 1).

2. *Public pressure:* The second argument in the Wellington and Winter analysis is that public pressure on city officials forces them to make quick settlements. The validity of this argument depends on whether the service is essential. Using as a criterion whether the service is essential in the short run, we believe a priori that services can be divided into three categories: (1) essential services—police and fire —where strikes immediately endanger public health and safety; (2) intermediate services—sanitation, hospitals, transit, water, and sewage —where strikes of a few days might be tolerated; (3) nonessential services—streets, parks, education, housing, welfare and general administration—where strikes of indefinite duration could be tolerated.* These categories are not exact since essentiality depends on

---

*We consider education a nonessential service. However, because our portion of the Brookings Institution study excludes education, our analysis in this article will also largely exclude education.

the size of the city. Sanitation strikes will be critical in large cities such as New York but will not cause much inconvenience in smaller cities where there are meaningful alternatives to governmental operation of sanitation services.

Statistics on the duration of strikes which occurred in the public sector between 1965 and 1968 provide evidence not only that public services are of unequal essentiality, but also that the a priori categories which we have used have some validity. As can be seen from table 1, strikes in the essential services (police and fire) had an

Table 1*
Duration of Strikes by Essentiality of Function

	Average duration in days	Standard deviation† in days
Essential	4.7	7.9
Intermediate	10.3	18.5
Nonessential	10.6	20.1
Education	7.2	8.9

*Based on data collected by the Bureau of Labor Statistics on strikes during 1965-68 involving employees of local government.

†Standard deviation is a measure of dispersion around the average or the mean.

average duration of 4.7 days, while both the intermediate and the nonessential services had an average duration of approximately 10.5 days. It is true that the duration of strikes in the intermediate and nonessential services is only half the average duration of strikes in the private sector during these years (U.S. Bureau of Labor Statistics 1969). However, this comparison is somewhat misleading since all of the public sector strikes were illegal, and many were ended by injunction, while presumably a vast majority of the private sector strikes did not suffer from these constraints. It would appear that with the exception of police and fire protection, public officials are, to some degree, able to accept long strikes. The ability of governments to so choose indicates that political pressures generated by strikes are not so strong as to undesirably distort the entire decision-making process of government. City officials in Kalamazoo, Michigan, were able to accept a forty-eight day strike by sanitationmen and laborers; Sacramento County, California, survived an eighty-seven day strike by welfare workers. A three month strike of hospital workers has occurred in Cuyahoga County (Cleveland), Ohio.

3. The strike as a unique weapon: The third objection to the strike is that it provides workers with a weapon unavailable to the employing agency or to other pressure groups. Thus, unions have a superior arsenal. The Taylor Report (p. 15) opposes strikes for this reason, among others, arguing that "there can scarcely be a counter-vailing lockout." Conceptually, we see no reason why lockouts are less feasible in the public than in the private sector. Legally, public sector lockouts are now forbidden, but so are strikes; presumably both could be legalized. Actually, public sector lockouts have occurred. The Social Service Employees Union (SSEU) of New York City sponsored a "work-in" in 1967 during which all of the case-workers went to their office but refused to work. Instead, union-sponsored lectures were given by representatives of organizations such as CORE, and symposia were held on the problems of welfare workers and clients. The work-in lasted for one week, after which the City locked out the caseworkers.

A similar assertion is made by Wellington and Winter, who claim that no pressure group other than unions has a weapon comparable to the strike. But this argument raises a number of questions. Is the distinctive characteristic of an inappropriate method of influencing decisions by public officials that it is economic as opposed to political? If this is so, then presumably the threat of the New York Stock Exchange to move to New Jersey unless New York City taxes on stock transfers were lowered and similar devices should be outlawed along with the strike.

4. Distortion of the political process: The ultimate concern of both the Taylor Committee and Wellington and Winter is that "a strike of government employees . . . introduces an alien force in the legislative process" (Taylor Report, p. 15). It is "alien" because, in the words of the Taylor Report (pp. 18-19):

Careful thought about the matter shows conclusively, we believe, that while the right to strike normally performs a useful function in the private enterprise sector (where relative economic power is the final determinant in the making of private agreements), it is not compatible with the orderly functioning of our democratic form of representative government (in which relative political power is the final determinant).

The essence of this analysis appears to be that certain means used to influence the decision-making process in the public sector—those which are political—are legitimate, while others—those which are economic—are not. For several reasons, we believe that such distinctions among means are tenuous.

First, any scheme which differentiates economic power from political power faces a perplexing definitional task. The *International Encyclopedia of the Social Sciences* (1968, vol. 12, p. 265) defines the political process as "the activities of people in various groups as they struggle for—and use—power to achieve personal and group purposes." And what is power?

Power in use invariably involves a mixture of many different forms—sometimes mutually reinforcing—of persuasion and pressure . . . .

Persuasion takes place when A influences B to adopt a course of action without A's promising or threatening any reward or punishment. It may take the form of example, expectation, proposals, information, education, or propaganda . . . .

Pressure is applied by A upon B whenever A tries to make a course of action more desirable by promising or threatening contingent rewards or punishments. It may take the form of force, commands, manipulation, or bargaining . . . .

Physical force is a blunt instrument . . . . Besides, more flexible and reliable modes of pressure are available. Rewards, in the form of monetary payments, new positions, higher status, support, favorable votes, cooperation, approval, or the withdrawal of any anticipated punishment, may be bestowed or promised. Punishment, in the form of fines, firing, reduction in status, unfavorable votes, noncooperation, rejection, disapproval, or withdrawal of any anticipated reward, may be given or threatened . . . .

Bargaining is a still more fluid—and far more persuasive—form of using pressure. In bargaining, all sides exercise power upon each other through reciprocal promises or threats . . . . Indeed, force, command, and manipulation tend to become enveloped in the broader and more subtle processes of bargaining. (pp. 269-70)

We have quoted at length from this discussion of the political process because we believe it illustrates the futility of attempting to distinguish between economic and political power. The former concept would seem to be encompassed by the latter. The degree of overlap is problematical since there can be economic aspects to many forms of persuasion and pressure. It may be possible to provide an operational distinction between economic power and political power, but we do not believe that those who would rely on this distinction have fulfilled their task.*

---

*It is interesting to note that some who would differentiate between economic and political considerations apparently view public sector strikes as *politi-*

Second, even assuming it is possible to operationally distinguish economic power and political power, a rationale for utilizing the distinction must be provided. Such a rationale would have to distinguish between the categories either on the basis of characteristics inherent in them as a means of action or on the basis of the ends to which the means are directed. Surely an analysis of ends does not provide a meaningful distinction. The objectives of groups using economic pressure are of the same character as those of groups using political pressure—both seek to influence executive and legislative determinations such as the allocation of funds and the tax rate. If it is impossible effectively to distinguish economic from political pressure groups in terms of their ends, and it is desirable to free the political process from the influence of all pressure groups, then effective lobbying and petitioning should be as illegal as strikes.

If the normative distinction between economic and political power is based, not on the ends desired, but on the nature of the means, our skepticism remains undiminished. Are all forms of political pressure legitimate? Then consider the range of political activity observed in the public sector. Is lobbying by public sector unions to be approved? Presumably it is. What then of participation in partisan political activity? On city time? Should we question the use of campaign contributions or kickbacks from public employees to public officials as a means of influencing public sector decisions? These questions suggest that political pressures, as opposed to economic pressures, cannot *as a class* be considered more desirable.

Our antagonism toward a distinction based on means does not rest solely on a condemnation of political pressures which violate statutory provisions. We believe that perfectly legal forms of political pressure have no automatic superiority over economic pressure. In this regard, the evidence from our field work is particularly enlightening. First, we have found that the availability of political power varies among groups of employees within a given city. Most public administrators have respect for groups which can deliver votes at strategic times. Because of their links to private sector unions, craft

---

cal activity. Stieber (1967) states: "The basic question is whether the strike, which in the United States has been viewed primarily as an economic weapon, is equally appropriate when used as a political weapon." If Stieber's characterization of public sector strikes is correct, then presumably the rationale of the Taylor Report should make these strikes legal.

unions are invariably in a better position to play this political role than a union confined to the public sector, such as AFSCME. In Chicago, Cleveland, and San Francisco, the public sector craft unions are closely allied with the building trades council and play a key role in labor relations with the city. Prior to the passage of state collective bargaining laws such unions also played the key role in Detroit and New York City. In the no-strike model, craft unions clearly have the comparative advantage because of their superior political power.

Second, the range of issues pursued by unions relying on political power tends to be narrow. The unions which prosper by eschewing economic power and exercising political power are often found in cities, such as Chicago, with a flourishing patronage system. These unions gain much of their political power by cooperating with the political administration. This source of political power would vanish if the unions were assiduously to pursue a goal of providing job security for their members since this goal would undermine the patronage system. In Rochester, for example, a union made no effort to protect one of its members who was fired for political reasons. For the union to have opposed the city administration at that time on an issue of job security would substantially have reduced the union's influence on other issues. In Chicago, where public sector strikes are rare (except for education) but political considerations are not, the unions have made little effort to establish a grievance procedure to protect their members from arbitrary treatment.

Third, a labor relations system built on political power tends to be unstable since some groups of employees, often a substantial number, are invariably left out of the system. They receive no representation either through patronage or through the union. In Memphis, the craft unions had for many years enjoyed a "working relationship" with the city which assured the payment of the rates that prevailed in the private sector and some control over jobs. The sanitation laborers, however, were not part of the system and were able to obtain effective representation only after a violent confrontation with the city in 1968. Having been denied representation through the political process, they had no choice but to accept a subordinate position in the city or to initiate a strike to change the system. Racial barriers were an important factor in the isolation of the Memphis sanitation laborers. Similar distinctions in racial balance among functions and occupations appear in most of the cities we visited.

Conclusions in Regard to Strikes and the Political Process

Wellington and Winter and the Taylor Report reject the use of the strike model in the public sector. They have endorsed the no-strike model in order "to ensure the survival of the 'normal' American political process" (reading 15). Our field work suggests that unions which have actually helped their members either have made the strike threat a viable weapon despite its illegality or have inter-twined themselves closely with their nominal employer through patronage-political support arrangements. If this assessment is cor-rect, choice of the no-strike model is likely to lead to patterns of decision making which will subvert, if not the "normal" American political process, at least the political process which the Taylor Re-port and Wellington and Winter meant to embrace. We would not argue that the misuse of political power will be eliminated by legaliz-ing the strike; on balance, however, we believe that, in regard to most governmental functions, the strike model has more virtues than the no-strike model. Whether strikes are an appropriate weapon for all groups of public employees is our next topic.

Differentiation Among Public Sector Functions

The most important union for local government employees, The American Federation of State, County, and Municipal Employees (AFSCME), issued a policy statement in 1966 claiming the right of public employees to strike:

AFSCME insists upon the right of public employees . . . to strike. To forestall this right is to handicap the free collective bargaining process. Wherever legal barriers to the exercise of this right exist, it shall be our policy to seek the re-moval of such barriers. Where one party at the bargaining table possesses all the power and authority, the bargaining becomes no more than formalized petition-ing. (International Executive Board, AFSCME, Policy Statement on Public Em-ployee Unions: Rights and Responsibilities (July 26, 1966))

Significantly, AFSCME specifically excluded police and other law enforcement officers from this right. Any local of police officers that engages in a strike or other concerted refusal to perform duties will have its charter revoked.

Can a distinction among functions, such as is envisioned by AFSCME, be justified? In view of the high costs associated with the suppression of strikes, could each stoppage be dealt with, as Theodore Kheel suggests, only when and if it becomes an emergency?

Despite arguments to the contrary, we feel that strikes in some essential services, such as fire and police, would immediately endanger the public health and safety and should be presumed illegal. We have no evidence from our field work to support our fears that any disruption of essential services will quickly result in an emergency. But the events which occurred on September 9, 1919, during a strike by Boston policemen provide strong proof; those which occurred on October 7, 1969, following a strike by Montreal policemen would appear to make the argument conclusive. Contemporary accounts amply describe the holocausts:

Boston, 1919

About me milled a crowd of aimless men and women, just seeing what they could see . . . . There was an air of expectancy without knowing what was expected.

Then came the sound of two hard substances in sharp impact, followed a second later by a louder one and the thrilling crash of falling splintering glass. A plate show-window had been shattered. Instantly the window and its immediate vicinity were filled with struggling men, a mass of action, from which emerged from time to time bearers of shirts, neckties, collars, hats. In a few seconds the window was bare. Some with loot vanished; others lingered.

Lootless ones were attacking the next window. Nothing happened. That is, the fear of arrest abated after the first shock of the lawless acts. I saw men exchanging new shirts each with the other, to get their sizes . . . good-looking men, mature in years, bearing all the earmarks of a lifetime of sane observance of property rights. (Wood 1971)

Montreal, 1969

"You've never seen the city like this," said the owner of a big women's clothing store surveying his premises, strewn with dummies from which the clothing had been torn. "It's like the war." (New York Times, October 9, 1969, p. 3)

A taxi driver carrying a passenger up Sherbrooke Street in Montreal today blamed the police for "not knowing the effect their absence would have on people." He continued: "I don't mean hoodlums and habitual lawbreakers. I mean just plain people committed offenses they would not dream of trying if there was a policeman standing on the corner. I saw cars driven through red lights. Drivers shot up the wrong side of the street because they realized no one would catch them." (New York Times, October 10, 1969, p. 2)

In the case of strikes by essential employees, such as policemen, the deterioration of public order occurs almost immediately. During the first few hours of the police walkout in Montreal, robberies occurred at eight banks, one finance company, two groceries, a jewelry store, and a private bank (*New York Times,* October 8, 1969, p. 3). In the case of the Boston police strike of 1919, outbreaks began within four hours after the strike had commenced. Such consequences require that strikes by police and other essential services be outlawed in advance. There is simply no time to seek an injunction.

Even if a distinction in the right to strike can be made among government functions on the basis of essentiality, is such a distinction possible to implement? The Taylor Report based its argument against prohibiting strikes in essential functions but allowing them elsewhere on this difficulty:

We come to this conclusion [to prohibit all strikes] after a full consideration of the views . . . that public employees in nonessential government services, at least, should have the same right to strike as has been accorded to employees in private industry. We realize, moreover, that the work performed in both sectors is sometimes comparable or identical. Why, then, should an interruption of nonessential governmental services be prohibited?

To begin with, a differentiation between essential and nonessential governmental services would be the subject of such intense and never ending controversy as to be administratively impossible. (p. 18)

Despite the conclusion of the Taylor Report it appears that in practice a distinction is emerging between strikes in essential services and strikes in other services. Employee organizations and public officials do in fact treat some strikes as critical, while other strikes cause no undue concern.

Our analysis of the Bureau of Labor Statistics strike data pertaining to the last four years suggests that it is possible to devise an operational definition of essential service. First, as we have indicated above, strike duration was considerably shorter in the essential services than in the intermediate or nonessential services (see table 1). These data suggest that, except in police and fire services, public officials have some discretion in choosing to accept long strikes. Second, the statistics reveal that managers have been able to distinguish between essential and nonessential services in their use of counter sanctions. In strikes involving essential services, injunctions were sought more frequently and employees, because of their short run indispensability, were fired less frequently. Injunctions were granted in 35 percent of the essential strikes, and in 25 percent of the intermediate, but only in 19 percent of the nonessential strikes. Third, partial operation was attempted more frequently in essential services (see table 2). By using nonstrikers, supervisors, replacements, or volunteers, local governments were able to continue partial operation during 92 percent of the essential strikes, but in only 80 percent of the intermediate, and 77 percent of the nonessential strikes. Such data suggest that it may be administratively feasible to differentiate among public services so as to permit some, but not all, public employees to strike. Indeed, public administrators already seem to be making such distinctions.

The idea that distinctions among functions are appropriate is also beginning to emerge among legislators. The first state to move in this direction has been Vermont (Vermont Stat. Ann. title 21, §1704 (Supp. 1969)), which apparently restricts municipal employee strikes only if they endanger the health, safety, or welfare of the public. Unfortunately—at least from the viewpoint of researchers —there has been no experience under the statute. Montana (Rev. Codes of Montana title 41, §2209 (Supp. 1969)) prohibits strikes in private or public hospitals only if there is another strike in effect in a hospital within a radius of 150 miles. Study commissions in other states have accepted the distinction between essential and nonessential services. In 1968, the Governor's Commission in Pennsylvania recommended a limited right to strike for all public employees except police and firemen (Governor's Commission to Revise the Public Employee Laws of Pennsylvania, Report and Recommendations, 251 Gov. Emp. Rel. Rep. E-1 (1968)). In 1969, the Labor Law Committee of the Ohio State Bar Association recommended repeal of the Ferguson Act, which prohibits strikes by public employees (Ohio Rev. Code §§4117.01-4117.05 (1964)). They proposed a Public Employment Relations Act which would permit strikes by recognized employee organizations in nonessential occupations following mandatory use of factfinding procedures (42 Ohio Bar 563 (1969)). The proposed statute states:

In the event a public employer and a certified labor organization are unable to reach an agreement within forty-five days following the date of the receipt of

Table 2*
Partial Operation by Essentiality of Function
(Noneducation)

	Essential		Intermediate		Nonessential		Total†	
	Number	Percentage	Number	Percentage	Number	Percentage	Number	Percentage
Total number of strikes‡	37	100.0	221	100.0	43	100.0	301	100.0
Partial operation	34	91.9	175	79.2	33	76.7	242	80.4
Supervisors	(28)	(75.7)	(154)	(69.7)	(29)	(67.4)	(211)	(70.1)
Nonstrikers	(27)	(73.0)	(137)	(62.0)	(28)	(65.1)	(192)	(63.8)
Replacements	(3)	(9.1)	(34)	(15.4)	(4)	(9.3)	(41)	(13.6)
Volunteers	(5)	(13.5)	(16)	(7.2)			(21)	(7.0)
No partial operation	3	8.1	46	20.8	10	23.3	59	19.6

*Based on data collected by the Bureau of Labor Statistics on strikes during 1965-68 involving employees of local governments.

†Twenty-eight strikes in such miscellaneous functions as libraries, museums, and electric or gas utilities were not classified. There was partial operation in 18 (43.3 percent) of these strikes.

‡The subtotals for partial operation do not add to 100 percent because more than one method may have been used in each strike.

the recommendation of the factfinding board, the public employees in the bargaining unit . . . and/or the labor organization shall not thereafter be prohibited from engaging in any strike until such time as the labor organization and the public employer reach agreement on a collective bargaining agreement.

Implications for Public Policy

We have expressed our views on the market restraints that exist in the public sector, the extent of the public pressure on public officials to reach quick settlements, the likely methods by which decisions would be made in the no-strike model, and the desirability and feasibility of differentiating among government services on the basis of essentiality. In this light, what public policy seems appropriate for strikes at the local government level?

In general, we believe that strikes in the public sector should be legalized for the same reasons they are legal in the private sector. For some public sector services, however—namely, police and fire protection—the probability that a strike will result in immediate danger to public health and safety is so substantial that strikes are almost invariably inappropriate. In these essential functions, the strike should be presumed illegal; the state should not be burdened with the requirement of seeking an injunction. We would, however, permit employees in a service considered essential to strike if they could demonstrate to a court that a disruption of service would not endanger the public. Likewise, we would permit the government to obtain an injunction against a strike in a service presumed nonessential if a nontrivial danger to the public could be shown.*

The decision to permit some, but not all, public employee

---

*The Labor Management Relations Act (Taft-Hartley Act) is a statute which presumes strikes are legal unless an emergency is involved. 29 USC §§176-180 (1969). The President may delay or suspend an actual or threatened strike which if permitted to occur or continue will constitute a threat to the national health or safety. The emergency procedures have been invoked 29 times since 1947. This experience should provide some guidance in formulating an operational version of our policy which would permit strikes in nonessential functions unless a nontrivial danger to the public could be shown. We realize that it may be more difficult to formulate an operational version of our policy for essential functions. We are not aware of any experience with a statute which permits the presumption of illegality for strikes to be rebutted under appropriate circumstances.

strikes cannot, of course, take place *in vaccus publicum jus.* Mediation, factfinding, or advisory arbitration may be appropriate for those functions where strikes are permitted. Where strikes are illegal because of the essential nature of the service, it may be necessary to institute compulsory arbitration.* The choice of a proper role for third parties in the public sector is difficult, and we do not wish to leave the impression that we are unaware of the problem. In our portion of the Brookings Institution study, we will examine the experience which many cities have had in the use of neutral third parties. Our initial reaction is that such experience does not undermine the feasibility of a public policy which would permit some, but not all, public employees the right to strike, and include that decision in a comprehensive public policy for collective bargaining.

While we have indicated our support for the right of public employees to strike, we do not mean to suggest that all strikes are desirable. In particular, strikes which are necessary solely because the employer refuses to establish a bargaining relationship seem anachronous. The right of employees to deal with their employer through a representative of their choosing should be reflected in our public policy. The obligation on employers to recognize and to bargain with properly certified unions has eliminated many strikes in the private sector. The evidence in table 3 suggests that, in the public sector, strikes on such issues can be sharply reduced. In those states in which local governments are required to recognize and to bargain with unions representing a majority of their employees, strikes to establish the bargaining relationship have been virtually eliminated. States with permissive laws, which require minimal recognition of unions and which require only that employers "meet and confer," as opposed to "bargain," with these unions, have perhaps aggravated the strike problem.

Similarly, our general endorsement of public sector strikes does not mean that we are unconcerned about the circumstances under which such strikes take place. Public policy has an important role to

---

*Michigan has recently enacted a statute applicable to public police and fire departments which imposes penalties on striking employees and establishes a binding arbitration procedure for negotiating disputes. Arbitration is available upon the request of either party in the dispute. Michigan Comp. Laws §§ 423.232-.247 (1948).

Table 3
Local Government Strikes by Public Policy and Issue*

	Noneducation strikes		Education strikes	
	Number	Duration in days	Number	Duration in days
Mandatory Law				
Strikes to establish				
bargaining relationship†	1	10.0	5	3.4
Other strikes	56	6.7	104	8.7
Permissive Law				
Strikes to establish				
bargaining relationship	20	19.6	2	7.0
Other strikes	34	10.4	16	6.5
No Law				
Strikes to establish				
bargaining relationship	68	21.6	29	5.9
Other strikes	150	5.8	93	6.2

*Based on data collected by the Bureau of Labor Statistics on strikes during 1965-68 involving employees of local governments.

†Includes strikes where union was demanding recognition as well as strikes where union was demanding bona fide collective bargaining.

play in shaping the structure and, hence, influencing the outcome of collective bargaining (for a discussion of collective bargaining structure, see Weber 1967). An example is the inclusion or exclusion of supervisors in the bargaining unit. As indicated in table 2, supervisors are often used during strikes to provide partial operation. Presumably, this enhances the ability of local governments to resist union demands. Some states, such as Wisconsin,* have wisely stipulated that supervisors are to be excluded from bargaining units, while other states, such as New York, have not. A supervisor who belongs to a striking union is likely to be of limited usefulness to management in attempting to counteract the strike. Another way in which a state's public policy could enhance local government's ability to resist strikes would be to enact a statute prohibiting public employers from signing away their right to subcontract. The absolute right to subcontract operations would thereby be preserved. While it is unlikely that some services, such as police and fire protection, will ever be

---

*Wisconsin Stat. Ann. §111.81(12) (Supp. 1969) relates to state employees.

placed under private management, other services can be subcontracted if union demands raise the cost of a public service to a level at which private service becomes competitive. Excluding the education sector, subcontracting was threatened by management in 16 local government strikes and implemented in five between 1965 and 1968.

Conclusion

This article has offered a policy to deal with public sector strikes. It has also examined several propositions concerning public sector strikes which have been based largely on logical analysis. The assertions that strikes by public employees inevitably distort the decision-making process in the public sector and that differential treatment of public employees in their right to strike would be infeasible have been found to be wanting when evaluated in the light of our actual experience with public sector strikes. This evaluation suggests that logic alone is an inadequate basis for public policy in this area. Yet we would not want to suggest that a literal interpretation of Holmes' view on the relative merits of logic and experience is appropriate. If we were forced to choose a mentor in any debate concerning the proper bases for law, we endorse Cardozo:

My analysis of the judicial process comes then to this, and little more: logic, and history, and custom, and utility, and the accepted standards of right conduct, are the forces which singly or in combination shape the progress of the law.

References

Cartter, A. M., and Marshall, F. R. *Labor Economics: Wages, Employment, and Trade Unionism*. Homewood, Ill.: Irwin, 1972.

Chamberlain, N. W., and Kuhn, J. W. *Collective Bargaining*. New York: McGraw-Hill, 1965.

Governor's Committee on Public Employee Relations. *Final Report*. Albany: State of New York, 1966.

Kheel, T. W. "Resolving Deadlocks Without Banning Strikes." *Monthly Labor Review* 92 (July 1969): 62-63.

McLennan, K., and Moskow, M. "Multilateral Bargaining in the Public Sector." *Industrial Relations Research Association Proceedings* 31 (1968).

Rees, A. *The Economics of Trade Unions*. Chicago: University of Chicago Press, 1962.

Stieber, J. "Collective Bargaining in the Public Sector." *Challenges to Collective Bargaining*, edited by L. Ulman. Englewood Cliffs, N.J.: Prentice-Hall, 1967.

U.S. Bureau of Labor Statistics. *Analysis of Work Stoppages 1967* (Department of Labor Bulletin no. 1611). Washington, D.C.: The Bureau, 1969.

Weber, A. "Stability and Change in the Structure of Collective Bargaining." *Challenges to Collective Bargaining*, edited by L. Ulman. Englewood Cliffs, N.J.: Prentice-Hall, 1967.

Wood, C. "Reds and Lost Wages." Quoted in *One Thousand Strikes of Government Employees*, by D. Ziskind. New York: Arno Press, 1971. Reproduction of 1940 edition.

Reading 17
Why Teachers Need the
Right To Strike

Albert L. Shanker

Instead of talking about alternatives to strikes, we ought to be talking about *trying* to strike in the public sector. It has not been tried. In the private sector, we have paid a price for strikes. We have paid a price for the process of collective bargaining, because the only alternative is an unfree society—and the price that we pay for strikes is one that we generally are willing to pay.

Collective bargaining has never been sold as an ideal answer to anything, but it is the lesser of a number of evils that exist in the private sector and, in a somewhat modified form, in the public sector. Management and labor have to go through some sort of messy process to find a way of agreeing with each other for a period of time, and the only alternatives are unilateral determination by management—which leads to exploitation—or arbitration—which leads to the imposition by a third party of his views.

There are some differences in the public sector, but these are not adequate justification to abolish or modify the bargaining process. The notion, constantly stated, that in the public sector there

Reprinted by permission from *Monthly Labor Review* 99 (September 1973), pp. 48-51.

is no profit motive is in a sense true. But in a sense it is irrelevant, because there is no question that the public employer bargains just as hard, if not harder, than the private employer. The question of being reelected, the fear of being accused of throwing away public money —"giving it away" to public employees—and also the very fact that he is involved in a public activity in many ways makes it more difficult for public management to bargain than for private management. No one fought a tougher battle against labor unions than philanthropists who were involved in donating their own time as managers in hospitals in the City of New York. They spent many hours in getting many billions of dollars to see to it that these hospitals could be made viable. But when it came to providing an effective union for employees earning $24 or $25 a week, they felt that those employees should donate their time, too, since the philanthropists were. This happens frequently in public sector management.

Another issue in the public sector, somewhat more difficult to resolve, is that top public management is elected by the people, put there in order to effectuate public purposes. We do run into a conflict in the question of bargaining and it is just that—who is making these public decisions? Can public management make the decision on the basis of their platform, on the basis of their promises? Or will elections become relatively meaningless, because whatever the politician says he's going to do, eventually he's going to the bargaining table and be forced to do, not what the people or the general public want him to do, but what he is compelled to do. Who's really running the city, the Board of Education? the Department of Sanitation? Is it the people in a democracy, or is it the unions—here viewed as a greedy and private interest, compelling government to do for its purposes rather than those of the people. These are some of the issues in this sector.

As we look at alternatives, it is important to acknowledge that strikes originally were widespread in obtaining recognition for unions. No one has mentioned that the majority of states still do not recognize any form of collective bargaining for public employees. Here in California there is an ineffective "meet and confer" law, which does not result in binding written agreements or anything resembling collective bargaining.

Instead of talking about alternatives to the strike in the public sector, I would say that the teachers and other public employees in the State of California, and the majority of other states in the United States, would be wise to follow the trends of teachers and other public workers in New York, Chicago, Philadelphia, and elsewhere— because if they do not in fact exercise the right to strike, the government may never create the machinery that employees have in other states. It is not accidental that in states in which public employees have engaged in strikes the legislatures have found it possible to create mechanisms for collective bargaining.

Among the alternatives that have been offered, the State of New York has one of the most comprehensive. The process under the Taylor Law is essentially that there is a procedure for recognition and a timetable based on the budgetary submission process of negotiations. There is a procedure for mediation and a procedure for factfinding. Factfinding was expected to be the answer in the public sector, because the weight of the factfinder's opinion would be so strong in bringing public pressure to bear on public officials that the public officials would immediately just roll over, raise the white flag, and say "Well, if the factfinder's report is printed in *The New York Times*, I have absolutely no choice but to see to it that the employees receive justice."

We might have realized some time ago that this would not happen. By and large, the general public believed for many years that teachers were underpaid and that other public employees were, but that belief didn't move the government toward providing adequate salaries and working conditions.

The terminal process in the Taylor Law is the legislative hearing. After the factfinder presents his report, the elected representatives of the people hold a hearing based upon this factfinding report and make the final decision. In any of 800 school districts in the State of New York, this means that the teachers first present their demands and then go through a process of negotiations; the mediator comes in and they go through that process; the factfinder comes in; the factfinder issues his report, and 99 times out of 100 the board of education turns it down; then there is a hearing before the legislative body for the teachers in that district—which is the very same board of education that they have been negotiating with all along. The same is true of the Transit Authority in the City of New York. The same is true of state employees with respect to the state legislature. What we have is philosophically a very brilliant concept, that in a democracy ultimately those elected by the people to represent them will make these determinations on the basis of the facts given to them. But it turns out that the supposedly impartial legislative body representing the people is the very same government employer that the worker has been involved with all along. So we have a process of unilateral determination by the employer.

Laws like the Taylor Law provide very strict penalties—penalties like two days' fine to be paid by each employee for each day out on strike, unlimited financial penalties against the unions, unlimited suspension of dues check-off privileges, and jail sentences for all those found guilty of violating the injunction. Instead of preventing strikes, the existence of such legislation actually provokes strikes.

The public employer, knowing that this arsenal of weapons under the law must be used, sits back with the feeling that under no circumstances can the public employees go out on strike, because this battery of weapons is so strong. If they do go out on strike, facing this punishment once will solve the problem, and we won't have to worry about strikes next time, the time after that, or the time after that. Once the strike takes place, negotiations stop and government has to engage its entire machinery in the process of punishment.

Differences do exist with respect to strikes in the public sector and in the private sector. First, by and large a strike in the public sector is not economic—it is political. In the private sector, both management and labor are losing money each day. At times we have suspected that teachers' strikes and other public sector strikes have been permitted to go on for a long time in order to help the city balance its budget.

One of the greatest reasons for the effectiveness of the public employees' strike is the fact that it is illegal. When the public sees a group of teachers—whom they tend to see as rather docile human beings who have never done anything wrong and who chose to become teachers rather than meet the conflicts that exist in the rest of the world—when they see these teachers out on picket lines for three weeks, five weeks, or seven weeks, when they see them being picked up by police and being sent to jail, frequently the public, instead of turning against the teachers, turns the other way. They say, "Now, if those little old ladies (of both sexes, sometimes they say) are willing to engage in this sort of thing, somebody must have done something wrong to them." We have found that opinion in many strikes by teachers across the country. The teachers may not have majority support. But in the political sector, if you've got 25 percent of the public strongly on your side, any mayor would have to consider that the next time he runs (unless he won by a margin much bigger than that, and not too many mayors do that these days).

Another problem of public employee bargaining is whether you negotiate salaries and working conditions, or whether you are really determining public policy. Take something in a school situation like class size. There is no question that keeping class size small is a working condition for the teacher, and yet the question of the desirable size of the classroom is also a question of public policy. Is reducing class size the most effective way of spending public funds?

One outstanding example of a clash between public policy and collective bargaining came when we were negotiating a contract for 10,000 paraprofessionals who came from the poverty rolls and were welfare recipients and had come to work as assistants to teachers in the classroom, most of them making about $2,000 a year for part-time employment. In the negotiations we were confronted with government spokesmen saying they could not give these employees more money because it would ruin the program, that the whole value of paraprofessionals was that children from poor neighborhoods couldn't relate to the teacher because the teacher was a middle-class person who left school at the end of the day and got on the subway or into a car and went away to another neighborhood or suburb. But the children could identify with some other poor person from that very same neighborhood, and if we succeeded in getting higher salaries for the paraprofessionals, they too would become middle class and would move out of the neighborhood, and the entire educational value would be destroyed.

I have never heard arguments like this used in the private sector.

Finally, one other difference should be mentioned, that the argument of ability to pay doesn't really count in public sector negotiations. A private employer could pull out his books and show that he's going to go out of business if he pays more, but government can't.

There is no question that bargaining in the public sector is not a clear kind of issue. It's messy. If you try to push these arguments about sovereignty, if you try to push these arguments about who determines public policy, if you try to push arguments about how to get finality in this whole thing, we are going to end up with a whole mess of contradictions and we are going to try to impose solutions where solutions cannot be imposed.

In 1960, we had a very small teachers' union in New York City. We represented only 5 percent of the entire staff. We asked for a collective bargaining election, and at the time there was no collective bargaining for any teachers anywhere in the United States. The Board of Education took the position that the board was a governmental agency, government had sovereignty, and the sovereign could not sit down and treat his subjects as equals; therefore, no collective bargaining. We had a one-day strike on November 7, 1960, and the Board of Education changed its mind. Essentially, it said: We are the Board of Education, we are a government agency, government enjoys sovereignty, sovereignty is king, and a king is all powerful; he is so powerful that if he *wants* to treat his subjects as equals (and bargain with them), no one can prevent him from doing so.

Some years ago, under the concepts of sovereignty, no subject could sue the government, but in a democratic society we found ways in which citizens can sue the government. In a democratic society we also ought to find ways in which public employees can engage in strikes against the government without raising the question of whether they are engaged in a revolution.

Reading 18

Impasse Issues in Teacher Disputes Submitted to Factfinding in New York

Barbara Doering

In New York as in most other states where collective bargaining has been mandated for public employees, the strike remains illegal. As an alternative to the use of strikes many states provide a procedure to help the parties at impasse reach settlement. In New York the impasse procedure calls for mediation followed, if necessary, by factfinding with recommendations. The factfinder's recommendations are not binding on the parties; it was feared that to make them binding might deter meaningful bargaining. It was hoped, however, that the recommendations, even if not accepted in full, would be the basis for a settlement.

In 1969, more than half of New York's 800 districts bargained to impasse and requested the services of a mediator, or factfinder, or both.* In 200 cases a written factfinding report was issued. In 149 of these cases the report was either accepted or was the basis for further

Reprinted by permission from *The Arbitration Journal* 27, no. 1 (March 1972), pp. 1-17.

*According to information taken from the files of the Public Employment Relations Board (PERB), Albany, N.Y., some 452 school district disputes were referred to the board for assignment of a conciliator in 1969.

negotiation which culminated in settlement. In 33 cases another neutral party was sent in for conciliation after factfinding, and the remaining 18 cases were still open at the year's end.*

Since factfinders have been instrumental in helping parties reach settlements in nearly a quarter of these cases, it seems worthwhile to take a closer look at factfinding and factfinders' recommendations, in order to get an idea of how the process works.

By examining factfinders' reports and recommendations it is possible to draw some conclusions about the kind of issues they deal with (and those they try to avoid); the way in which different factfinders deal with particular issues; and the major criteria upon which their recommendations are based.

In order to produce a uniform basis for comparison, this study considered only cases involving teachers who, as "professional" public employees in collective bargaining, present special problems. A sample of fifty 1969 teacher cases was selected from the 200 cases in which factfinding reports were issued.† The recommendations were carefully studied and the factfinders' treatment of the major issues is summarized below. The factfinders were also questioned‡ regarding the criteria upon which they made their recommendations and the degree of confidence they had in the acceptability of their reports. This information is presented in the conclusion.

Attention is focused on the specific issues in order to bring out the degree of consistency or inconsistency of the recommendations of different factfinders. The issue-by-issue summary also lends itself to an examination of the criteria implicit in the recommendation, suggesting the frequency with which factfinders rely upon certain criteria for the resolution of the various issues.

---

*Information obtained from PERB's Director of Public Employment Research, Dr. Thomas E. Joyner, by letter to the author, January 7, 1970.

†The sample of fifty cases was stratified to reflect the relative unit size of all 200 cases in the population, with the cases in each stratum randomly drawn. Coincidentally, the sample selected was also relatively representative of the geographical distribution of teacher cases in New York State for 1969.

‡The author participated, to the extent of studying and summarizing these fifty cases, in a study conducted by Yaffe and Goldblatt on the factfinding. Their study culminated in a book: *Factfinding in Public Employment Disputes in New York State: More Promise than Illusion* (1971).

Special Problems of Teachers in Collective Bargaining

Before turning to the specific issues in teacher impasses, certain profession-related problems which teachers as a group present when they participate in collective bargaining ought to be noted. The very idea of professionals bargaining collectively seems to be a contradiction in terms, and it is from this contradiction that problems arise.

Because the public does not have the training to judge professionals, members of the professions argue that they must set their own standards. As a corollary, they usually also set their own conditions of employment. Clients can choose between the several members of any profession on the basis of the individual's record of success (e.g., cases won, buildings which stand up, cured patients, etc.).

Teaching differs from other professions, not so much in degree of advanced preparation, but in that it is difficult, if not impossible, to establish individual records of success. Partly because of this a standard salary schedule based upon objective and measurable criteria has become the accepted mode of employment. Additionally, because of the breadth of public experience with education and interest in it, teachers are not in the same revered standard-setting position as members of the other professions.

Thus, when the Taylor Law opened up salaries and working conditions to collective negotiations, some teacher groups felt this was also an opportunity to increase teacher influence as professionals in educational policy areas. Even where teacher groups have restricted their demands to salaries and working conditions, the question of the teacher's role in policy decisions arises since some teacher working conditions overlap, and depend upon, educational policy matters.

The Issues

"Negotiability"

In 1969 "negotiability" itself was an issue. Many school boards were beginning to worry about what they saw as an erosion of their decision-making function, particularly in policy areas other than the strictly money items of salaries and benefits. Boards feared that the mere discussion or "negotiation" of an item during bargaining might be held by the teachers as a precedent for inclusion of that item within the ever broadening area in which the board was no longer allowed to take unilateral action. School boards thus refused even to discuss some subjects during negotiations lest they set new self-imposed limits on old "managerial prerogatives."

Most of the problems cropped up over what issues could or should be construed to involve working conditions (which under the Taylor Law the board is legally obliged to negotiate) and what issues remained within the sole prerogative of the board under the Education Law. Factfinders were generally reluctant to rule on the "negotiability" of an item per se. They tended rather to talk around the "negotiability" problem and discuss the item itself.

The most common items which sparked "negotiability" debates were: the establishment or elimination of positions, and the related issue of class size; program decisions; board policy changes; and budget cuts affecting educational equipment and supplies.

Most factfinders agreed that the creation or termination of positions is a board prerogative, although the impact of such decisions upon specific individuals within the bargaining unit may be negotiable. This interpretation was affirmed in the PERB decision in the *New Rochelle* case (Case no. U-0249) in July 1971. Factfinders also generally held that the obligation to bargain does not include explaining or justifying the budget or cuts in it. This is logical: not only does the budget encompass matters beyond the scope of teacher bargaining, but in New York State, teachers' salaries do not depend upon budget approval. Even if the budget is defeated, "the board of education is empowered to levy a tax sufficient to defray the cost of those items specifically authorized by statute (e.g., teachers' salaries —Education Law § 2023), and the cost of those items determined by the board of education to constitute 'ordinary contingent expenses'" (New York State Department of Education (1968); sections of law referred to are: Education Law § 1718 and § 2023). Thus in one case (M69-279),* teacher demands to negotiate not only

---

*Cases will be cited by their PERB index number. The factfinders' reports can be found in PERB's files in Albany, or at the New York State School of Industrial and Labor Relations Documentation Center at Cornell University. Some reports are published (under different identification numbers) in: *Official Decisions and Related Matters, Public Employment Relations Board of the State of New York* (vol. 3, 1970).

their own salaries and working conditions but also the school budget were rejected as beyond association jurisdiction.

One factfinder pointed out that in spite of possible advantages in discussing budget cuts with teachers, school boards may well shy away from such discussion if it appears that the teachers are only interested in haggling over the amount of the cuts and board justification for making them (cf. M69-260). The converse of staff cutting, the question of hiring additional teachers, also came up in a number of cases. One factfinder (cf. M69-484) noted that, although creation of positions was normally a board prerogative, in cases where there is a contractual provision for maximum class size the matter of additional personnel can be dealt with through the grievance procedure if contractual maximums have been exceeded.

The class size issue as one aspect of creation of new positions was often raised as a negotiability problem. Factfinders tended to agree with the teacher groups that class size has a definite impact on working conditions, but were reluctant to set hard and fast limits because of other considerations beyond teacher working conditions which are affected by class size. The result in many cases (cf. M69-279, M69-428, M69-63, M69-188, M69-166) was that a loosely worded clause setting forth desirable limits or "guidelines," to be observed "where possible," was recommended for inclusion in the contract. The inclusion of the clause in the contract demonstrated the factfinder's belief that class size was a negotiable item; however, the language was left loose deliberately to protect the interests outside of the jurisdiction of the teacher negotiating unit.*

In addition to creation and termination of positions, the deployment and assignment of personnel was recognized by factfinders as a board prerogative. One group of teachers (cf. M69-51) requested the establishment of a study committee to investigate the need for more administrative personnel and the possibility of evening hours for guidance counselors, etc. The factfinder refused to recommend

---

*Statistics on the number of 1969 contracts including clauses on class size can be found in Sabghir (1970, p. 84).

Note also: negotiability of this issue has recently been dealt with by PERB in an improper practice case, Case no. U-0145, September 1971. The Board ruled in a split decision that class size is not a mandatory subject of negotiations, but the impact of class size is. For details see PERB *Newsletter*, September 30, 1971, or the *West Ironequoit* case (Case no. U-0145).

formation of the committee since he viewed this as a board responsibility. He did, however, recommend that, should the board in future
form such a committee,* the teachers be entitled to representation.
Several other factfinders suggested in the matter of deployment of
personnel that if certain individuals felt unjustly treated their complaints were more properly a matter for the grievance procedure than
for the negotiating session.

Thus in questions of negotiability, factfinders appeared to
examine the directness and degree of effect upon teacher working
conditions relative to the degree to which the issue affected other
groups and other responsibilities beyond the teacher interest. Where
possible, factfinders recommended language which would solve the
particular problem with reference to teacher working conditions
without unduly restricting the board of education in terms of its
broader responsibilities. In areas where overlap between board responsibilities and negotiable working conditions was less clear, or
where the overlap involved the teachers' professional expertise rather
than the employment relationship, factfinders often recommended
the use of joint committees, with professional terms of reference
separate from the bargaining experience. (For further discussion of
the scope of bargaining as evidenced in the contracts themselves
rather than as viewed by factfinders, see Sabghir 1970, pp. 58-67,
83-88).

Compensation for Extra Duty

One of the common items in the 1969 factfinding reports is the
matter of compensation for extra duty. On rates for extracurricular
supervision of clubs and sports activities factfinders' recommendations differ widely. This variation appears to reflect a difference in
the way factfinders view the after-school supervision of extracurricular activities. Before a factfinder can recommend a pay rate for such
duties he must come to some conclusion as to what these activities

---

*Study committees themselves presented a bit of a problem. Although a
useful solution to particularly difficult issues, the effectiveness of such committees is likely to be limited by the parties' disinclination to compromise future
bargaining positions. One factfinder (in M69-427) recognized this problem and
recommended that the committee he was proposing to study nonteaching duties
". . . will not discuss negotiations nor grievance procedure as part of their function."

are, in terms of who or what determines which after-school activities will be offered each year, and whether the supervision of after-school activities is voluntary or compulsory at the discretion of the board. Is it up to the math teacher whether or not there is a math club? Is the English teacher required to supervise a school newspaper? If more than one teacher wants a certain coaching position, who decides which one gets it?

Factfinders who found that performance of these duties was voluntary and that number and type of activities offered were discretionary with the board tended to recommend the board's suggested rates if these did not seem unreasonably low (cf. M69-226, M69-469). "Unreasonably low" in this context appeared to refer to whether or not past rates had been increased to offset inflation. Some factfinders also made comparisons with neighboring districts.

Factfinders who felt that supervision of these activities was an involuntary extension of the teaching day, a form of overtime, recommended rates closer to demands of the teachers (M69-191).

Factfinders who did not comment on the nature of the activities one way or the other, viewing the matter as an extension of the salary question, tended, as in their salary recommendations, to rely largely upon comparisons with neighboring districts.

Another money question which came up with reference to extracurricular duties was the question of whether or not all activities and sports should be compensated at the same rate. Many districts distinguish between actual activity supervision and crowd control. Some districts also make distinctions in the pay rates for different activities. One factfinder (in M69-427) recommended against continuing a differential between coaching rates for various sports.

In addition to the money questions there were cases in which the amount and nature of the activities offered were issues in dispute (cf. M69-155). Are these activities offered only at the discretion of the board? Is there any reason why the number of activities offered should be competitive with other area school districts? Should the number of offerings be increased to accommodate expanding enrollment? What kind of activities should be represented, and if more than one teacher volunteers for an activity, who shall decide which teacher takes it?

These were a few of the questions which arose. There was no particular pattern in the factfinders' recommendations. While some factfinders cited comparability with neighboring school districts as a rationale for their recommendations (cf. M69-370, M69-191), others specifically pointed out that they felt that comparability was inappropriate ". . . because of variations in the extent of duties or responsibilities . . ." (M69-314), and because of ". . . individual differences in the importance attached by the Boards to these activities" (M69-318). Past practice, particularly the pattern of recent raises, and persuasive arguments by the parties, such as the one relating the number of activities to enrollment, seemed to be decisive where comparability was not used as a standard.

Teacher Workload and Length of School Day

Somewhat related to the matter of extra duty after school was the issue of workload during the school day. This issue included limiting the number of teaching periods, specifying preparation periods, limiting class size, covering classes for absent colleagues, release from nonteaching duties, and length of the school day.

These matters, like the preceding issues, involve policy as well as money. The policy considerations here involve creation of additional positions to lessen the load on current staff, implementation of aide programs, and in some cases questions of scheduling and classroom space. Most factfinders accepted the issues listed above as proper areas of concern for teacher negotiations, but on account of the impingement on broader board responsibilities recommendations usually took the form of maximum or minimum tolerable levels to be observed "where possible" (cf. M69-28, M69-379, M69-166, M69-428). In this way a general maximum or minimum standard could be established without overly restricting the board's flexibility to meet unusual circumstances.

Release from nonteaching duties is often complicated by the related question of teacher aide programs. In addition to the reasonableness of the requests with regard to scheduling and available resources, factfinders considered past practice in the district (cf. M69-227, M69-155). One case was unusual in that the board suggested a trade rather than outright release from nonteaching duties. Board negotiators suggested substituting an additional teaching period instead of daily nonteaching chores. The factfinder, for his part, recommended that the issue be taken up by the Teachers' Advisory Cabinet for further study and resolution (M69-226).

Regarding length of school day, the "teaching day" is set by the board as a matter of educational policy. The question which often came up in collective bargaining was how long should teachers be required to stay in school buildings once the "teaching day" was over? Factfinders generally tended to accept teacher proposals to shorten this time, usually from a half hour to fifteen minutes.

In some cases teachers asked for extra compensation for covering classes when no substitute was available. Most factfinders rejected the demand, one commenting that refusing to cover classes was unprofessional, another suggesting that if teachers feel their services are being abused they should keep records of the number of instances when substitutes are not hired, to show whether or not the district was making sufficient efforts to provide substitutes.

Association Rights

Release time for association officers was an issue in a few cases (cf. M69-279, M69-328, M69-227, M69-370, M69-93, M69-166). Teachers asserted that a certain amount of release time was necessary in the interest of the responsible management of association business. Common association requests, other than time off, were for use of faculty mailboxes, participation in annual teacher orientation, and dues checkoff privileges. Factfinders usually recommended acceptance of these requests, while in the matter of release time there was less consistency in their recommendations. In those cases where release time was recommended, there was variation in the amount of time considered necessary for this function as well as differences in the number of officers regarded as necessary to perform the work. In one case (M69-328) it was recommended that the association president, vice president, and building representatives be released from all nonteaching duties, while in another case (M69-279) it was recommended that the president alone be released from homeroom duties plus two teaching periods per day.

Grievance Procedure

A number of reports deal with grievance procedure, particularly with the definition of a grievance and whether to use arbitration as a final step. Most factfinders recommended that grievances be limited to matters of contract interpretation, although one factfinder (M69-49) suggested that in the interest of good communications anything be allowed at the lower levels of the procedure, while only contract questions could be taken to an arbitrator.

The question of arbitration and whether it be only advisory or final and binding was an important issue in many of the cases. Generally factfinders favored binding arbitration, although several recommended advisory arbitration for the time being. One factfinder (M69-63) compared advisory arbitration to factfinding and commented that the latter works well enough even though the recommendations are not final and binding.

The arbitration problem also came up in an indirect way through the no-strike clause. Although the no-strike pledge was usually a part of the recognition clause, it appears that a number of teacher groups in 1969 tried to withdraw this pledge in an effort to trade it back for binding grievance arbitration. This trade is commonly made in private industry. However, no-strike clauses are more meaningful in the private sector, since strikes by public employees are banned by law.

Salary

In cases where salary disputes were essentially over the amount of new money, factfinders generally relied upon a standard of comparability with neighboring districts of similar size and wealth rather than a standard of compromise or of splitting the difference. In some cases where area patterns were not yet established, the factfinders cited cost of living increases as a guide.

Some more specific problems in salary disputes beyond general questions of the amount of new money include: the level of the base or recruiting salary, the length of the vertical scale, use of percentage (index) versus lump sum amounts, and the controversial matter of "merit" or nonautomatic increments.

Before taking up the more specific issues a word of explanation about the terminology is in order. Base salary is the amount which would be paid to a first year teacher with a bachelor's degree. This figure usually appears in the upper left-hand corner of the salary schedule. From this base salary the schedule has increments downwards (the vertical scale) for years of experience (until 1971, at least twelve such increments were required by law) and also columns across (the horizontal scale) for advanced training in the form of graduate credits and master's or doctor's degrees. Some salary schedules have increments in lump sum amounts (e.g., $300) while others have increments indexed (a certain percentage of) to the base salary.

One factfinder (M69-116) took an interesting approach to hiring or base salary. The board had argued that its current base salary was entirely adequate for competitive recruitment of staff. The factfinder recommended that since recruitment is a board responsibility, the board be allowed to set the hiring salary. He then directed his recommendations further along the scale in an effort to correct inequities which have a greater effect on teachers already in the district who are members of the bargaining unit. The board was thus allowed to effect a savings at the expense of prospective teachers, but not at the expense of current staff.*

The question of the length or number of increments on the vertical scale is of interest simply because of the different opinions factfinders appear to have on the subject. While some factfinders recommended condensing 18- or 20-step schedules into fewer (13-15) steps, others recommended lengthening 12- or 13-step schedules to 15 or more steps (cf. M69-279, M69-312, M69-393, M69-227). In one case (M69-279) a factfinder recommended that the 20-step schedule recommended by factfinders in 1968 be condensed to 15 steps. Such conflicting recommendations might suggest a strategy to the teachers of one year demanding an extra step or two and the following year asking that the money be paid out sooner in fewer steps. At present 15 steps with longevity increments at the 20th and 25th years appears to be about the average.

Factfinders differed on the issue of "merit," or nonautomatic increment. For the most part, they were reluctant to recommend changes from current practice. The feeling seems to be that long term implications as well as the more immediate complications of a "merit" system are such that changes from or implementation of

---

*The factfinder in this case returned a questionnaire in the Yaffe-Goldblatt (1971) study. He commented: "In the case under study the Board made much of the assertion that it was in fact competitive with other school districts. According to the Superintendent's testimony he was being deluged by applications from new teachers. It was on this basis that I recommended adoption of the Board's proposal for first and second step personnel, but, in doing so, I rather suspected the Board would voluntarily raise these levels because it would, in fact, have had recruiting difficulties under its own proposal. I believe my expectations materialized."

such programs ought to be arrived at by agreement of the parties rather than by third-party ruling (cf. M69-368, M69-134, M69-312, M69-370, M69-490).

"Indexing" or substituting percentage of base for lump sums came in for the same kind of treatment by factfinders as the "merit" issue. Factfinders were loath to recommend changes in present practice (cf. M69-319, M69-226, M69-456, M69-440, M69-90, M69-227, M69-314, M69-166, M69-484). Even those factfinders who made their salary recommendations in the form of flat percentage increases were disinclined to change the increment structure from flat dollar amounts to percentages or the reverse.

As to the criteria used by factfinders when arriving at a salary figure, it is clear that geographical proximity, size of community, and comparable tax base (measured by wealth per pupil in WADA)* were the major considerations. Many factfinders also considered the history of tax rate increases and budget defeats in the community and in its neighbors with which it was being compared. (For a more detailed picture of factfinders' salary recommendations and the underlying rationale see Pegnetter 1971).

Fringe Benefits and Paid Leaves

The amount factfinders recommended the district contribute toward health insurance for teachers and their dependents usually followed the general pattern for the geographical area of the district. While the trend was generally upward, the specific amount of recommended increase appeared to be flexible, often tailored to the size of other money items in the recommendations.

In some districts, particularly in the downstate region, dental insurance plans were requested by the teachers. Since there is not yet a pattern of providing such coverage, factfinders in two of the three cases in this sample (M69-110, M69-70) denied the requests. In the third case (M69-28) the factfinder recommended a plan with 25 percent district contribution. Life insurance was also an issue in several cases (cf. M69-279, M69-117, M69-110). Factfinders were more disposed to recommend the life insurance coverage than the dental plans. The recommendations were generally for noncontributory group plans in the range of $2500 to $5000.

---

*This refers to total true value of taxable property in the district divided by the number of pupils in weighted average daily attendance.

Paid leaves including sick leave, family and personal leave, professional leave, and sabbatical leave were frequently among the issues at impasse. Recommendations on sick leave and personal leave usually followed area standards with consideration for past practice, both in terms of amount and accumulation, and in the case of personal leave in terms of whether or not a reason and/or prior approval would be required. In one unusual case, the board wanted teachers who take unauthorized leave to be required to pay all resultant expenses incurred by the board. The factfinder pointed out that such a policy might tempt teachers to "buy days off" and that such cases were better left to disciplinary action (cf. M69-227).

Professional leave recommendations—that is, the number of professional and/or association conference days with or without pay to be allowed—followed no set pattern and depended to a large extent on past practice in the district.

Issues also arose concerning the number of sabbatical leaves to be granted, the length of such leaves, and the percentage of salary which would be paid. The procedures which have been developed in the various school districts for granting sabbatical leaves vary considerably. Factfinders' recommendations based on the existing procedures and the parties' proposals for changes therefore were equally disparate. The recommendations tended to reinforce current programs, occasionally calling for some increases. There was, however, no pattern to either the amount or type of increase suggested. One factfinder (M69-110) recommended an increase from 50 percent to 55 percent of salary for teachers on sabbatical, while others (M69-117, M69-93) recommended increasing the percentage of teachers to be given sabbaticals each year or the amount of money to be set aside for this purpose. Another factfinder (M69-469) suggested shortening the required period of service in the district from seven years to five. Factfinders tended to approve teacher requests for an option of a half year at full pay, rather than a full year at half pay when the individual so desired.

Summary

The Criteria

What then are the criteria upon which factfinders base their recommendations? There seem to be two major considerations involved, and one or both may be operative in any one situation. The standards of "acceptability" (what the parties will agree to) and of "equity" (the requirements of the factfinder's notions of fairness and good labor relations) appear to be determinative.

The weighting of these criteria will depend to some extent upon the factfinder's view of his own role: whether he sees his primary function as making proposals which will produce a settlement, or as a neutral third party whose major role is to make public the facts of the dispute and try to suggest an "equitable" (not merely "acceptable") resolution of issues. Actually both of these functions are part of the factfinder's role (Governor's Committee on Public Employee Relations 1966, pp. 37-38; Public Employees' Fair Employment Law, ch. 392 of the Laws of 1967, § 209), and they need not necessarily be conflicting. If, however, they are not entirely compatible, the factfinder must choose which criterion to modify in light of the other.

Acceptability

"Acceptability" as an abstract criterion by which to decide the issues in dispute is fairly self evident—"to the lion shall go the lion's share." It means convincing the parties that the recommendations represent the best bargain they could have gotten based upon the power balance between them in free collective bargaining if stoppages were not illegal.

While the concept of "acceptability" is easily defined in the abstract, specific definition of the "acceptable" solution for any set of circumstances is often difficult. The neutral party must get the sense of the situation from the parties themselves and from that try to gauge the area of possible settlement. In addition to correctly judging what the area of settlement is, he must convince the parties that his interpretation is accurate and that the recommendations based upon it represent the best they will be able to get.

Sometimes the problem of persuasion becomes part of the criterion itself. A recalcitrant individual on one of the negotiating teams may have to be taken into consideration in defining the area of settlement, and the criterion of "acceptability" may end up relating as much to personalities and emotions around the bargaining table as to the facts in the case. The situation is peculiar to public sector bargaining. In a private sector strike situation, the personalities and rhetoric of the negotiators soon give way to a test of economic strength. In public employment impasse procedures are designed to avoid such tests, and it is more difficult to call a bluff. Personalities and emotions creep into the process and cannot be ignored if settlement is the object. Another factor which may make the neutral person's job more difficult is the fact that in the public sector there are politics on both sides of the table. Management as well as union spokesmen are elected officials.

Although some pressure can be brought to bear through publication of the factfinder's report, research (Yaffe and Goldblatt 1971) indicated that attempts to arouse public interest have had only minimal effects on the actual settlement of the dispute. Thus the factfinder looking for a settlement is pretty well limited to the facts, both economic and political, and the personalities at the table.

Equity

In addition to his appraisal of acceptability, the factfinder usually arrives at some notion of the "equity" involved before making his recommendations. The term equity here denotes considerations by the neutral party which are not influenced by the power balance between the parties, but by the argument put forward and such abstract standards of justice as the factfinder may have.

From the presentations made by the parties the factfinder usually obtains several indications as to the equity of their proposals. Perhaps the most useful of these indicators are past practice within the district, and present practice in other neighboring and/or similar districts, with emphasis usually on the latter. Past practice within the district, except where a district has been a leader in a certain field, is usually de-emphasized because it is no longer current. Furthermore, the practices may be in dispute. Comparison with similar and neighboring districts has the advantage of being both an outside standard and a current one.

Through comparisons with neighboring and similar districts the factfinder can ascertain the level of settlements (or at least the relative positions of the parties if bargaining is incomplete) in other districts faced with the same geography, similar tax problems, and the same increases in the cost of living. From this the factfinder gains an idea of the "going rate" and also of the competitive recruiting salaries. If neighboring districts are dissimilar in terms of size or tax base, the factfinder may modify or weight the criterion of comparability accordingly.

In addition to comparability, past practice, and other arguments presented by the parties, the factfinder himself has professional standards from his training and experience in labor relations which may influence his findings. Certain issues may be handled from the point of view of good labor relations rather than on a basis of comparability, past practice, or even acceptability.

The Weighting of the Criteria

Acceptability and equity are most likely to conflict when acceptability is less dependent on economics, and more a matter of personalities or politics. If agreement is to be achieved, such needs and individuals must be accommodated, sometimes at the expense of equity. Where acceptability is measured in economic terms it usually produces contracts similar to those negotiated in comparable districts if only because those districts also had to find acceptable solutions.

In mediation, which precedes factfinding, settlements (if they are achieved) are achieved on the basis of acceptability. If the mediator is successful in convincing the parties of his impression of the "acceptable" solution, there is no need to go on to factfinding. The disputes most likely to be carried further are those in which acceptability depends upon the personalities at the bargaining table, or on political rather than economic factors; in these disputes there is the greatest conflict between acceptability and equity and one party will undoubtedly feel aggrieved. One or both of the parties may opt for factfinding in hopes of finding someone with a different appraisal of acceptability, or someone who will modify what has already been identified as the "acceptable solution" in light of some higher equity. That is, teachers sometimes feel that if a position is morally right and equitable it should prevail even if the power balance in the community would not support such a position. They occasionally go to factfinding in the hope that the factfinder will lend his support to their position.

Factfinding gives the parties a second neutral interpretation of the "acceptable solution" and often an opinion of the equity as well. Having thus identified acceptability and equity as the major criteria, and having suggested that acceptability may be the more important since factfinding is a dispute settlement procedure, it would be interesting to know with what accuracy factfinders judge the area of settlement. If factfinders cannot be reasonably sure of correctly assessing acceptability, it would suggest that they ought not to place inordinate weight on this criterion, or that they should at least give equity the benefit of the doubt in situations where they perceive a conflict between the two criteria.

Yaffe and Goldblatt (1971) have utilized these fifty teacher cases along with fifty-six nonteacher cases in a study of factfinding effectiveness. In their questionnaire factfinders were asked, among other things, if they were confident about the acceptance of their recommendations. The question was divided to deal with employee organization acceptance and employer acceptance separately. Using the results of the questionnaire with reference to these fifty teacher cases, plus information from PERB's files regarding the disposition of the cases, we find the following information about factfinders' ability to predict settlement.

In the sample of fifty cases thirty-eight factfinders returned completed questionnaires. In these thirty-eight cases, factfinders were confident that the whole report and recommendations would be accepted by the board in twenty cases and by the teachers in twenty-two cases. On the whole their confidence was well founded. Of the twenty cases where factfinders expressed confidence in board acceptance, there were only three cases where the board did not accept the recommendations. Of the twenty-two cases where factfinders expressed confidence in teacher acceptance there were four cases where teachers rejected the reports. Thus in 83 percent of the cases where factfinders expected their recommendations to be accepted, they had correctly judged "acceptability." It would appear that reliance upon acceptability does actually produce settlements.

Conclusion

In terms of this study, the obvious question is whether there is a pattern to factfinders' recommendations on particular issues— whether they are consistent—and if so, to what extent the operative criteria and the weighting of those criteria can be identified.

Where the recommendations tend to be consistent, it may be assumed that factfinders either have similar notions of good educational or labor relations policy, or that they have used a standard of comparability which reproduces the general pattern of other recommendations and agreement around the state. On the other hand, where the recommendations are inconsistent, it is obvious that comparability at least was not the determinative standard. Inconsistency indicates differing interpretations of equity, or possibly greater concessions to acceptability.

In the course of examining the fifty factfinding reports for the teacher impasses included in this study it was found that, with some allowances for modifications in the interest of acceptability, factfinders were relatively consistent in their treatment of the following issues: (1) negotiability problems: factfinders consistently tried to deal with the disputed items rather than the more abstract question of negotiability; (2) scope of bargaining: factfinders identified certain areas as management responsibility such as creation or elimination of positions, the budget, program decisions, deployment of personnel; (3) working conditions: consistency here even included reluctance to recommend clauses which might deprive the board of its flexibility in areas of overlap between teacher working conditions and broader board responsibilities, notably class size; (4) assignment of educational policy issues to joint committees for resolution, often outside of the bargaining relationship; and (5) salary levels and fringe benefits, including personal leave days and sick leave.

While consistent findings in the first four of the above issues would appear to reflect reliance upon current notions of adequate working conditions and practicality of implementation, consistent findings in the matter of leaves and money issues more probably stems from use of a standard of comparability.

The issues in which factfinders were least consistent in their recommendations were: (1) changes in board policy; (2) grievance arbitration, whether advisory or binding; (3) release time for association officers; (4) professional leave policy; (5) extracurricular rates; (6) salary structure, particularly the length of the vertical scale. These issues appear to represent the risk areas in going to factfinding.

Thus, factfinding involves some areas in which the factfinder's response cannot be anticipated. Beyond mediation it offers a second and perhaps different interpretation of acceptability and the chance that the factfinder will weight equity, as he perceives it, higher than acceptability, especially on the risk issues. Moreover, factfinding offers a neutral opinion which will be made public.

References

Governor's Committee on Public Employee Relations. *Final Report.* Albany: State of New York, 1966.

New York State Department of Education, Division of Educational Management Services. *Board of Education Responsibility for the Determination of "Ordinary Contingent Expenses."* Albany: University of the State of New York, 1968.

Pegnetter, Richard. "Fact Finding and Teacher Salary Disputes." *Industrial and Labor Relations Review* 24, no. 2 (January 1971).

Public Employment Relations Board of the State of New York. *Official Decisions and Related Matters* (vol. 3). New York: Lenz & Riecker, 1970.

Sabghir, Irving. *The Scope of Bargaining in Public Sector Collective Bargaining.* Albany: PERB, 1970.

Yaffe, B., and Goldblatt, H. *Factfinding in Public Employment Disputes in New York State: More Promise than Illusion.* Ithaca: New York State School of Industrial and Labor Relations, 1971.

Reading 19

Preintervention Effects of Mediation versus Arbitration

Douglas F. Johnson and Dean G. Pruitt

This study was basically concerned with the impact that the anticipation of third-party intervention has on concession making in negotiation. Two major kinds of intervention can be identified in formal negotiation: arbitration and mediation. These differ on at least two dimensions: (1) the extent to which the intermediary's recommendations are binding, and (2) the amount of information potentially available to the intermediary about the issues being negotiated. An arbitrator's decisions are usually binding; and because he can subpoena witnesses and documents, he has the potential for gaining considerable information about the issues. A mediator's decisions are usually nonbinding, and he typically has less access to information.

Several authors (Bernstein 1954; Elkouri 1952; Trotta 1961), basing their conclusions on case studies, have observed that negotiators tend to reach agreement more easily (i.e., concede more rapidly) when they anticipate future arbitration than when they anticipate future mediation. This may or may not be a valid conclusion. If

Reprinted by permission from *Journal of Applied Psychology* 56, no. 1 (1972), pp. 1-10.

valid, there are at least two reasons why it may be correct, based on the dimensions distinguished earlier.

The supposedly greater speed of concession under the threat of arbitration may be due to efforts to avoid a binding third-party decision. A negotiator may fear such a decision because it forecloses the possibility of developing further bargaining power. Furthermore, there is a danger that the arbitrator will make erroneous judgments as a result of prejudice or a lack of responsibility for living with the implications of the decisions he makes. In addition, the loss of control implied by a binding decision may be unpalatable to the negotiator because it carries the implication to himself and others that he is weak or has failed in some way. For all these reasons, negotiators may try to avoid arbitration by moving rapidly toward agreement before the time at which the arbitrator is supposed to intervene.

Alternatively, arbitration may produce more rapid concessions than mediation because of the amount of information available to the intermediary. When, as in mediation, the intermediary has little information about the issues, the negotiators may expect him to base his recommendations primarily on their bargaining positions at the time of intervention. For example, they may expect him to propose simply splitting the difference between their current positions, since he has little else to go on. A negotiator who expects this may concede very little before intervention so that splitting the difference will favor his interests as fully as possible. On the other hand, when the intermediary is fully capable of informing himself about the issues, as in arbitration, the negotiators may view their bargaining positions as irrelevant to his decision processes. Hence, they will be less likely to maintain rigid, uncompromising bargaining positions in an effort to influence his decisions.

It was possible in this study to manipulate independently the two dimensions that distinguish arbitration from mediation and to observe their separate impact on preintervention concession making. On the basis of the arguments just presented, we hypothesized that:

1. Concessions will be more rapid under the threat of binding, as opposed to nonbinding, third-party intervention, and

2. Concessions will be more rapid when informed, as opposed to uniformed, intervention is anticipated. If either hypothesis should

receive support, we were ready to conclude that the anticipation of arbitration produces faster concessions than the anticipation of mediation, but we would draw differing conclusions about the process underlying this phenomenon, depending on which hypothesis was supported.

Method

Subjects

The Ss were 50 male graduate students from a course on collective bargaining. These advanced students were used because of their presumed sophistication about negotiation. It was assumed that they would learn the task rapidly and be able to anticipate realistically the implications of third-party intervention. The Ss were told that they were going to participate in a collective-bargaining simulation for two reasons: (1) to gain experience and insight into the bargaining process as a supplement to their course; and (2) to contribute to a controlled study of the bargaining process.

Variables and Design

A basic 2 X 2 design was employed, involving anticipation of binding (B) versus nonbinding (NB) third-party intervention and anticipation of well-informed (I) versus poorly-informed (NI) intervention. In addition, a control condition was employed in which no third-party intervention was anticipated. The Ss were randomly assembled into dyads that were randomly assigned to the five conditions. Five dyads were run in each condition.

A third variable was role. Within each dyad, one S was randomly designated as the union representative (U) and the other as the management representative (M). A fourth variable, time (divided into 10 time segments) was used in the analysis of the behavioral data.

Task and Materials

The experiment made use of a simulation of collective bargaining which resembled in some ways a procedure developed by Druckman (1967). The task involved face-to-face bargaining between the two Ss in a dyad. Enough background information was introduced to maintain the interest of the Ss. This information, which was based on a composite of several cases drawn from the west coast airframe industry (Levinson 1966), consisted of data on economic trends and production and statements about union problems and the attitude of management toward labor organizations. The negotiators bargained over two issues simultaneously: a major issue, wages, and a minor issue, which was aid to education in the practice session and hospitalization in the main bargaining session. Background materials were given to all negotiators, some of which were labeled "not to be shown to your opponent." The unrestricted background material consisted of the history and the economic trends for the company and industry. Included in the restricted material were scales that delimited the offers that could be made to the other side (see tables 1 and 2). Below each possible offer was a utility value. For U, this consisted of a scale of psychological satisfaction values that the average worker was expected to feel for each possible agreement. M's utility scale consisted of the expected earnings per share accruing to the stockholders as a function of each possible agreement.

Both bargainers were given a figure that was obtained by that side in the last contract negotiation. It was assumed that this status quo figure would serve as a psychological zero point below which the negotiator would be quite reluctant to go. So as to avoid premature agreements, the scales were constructed in such a manner that it was impossible for both sides to achieve their status quo.

Each S also received a sheet outlining the procedure to be followed in case the bargainers failed to reach agreement. These sheets introduced the independent variables in the study. All sheets stated that if an agreement had not been reached after 25 minutes of bargaining, the negotiation would be considered deadlocked. In this case, a third party would be brought in. The sheet also stated the general qualifications of the third party: He would be an advanced industrial relations student with a great deal of general knowledge but no specific information regarding this simulation. The final two points on the sheet dealt with the independent variables. In the NI condition it was stated that the third party would remain fairly uninformed regarding this simulation, that is, he would receive only the last offers made by each bargainer and the range of potential offers on their offer forms. In the I condition, the third party would receive the offers that each bargainer had made plus *all* of the information presented to each bargainer in the simulation (e.g., background, utility scales, etc.). The B-NB variable was introduced by stating in the B

Table 1
Union's Scales of Possible Offers with Corresponding Value of Each Offer

I. Wages

5	6	7	8	9	10	11	12	13	14	15	16	17	18	19	20	21	22	23	24	Possible wage increases in cents per hour
0	5	10	15	20	25	30	35	40	45	50	53	56	59	64	69	75	79	85	90	Index of employee satisfaction for each possible wage increase

II. Hospitalization

30	40	50	60	70	80	90	100	Percentage of possible management contributions
0	1	2	3	4	5	6	7	Increase in employee satisfaction

Note: Current index shows employee satisfaction at about 60.

Table 2
Management's Scales of Possible Offers with Corresponding Value of Each Offer

I. Wages

5	6	7	8	9	10	11	12	13	14	15	16	17	18	19	20	21	22	23	24	Possible wage increases in cents per hour
62	61	60	59	58	55	54	53	52	51	45	39	36	34	33	32	28	27	26	25	Projected earnings in cents per share if wage increase indicated above is agreed upon

II. Hospitalization

30	40	50	60	70	80	90	100	Percentage of possible management contributions
1½	2	2½	3	3½	4	4½	5	Decrease in earnings in cents per share

Note: Last year's gross earnings per share were 35.7¢.

condition that the third party's decision would be final and that a contract would be signed according to that decision. In the NB condition it was stated that the third party's decision would be merely a recommendation and that the bargainers could accept or reject it as they pleased. In the control condition, the sheet stated that if an agreement were not reached in 25 minutes the bargaining would be interrupted to allow the bargainers to collect their thoughts and reappraise the situation. After doing so, they would resume bargaining.

The final piece of material presented was a blank contract which was to be filled in upon reaching an agreement (or when the arbitrator dictated an agreement).

Procedure

Each bargaining session lasted 2 hours. Two Ss who had previously participated in the simulation (the evaluators) and two new Ss (the negotiators) were used in each session. The negotiators were seated face-to-face across a table in the center of which stood a 12-inch barrier which served to prevent one from seeing the materials of the other. One negotiator was randomly designated as the U representative and the other as the M representative. The job of the evaluators was said to be one of judging the adequacy of the negotiators' performance. The instructions indicated that permanent records of the evaluators' judgments would be kept so that the Ss could get feedback at the end of the study concerning their standing in comparison with all of the industrial relations students who had participated in the study. There were two related reasons for using evaluators. One was to simulate a critical element of most negotiations, the existence of constituents who oversee the activities of the negotiators. The other was to motivate Ss to think seriously about how they should behave in this situation and, hence, come to grips with the implications of future third-party intervention. We were afraid that, without such a motivational device, Ss would attend mainly to current situational demands and ignore the future—a fear that was reinforced by earlier experience in laboratory research on negotiation (Pruitt and Drews 1969).

In the four conditions where third-party intervention was anticipated, a fifth person was introduced as the third party. The third party was actually a confederate employed by E for this study. He was billed as an advanced Ph.D. candidate in the industrial relations program who, although engaged in another task, would help out in this simulation should the need arise.

General instructions were read to the five people in the room. The evaluators were then seated at a table in the back of the room, and the third party was taken out to his other task. (Actually, the third party had no other task, but it seemed desirable to tell this to Ss so that they would not feel pressure to fail to reach agreement so that the third party would have something to do in the experiment.) The negotiators were then given the materials for the session. The U and M representatives had different materials and were instructed not to show them to their adversary. The evaluators had a copy of both U and M materials.

After the materials had been studied, the negotiators began a 20-minute bargaining session which ended in practice with the dead-lock procedure. After this session was over they were told that it had only been for practice in order to familiarize them with the back-ground materials and with bargaining techniques in the laboratory. They were then given the materials to be used for the second session. These materials were the same as those used in the first session ex-cept that the specific issues and their utilities had been changed. After this material had been studied, a questionnaire was adminis-tered concerning S's plans and expectations about the final session about to begin. This questionnaire had a dual purpose. It was de-signed both to gather data and to force Ss to think ahead and weigh the implications of the deadlock procedure. To the latter end, ques-tions were included on such qualities of the third party as his hon-esty, capability, helpfulness and level of information, and on the importance of reaching agreement before institution of the deadlock procedure. Again the rationale behind use of this questionnaire was a fear that, otherwise, Ss would attend mainly to current situational demands and fail to think ahead.

The final session lasted 25 minutes. The bargainers were told that they could handle the session in any way they desired; they could make offers and counteroffers whenever they pleased. The only restrictions were that they could not show each other any re-stricted material and had to refrain from discussing issues that were unrelated to the materials provided. Questionnaires were again ad-ministered to all Ss. In the control condition and the conditions involving an NB third-party decision, Ss were given an additional 5 minutes of bargaining time after the administration of the questionnaires. At the end of the session all Ss were debriefed, and the two Ss who served as negotiators were recruited to return at a later time to serve as evaluators.

Results

Behavioral Data

So that it would be possible to study trends over time, the 25-minute negotiation session was divided into 10 equal segments. The raw score used to describe an S's behavior in a time segment was the utility of the most lenient offer he made during that segment (i.e., the offer which had the lowest utility to him). For the U data, the utility of an offer consisted of the index of employee satisfaction on wages plus the index of employee satisfaction on hospitalization. For the M data, the utility of an offer consisted of the projected earnings per share on wages minus the cost per share of the hospitalization plan. Because the raw scores for U and M were expressed in different units, they were transformed in an effort to reconcile the scales. The following formula was used for this transformation: $Y = 100 (H-X)/(H-Q)$, where Y is the transformed utility score, H is the highest utility obtainable by the negotiator in question (97 for U and 57¢ for M), X is the raw utility score, and Q is the status-quo point (60 for U and 35.7¢ for M). It will be seen that this index expresses a score as the percentage moved of the utility distance between the most extreme demand a negotiator can make and his status quo point. Note that this is an index of the extent of concession embodied in the current offer rather than an index of the value of the current offer. Hence, when a negotiator makes his largest possible demand, he gets a score of zero, that is, no concession. When his offer is at his status quo point, he gets a score of 100: he has moved all the way to what we assumed to be his point of psychological zero utility. It is possible, of course, for an S to go further than his status quo point; hence, this index can be (and was in some of the conditions of this experiment) greater than 100.

The results for the transformed index are shown in figures 1 and 2. A two-between and two-within, $2 \times 2 \times 2 \times 10$ analysis of vari

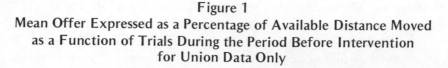

Figure 1
Mean Offer Expressed as a Percentage of Available Distance Moved
as a Function of Trials During the Period Before Intervention
for Union Data Only

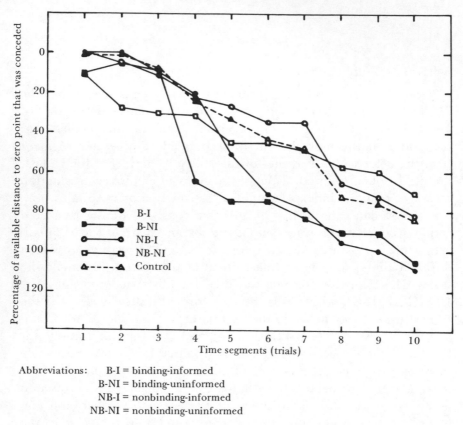

Abbreviations: B-I = binding-informed
                  B-NI = binding-uninformed
                  NB-I = nonbinding-informed
                  NB-NI = nonbinding-uninformed

ance was performed on these data, with trend comparisons up to the cubic across the 10 time segments.* The results of this analysis are shown in table 3.

The highly significant linear trend effect is reflected in the pronounced downward trend over time segments that can be seen in

_____

*Higher order trends were not investigated, since it seemed unlikely that they would appear. It should be noted that the kind of analysis employed here does not assume homogeneity of covariance and, hence, is superior in this respect to ordinary univariate repeated-measures analysis.

Figure 2
Mean Offer Expressed as a Percentage of Available Distance Moved as a Function of Trials During the Period Before Intervention for Management Data Only

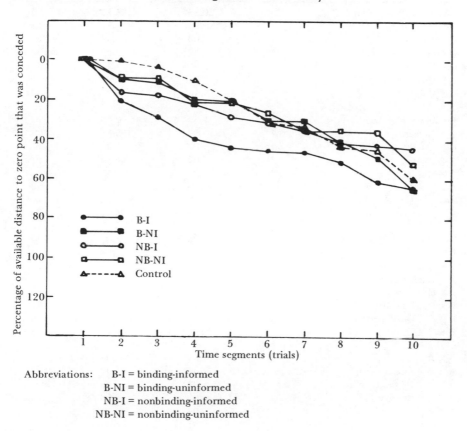

Abbreviations: B-I = binding-informed
                   B-NI = binding-uninformed
                   NB-I = nonbinding-informed
                   NB-NI = nonbinding-uninformed

figures 1 and 2. This indicates that the negotiators made fairly regular concessions over time. The significant C main effect can be interpreted most adequately in conjunction with the significant C X Linear Trend interaction. What happened is that both negotiators started at or near their maximal demands. Thereafter, U conceded more rapidly than M, in terms of the proportion of the maximum available utility embodied in their offers. Indeed, a number of the U representatives went below their status quo point in time segment 10 in an effort to reach agreement while this was seldom true for the M representatives.

Table 3
Trend Analysis on the Transformed Utility-of-Offer Index

Source	df	MS	F	p
Linear trend over trials	1	20.18	135.87	.001
Quadratic trend	1	.06	.71	ns
Cubic trend	1	.00	.04	ns
Union-management (C)	1	3.32	7.05	.02
C × Linear trend	1	1.82	40.45	.001
C × Quadratic trend	1	.01	.04	ns
C × Cubic trend	1	.16	6.27	.02
Binding-nonbinding (A)	1	1.55	2.03	ns
A × Linear trend	1	.87	5.85	.03
A × Quadratic trend	1	.07	.95	ns
A × Cubic trend	1	.03	1.19	ns
A × C	1	.26	.55	ns
A × C × Linear trend	1	.28	6.13	.02
A × C × Quadratic trend	1	.12	2.00	ns
A × C × Cubic trend	1	.15	5.91	.02
Informed-uninformed (B)	1	.00	.01	ns
B × Linear trend	1	.13	.88	ns
B × Quadratic trend	1	.00	.02	ns
B × Cubic trend	1	.02	.67	ns
B × C	1	.57	1.20	ns
B × C × Linear trend	1	.24	5.24	.04
B × C × Quadratic trend	1	.23	4.01	.06
B × C × Cubic trend	1	.04	1.44	ns
A × B	1	.04	.06	ns
A × B × Linear trend	1	.01	.02	ns
A × B × Quadratic trend	1	.01	.10	ns
A × B × Cubic trend	1	.00	.03	ns
A × B × C	1	.05	.11	ns
A × B × C × Linear trend	1	.01	.30	ns
A × B × C × Quadratic trend	1	.02	.35	ns
A × B × C × Cubic trend	1	.01	.40	ns
Between-dyad-totals error	16	.76		
Linear trend error	16	.15		
Quadratic trend error	16	.08		
Cubic trend error	16	.02		
C error	16	.47		
C × Linear trend error	16	.05		
C × Quadratic trend error	16	.06		
C × Cubic trend error	16	.02		

Note: For organization of this table, eight separate between-dyad analyses were performed, one for each error term listed in the last group of terms. The first term from each of the eight analyses is given in the first group of terms (with the exception of the test for the grand mean, which is uninteresting); the second terms are in the next group, etc.

Several significant interactions are found between the B-NB variable and the within variables. The A X Linear Trend and A X C X Linear Trend interaction results indicate the following: Negotiators faced with a B decision made larger and more frequent concessions than those faced with an NB decision, and this was particularly true for the U as opposed to the M representatives. The A X C X Cubic Trend interaction result reflects the pronounced S-shaped curve that is seen only in the B-U data, involving a relatively constant level of demand over the first three or four trial blocks and then a sudden drop in demand around blocks 4 and 5. The significant B X C X Linear Trend interaction result and nearly significant B X C X Quadratic Trend interaction result can be interpreted as follows: M tended at first to concede more rapidly in the I as opposed to the NI condition, while U tended to concede at first more rapidly in the NI than in the I condition.

Because of the many interactions involving the U-M variable, separate analysis of variance were performed on the U and the M data. These tended to confirm the conclusions stated above. Significant A X Linear Trend interaction (F = 9.13, p < .01) and A X Cubic Trend interaction (F = 4.85, p < .05) results were found for U but not for M. A nearly significant B X Linear Trend interaction effect (F = 3.09, p < .10) was found for U, and a nearly significant B X Quadratic Trend interaction effect (F = 3.60, p < .10) was found for M.

The behavior of negotiators in the control condition was compared to that of negotiators in the other four conditions. The only significant differences were found between the control condition and the B condition: a linear trend interaction (F = 8.00, p < .01) and a cubic trend interaction (F = 4.13, p < .05). In conjunction with the curves shown in figure 2, these findings indicate that negotiators who anticipated B intervention conceded more rapidly than those who anticipated no intervention, especially after the first few time segments.

Questionnaire Data

The main questionnaire was administered between the practice session and the main negotiation. The means for most of the items are shown in table 4. A 2 X 2 X 2 analysis of variance was performed on the data from each item.*

---

*The U-M variable was treated as a between variable in this analysis since the questionnaire was employed before the main negotiation.

Table 4

Means of Questionnaire Items Measuring Anticipations about the Main Negotiation

Question	Binding				Nonbinding			
	Informed		Uninformed		Informed		Uninformed	
	Union	Management	Union	Management	Union	Management	Union	Management
See third party as honest	5.8	6.8	5.8	5.8	6.8	6.4	6.4	5.6
See third party as informed	3.2	5.4	3.4	3.0	4.0	5.4	1.6	2.6
See third party as helpful	2.8	3.8	4.0	3.2	4.2	4.8	4.6	3.6
See third party as fair	4.2	5.2	2.6	3.4	4.8	4.8	4.6	4.2
See third party as unyielding	4.8	3.8	4.2	5.4	3.0	3.2	4.6	3.6
Importance to agree quickly	3.2	4.2	3.4	4.0	3.6	2.8	1.8	2.8
Influence of third party	4.4	3.2	3.2	3.6	2.4	3.6	3.0	2.4
Capability of third party to make an equitable decision	4.8	5.4	2.8	4.8	5.0	5.2	3.6	4.8
Importance of agreement before intervention	2.0	3.2	4.0	3.2	2.2	2.6	1.8	3.4

Note: All are 7-point scales.

Two of the questions demonstrate the adequacy of the I-NI manipulation: In the I condition, the third party was seen as better informed ($F = 13.23$, $p < .001$) and more capable of determining an equitable solution ($F = 10.08$, $p < .01$) than in the NI condition. These two questions also produced U-M differences: M saw the third party as better informed ($F = 4.26$, $p < .05$) and more capable of determining an equitable solution ($F = 8.33$, $p < .01$) than did U.

The adequacy of the B-NB manipulation is confirmed by the fact that negotiators in the B condition felt that the third party would be less yielding ($F = 6.13$, $p < .02$) and more influential ($F = 3.13$, $p < .10$) than negotiators in the NB condition. A significant three-way interaction in the data from the question on yielding ($F = 4.94$, $p < .05$) indicated that M anticipated a more yielding third party than did U in the B-I and NB-NI conditions, and U anticipated a more yielding third party than did M in the B-NI and NB-I conditions.

Another question inquired about how important it was to reach agreement before third-party intervention. Negotiators in the B condition indicated that it was more important than did those in the NB condition ($F = 3.32$, $p < .10$). A significant A $\times$ B $\times$ C interaction was found for this item ($F = 5.07$, $p < .05$), indicating that M felt it more important to reach agreement than did U, except in the B-NI condition where U felt it to be especially important to reach agreement before intervention. Within-cell correlations were computed between the answers to this question and behavior. For the most part, these coefficients showed that negotiators who felt that it was more important to reach agreement before intervention conceded more rapidly. This was especially pronounced in the B-NI condition for U ($r = -.88$).

The other findings from the analysis of the questionnaire data can be summarized as follows: In the NB as opposed to the B condition, the third party was seen as more helpful ($F = 3.28$, $p < .10$) and more fair ($F = 6.17$, $p < .02$). In the I as opposed to the NI condition, the third party was viewed as more honest ($F = 3.78$, $p < .06$) and more fair ($F = 6.35$, $p < .02$). The interactions between I-NI and U-M indicate that U saw an informed third party as less wise ($F = 3.31$, $p < .08$), less helpful ($F = 3.28$, $p < .10$), less necessary ($F = 3.36$, $p < .08$), and less capable of making an equitable decision ($F = 3.00$, $p < .10$) than did M.

Discussion

The purpose of this study was not to simulate interesting conditions that have an exact correspondence to the real world but, rather, to operationalize variables that seem to be of theoretical interest. Sometimes, in such operationalization, one constructs a condition that has no analogue in the real world. But one may still learn something from that condition about the impact of certain variables on human behavior. Vaughn and Bass (1967) assert that although simulations cannot reproduce real-life operations in every detail, "business games" often make it possible to make measurements on purportedly important variables.

The experimental results provide support for hypothesis 1: bargainers faced with a B third-party decision were more conciliatory, that is, making more concessions and making them faster, than were negotiators faced with an NB decision or negotiators not faced with third-party intervention. However, two qualifications have to be made: Hypothesis 1 received strong support from the U data but only marginal support from the M data. Furthermore, the differences between B-NB can be clearly seen only during the later trials. Hypothesis 2 stated that concessions would be more rapid when I, as opposed to NI, intervention is anticipated. The I-NI distinction did appear to have an impact during the early trials but, again, this was a function of the U-M variable. M conceded faster, at first, under I as opposed to NI, while U conceded faster under NI than under I.

Some insight into the causes of the behavior just described can be obtained from the questionnaire data. The questionnaires were given just before the negotiation and, hence, their results seem most appropriate for explaining early behavior in the negotiation. More specifically, they seem particularly useful for understanding the early, rapid concessions that were found for U in the B-NI condition. Understanding the roots of this behavior seems, in turn, to open the way to interpreting the particularly strong, later impact of the B-NB variable on the U negotiators.

One of the ideas broached earlier was that a negotiator may concede rapidly *in an effort to avoid intervention*. Support for this assumption can be found in the high correlation between rate of concession and the perceived importance of reaching agreement before intervention. The more desirable it seemed to avoid intervention, the faster the subsequent concessions. Table 4 shows that U negotiators in the B-NI condition were particularly impressed by the importance of reaching agreement before intervention, which presumably explains their fast movement during the early trials.

But why were the U negotiators impressed by the importance of avoiding intervention in the B-NI condition? The answer to this query may emerge from the data on the perceived capacity of the third party to make an equitable decision, that is, the perceived bias of the third party. It is seen in table 4 that U saw the third party as especially biased in the NI condition. These are the lowest averages in the table. A B decision from a biased third party is clearly something to avoid; hence, U moved fast in the B-NI condition.

It is also necessary to explain why U may have perceived the third party to be especially biased in the NI condition. One possible basis for this perception lies in the *structure of the offer scales,* as seen in tables 1 and 2. It can be seen that M is able to move well beyond the midpoint of the all-important wage scale before reaching his status quo point while U cannot do so. Hence, M can make more concessions than U. In the I condition the third party can presumably see U's predicament and make allowances for it. But in the NI condition U may fear that if intervention occurs, the third party will be biased against him because his few concessions appear to be a violation of a *norm of equal concessions.*

The above reasoning can explain U's early movement in the B-NI condition, but it does not account for the rapid movement that also eventually developed for U in the B-I condition. Evidence from verbalizations during negotiation suggest that this was due to events that happened later in the negotiation which were not foreshadowed in the questionnaire. In both B conditions, M *often argued* that the third party would be biased against U because he had not moved far enough and, therefore, did not appear to be negotiating in good faith. Hence, the fears that presumably originally beset U in the B-NI condition were eventually also activated in the B-I condition as a result of M's arguments.

In summary, the major elements of U's behavior in this study are interpreted as follows: U's initial rapid movement in the B-NI condition presumably resulted from a desire to reach agreement to escape a B judgment from a third party who was presumed to be biased. This presumption of bias resulted from the fact that the NI third party could not see the structure of the offer scales and, hence, presumably could not appreciate the fact that U was unable to make as many concessions as M. As the negotiation went on in both B conditions, the M negotiator often made a big point of the fact that the third party would see the U negotiator's concessions as inadequate. Hence, the U negotiators in the B-I condition were eventually motivated to make large concessions for reasons similar to those that motivated the earlier large concessions by negotiators in the B-NI condition. This explains why, in the long run, U made many more concessions in both B conditions than in either NB condition. This explanation implies that U faced an added dilemma in the B conditions: U is less able to concede than M but, hence, paradoxically more in need of making concessions to avoid intervention. In an apparent effort to resolve this dilemma, many U negotiators conceded well beyond their status quo point.

Another possible explanation for U's perception of bias in the third party and, hence, for U's especially rapid movement in the B condition is that the third party had been introduced as an "advanced management trainee" and appeared likely to be prejudiced against unions in general. Akin to this is the idea that all Ss, whether assigned the M or U role, are biased against the U position and projected their own bias onto the third party. However, the first explanation offered—that the structure of the offer forms put U in a position of appearing to violate general bargaining norms—explains more and is preferred by the present authors.

Another idea presented in the introduction was that negotiators faced with B intervention would fear loss of control over the situation because the issues could be removed from their hands and settled by an outsider. Such a settlement might cause the negotiators to feel that they had failed, to some extent, in doing their jobs. The questionnaire results provide suggestive, but by no means strong, support for this assertion. Among the items showing a trend in this direction is a question that asked: "How much will it be a sign of your failure as a negotiator if you do not reach agreement before intervention?" The results indicated that Ss in the B condition felt that it would be a sign of their failure to a greater extent than did those in the NB condition ($p = .24$). Because the evidence is only suggestive, this theory must still be considered tentative.

In the present study, the evidence from the U data and the

tendency of the M data in the same direction leads one to speculate on an applied level. The results might be taken to indicate that in certain areas of the public interest, for example, matters that involve the police and fire departments or the public school system, labor relations might progress more smoothly, involve less conflict, and culminate in more mutually beneficial results if the issues were made subject to a B arbitration procedure rather than merely to mediation or to the activity of a factfinding board. However, it is evident that further research is needed in such areas as the biases that bargainers may project onto third parties, differences in the degree to which the bargainers feel they can be flexible in making concessions, and replicating the present study under other conditions and settings before such a generalization can be confidently made.

References

Bernstein, I. *Arbitration of Wages.* Berkeley: University of California Press, 1954.

Druckman, D. "Dogmatism, Prenegotiation Experience, and Simulated Group Representation as Determinants of Dyadic Behavior in a Bargaining Situation." *Journal of Personality and Social Psychology* 6 (1967): 279-90.

Elkouri, F. *How Arbitration Works.* Washington, D.C.: Bureau of National Affairs, 1952.

Fleming, R. W. *The Labor Arbitration Process.* Urbana: University of Illinois Press, 1965.

Levinson, H. M. *Determining Forces in Collective Wage Bargaining.* New York: John Wiley & Sons, 1966.

Pruitt, D. G., and Drews, J. L. "The Effect of Time Pressure, Time Elapsed, and the Opponent's Concession Rate on Behavior in Negotiation." *Journal of Experimental Social Psychology* 5 (1969): 43-60.

Trotta, M. *Labor Arbitration: Principles, Practices, Issues.* New York: Simmons-Boardman, 1961.

Vaughan, J. A., and Bass, B. M. "Putting the Business World into a Test Tube." *Transaction* 5 (1967): 50-52.

Reading 20

The Chapter Chairman and School Grievances

Alan M. Glassman and James A. Belasco

Previous research has stressed that the shop steward often controls access to the grievance process (Sayles and Strauss 1967). He is the first union official to evaluate grievances, and, under normal circumstances, he decides which grievances are to be pursued and either settles them at the local level or is involved in the decision to appeal to a higher level.

This article focuses on teacher chapter chairmen, individuals who perform the same role in schools as stewards do in industrial plants. It considers how chairmen's backgrounds and attitudes affect the rate at which they file and appeal grievances; data indicate that these factors explain most of the variance in grievance activity among schools. It appears that filing grievances may be a strategy adopted to improve the status of the teaching occupation in general and the prestige of the chapter chairmen in particular, while the appeal of grievances appears designed to exert pressure for even more fundamental changes in the system, for example, reallocation of resources to core area schools, increased state aid for special educational programs, and larger budgets for educational materials.

Reprinted by permission from *Industrial Relations* 14, no. 2 (May 1975), pp. 233-41.

The Research Site

Our research site was an urban school district in western New York. The district was comprised of approximately 620,000 people, 68,000 students, and 4,000 teachers. The teachers were represented by a branch of the National Educational Association and were covered by a negotiated collective bargaining agreement which contained a grievance procedure comparable to many found in the private sector. This provision recognized the need to resolve grievances at the lowest possible level, contained an extensive appeals procedure, and terminated in binding arbitration.

Although the study occurred four years after the commencement of formal bargaining, the relationship between the city's Board of Education and the local teacher association was strained. Initially, the board refused to recognize the legitimacy of the teacher association, and during the ensuing years the two parties disagreed on (1) the role of the teacher association in the development of educational programs, (2) the need for school busing, and (3) the steps needed to curb violence within the schools and to protect the teaching staff. Moreover, the superintendent of schools and the president of the teacher association had adopted an adversary relationship. Each blamed the other for many of the system's problems and often used the media to elicit public support.

In this atmosphere, it is understandable that the grievance rate was high. During the year studied, chapter chairmen filed more than 1,500 grievances and appealed 873 beyond the local level. More than 40 percent of these grievances alleged inadequate classroom supplies, while another 20 percent concerned improper working conditions. While many grievances appeared trivial, they were, in fact, part of a general strategy by the teacher association to achieve greater participation in the educational decision-making process and to enhance the support of its membership (Glassman and Belasco 1974).

Methodology

Our findings are based on a questionnaire sent to the teacher association's 80 chapter chairmen and returned by 59 (74 percent). An analysis of the demographic characteristics of respondents and nonrespondents revealed no significant differences in such common traits as age, sex, marital status, and length of service as chapter chairman.

The data were first analyzed by dividing the sample into two groups, one comprised of chapter chairmen with high rates of grievance filing (N = 29) and the other of chapter chairmen with low rates of grievance filing (N = 30). Analysis of variance was computed to determine which factors could differentiate the two groups. Then, the sample was again divided into two groups, one consisting of chapter chairmen with high grievance appeal rates (N = 20) and the other of those with low grievance appeal rates (N = 39). Again, analysis of variance was computed. As indicated in table 1, there was relatively little relationship between these two forms of grievance activity.

Table 1
Numbers of Chapter Chairmen with Various Degrees
of Grievance Activity

		Grievances filed	
		High	Low
	High	12	8
Grievances appealed			
	Low	17	22

Finally, in an effort to develop more parsimonious predictive models which could explain the variance in grievance filing and appeal rates, stepwise multiple regressions were computed, utilizing first the number of grievances filed and then the number of grievances appealed as the dependent variable. This analysis explained 74.5 percent of the variance in the grievance filing rate and 66 percent of the variance in the grievance appeal rate. Again, there was no significant relationship between the two rates.

The questionnaire dealt with four dimensions:

Decisional deprivation. For each of 15 key local issues (e.g., faculty assignments, new curriculum materials, use of school aides), each chapter chairman responded to a Guttman-type scale, indicating perceived and preferred levels of interaction between himself and the building principal (the local management representative). Deprivation scores were derived by summing the differences between perceived and preferred rates of communication, consultation, and joint decision making. The higher the score, the greater the assumed level of deprivation.

Attitudes. Attitudes were measured by use of semantic differential scales (Osgood, Suci, and Tannenbaum 1957). To measure important connotative meanings, chapter chairmen were asked to respond to 12 bipolar adjectives arranged on seven-point scales, concerning such employment conditions as teacher militancy, teacher grievances, principal-chapter chairman cooperation, the school system and the building principal. When taken together these scales yielded three factors: one factor indicating the chapter chairman's judgment concerning the *desirability* of each of these employment conditions, another factor indicating his judgment concerning the extent to which each condition existed (*existence*), and a third factor indicating its *importance.*

Personality traits. Two personality traits were studied. *Interpersonal* trust was measured by a six-item scale, which focused on beliefs concerning the fundamental cooperativeness or trustworthiness of human nature (Kluckhohn and Murray 1967, pp. 146-84). The higher the score, the greater the level of interpersonal trust. To measure *authoritarianism,* we utilized a shortened 15-item version of the California F-scale (Rokeach 1960).

Other data. The questionnaire collected a variety of personal and institutional data including sex, marital status, years at present school, percent of teachers in the teacher association, number of minority teachers and students, and desire to advance within the teacher association or to become a principal.

Decisional Deprivation

Our findings were consistent with other studies which had identified a strong relationship between the use of the grievance process and the perceived ability of management to satisfy the stewards' needs for communication, consultation, and joint decision making. (For examples, see Harbison and Dubin 1947; Dean 1954; Weickhardt 1959; Wagner 1968.) As table 2 indicates, grievance filing and grievance appealing were both associated with relatively high levels of perceived decisional deprivation.

Somewhat surprisingly, decisional deprivation contributed significantly to the variance in grievance filing, but not for appealing. The chapter chairmen's desire for additional consultation and joint decision making accounted for more than 42 percent of the variation in grievance filing, but it was not significant in explaining the varia-

Table 2
Analyses of Variance, Grievance Filing, and Appealing

	Grievance filing			Grievance appealing			Regression analysis[a]	
	Within-group means		Correlation (R)	Within-group means		Correlation (R)	Grievances filed	Grievances appealed
	Low	High		Low	High			
Decisional deprivation								
Communication	3.87	8.19†	.524†	5.13	7.75*	.285*	0	0
Joint consultation	5.40	9.55†	.618†	6.38	9.45†	.408†	+	0
Joint decision making	5.50	10.21†	.598†	7.03	9.35*	.273*	+	0
Attitudes toward								
School system:								
Desirability	48.47	39.31*	−.222	43.44	45.00*	.084	−	0
Existence	52.47	45.71	−.063	47.48	51.80	.204	0	+
Importance	6.23b	6.24†	.113	5.92	6.15	.097	+	−
Cooperation:								
Desirability	59.60	55.24	−.113	57.80	56.30	−.047	+	−
Existence	53.63	52.57	−.143	56.25	49.90	−.215	0	−
Importance	6.53	5.86	−.003	6.15	6.30*	.099	+	+
Teacher grievances:								
Desirability	61.87	56.83	−.120	59.90b	58.90†	−.096	−	0
Existence	59.53	55.17	−.100	56.92	58.60*	.006	0	0
Importance	6.60	6.41	−.059	6.15	6.20	−.112	0	0
Teacher militancy:								
Desirability	54.73	57.01*	.052	54.82	57.90	.105	+	0
Existence	59.20	57.17	−.132	57.41b	57.80†	−.066	0	+
Importance	6.10b	6.31†	.012	6.15	6.30*	.036	0	−
Building principal:								
Desirability	54.86	44.97†	−.279*	52.46	45.20	−.251*	0	0
Existence	55.66	44.62*	−.253*	51.39	48.00	−.101	0	0
Importance	5.60	4.62†	−.140	5.46	4.35*	−.231	+	0
Personality traits								
Trust	14.60	14.00†	−.078	14.33	14.25†	−.019	−	0
Authoritarianism	30.73	32.42	.083	32.13	30.50	−.087	0	0

Desire to								
Become principal	3.70	3.66	.150	3.97	3.20*	-.239	+	—
Advance in teacher organization	3.70	4.00	.159	3.74[b]	3.75†	-.100	+	0
Demographic data								
Sex[c]	.50	.52	-.115	.54[b]	.60*	-.035	+	—
Age	36.33	30.72	.022	33.51[b]	33.50†	.068	0	0
Years at present school	6.67	4.66	-.086	5.72	5.60†	-.074	+	—
Marital status[d]	.80	.55*	-.122	.69	.60	-.151	0	—
Institutional								
Type of school[e]	.17	.31	.134	.26	.20*	-.066	0	0
Age of school	44.30[b]	46.52†	.048	40.69	51.00	.223	0	0
Population (%)								
Male teachers	24.21	31.96*	.065	28.93	25.45	-.051	0	0
Members of teacher organization	64.71	67.32	.075	65.98[b]	67.54†	.043	—	0
Minority teachers	9.67[b]	9.51†	.010	11.52	7.50	-.233	0	+
Minority students	3.65	4.32	.043	4.28	3.74	-.153	—	+
Teacher organization members opposed to teacher organization policy	3.07	5.76	.084	4.59	3.25	-.103	0	—
Nonteacher organization members opposed to teacher organization policy	9.17	7.76	-.168	10.05	5.15	-.162	—	0

*Significant at .05 level.

†Significant at .01 level.

[a] Variables contributing significantly to prediction of numbers of grievances filed and appealed. + means significant (.05) positive relationship; — means significant (.05) negative relationship; 0 means no significant relationship.

[b] Those variables where the mean is very close between groups but the F value is highly significant are explained by the very small "within-group" mean square relative to the "between-group" mean square. This, in turn, is due to the large number of degrees of freedom, 57 in this case, available to estimate the variation with the groups.

[c] 0 = female, 1 = male.

[d] 0 = single, 1 = married.

[e] 0 = elementary, 1 = secondary.

tion in grievance appealing. Possibly chapter chairmen who frequently filed grievances were attempting to force the principal to include them in employee-related matters, while those who frequently utilized the appeals procedure were convinced that local level interactions were ineffective and that it was necessary to bring in higher levels.

Attitudes

One set of attitudinal variables differentiated between those with high and low grievance filing rates and another set differentiated between those with high and low grievance appeal rates. Grievance-filing chapter chairmen had more negative attitudes toward their building principal, had more positive attitudes toward teacher militancy, felt that the school system was more important, but were less favorable toward it. This finding suggested that the filing of a grievance was probably considered a militant activity, as well as an outlet for negative feelings.

The regression analysis indicated that within the grievance filing group a roughly similar pattern existed. High grievance filing was associated with a feeling that the school system and building principals were important, that teacher militancy was desirable, and that grievances themselves were relatively less desirable, the last point being somewhat ironical. These attitudes, when combined with the desires for principalships and more responsible positions in the teacher association, suggested that grievance-filing chapter chairmen were ambitious to rise within the school system and viewed the filing of grievances as an opportunity to draw attention to themselves and to enhance their status and opportunity for promotion. Too, the data indicated that this strategy was considered risky.

The attitudes of grievance-appealing chapter chairmen reflected a desire to improve the school system and a personal frustration with the need to utilize teacher militancy and grievances. In fact, the regression analysis indicated an attitudinal profile which suggested that those chapter chairmen who frequently appealed grievances rejected (1) cooperation with the building principal, (2) local teacher militancy, and (3) established school system procedures, seeing none of these as effective means for improving conditions. These chapter chairmen may have been looking beyond the institutional setting of the school system, seeking to obtain their goals in other arenas (e.g., the state legislature).

Personality Traits and Other Data

Our findings supported Walton and McKersie's (1965, pp. 357-59) contention that interpersonal trust is vital to conflict resolution. As indicated in table 2, grievance filing and grievance appealing were both related to lower propensities toward interpersonal trust.

While few personal characteristics distinguished between high and low grievance filers, a number of personal characteristics paralleling the traditional militant teacher profile (i.e., younger, male, fewer years service) did differentiate between the two grievance appeal groups. (For examples, see Cole 1969; Belasco and Alutto 1969.) Thus, while grievance-filers seemed to view their activities as militant, this finding suggested that grievance appealing was more closely related to other forms of teacher militancy (e.g., slowdown, strike). Unexpectedly, however, (since other research had linked teacher militancy with secondary schools and organizational marginality) chapter chairmen in elementary schools and in schools with a relatively high percentage of teacher association members had relatively more grievance appeals. (For examples, see Cole 1969; HEW Task Force 1970.) This may be explained, in part, by the political control the teacher association leadership maintained over the appeal procedure (Glassman and Belasco 1974).

The regression analysis indicated additional differences between those who frequently filed grievances and those who frequently appealed them. Grievances tended to be filed more frequently in schools with a relatively low percentage of minority teachers, a low percentage of teacher association members, and little opposition from rival organizations. The high rate of grievance filing may have represented the teacher association's attempt to demonstrate the utility of membership to nonmembers.

Chapter chairmen with a higher rate of grievance appeal tended to be employed in schools with a relatively high percentage of both minority teachers and minority students, and relatively less opposition from other organizations. Schools of this sort tend to be concentrated in core areas. Furthermore, since many of the problems associated with core area schools are beyond the control of local school officials, these findings suggest that chapter chairmen utilize the appeals procedure as a means of publicizing problems.

Summary and Implications

Three implications emerged from this study.

1. Sayles and Strauss's (1967) contention that the local employee representative controls access to the grievance procedure is supported by the fact that a large proportion of the rates of both grievance filing and appealing are explained by chapter-chairman based variables. This contention is reinforced by the relatively low explanatory power associated with institutional variables, indicating that local constituencies tend to give chapter chairmen a great deal of freedom.

2. Perceived decisional deprivation explains a great deal of the variance in initial grievance filing. These data extend the TVA findings of Patchen (1970) and Wagner (1968) and support their contention that increased participation results in lower grievance rates. The chapter chairmen's strong desires for increased communication, consultation, and joint decision making may reflect the rising aspirations of teachers for more participation in both instructional and non-instructional matters, aspirations that are likely to be crystallized in the actions of the chapter chairmen.

3. Chapter chairmen pursued grievance strategies which were compatible with their own objectives. The higher grievance filers tended to be quite upwardly mobile and to feel strong decisional deprivation. For them the frequent filing of grievances seemed to represent an effort to draw attention to themselves and/or to improve their status. Note that these individuals were unlikely to appeal grievances, since this might embarrass their principals, and principals were responsible for promotional recommendations. Instead, these chairmen might exert pressure on individual grievants to "be reasonable" and accept solutions that do not fully meet their expectations.

The profile of high grievance appealers was very different. These chapter chairmen tended to be single, female, to have been at their present school for a relatively short period of time, and to be employed in a school with a relatively high percentage of minority teachers and students, suggesting a core area school. For these chapter chairmen, appeal represented an effort to exert pressure beyond the local level. Thus grievance appealing may be a technique used by minorities and their supporters to effect organizational change.

References

Belasco, James, and Alutto, Joseph A. "The Organizational Impact of Collective Negotiations in Educational Institutions." *Industrial Relations* 9 (October 1969): 67-79.

Cole, Stephen. "Teacher Strikes: A Study of the Conversion of Predisposition into Action." *American Journal of Sociology* 5 (March 1969): 506-20.

Dean, Lois R. "Union Activity and Dual Loyalty." *Industrial and Labor Relations Review* 7 (July 1954): 529-30.

Glassman, Alan M., and Belasco, James A. "Appealed Grievances in Urban Education: A Case Study." *Education and Urban Society* 7 (November 1974): 83-86.

Harbison, Frederick, and Dubin, Robert. *Patterns of Union-Management Relations.* Chicago: Science Research Association, 1947.

HEW Task Force. *Urban School Crisis: The Problem and the Solution.* Washington, D.C.: Department of Health, Education, and Welfare, 1970.

Kluckhohn, Clyde, and Murray, Henry. *Personality in Nature, Society, and Culture.* New York: Knopf, 1967.

Osgood, C.; Suci, C.; and Tannenbaum, P. *The Measurement of Meaning.* Urbana: University of Illinois Press, 1957.

Patchen, Martin. *Participation and Involvement on the Job.* Englewood Cliffs, N.J.: Prentice-Hall, 1970.

Rokeach, Milton. *The Closed and Open Mind.* New York: Basic Books, 1960.

Sayles, Leonard, and Strauss, George. *The Local Union.* New York: Harcourt, Brace, & World, 1967.

Wagner, Aubrey J. "TVA Looks at Three Decades of Collective Bargaining." *Industrial and Labor Relations Review* 22 (October 1968): 29-30.

Walton, Richard E., and McKersie, Robert B. *A Behavioral Theory of Labor Negotiations.* New York: McGraw-Hill, 1965.

Weickhardt, L. S. "Joint Consultation in the Imperial Chemical Industries of Australia and New Zealand." *Journal of Industrial Relations* 1 (October 1959): 69-70.

PART IV

Economic, Political, and Organizational Outcomes

Overview

The significance of collective bargaining in schools is largely measured by its effects. Therefore, an examination of outcomes is a key element in the analysis of collective bargaining in the schools. The term "outcomes" is used here broadly to mean the effects of collective bargaining which relate to the operation of the school. A concept this broad implies a wide variety of possible effects, such as an increase in local taxes to cover a teacher salary settlement or a higher level of interpersonal conflict between teachers and administrators. Such effects can be considered feedback if they have consequences for future bargaining or other aspects of school operation.

The consequences can be a result of some change in the school system itself (e.g., a new grievance procedure), or some change in the environment (e.g., increased voter resistance to school tax increases). Since the outcomes are central to both the effectiveness of the school and its future directions, outcomes comprise a major section of this work.

Unfortunately, a full examination of outcomes and feedback in school systems is not possible here. (For a more complete treatment of feedback in school systems, see Wirt and Kirst 1972, and Herriot and Hodgkins 1973.) Certainly, the conceivable number of interesting outcomes is great, but only a relatively small number have been researched. The topics of primary interest here fall into three rough categories: economic, political, and organizational. The categories are rough, since the outcomes in one area link to the others. But the individual readings tend to focus on a narrow range of topics, and illustrate how the outcomes of bargaining can be explored. Part IV is thus an assemblage of works which treat a small set of outcomes, each from a single perspective. So along with our review of the individual articles, we will devote some attention to the general content of each of the three categories.

Economic Outcomes

The literature on economic outcomes of collective bargaining is abundant, particularly in the study of effects on teacher salaries. This may be due to several factors.

1. The major goal of teacher unions is supposedly to increase salaries and benefits.

2. Salary rates and other economic variables are somewhat easier to measure than political and organizational ones.

3. The study of behavior of public employee unions is often guided by concepts developed in economics (and especially labor economics). Therefore, it is not surprising to find empirical inroads into the study of teacher unionism carrying an economic bias.

4. With rising tax rates and the fact that education is a labor intensive industry, the effect of bargaining on wage rates has been watched carefully by those concerned with the cost and control of public edcuation.

Inasmuch as the economics of teacher unions is understood in terms of union behavior generally, it is well to begin a review of economic outcomes of bargaining in the private sector. Modern wage theory has its roots in the work of the English economist, Alfred Marshall. (For a discussion of Marshall's work, see Bloom and Northrup 1969.) A central concept in this theory, *marginal productivity,* forms the basis for wage rate explanation. Employers seek to maximize profits, so they hire additional workers for a given production process until the marginal value product (marginal productivity) of the last worker hired equals marginal product returns. That is, the value added to production by the "last" worker will be equivalent to his wage rate. The theory is based on the assumption of complete interchangeability of a class of workers; it assumes that the wage rate paid to the "last" will be the same as paid to all other workers in the same category. Wage rates for the whole class of workers are adjusted, in this theory, to equal the value added by the last worker. While this may not be strictly true for any particular firm, the theory is expected to hold for a class of workers in an industry.

The theory assumes further that productivity is affected by the mix of labor and capital. If capital, tools, and machinery are unchanged and the size of the labor force is increased, the productivity of each marginal increment of labor diminishes accordingly. Alternately, if capital investment is increased and the labor force held constant, the productivity of each member of the labor force increases accordingly, although at a diminishing rate. The theory would argue that as the productivity of labor increases, the wage rate paid to each worker will be increased and as the productivity of labor decreases the wage rate also decreases. If workers, through unionism or some other mechanism, succeed in pushing wages up, the theory holds that employers will reduce the size of their work force again until the "last" worker's marginal value product is again in equilibrium with returns. (For a discussion of wage theory, see Chamberlain and Kuhn 1965, pp. 310-39.)

On the basis of this theoretical position economists have argued that union attempts to affect wage rates are futile. Wages are determined in the labor marketplace. It is impossible for unions to generate sufficient pressure on wages to overcome the compensating pressures set in motion by the market. Hence, over time wage rates would tend to stabilize and maintain a market equilibrium based on the workers marginal contribution.

During the 1930s, economists began to modify their argument, suggesting that it might be possible for unions to generate sufficient pressure to drive wage rates up, but only by sacrificing some jobs. That is, if unions succeeded in driving the wage rate up, employers would reduce the work force, substituting capital investment for the more expensive labor. In the reformulation of the theory, unions might be able to hold the wage rate at this artificial level, hence preventing unemployed workers from bidding the wage rate down to its level of equilibrium (usually called the competitive wage rate). This explanation was offered to account for the "hard core" unemployment in the United States during this period.

As with all theories, marginal productivity wage theory relies on certain simplifying assumptions:

1. The market is competitive, that is, there is a sufficient number of firms to maintain competition, none large enough to measurably influence the marketplace.

2. Firms strive to maximize profits, workers seek to maximize wage returns to labor.

3. Costs of production are constant or increasing.

4. There is only "fractional" unemployment, i.e., the unemployed are workers temporarily between jobs.

5. Most workers are mobile.

6. Methods of production are variable overtime, so that labor and capital may be used in different mixes.

7. The work force is sufficiently homogeneous to ensure that workers are relatively interchangeable.

8. Both employers and workers have considerable knowledge of the state of the product, labor, and capital markets.

Marginal productivity is, then, dependent on the operation of free market conditions; that is, firms are in competition for product markets, and workers are competitive in the labor market. Marginal productivity does not determine wage rates when free market assumptions do not hold. Principal examples are cases where a firm enjoyed product monopoly and could set prices without concern for competition, or in cases where employers enjoyed monopsony (i.e., where a firm is the only source of employment for workers in the region). In both of these cases, wage rates can be established by other than purely market forces. In monopsony conditions, employers can pay less than the prevailing wage rate since the worker has no alternative source of employment. Neoclassical economic theory holds that it is only in cases of monopsony that unions can exercise long-term wage impact. These are important concepts to the study of wage rates in public employment and are now receiving more attention in explanations of teacher salary rates.

The Impact of Unionism on Wage Rates

In addition to theoretical difficulties previously described, it is empirically difficult to estimate the impact of union activity on wage rates. The major problem is that wages from any one employer, unionized or not, are affected by interactions among wage rates offered by other employers. Unionized and nonunionized employers alike must bid for the same workers and hence must pay prevailing wage rates. If the employer seeks to minimize the possibility of his firm being unionized, he may well be willing to pay a wage rate slightly above the union wage rate in order to minimize the attractiveness of organizing a union. This spill-over effect, therefore, has greatly complicated any comparative study attempting to isolate the impact of unions on wage rates. The long-held view that unions cannot override wage pressures in the market, coupled with this empirical difficulty, has discouraged private sector economists in their attempts to analyze the wage impact of unions.

There are even greater theoretical and empirical difficulties when the examination is extended to the public sector. For example, teacher salaries appear to be regionally interdependent. It has long been the practice of school boards and school administrators to canvass the region in order to estimate competitive wage rates (see Gerwin 1973). The comparisons do not seem to be limited to either union or nonunion school systems. Among the readings included here, Baird and Landon (reading 23) make an excellent case for considering teacher salaries as regionally competitive, and do much to link analyses of teacher wage rates to classical economic wage theory. Hall and Carroll (reading 22) also consider this integration in their argument. There is some evidence that salaries are less important motivators in teacher mobility than nonpecuniary factors such as class size and pupil social class (see Greenberg 1974 and Alexander 1974). Differences between starting teachers' salaries in adjacent districts will not typically exceed 2 percent. This is in contrast to the differential wage rates within a given school district, which may differ by 100 percent, i.e., the highest paid teacher in the district can earn twice what the beginning teacher earns.*

---

*For example, in several school systems in the Chicago area, salary schedules start at around $9000 and go to well over $20,000 (Office of the Superintendent of Public Instruction 1975).

Empirical Studies of Teacher Salaries

In recent years there have been reported a number of studies seeking to explain differences in teacher wage rates. One of the variables inevitably used is some measure of union activity. Typically these measures have been reflections of whether organized teachers engaged in collective bargaining in the district. Three major findings emerge from these studies:

1. Community characteristics including wealth, educational levels, and number of white collar workers are related to teacher wage rates. These findings are consistent with earlier findings of James, Kelly, and Garms (1966), and Dye (1966).

2. There is some evidence that the state of competition between school systems for teachers in the area affects wage rates, i.e., in cases of monopsony, wages tend to be lower. Baird and Landon represent this argument here.

3. Teacher wage rates tend to reflect general wage levels in the region. Studies which compare per capita income and teacher wage rates have revealed that teacher wage rates increased no faster or slower than per capita income. This suggests that competition for teachers is generally conditioned by the competition for workers in the area. Murphy and Hoover (reading 24) take this perspective in their paper.

4. Taken together, the studies show that unionism has at most a modest impact on teachers' salaries. Current estimates range from 0-4 percent higher wage rates in union-active school districts than in nonbargaining counterparts. The research in this area is reviewed by Lipsky and Drotning (reading 21).

These findings and their underlying assumptions bear striking resemblance to theories of wage determination from private sector studies. First, there seems to be general consensus that teacher unions have only marginal impact on the general structure of wage rates in public education. Regression studies of teacher salary determinants suggest that teacher unions have not been able to produce sufficient pressure to offset community factors in determining wage rates. Second, in some regions, such as sparsely settled rural areas or large county school systems, one board will be the only employer. Such a condition of monopsony nullifies general labor market pressures and the employer may pay lower wages. Generally lower rates are found in regions where school boards operate in monopsonistic conditions. Regional competition for teacher services is related to higher salaries (see Landon and Baird 1971). Competition and higher salaries seem to be tied to teacher quality as well. At least one researcher has found community and regional factors to be the principal determinants of teacher salaries. Teacher quality was shown to be part of a causal chain, with higher salaries associated with better teachers. Overall, labor market competition for teachers seems more important to both salary levels and teacher quality than union activity alone. These findings, while not conclusive, suggest the same basic theories of wage determination may apply across both the public and private sector.

However, these findings must be viewed with considerable caution. All of the data on which they are based come from a period when the supply of teachers was generally short of the demand. These conditions no longer apply. The U.S. Office of Education projects a substantial oversupply of teachers well into the 1980s (National Center for Educational Statistics 1975, p. 74). This could be expected to substantially reduce the levels of competition for teachers in the labor market. How this oversupply will affect the salary levels for teachers depends on whether market competition or unions have more importance in the wage determination process. The current data suggest that competition is more important. Thus, real wages would be expected to decline, or at least grow less rapidly. If wages continue to rise at current or higher rates, this could be taken as evidence of influence of union activity. Teacher unions could, in the presence of an oversupply of teachers in general, sacrifice jobs for wage gains. This is precisely what was done in a recent wage settlement in Chicago. It remains to be seen, of course, whether this behavior becomes a general pattern.

Organizational Outcomes

The union activities of teachers do, of course, have impact on more than salaries. Labor relations may potentially influence all aspects of school operations, as they relate to the work of the teachers in the classroom. Therefore, in addition to wage impacts, Part IV discusses how bargaining and related activities affect the decision-making and control structures, staff patterns, and interpersonal relations in the schools. Relatively few of the possible interactions have been studied. The readings included here are limited in scope and tend to be suggestive rather than definitive as they deal with key concepts of professionalism, teacher participation in administration, and changes in formal structures. Professionalism and union activity are key elements in the bargaining-organization dynamic. The most able teachers are often in the forefront of union organizing (see Corwin 1966, 1968). One side effect of militant behavior and collective bargaining activity may be increased professionalism in teachers. The mechanism for this is outlined by Murphy and Hoover (reading 24), who suggest that collective bargaining increases the amount of teacher participation in decision making and tends to democratize a public school, e.g., the hierarchical authority system associated with bureaucratic organization is diminished. Some research (see Belasco and Alutto 1969) has shown increased teacher participation in the decision making of a bargaining district. Thus, it may be that collective bargaining can modify the organizational structure of schools, which will in turn modify the structure of collective bargaining, and so forth. With few exceptions, organizational studies of the impact of collective bargaining indicate positive effects on the organization.

Political Outcomes

Labor relations are a major element in the overall process of allocating resources, power, and status in the school system. Setting salaries involves the major part of the budget. Participation in the bargaining means access to these important decision-making and information channels. Work rules and other terms of the labor agreement (such as the control of personal-leave days) confer power and status among the persons in the school system. Although this is just a partial list of elements in the bargaining, their importance indicates that labor policies and practices are central to the power and control processes of the school. Links between the labor relations process and the political process of the school are many and intimate. Therefore, bargaining and its outcomes will have an impact on the school political system.

Outlining political impacts requires some scheme to identify the parts of the political system which are of interest. The basic question is: what is different about the ways schools are governed as a result of collective bargaining? We might ask further:

1. How do the participants vary?
2. How does their relative power to influence policy vary?
3. How do the issues vary?
4. Are there new constraints or resources supplied to the governance system?

To the extent that these (or related changes) flow from bargaining phenomena they are political impacts.

Of course, changes in the political system can result from a variety of sources, such as changes in the demography of the school system, new fiscal constraints imposed by economic conditions, or rearrangements in state or federal policies which apply to the schools. As in the other parts, we are interested in illustrating the general concepts involved in political impacts and examining in part the interactions among the collective bargaining process, the school political system, and other features of the environment. Both the direct impacts and the possible interactions are of immediate interest and worth some attention. We have chosen two for particular emphasis: (1) school finance reform and labor relations, and (2) participation in decisions. These topics provide a means for examining important policy interactions.

How financing and labor relations are linked is a question which touches on most of the significant political dimensions of school governance. In our terms, finance reform is a change in state school financing policy which results in a fairer distribution of resources among the school districts of a state. Usually, substantial shifts in resources occur (from richer to poorer school districts) and new fiscal constraints apply to school revenues. Finance reform might also apply to the manner in which resources are allocated within the school district, extending some criterion of fairness to building, classroom, or even pupil-by-pupil allocations. School board decisions are affected, since revenues may not match local desires, or great increases in resources may spark increased demands. Taxpayer resistance to teacher salary increases will be affected (either upward or downward). Teacher political activity in local or state policy making will certainly intensify where great resource shifts are involved. As state influence in local financing increases, the pressures for state-wide bargaining of one form or another may grow, so state-local relations may be affected. In districts where tighter financial constraints result, teachers may seek higher salaries at the cost of fewer teaching positions, or trade off higher salaries for greater voice in school governance, or simply demand cutbacks in nonsalary expenditures to maintain or improve salaries in shrinking budgets. In each of these cases, fiscal changes affect the bargaining process, which in turn can influence the basic educational and financial policies of the local district. None of these possible interactions are well understood, and the possible research agenda is a long one. Since both school financing and labor relations are involved with statute and case law, the article by Murphy, Barton, and Mills (reading 25) was chosen to outline the basic dimensions and nature of the interactions.

A basic question here involves the impact of school finance decisions by courts on the collective bargaining and policy-making structures of the school. Reform mandates of state or federal courts will change the basic relationships between the state and local school districts, and trends toward state-wide collective bargaining are initiated or accelerated by reforms. As reform increases the state role in financing schools, fiscal control shifts toward the state capitol, and the teacher unions and school boards alike will favor centralized bargaining. The centralization will in turn change the participants in educational policy making by involving the state government much more directly in negotiations and fiscal policy making.

The main problem with such an analysis is that the direction of causal relationships is consistently biased in terms of one interpretation of events: that the courts or legislatures change laws, and the school systems and unions respond. That is only one of several alternative interpretations. One could say that the actions of the courts and legislatures are simply reactions to changes in political demands and conditions in the state and local arena. Or more plausibly, one could argue that there are multiple interactions between the legislatures, courts, schools, and the public. The directions of cause and effect are seldom clearly known, and seldom consistent. For example, it is plausible to hypothesize that the increased unionization and militancy of teachers has led to their increased activity in state government, which has in turn led to pressures for state-wide bargaining. Or it could be argued that the pressures for finance reform in some areas are a consequence of increased pressures on the local budget caused by teacher militancy. Each of these are possible political impacts of teacher collective bargaining, rather than results of finance changes.

The collective bargaining relationship assumes a position of major importance in the web of connections between the school and its clientele, as well as affecting internal governance structures. Wellington and Winter (reading 15) argue that the possibility of strikes and other militant actions give the teachers increased power in the school policy-making process and that increased conflict and public dissatisfaction with the schools may result. Although they agree on possible political power distortions of collective bargaining mechanisms, Love and Sulzner (reading 26) take a more moderate and hopeful analytical posture. To them, politics is central to collective bargaining because collective bargaining functions as a system of governance. It is a political system. In the private sector, bargaining is the governance mechanism which allows workers to participate meaningfully in decisions affecting their work existence. Public sector decision structures, according to Love and Sulzner, add complexity to this industrial-democratic explanation. In public sector management, the locus of decision authority often shifts in accordance with the political significance of issues, making collective bargaining difficult to organize and manage. In the course of their analysis, Love and Sulzner raise some thoughtful questions which can guide research in this area.

References

Alexander, Arthur J. *Teachers, Salaries, and School District Expenditures.* Santa Monica, Calif.: RAND, 1974.

Belasco, James A., and Alutto, Joseph A. "Organizational Impact of Teacher Negotiations." *Industrial Relations* 9, no. 1 (October 1969): 67-79.

Bloom, Gordon, and Northrup, Herbert R. *Economics of Labor Relations* (6th ed.). Homewood, Ill.: Irwin, 1969.

Chamberlain, Neil W., and Kuhn, James W. *Collective Bargaining.* New York: McGraw-Hill, 1965.

Corwin, Ronald G. *Staff Conflicts in the Public Schools.* Columbus: Ohio State University Press, 1966.

Corwin, Ronald G. "Teacher Militancy in the United States: Reflections on Its Sources and Prospects." *Theory into Practice* 7 (April 1968): 96-102.

Dye, Thomas. *Politics, Economics and the Public Interest.* Chicago: Rand McNally, 1966.

Gerwin, Donald. "An Information Processing Model of Salary Determination in a Contour of Suburban School Districts." *American Educational Research Journal* 10 (Winter 1973).

Greenberg, David H., and McCall, John J. *Analysis of the Educational Personnel System: VII, Teacher Mobility in Michigan.* Santa Monica, Calif.: RAND, 1974.

Herriot, Robert E., and Hodgkins, Benjamin J. *The Environment of Schooling: Formal Education as an Open Social System.* Englewood Cliffs, N.J.: Prentice-Hall, 1973.

James, H. Thomas; Kelly, James A.; and Garms, Walter I. *Determinants of Educational Expenditures in Large Cities of the United States.* Stanford, Calif.: Stanford University Press, 1966.

Landon, John H., and Baird, Robert N. "Monopsony in the Market for Public School Teachers." *American Economic Review* 61, no. 5 (December 1971): 966-71.

National Center for Educational Statistics, Department of Health, Education, and Welfare. *The Condition of Education.* Washington, D.C.: U.S. Government Printing Office, 1975.

Office of the Superintendent of Public Instruction. *Illinois Teacher Salary Schedule and Policy Study, 1974-75.* Springfield, Ill.: OSPI, 1975.

Wirt, Fredrick W., and Kirst, Michael W. *The Political Web of Schools.* Boston: Little, Brown, 1972.

Reading 21

The Influence of Collective Bargaining on Teachers' Salaries in New York State

David B. Lipsky and John E. Drotning

What impact, if any, has teacher unionism had on teachers' salaries? Others have asked this question, but to date research results have been inconsistent.* In part, this may be attributed to different research designs and methods; but whatever the reasons for the inconsistencies, the relationship between teacher unionism and salaries is not yet completely clear.†

This paper analyzes the influence of collective negotiations on teacher salaries in New York state in the first year in which the Taylor Law, governing public employer-employee relations, was in effect. (For a thorough discussion of the Taylor Law, see Oberer, Hanslowe, and Doherty 1970.) Many economists believe that the

Reprinted by permission from *Industrial and Labor Relations Review* 27, no. 1 (October 1973), pp. 18-35. Copyright 1973 by Cornell University.

*Four principal studies have been published during the past three years. They are, Kasper (1970); Baird and Landon (1972); Thornton (1971); and Hall and Carroll (reading 22). See also Kasper (1971).

†Three significant studies that deal with determinants of teacher salaries (but not with the effect of collective bargaining) are Levin (1970); Owen (1972); and Landon and Baird (1971).

union's impact on wages is likely to be greatest in the initial stages of organization. More than forty years ago, Paul Douglas (1930, p. 564) concluded,

Unionism, in other words, very probably does give an appreciable increase in earnings during the early period of effective organization, but during the later and more mature years of union development, the relative rate of further progress seems, to say the least, to be no more rapid on the whole for unionists than for non-unionists.

Thus, the passage of the Taylor Law in 1967 presents a unique opportunity for a study of the type undertaken here. Most New York school districts entered bargaining for the first time in the spring of 1968. Information for 696 districts reveals that about 63 percent signed collective agreements in 1968. All but a handful had never been organized for bargaining before the passage of the Taylor Law.*

Did New York districts with collective bargaining contracts in 1968 have significantly higher salaries than districts without contracts? Did organized districts win larger salary increases than districts not yet organized? In answering these basic questions, this study also sheds light on other factors that influence the determination of teacher salaries.

Preliminary Analysis

Table 1 shows differences in salary levels between districts with contracts in 1968-69 (441) and districts without contracts (255). Teachers are normally paid according to a salary schedule based on two factors: years of experience and college credit hours earned beyond the bachelor's degree. Data were gathered for three salary points in the schedule for each New York district: (1) the salary paid to first-year teachers with only a bachelor's degree (base or BS minimum); (2) the salary paid to a teacher with seven years of experience and thirty hours of earned credit beyond the bachelor's degree (BS +

---

*New York City is not included in this study. New York City is obviously exceptional in many ways. For example, although only one of more than 700 districts in the state, it has more than one quarter of all pupils enrolled in the state and spends approximately 30 percent of all money expended on primary and secondary public education.

Table 1
Difference in Salary Levels Between New York School Districts with and Without Collective Bargaining Contracts, 1968-69

Salary level	Districts with contracts (N = 441)		Districts without contracts (N = 255)		Percentage difference $(1) - (3) \div (3)$
	Mean (1)	Standard deviation (2)	Mean (3)	Standard deviation (4)	(5)
Base salary	$ 6,485	$ 275.9	$ 6,420	$ 299.1	1.01
BS + 30, 7th step	9,091	615.8	8,943	652.0	1.65
BS + 60, 11th step	10,931	1,166.0	10,691	1,016.5	2.24
Mean salary	8,539	1,093.6	8,385	1,190.4	1.84

30, 7th step); and (3) the salary paid to a teacher with eleven years of experience and sixty hours of earned credit beyond the bachelor's degree (BS + 60, 11th step).

These three salary points give a representative picture of the salary schedule in each district.* Note that these salary figures may not represent the average salary actually paid in any given district, for that depends on the placement of teachers within the schedule, i.e., the characteristics of the specific teacher work force in terms of experience and earned credits. Yet the use of the teacher salary scale is particularly appropriate, since this is normally the subject of direct negotiation in collective bargaining.

In addition, however, information was obtained on the mean salary actually paid in each district in 1968.† Average salaries are not likely to be the direct subject of collective negotiations, but they are a measure of actual compensation received by teachers and therefore are useful in judging the real economic benefit of unionism.

In previous studies, both salary scales and mean salaries have been analyzed—but never in the same study. The differences between the two types of measure are important: later, it will be shown that,

---

*For some purposes, the Public Employment Relations Board uses these points as a shorthand for describing a given teacher salary schedule. In a sense, these points describe a "normal" career path for a teacher.

†Unfortunately, we were not able to obtain mean salary figures for all districts in earlier years.

in certain respects, the determinants of the salary scale are different than the determinants of average salary.

Table 1 indicates that there were indeed differences in salaries at all levels between districts with and without contracts. This, however, does not take one very far. First, the salary differences between districts are not very large: from about one percent ($65) at base to 2.24 percent ($240) at the BS + 60, 11th step. Second, of course, we are not controlling for any other variables influencing teacher salaries.

It is possible, for example, that organized districts had *always* been higher-paying districts and that high salaries lead to organization, rather than the reverse. In fact, it is true that districts organized in 1968 had tended to pay higher salaries in 1967 than unorganized districts, but these differences in 1967 were much smaller than those existing in 1968, ranging from $25 at base to $125 at the BS + 60, 11th step. This implies that unionism did produce salary gains for teachers in 1968, as table 1 suggests, but clearly this hypothesis needs a more rigorous testing that allows for the effect of other determinants of teacher salaries.

A Model of Salary Determination for Public School Teachers

In a perfectly competitive labor market—where there are no barriers to worker mobility, and workers and employers possess no monopoly power with respect to wages—workers in the same occupation, possessing the same level of skill and having all other relevant characteristics (experience, age, sex, etc.) in common, should receive the same wage. Intraoccupational wage differentials will exist if any of the above conditions are not met. For example, similar jobs may involve different levels of effort with different employers. Second, the assumption of a homogeneous labor supply is usually violated in the real world. Workers possess different levels of skill and experience, and wage levels can be expected to reflect these differences. Third, workers are not optimally mobile; movement is not without cost. Moreover, workers may also be tied to their jobs by nonwage considerations, such as preferences for certain work settings, satisfaction with present work associations, etc. Fourth, other market imperfections may also exist. Employers may not be "price takers"; rather they may possess some monopsony power. Workers may also exercise monopoly power. Different market structures will cause wage differences to occur within the same occupation.

The model used in this study to explain differences in teacher salaries is derived from these considerations. One must first consider the fact that "teaching" involves different duties in different districts, so the quality of the position will vary. The pupil-teacher ratio (P/T) is one measure of difference in the quality of jobs available to teachers. Although there may be better measures, differences in average class size are common indicators of quality differences in schools.*

The use of P/T, however, can be perilous. As Hall and Carroll (reading 22) have pointed out, teachers often bargain just as hard for class size limitations as for higher salaries. Salaries and pupil-teacher ratios may be determined simultaneously through bargaining. Nevertheless, P/T will be used as an independent variable in the analysis, because in the first year of bargaining under the Taylor Law, class size was not a major issue. Even in 1970, according to the New York State Teachers Association (*Information Service Memorandum,* November 30, 1970), only 255 districts in New York had contracts containing *any* sort of class size provision, and the great majority of these were simple statements of intent that were not binding on the school district.

In another sense, class size is a double-edged variable: Kasper (1971), for example, implicitly considers P/T a measure of teacher productivity. If a low P/T is an indication of a high-quality district, one would expect a negative relationship between P/T and salaries. On the other hand, if one expects a correlation between salaries and physical productivity, as measured by class size, then there should be a positive relationship between P/T and salaries. In addition, if teachers prefer smaller to larger classes, the relationship might be positive, indicating that teachers are compensated for the disutility of larger workloads.

Another measure of difference in the quality of districts may be the district's enrollment. Total enrollment, E, may reflect both

---

*The "quality" of a school has been measured by student achievement test scores, percentage of college entrants, and similar indices. See Barron (1967, pp. 279-309). The pupil-teacher ratio may be more subject to control by school administrators than other quality indices.

differences in quality and differences in market structures, as Kasper (1970, p. 63) has pointed out. Larger districts may have more specialized programs (art, music, special education, etc.) requiring teachers of higher skill levels. Larger districts, especially those in the affluent suburbs, may have brighter students and conduct more enriched programs. Moreover, larger districts are likely to be in or near metropolitan areas where competition for teachers may be keen. Conversely, smaller districts may have more monopsony power, because, as Kasper (1970) puts it, "There may be no nearby school districts to stimulate competition." Thus, we expect there to be a positive relation between enrollment, E, and salaries.

At the same time, one does not expect district size and salaries to be linearly related. This is partly based on Kasper's (1970) finding of an "urban turnaround." In the very largest urban school districts, teachers may need skills less of a pedagogic than of a disciplinary variety. Moreover, large city school districts may need to compete more intensely with other public services (welfare, transportation, sanitation, etc.) for a piece of the taxpayer's dollar.

It might be argued that teachers prefer to work in smaller districts, and, therefore, larger districts must pay higher salaries to entice teachers away from preferred smaller districts. Disutilities may result from working in larger districts because of a more impersonal atmosphere, the encumbrances of a large bureaucracy, and disciplinary problems. Many of the larger districts in New York state, however, are suburban communities offering highly attractive working conditions much coveted by teachers. If disutilities result in higher salaries, the highest salaries should be found in central city districts that reputedly have the least attractive jobs. Consequently, the expected "urban turnaround" would not materialize.

Salary Schedule and Teacher Characteristics

The next elements of our model relate to differences in teacher characteristics. Districts differ in the mix of teachers on their staffs. Salary schedules usually require districts to pay higher salaries to teachers with more experience or more earned college credits; therefore, one would expect a positive relation between, for example, mean salary and the percentage of teachers in a district with advanced degrees (master's or better); this variable will be labeled ADV.

Some interesting questions arise, however, when one considers the relation between points on the salary schedule and teacher characteristics. For example, does a district with a high ADV necessarily have a high base salary? The hypothesis here is that a district desiring high-quality teachers (as measured by ADV) will tend to pay high salaries at every point in the salary schedule in order to recruit and retain high-quality teachers, regardless of degree level.

The teacher experience variable tested in our model is the percentage of teachers in a district with three years of seniority or less (SEN 3). This form is chosen for several reasons. For example, it can be argued that districts that recruit heavily (and thus have a high SEN 3) will tend to shift the entire salary schedule upward in order to attract young teachers not only by a high base salary but by the promise of substantial increments throughout their careers, especially since the full cost impact of this shift will not be felt immediately. Districts with low salary schedules may suffer from high turnover. Since younger workers are usually the most mobile, high turnover may result in a low SEN 3.* Hence, SEN 3 and salaries would be positively correlated.

On the other hand, one would not expect a positive relation between salaries actually paid by districts (for example, mean salaries) and SEN 3, because of the requirements of the salary schedule. A district with a teaching staff with extensive experience will necessarily tend to pay higher *actual* salaries (as opposed to salaries listed in the schedule). Therefore, it is expected that mean salary and SEN 3 will be negatively related.

The preceding discussion highlights the possible uses of a teacher salary schedule. A district can adjust a schedule to show, for example, relatively high salaries at the base level but relatively low salaries at subsequent steps. If the district's teachers are employed mainly at the higher steps and no hiring is being done, the average salary actually paid by the district will tend to be lower than other districts with, possibly, a lower base salary but a different age-distribution of teachers. Thus, the common practice of using the base salary as a comprehensive index of a district's average salary level can be quite misleading.† Both administrators and teacher organizations

---

*For an analysis of the relationship between turnover and the seniority distribution of employed workers, see Stoikov (1972).

†Baird and Landon use only the base salary in their two studies.

can manipulate the salary schedule to serve various purposes—public relations, politics, recruiting, etc.

Some degree of monopsony is likely to exist in teacher labor markets.* As pointed out above, the enrollment variable is likely to pick up some monopsony effects. In addition, a dummy variable, DWN, is added to the model to capture additional monopsony effects. (DWN takes a value of 1 if a district is in downstate New York, 0 otherwise.) Approximately one quarter of the state's districts are in the three downstate counties, Nassau, Suffolk, and Westchester.† An apparently substantial salary differential, favorable to downstate teachers, has persisted in New York state over many years. There may be several reasons for this differential. The argument presented here is that the competitive market structure in the downstate counties is responsible for a large part of the differential. The downstate districts are goegraphically more concentrated than New York's upstate districts. It is conceivable that a teacher living downstate can change jobs (and districts) many times without changing his place of residence. Most teachers living upstate who change jobs must also necessarily change residences. This means that the downstate teacher is potentially more job-mobile than the upstate teacher, and this gives the upstate district a monopsonistic edge in the labor market.‡

In addition, downstate districts must compete for teachers in a labor market that affords teachers many more opportunities outside the teaching profession than are available in upstate New York. In summary, the downstate market for teachers is likely to be significantly more competitive than the upstate market.**

---

*This is true because a public school system obviously does not operate in a competitive product market but has a virtual monopoly on the provision of educational services within a given geographic area. Thus, teachers are limited in the number of employers with whom they may deal. The most explicit discussion of the monopsony question is in Landon and Baird (1971).

†Arguably, Rockland might also be considered a downstate county. Since it has only nine districts, its inclusion or exclusion does not affect the analysis to any great extent.

‡This is a generalization that probably does not hold for the Buffalo metropolitan area. There are forty-one districts in western New York (Erie and Niagara Counties) competing for teacher services. The next largest upstate county, Monroe (Rochester), has eighteen districts.

**Landon and Baird argue that the (log of the) number of districts per county is directly related to the competitiveness of the teacher labor market.

There are other possible, but less plausible, causes of the downstate differential. First, downstate districts tend to be wealthier than upstate districts, and, thus, their ability to pay higher salaries is greater. Wealth variables will be incorporated into the model.*

Second, consumer prices are higher in the downstate area than upstate, and teacher salaries may reflect differences in living costs, but recent research indicates that is unlikely (Owen 1972). Also, there does not appear to be enough variation in the cost of living between upstate and downstate communities to produce the sizable downstate salary advantage.

Third, some argue that strong teacher organizations in the downstate area, particularly in New York City, generate patterns that have lifted the salaries of all downstate districts, both organized and unorganized. Later, this study will correct for some of the pattern-spillover effects that apparently do exist in teacher bargaining, and it will be seen that our results do not support the contention that a few strong organized districts lift the salaries of all districts in the area. Also, this argument would be more persuasive if the downstate differential had not existed in the prebargaining era, as it clearly did.

Thus, the downstate advantage is probably the result of the more competitive labor market conditions in that area, and any analysis of teacher salaries in New York should allow for this differential.

The Regression Models

The first variant of the model tested is completed by the addition of a union variable, CTRCT, which takes a value of 1 if a district had a contract for the year 1968-69, and 0 otherwise.[†]

In summary, the first model tested takes the form:

Since the downstate New York counties have, by far, the highest number of districts apiece in the state, DWN can be viewed simply as a dichotomized version of the Landon and Baird variable. See Landon and Baird (1971).

*Although there is a positive correlation between DWN and the wealth variable considered here (true value per pupil), it is not high enough to cause a problem of multicollinearity.

[†]Approximately 70 districts engaged in some form of negotiations in 1968 but did not sign contracts.

$$S = b_0 + b_1 \, (P/T) + b_2 \, E - b_3 \, E^2 + b_4 \, ADV$$
$$+ \, b_5 \, SEN \, 3 + b_6 \, DWN + b_7 \, CTRCT + e \, . \tag{1}$$

S is the salary variable; e is the error term; and the other variables have previously been defined. Note that the preceding discussion leads to some uncertainty concerning the signs of b_1 and b_5. Essentially, this first model consists of structural characteristics (P/T, E, DWN), teacher characteristics (ADV, SEN 3), and the contract variable.

A second, extended version of the model is also reported here. Added to equation (1) are variables representing the district's ability to pay and its willingness to pay. A common and accepted measure of ability to pay is "true value per pupil" (TV/P).* True value is an estimate (admittedly, often a poor one) of the market value of the property in a school district. Since school revenues are based primarily on local property taxes, the value of a district's property wealth behind each pupil is considered a good index of ability to pay.

There is generally less agreement on the appropriate index for a district's willingness to pay. David B. Ross (1969) has suggested, "An idea of the effort a community has made to supply public services comes from comparing its ability to pay, measured by its taxable resources, and the amount of tax revenues which actually have been collected and spent on services." (For further discussion, see Drotning and Lipsky 1971.) Following Ross's lead, this study considers the ratio of current expenditures to true value a useful measure of a district's "willingness to pay" or "effort."† Current expenditures are defined as instructional costs (IC), and the following identity is noted:

---

*See Benson (1968, p. 111). Other labels for the same concept are "full value," "fair value," "fair market value," and "actual value."

†Landon and Baird (1971) use the "effective property tax rate" as their measure of willingness to pay. This is sometimes called "tax on true," and is equal to property tax revenue divided by true value (x1,000). Thus, the difference between our measure of "effort" and Landon and Baird's is a question of the relation of instructional costs to property tax revenue. For example, in 1969 in New York, property revenue was approximately $2.1 million and instructional costs were $2.6 million.

$$\frac{IC}{P} \equiv \frac{TV}{P} \cdot \frac{IC}{TV} .$$

Hence, it can be argued that the level of instructional costs per pupil reflects both a district's ability and its willingness to pay. It might be noted that the simple correlation between TV/P and IC/TV is insignificant for New York school districts and slightly negative (r = −.086). Nevertheless, it is hypothesized that both TV/P and IC/TV will have a positive influence on salaries.

The final variable tested in the extended version of the model is debt service per pupil (DEBT/P). The addition of DEBT/P gives a more comprehensive picture of the true costs of educating a district's pupils.* School districts are limited, for the most part, to using borrowed funds for capital expenditures. It is expected that DEBT/P will have a positive influence on teacher salaries. Two reasons are suggested for this relation. First, a district with a high DEBT/P is likely to have undertaken a school building program in the recent past. New buildings may result in a higher quality system or an expanded system, both results calling for additional teachers and thus being likely to have a positive influence on salaries. Second, to the extent that new buildings are financed with borrowed funds rather than current tax revenues, the amount of tax revenue available for teacher salaries is not diminished, at least in the short run.

The hypothesis is that a high DEBT/P indicates a system that is growing or being improved, and this creates upward pressure on salaries. Obviously, the existence of debt service in a district's budget may reflect borrowings made many years in the past. Yet, given the rapid acceleration of both construction costs and interest rates in the 1960s, a high DEBT/P almost inevitably reflects recent bond issues.

The extended model takes the form:

$$S = b_0 + b_1 (P/T) + b_2 E - b_3 E^2 + b_4 ADV$$
$$+ b_5 SEN\ 3 + b_6 DWN + b_7 CTRCT + b_8 (TV/P) \qquad (2)$$
$$+ b_9 (IC/TV) + b_{10} (DEBT/P) + e .$$

*The sum of IC/P and DEBT/P, however, does not equal total expenditures per pupil. Omitted are items such as expenses related to the board of education and central administration, building maintenance expenses, and "undistributed" expenses. IC/P and DEBT/P combined average about 80 percent of total expenditures per pupil.

The extended model adds variables denoting the district's costs of producing a student, i.e., the "price of the product." The first model, then, is built on assumptions about the operation of the labor market, and the second adds "product" market variables.

Regression Results

Results from cross-sectional analyses of the two models, using data from almost 700 New York state school districts, are displayed in table 2. In general, the models test out well. About 45 to 60 percent of the variance in the dependent variables is explained. Note that the addition of the three financial or "product" market variables does not add much to the R^2. In fact, for each of the three points from the salary schedule, about one percentage point is added to the variance explained; for mean salary, about three percentage points are added to R^2. On the other hand, the coefficients of the three financial variables are, for the most part, significant and operate in the expected direction. Teacher salaries do appear to depend on both the district's ability and willingness to pay. DEBT/P is significant in all cases. True value per pupil and DEBT/P are particularly significant in the case of mean salary. Every $1,000 increase in TV/P adds $8 to average salary. A $1.00 increase in debt service per pupil is associated with an increase of $1.80 in average salary. The willingness to pay variable, IC/TV, has a significant impact on the salary scale, but it apparently plays no role in determining mean salaries. A district's willingness to pay must be determined through the political process. Community political preferences are apparently more likely to be reflected in the salary schedule than in average salaries paid.

Note also that the pupil-teacher ratio, P/T, is positively and significantly related to mean salaries, but negatively and insignificantly related (except for BS + 60, 11th step) to the salary scale. An extra pupil per teacher adds about $80 to average salary and, in a sense, this is a reward for higher productivity. On the other hand, high salary schedules are generally associated with low P/T ratios. If P/T is a measure of quality, it is reflected in the salary schedule, not in terms of salaries actually received by teachers. One can infer from these results that districts with high student-faculty ratios tend to have low salary schedules but older teachers.

Enrollment has the expected relation to the salary scale but not to average salary. Salaries in the schedule increase with district size but at a diminishing rate. The highest salaries at the BS + 60, 11th step, for example, seem to be associated with districts with about 25,000 pupils. At about 50,000 pupils, the net effect of enrollment on salaries is zero.* This is an example of the turnaround effect. At lower steps in the salary scale, however, the turnaround occurs only at an enrollment level that is outside the range of districts included in this study. Large central city districts may be required to pay higher starting salaries to compensate teachers for the disutilities associated with urban schools. More experienced teachers, however, may receive relatively lower salaries in urban districts. This implies that the salary structure in city districts may be more compressed than in outlying, suburban districts.

The variable ADV is significantly related to each of the dependent variables, but particularly to BS + 60, 11th step, and to mean salary. The Beta coefficients (not shown in table 2) reveal that ADV is the single most influential variable for mean salary, the second most important variable for BS + 60, 11th step. A high proportion of teachers with advanced degrees pulls up the entire salary schedule, even base salary. This might be called a reverse bumping effect. Of course, the impact is much greater at the higher steps and greatest in the case of mean salary. An increase of 10 percentage points in ADV adds an estimated $375 to $413 to mean salary.

SEN 3 is insignificant in the case of base and mean salary. A high proportion of *young* teachers does appear to be associated with an increase in the *higher* steps in the schedule. This effect is somewhat unexpected, but not perverse. Perhaps young teachers have long time horizons and are attracted to districts paying higher salaries at the higher steps. A growing district will probably have a high proportion of young teachers, and growth may put upward pressure on all points in the salary scale.†

The favorable salary differential enjoyed by downstate districts is quite substantial, even when other variables are controlled for. The DWN differential ranges from about $400 at base to $1,100 at BS + 60, 11th step. To some extent, downstate districts are purchasing more qualified teachers: the simple correlation between DWN and

---

*Aside from New York City, the only district with more than 50,000 pupils is Buffalo.

†The simple correlation between SEN 3 and DEBT/P, however, is only .14.

Table 2
Regression Coefficients for Determinants of Teacher Salaries in New York State, 1968

Independent variable	Base salary		BS + 30, 7th step		BS + 60, 11th step		Mean salary	
	Basic model	Extended model	Basic model	Extended model	Basic model	Extended model	Basic model	Extended model
P/T	−2.780	−2.969	−9.902	−7.827	−15.866	−14.818	79.971	83.460
	(2.388)	(2.381)	(7.160)	(7.215)	(9.330)*	(9.320)*	(10.212)***	(10.052)***
E	.0142	.0137	.0335	.0332	.0539	.0557	−.0093	−.0087
	(.0035)***	(.0035)***	(.0071)***	(.0072)***	(.0137)***	(.0138)***	(.0150)	(.0149)
E^2	−.0161	−.0152	−.0480	−.0464	−.1028	−.1042	−.0353	−.0334
	(.0071)**	(.0071)**	(.0140)***	(.0140)***	(.0279)***	(.0279)***	(.0305)	(.0301)
ADV	1.7431	1.6784	8.3823	7.6405	23.441	21.560	41.280	37.545
	(.952)*	(.973)*	(1.905)***	(1.971)***	(3.722)***	(3.807)***	(4.074)***	(4.106)***
SEN 3	.7124	.5543	7.7724	7.5011	17.093	17.214	−.1021	−.2022
	(.8797)	(.8819)	(1.7995)***	(1.8023)***	(3.438)***	(3.452)***	(3.763)	(3.7227)
DWN	414.58	403.88	842.06	806.28	1,157.81	1,157.81	843.98	691.53
	(25.92)***	(26.79)***	(52.71)***	(53.86)***	(101.30)***	(104.87)***	(110.88)***	(113.10)***
CTRCT	4.951	5.523	.4888	7.953	−12.832	−2.592	3.419	6.527
	(17.784)	(17.755)	(36.924)	(36.717)	(69.497)	(69.489)	(76.068)	(74.945)

Dependent variable

TV/P		.0003 (.0005)		.0018 (.0011)*		.0044 (.0019)**		.0080 (.0021)***
IC/TV		.0216 (.0088)**		.0318 (.0169)*		.0569 (.0344)*		.0013 (.0371)
DEBT/P		.2743 (.1283)**		.6934 (.2680)***		.6951 (.4020)*		1.807 (.5414)***
Constant	6,261.42	6,242.22	8,217.02	8,111.54	8,995.95	8,881.33	5,080.44	4,853.75
R^2	.537	.547	.615	.625	.526	.535	.442	.474
Standard error of estimate	198.10	196.59	396.30	392.48	774.15	769.45	847.34	829.86

***Significant at p < .01.
**Significant at p < .05.
*Significant at p < .10.

Note: Standard errors are in parentheses.

ADV is .61; this is the only point in the model at which a problem of multicollinearity exists.

Finally, it is clear that the model's measure of the effects of collective bargaining, CTRCT, has no significant relation to teacher salaries. The small size of the coefficients and the large standard errors indicate that the apparent differences displayed in table 1 are largely illusory—they are accounted for by other variables.

The evidence from this regression analysis would indicate that collective bargaining has no impact on salaries, but certain factors must be kept in mind in drawing any conclusions. First, the variable CTRCT is certainly not the only, and may not be the best, way of measuring the effects of bargaining. If it were possible, for example, to distinguish between "weak" and "strong" teacher unions, more meaningful results might be obtained. Such distinctions are difficult to draw and were not feasible for this study. Second, and more important, spillover effects may be blurring union impact and these can be corrected for, at least in part.

Spillover Effects

The existence of genuine collective bargaining in 60 percent of the districts in New York state in 1968 may have heavily influenced salary schedules among the 40 percent that were not effectively organized; that is, districts without formal negotiations and contracts may have chosen or been forced to follow the lead of organized districts and set their own salaries *as if* they were organized. It is well known that patterns are pervasive in public school bargaining (Pegnetter 1971). Unorganized districts may have been just as subject to the leadership of pattern setters as organized districts. Labor market pressures may have forced a district to match what its neighbors were paying or risk being unable to recruit and retain the teachers it needed. Districts wishing to avoid negotiations with a teacher organization may have elected to set salaries in line with comparable organized districts. All of this implies that if spillover effects are significant, the impact of the union will be seriously understated.

If spillover is a problem, how can its effects be corrected for? Assume that the amount of spillover is a function of the geographic proximity of school districts; that is, spillover will be greater among districts that are spatially clustered. A district that is isolated geographically will be relatively immune to pattern effects. The experience of the parties in negotiations provides some prima facie evidence to support this assumption: when comparisons are used as a standard for salary determination, it is inevitably nearby or adjacent districts that are used for the purpose. The more distant the district, the less relevance it has for the parties.

Earlier, it was argued that the spatial concentration of districts is a correlate of labor market competition; that is, spillover and competitiveness go hand-in-hand. In practice, it may be impossible to determine which effect accounts for a given salary pattern.

These considerations suggest a method of correcting for spillover. If a subsample consisting of relatively isolated districts can be selected, the influence of spillover will be reduced, if not eliminated. Furthermore, such a sample would consist of districts operating in less competitive, more monopsonistic labor markets. For example, a sample might be constructed consisting only of small-town districts or districts within a given enrollment range—that is, those relatively uninfluenced by geographically proximate districts and therefore less involved in any "orbit of coercive comparison."

Table 3 presents the results of running the basic model for districts with enrollments of 1,001 to 2,000 pupils. There are 188 districts in the sample, most of which are small, upstate communities, at some distance from major metropolitan areas. (Only 12 percent are downstate districts.) About 63 percent of these districts were organized in 1968, matching the extent of organization among all districts in the state. These small districts, however, tended to be poorer (the mean TV/P is $19,800) and to have larger average pupil-teacher ratios (P/T = 22.0) than the average district in the state. The willingness ratio, IC/TV, also tended to be lower than the average for the state.

The most interesting result shown in table 3 is the significant effect unionism appears to have on salaries; CTRCT is associated with $72 more on base to $313 more for BS + 60, 11th step. In percentage terms, dividing the CTRCT coefficients by the (unweighted) means of each of the dependent variables for districts in the sample results in the following:

Salary level	Percentage
Base salary	1.12
BS + 30, 7th step	2.15
BS + 60, 11th step	2.95
Mean salary	2.41

Table 3
Regression Coefficients for Determinants of Teacher Salaries in New York State Districts with Enrollments of 1,001 to 2,000 Pupils, 1968

Independent variable	Dependent variable			
	Base salary	BS + 30, 7th step	BS + 60, 11th step	Mean salary
P/T	−12.808	−34.843	−47.956	1.9467
	(2.897)***	(6.127)***	(9.649)***	(12.815)
ADV	−6.2310	−3.2261	.1198	32.328
	(2.034)***	(4.302)	(6.775)	(8.998)***
SEN 3	.1264	5.3414	8.6006	−6.4104
	(1.529)	(3.233)*	(5.092)*	(6.763)
DWN	405.31	793.15	1,267.71	660.05
	(60.09)***	(127.08)***	(200.13)***	(265.78)***
CTRCT	72.116	190.515	313.253	210.511
	(28.046)***	(59.315)***	(93.410)***	(124.057)*
TV/P	.00059	.00185	.00217	.00380
	(.0014)	(.00295)	(.0047)	(.0062)
DEBT/P	−.1866	−.4611	−.6924	.7159
	(.2256)	(.4772)	(.7515)	(.9981)
Constant	6,885.36	9,447.50	11,134.96	7,192.21
R^2	.522	.647	.666	.488
Standard error of estimate	160.43	339.30	534.34	709.65

***Significant at $p < .01$.
**Significant at $p < .05$.
*Significant at $p < .10$.

Note: Standard errors are in parentheses.

These union differentials are similar to, but slightly higher than, the differentials shown in the third column of table 1. Of course, in the analysis represented in table 3, other variables influencing salaries are controlled for, making the results far more meaningful. However, although the CTRCT regression coefficients are significant in a statistical sense, a 2 percent union differential is not likely to affect substantially the allocation of resources within a district. On the other hand, since the test employed here does not entirely eliminate spillover, the union effect may be understated.

The R^2s in table 3 are also similar to those in table 2. There are differences in how the model works with this particular sample. For example, the coefficients for the financial variables are not significant. Ability to pay and DEBT/P do not appear to influence salary determination in these districts.* If these districts do have greater monopsony power, they have greater discretion in setting salaries, regardless of financial indices of "ability" and "willingness."

It is significant that the IC/TV ratio was lower, on the average, for these districts than for the state as a whole. This implies that the districts were not exerting themselves to the same extent that other districts, both larger and smaller, were. In a sense, these districts were collecting monopsony rents. Under these circumstances, it is not surprising that collective bargaining appears to be more influential in this sample than elsewhere. Teachers organized for genuine bargaining can force monopsonistic districts to behave as price takers in the labor market, rather than discretionary price setters. In this way, the teachers can extricate some of the "economic rent" for themselves. Bargaining forces these districts into bilateral monopoly, in which power factors play a large role. At the same time, spillover effects are reduced, since the districts are scattered and relatively isolated.

It should be noted that the basic model was tested against other subsamples. When run on all districts with 1,000 or fewer pupils (N = 235), the coefficient for the CTRCT variable, with one exception, was not significant. The one exception was the BS + 60, 11th step. CTRCT was significant at the .05 level; the coefficient was $410, almost 4 percent of the mean salary at that level. At other salary levels, the coefficient ranged from $32 to $149, but the standard errors were too large to make the results significant.

---

*The "willingness" ratio, IC/TV, was tested in earlier runs but was not included in table 3.

These small, largely rural districts might be considered to have potentially as much monopsony power as those districts with 1,001 to 2,000 pupils and therefore to present the same prospects for union gains. In 1968, however, only 36 percent of these districts had contracts. Furthermore, in the districts where the teachers had organized, bargaining was largely unsophisticated; the contract was a simple document, seldom more than a few pages in length; and effective control often remained with the board of education. It is probable that, given the rapid extension of bargaining through 1969 and 1970 and the growing sophistication of negotiators on both sides, a strong union effect might be found in the smallest districts if data for 1970 or 1971 were to be tested.

For districts with more than 2,000 pupils, no significant CTRCT variables were discovered—the results being roughly equivalent to those in table 2. Furthermore, no significant effects were found when upstate and downstate districts were divided and tested separately.

Changes in Salary Levels, 1967-68

This section deals with the relation of collective bargaining to salary changes that occurred between 1967 and 1968. Table 4 shows that teachers who obtained collective agreements in 1968 seemed to win larger salary increases than teachers who did not have such contracts. For example, base salary increased by an average of $598 in districts with contracts in 1968 compared to $558 in districts without contracts. Base salary averaged $5,887 in 1967 in districts that

Table 4
Changes in Salary Levels, 1967-68: Differences Between New York School Districts with and Without Collective Bargaining Contracts

Salary level	Districts with contracts (N = 441)		Districts without contracts (N = 225)	
	Mean	Standard deviation	Mean	Standard deviation
Base salary	$598	$211.7	$558	$293.4
BS + 30, 7th step	782	297.6	704	402.2
BS + 60, 11th step	986	410.2	871	521.0

won contracts in 1968; in 1968, the base salary of these districts averaged $6,485. In unorganized districts, base salary averaged $5,862 in 1967 and $6,420 in 1968.

Once again, however, other variables influencing salary changes need to be controlled for. Therefore, the basic model was tested to determine if salary changes, rather than salary levels, might have been influenced by the presence of a collective bargaining contract. The movement of salaries from year to year is probably susceptible to a number of transient and random factors. Short-term changes cannot be explained so neatly by a reasonably compact model of the type used to analyze salary levels. It turned out that factors such as ability to pay, willingness to pay, and average class size were not related to salary changes. The most interesting results of the analysis are shown in table 5. Although only 6 or 7 percent of the variance in salary changes is explained by the regressions, in each case CTRCT is a highly significant variable.

The results indicate that the presence of a contract added about $83 to the amount by which base salary was increased from 1967 to 1968. The corresponding figures are $110 at the BS + 30, 7th step, and $131 at the BS + 60, 11th step. Thus, collective bargaining apparently resulted in salary increases that were approximately 15 percent greater than one would have expected otherwise.*

One variable not previously included in the analysis also appears to have influenced salary changes. MALES, the percentage of males in a district's teacher work force, had a positive and significant impact on salary changes. ADV is significant in two equations in table 5, but unexpectedly it was negatively related to the dependent variables. Enrollment, E, is positively related to salary changes, and significant in two equations, but E^2 is not significant. Apparently, there is no urban turnaround effect with respect to salary changes. DWN, an important factor in explaining salary levels, is insignificant here.

Given the low R^2s and relatively high standard errors of estimate, the equations in table 5 would not be useful for predictive purposes. Important variables may have been missed, and CTRCT

---

*If the coefficient, $83, is divided by the average increase in base salary in unorganized districts ($558), the result is 14.8 percent. At the BS + 30, 7th step, dividing $110 by $704 gives 15.6 percent; at the BS + 60, 11th step, $131 divided by $871 equals 15.0 percent.

Table 5

Regression Coefficients for Determinants of Changes in Teacher
Salaries in New York State, 1967-68

	Dependent variables		
Independent variables	Change in base salary	Change in BS + 30, 7th step	Change in BS + 60, 11th step
E	.0059	.0138	.0247
	(.0043)	(.0060)**	(.0080)***
E²	.0075	−.0019	−.0173
	(.0083)	(.0117)	(.0156)
ADV	−3.6752	−2.9907	−.6030
	(1.111)***	(1.512)**	(2.087)
SEN 3	−2.0562	−1.0098	−.4498
	(1.070)**	(1.510)	(2.004)
MALES	.2106	.4415	.5276
	(.1259)*	(.1762)**	(.2360)**
DWN	−12.730	−9.652	−2.4482
	(30.936)	(43.373)	(58.231)
CTRCT	83.039	109.837	130.591
	(21.573)***	(30.259)***	(40.660)***
Constant	655.924	624.149	582.519
R²	.070	.063	.066
Standard error of estimate	244.10	340.53	453.77

***Significant at $p < .01$.
**Significant at $p < .05$.
*Significant at $p < .10$.

Note: Standard errors are in parentheses.

may have captured some of the effects of these omitted variables. Nevertheless, the available evidence suggests that collective bargaining did result in larger negotiated increases in the salary scale than teachers would have gained in the absence of organization.

Comparison with Other Studies

Table 6 summarizes the principal studies now available on the influence of collective bargaining on teacher salaries. The table is virtually self-explanatory, although it provides no justification for the various regression models used by the several authors. In examining the table, one notices that the models have certain common variables. For example, district size is an explanatory variable in three studies. Each study has used an income or wealth variable, usually to serve as a proxy for ability to pay. The pupil-teacher ratio has also been considered by several authors.

A comparison of the conclusions reached through the various studies shows that the union variable was found to be statistically significant in the Thornton and the Hall and Carroll studies, but not significant in Kasper's research. The results are mixed in the study by Landon and Pierce and also in the present study, depending on (1) the dependent variable tested, (2) the specification of the union variable, and (3) the construction of the sample. It is more interesting to compare the range of the union effect in the various studies. Despite other differences, the percentage figures fall mainly into a rather narrow range, hovering between 2 and 4 percent. Kasper, for example, finds that teacher organizations increased average salaries by a maximum of about 4 percent. Landon and Pierce find almost no union effect in two tests but a maximum of 4.9 percent in a third. Thornton finds the effect to be between 1 and 4 percent, except for the "AM maximum" salary level in which the effect is a staggering (and unconvincing) 29 percent. Hall and Carroll's best estimate is just under 2 percent. The largest effect on salary level found in this study is just under 3 percent; without any correction for spillover, the effect is zero.

Thus, additional research has served to reinforce Kasper's initial findings, at least in terms of the magnitude of the union effect. As Kasper (1970, p. 71) put it, "Given these small estimates, it seems unlikely that bargaining has produced a significant or widespread reallocation of educational resources."

At the same time, it is hazardous to predict what the effect of teacher unionism will be in the future. This study's finding that bargaining added about 15 percent to salary increases, although subject to certain *caveats*, indicates that over time the cumulative effect of teacher bargaining might cause a substantial reallocation of educational resources. If the conclusion reached by Paul Douglas can be applied to the public sector, however, it seems unlikely that organized teachers can sustain their relative advantage into the indefinite future.

Summary and Conclusion

This study has been based on a model that makes certain assumptions about the teacher labor market. The model's independent

Table 6
A Comparison of Studies of the Influence of Collective Bargaining on Teacher Salaries

Matrix	Study				
	Kasper	Landon & Pierce	Thornton	Hall & Carroll	Lipsky & Drotning
Unit of observation	All states (including D.C.)	School districts with enrollments of 25,000 to 50,000, all of U.S.	School districts in cities with more than 100,000 population, all of U.S.	Elementary school districts in Cook County, Illinois	All school districts in New York state (except New York City)
Size of sample	51	44	83	118	696
Year(s) examined	1967-68	1966-67	1969-70	1968-69	1967-68
Dependent variable(s)	Average salary in state	Beginning salary (BS minimum)	BS minimum BS maximum AM minimum AM maximum	Average salary in district	BS minimum (base) BS + 30, 7th step BS + 60, 11th step Average salary, also changes in these salaries 1967-68
Significant independent variables	Per capita income, urbanization, percentage local revenue, expenditures per pupil	Number of districts in area, per capita income, percentage revenue from local sources	District size, average wage in area	District size, median family income, percentage male teachers, average seniority, state-aid per pupil as percentage of per pupil expenditures	District size, percentage teachers with advanced degrees, percentage teachers with 3 or fewer years service, pupil-teacher ratio, true value per pupil, "effort" ratio, debt service per pupil

"Union" variable(s)	(1) Percentage teachers represented by organization, (2) percentage of districts with representation, (3) percentage of teachers covered by agreements	(1) Dummy variable (1 = negotiations held), (2) percentage teachers members of NEA, (3) percentage teachers members of AFT	Dummy variable (1 = collective bargaining contract)	Dummy variable (1 = collective bargaining contract)	Dummy variable (1 = collective bargaining contract)
"Union" effect	Insignificant—adds 0 to about 4 percent	(1) Dummy variable significant—adds about 4.9 percent, (2) percentage NEA: barely significant, (3) percentage AFT insignificant	Significant—adds from 2.3 to 28.8 percent	Significant—adds about 1.8 percent	(1) Effect in entire sample insignificant, (2) effect in "small town" sample significant, (3) effect on salary change significant. Adds 0 to 3 percent to salary levels, 15 percent to salary changes

variables included teacher characteristics, structural factors, and financial variables, as well as a dummy variable representing the "bargaining effect." The dependent variables included both mean salary and rates taken from the salary schedule.

The model was first tested against all New York state school districts (excluding those in New York City) for the year 1968, the first year in which the Taylor Law was in effect. Collective bargaining was found to have had no effect on teacher salary levels, regardless of whether the dependent variable was a measure of actual earnings (mean salary) or of scheduled rates.

In an attempt to correct for spillover effects, the model was tested on certain subsamples of New York districts. For districts with enrollments between 1,001 and 2,000 pupils—essentially small town districts—the union effect was positive and significant for both types of salary measure. We argue that these districts were both relatively isolated from spillover and had a certain amount of monopsony power, so that a positive bargaining effect is more likely here than elsewhere.

Finally, estimates were made of the effect of collective bargaining on salary changes from 1967 to 1968, and the bargaining effect once again was found to be positive and highly significant, adding about 15 percent to salary increases.

Teacher unionism initially came to New York districts in which slightly higher salaries were already being paid. The effect of bargaining in the first year of the Taylor Law was to increase the favorable differential already enjoyed by the newly organized districts. The effect was probably greatest in small town, upstate districts, especially at the higher salary steps. The magnitude of the bargaining effect even at the eleventh step, however, was probably not more than 3 percent. For the state as a whole, without any correction for spillover, the salary effect of teacher unions was not significantly different from zero.

References

Baird, Robert N., and Landon, John H. "The Effects of Collective Bargaining on Public School Teachers' Salaries: Comment." *Industrial and Labor Relations Review* 25, no. 3 (April 1972): 410-17.

Barron, William E. "Measurement of Educational Productivity." *The Theory and Practice of School Finance*, edited by Warren E. Gauerke and Jack R. Childress. Chicago: Rand McNally, 1967.

Benson, Charles S. *The Economics of Public Education* (2nd ed.). Boston: Houghton Mifflin, 1968.

Douglas, Paul H. *Real Wages in the United States, 1890-1926*. Boston: Houghton Mifflin, 1930.

Drotning, John E., and Lipsky, David B. "The Outcome of Impasse Procedures in New York Schools Under the Taylor Law." *Arbitration Journal* 26, no. 2 (1971): 95-99.

Hall, W. Clayton, and Carroll, Norman E. "The Effects of Teachers' Organizations on Salaries and Class Size." *Industrial and Labor Relations Review* 26, no. 2 (January 1973): 834-41.

Kasper, Hirschel. "The Effects of Collective Bargaining on Public School Teachers' Salaries." *Industrial and Labor Relations Review* 24, no. 1 (October 1970): 57-72.

Kasper, Hirschel. "On the Effect of Collective Bargaining on Resource Allocation in Public Schools." *Economic and Business Bulletin* 23, no. 3 (Spring/Summer 1971): 1-9.

Landon, John H., and Baird, Robert N. "Monopsony in the Market for Public School Teachers." *American Economic Review* 61, no. 5 (December 1971): 966-71.

Levin, Henry M. "A Cost-Effectiveness Analysis of Teacher Selection." *Journal of Human Resources* 5, no. 1 (Winter 1970): 24-33.

Oberer, Walter E.; Hanslowe, Kurt L.; and Doherty, Robert E. *The Taylor Act Amendments of 1969: A Supplemental Primer for School Personnel (and Others Interested in Collective Negotiations)*. Ithaca: New York State School of Industrial and Labor Relations, 1970.

Owen, John D. "Toward a Public Employment Wage Theory: Econometric Evidence on Teacher Quality." *Industrial and Labor Relations Review* 25, no. 2 (January 1972): 213-22.

Pegnetter, Richard. "Fact Finding and Teacher Salary Disputes: The 1969 Experience in New York State." *Industrial and Labor Relations Review* 24, no. 2 (January 1971): 226-42.

Ross, David B. "The Arbitration of Public Employee Wage Disputes." *Industrial and Labor Relations Review* 23, no. 1 (October 1969): 6.

Stoikov, Vladimir. "The Effect of Changes in Quits and Hires on the Length-of-Service Composition of Employed Workers." *British Journal of Industrial Relations* 9, no. 2 (July 1972): 225-33.

Thornton, Robert J. "The Effects of Collective Negotiations on Teachers' Salaries." *Quarterly Review of Economics and Business* 11, no. 4 (Winter 1971): 37-46.

Reading 22

The Effect of Teachers' Organizations on Salaries and Class Size

W. Clayton Hall and Norman E. Carroll

In recent years, a growing body of literature on the effects of teachers' organizations on salaries has appeared. Unfortunately, by limiting themselves to a concern over salaries, the authors may have ignored other important effects of collective negotiations. Furthermore, limitations of the scope of the previous work suggest that some additional study of the salary issue may be appropriate. It is the purpose of this article to report on research concerning the relationships between collective negotiations and both teachers' salaries and class size. These two issues are related, and both are critical in formulating policy toward public school education.

The relevance of class size to the problems of financing education is emphasized in the *Final Report of the President's Commission on School Finance* (1972, p. xviii). The point is made repeatedly that there is no known relationship between class size and educational quality. The Commission, therefore, suggests that significant economic gains may be possible by increasing class size, without necessarily decreasing educational quality.

Reprinted by permission from *Industrial and Labor Relations Review* 26, no. 2 (January 1973), pp. 834-41. Copyright 1973 by Cornell University.

At least three earlier systematic analyses have been addressed to the question of the effects of collective negotiations on teachers' salaries. In the first of these, Hirschel Kasper (1970) was generally unable to find a consistent relationship between teachers' organizations and various measures of teachers' salaries. There were, however, serious weaknesses in his study which two later analyses have attempted to remedy. In both cases, statistically significant results were obtained. (See Thornton 1971; Baird and Landon 1972.) Nevertheless, several features of the design of these studies leave the answer to this critical question still in doubt.

The first problem stems from the districts included in the samples. In both studies, the samples were interstate and interregional in nature. As a result, it is not clear whether their findings reflected the impact of unions on salaries or whether they attributed the influence of variables such as state certification requirements, degree of urbanization, and regional income differentials to teachers' organizations.

In the second place, both samples apparently included large cities in which collective bargaining is relatively old and sophisticated. For this reason, it is not certain whether their findings could be carried over to suburban areas where teachers' organizations have become increasingly active in recent years but are still relatively inexperienced in the process of collective bargaining.

Finally, the salary measures employed were not actual amounts received but rather points on salary scales. Clearly this has some advantage, since it is these figures which are the direct subject of negotiations, but it also has the disadvantage of not directly reflecting the actual economic benefits of organization to teachers.

The research reported in this paper attempts to avoid some of the difficulties mentioned above. The analysis is based on data from the 118 elementary school districts in suburban Cook County, Illinois, for the school year, 1968-69. Information on finances, district size, student-teacher ratios, teacher qualifications, and salary figures are included. This is supplemented with community census data.* By

---

*In some instances school district borders do not coincide with community boundaries. Most districts, however, lie primarily within one community, and most communities are served largely by one school district. In the few exceptional cases where the political and district boundaries are not coextensive, the difference can introduce bias into the data. Therefore, we examined a sample

limiting the study to a single metropolitan area, we hope to eliminate any influence due to interstate or interregional differences. It also enables us to include variables representing teacher qualifications and community attitudes toward education.

The Basic Salary Model

The basic salary model argues that mean teacher salary (S) is a function of median family income (Y), the percentage of workers engaged in white-collar occupations (W), average daily attendance (A), the percentage of teachers who are male (M), the mean number of years of teaching experience (E), state aid per pupil as a percentage of per pupil expenditures (R), and the existence of a collective bargaining agreement (U). Symbolically this can be written as

$$S = S(Y,W,A,M,E,R,U) . \qquad (1)$$

Based on other work and a priori expectations, we hypothesized that salaries are positively related to income. High income presumably represents a greater ability to pay as well as demand for better teachers. In addition, both the school boards and the teachers themselves may come to expect to pay and receive the higher salaries which characterize a high-income area.

The percentage of workers engaged in white-collar occupations was taken as a rough measure of community attitudes towards education. It was assumed that when individuals derive their incomes from white-collar rather than blue-collar sources, they will have a higher demand for quality education, which will be reflected in teachers' salaries. For this reason a positive association was anticipated.

A positive relationship was also expected between salaries and district size as measured by average daily attendance. Large districts, as large organizations elsewhere, are likely to be characterized by formalized administrative procedures, bureaucratic inflexibility, and

---

of districts, comparing census track data with community data and found that the variations were too small to be meaningful. For example, the difference in median family income between the district and the community was on the average less than 1.5 percent. By contrast the community data for the median family income ranged from under \$5,000 to over \$20,000.

reduced opportunity for individual self-expression by teachers. For this reason higher salaries may be necessary to attract a sufficient number of qualified personnel. Furthermore, the larger districts may also find it feasible to conduct a larger number of special programs which require employing more specialized and highly paid individuals.

Since male teachers are more likely to be the primary breadwinners in their households and, hence, find it necessary to demand higher salaries, a positive association between the percentage of male teachers and mean teacher salary was expected. There was some doubt as to the precise mechanism by which this effect is transmitted. Formal salary schedules preclude outright sex discrimination. Nevertheless, it was felt that in some fashion, it is possible for male instructors to demand and receive higher remuneration; and districts which wish to hire and retain males on their staffs will have to pay somewhat higher mean salaries.*

The coefficient relating mean number of years of teaching experience to salaries was also expected to be positive, since most districts have salary schedules which reward experience.

Expectations concerning the sign of the association between state aid and salaries were a little less clear. One might first suspect a positive relationship, since state aid can increase the ability of districts to pay higher salaries. On the other hand, to the extent that state aid formulas include inadequate equalization and imperfect matching requirements, exactly the opposite effect may be observed. Financially affluent (but not necessarily high-income) districts may elect to spend virtually all their state funds on education, while less prosperous areas may reduce local support in response to more generous state contributions. In this case a negative association might very well be obtained. Such results have been obtained before (Kasper 1970).

When ordinary least-squares estimates were made of the basic salary model, the following results were obtained:

---

*It may be that a significant relationship merely reflects the possibility that male teachers are more likely to have extra compensations for academic hours beyond a bachelors degree. Since the necessary data were not available, we were unable to check on this possibility.

$$S = 6641.4853 + .0714Y^{***} + 6.0166W^* + .0916A^{***}$$
$$(2.8705) \qquad (1.8244) \qquad (5.0490)$$

$$+ 11.6335M^* + 170.3464E^{***} - 9.4193R^{***} + 167.1441U^{**}$$
$$(1.9600) \qquad (8.3676) \qquad (3.6320) \qquad (2.0095)$$

$R^2 = .7010$ t values in parentheses

*significant at the .10 level
**significant at the .05 level
***significant at the .01 level

In most cases the hypothesized relationships were confirmed. The regression coefficients indicate that salaries increase by approximately \$.07 for each one-dollar increase in median family income, by \$6.00 for each one-point increase in the percentage of workers engaged in white-collar occupations, by \$.09 for each additional student per district, by \$11.60 for each one-point increase in the percentage of teachers who are male, and by \$170.00 for each year of teaching experience. A salary decrease of \$9.40 was associated with each one-point increase in state aid per pupil as a percentage of per pupil expenditures. Of particular interest is the relationship between S and U which is significant at the .05 level. This regression coefficient suggests that teachers' contracts do indeed increase salaries by about \$167.00.

An Alternative Salary Model

For purposes of comparison, estimates were obtained for a model similar to one used by Kasper. Several of his more successful variables were irrelevant when applied to elementary schools at the district level. For example, the regional dummy variable for western states and the relative mix of elementary and secondary school teachers were clearly inappropriate. Similarly, the variables for degree of urbanization did not appear germane, since the entire sample of districts was taken from a single metropolitan area. Nevertheless, the districts in the present study did vary in size, and since some of the variation explained by degree of urbanization could be due to differences in the average size of employer units, average daily attendance was substituted for the urbanization variables.

Specificially, the second model took the form

$$S = S'(Y,X,A,R,U) \tag{2}$$

where X is operating expenditures per pupil, and the other variables are defined as before. The results were

$$S = 8504.2561 + .0965Y*** + .0620\,X + .0997A***$$
$$\qquad\qquad\quad (4.1859) \qquad\quad (.6030)\quad (4.3464)$$

$$\qquad - 19.9688R*** + 201.4427U*$$
$$\qquad\quad (7.0370) \qquad\qquad (1.9089)$$

$R^2 = .5093$ t values in parentheses

*significant at the .10 level
**significant at the .05 level
***significant at the .01 level

The relationship between S and U was significant at the .10 level.

Apparently part of the failure of Kasper's single-equation models to reveal an association between teachers' organizations and salaries was due to the aggregative nature of his data. Equation (2) which, after adjustments, is similar to Kasper's equation (1) yields a relationship which is significant at the .10 level, in contrast to Kasper's results. Although the R^2 for (2) is somewhat lower than most of the ones obtained by Kasper, this may be due to the local nature of the sample, which eliminates much of the interstate variation "explained" in the Kasper models. It is in line with results commonly obtained from local cross-sectional data.

Salaries are not the only issue in most negotiations between school boards and representatives of teachers' organizations. A variety of other matters are also included, many of which relate to working conditions, matters of educational quality, and faculty participation in decision making. Of these, perhaps the most frequently considered question relates to class size. Teachers' organizations often insist that they are bargaining for smaller classes in the face of opposition by school boards. For this reason, it is important to investigate the effect of collective negotiations upon class size in order to get a more complete picture of the total impact of collective negotiations. Indeed, as salaries and class size may be simultaneously determined, an unbiased estimate of the effect of one requires consideration of the effect of the other.

A survey of the literature indicates that while there has been a relatively large amount of work done on the topic of the relationships between class size and quality of education, there appears to be little previous research on the determinants of class size. However, based upon this literature and a priori expectations, a model was constructed which was able to explain a large portion of the observed variation. Specifically it is argued that class size as measured by the student-teacher ratio (Z) depends upon community population (P), the percentage of workers engaged in white-collar occupations (W), average daily attendance (A), state aid per pupil as a percentage of per pupil operating expenditure (R), and the existence of a collective bargaining agreement (U). Symbolically this takes the form

$$Z = Z(P,W,A,R,U) .\tag{3}$$

It was hypothesized that a larger community population would generally lead to larger classes. This was based upon the admittedly casual observation that larger classes are commonly found in the larger suburbs, although the reason for this was not clear.

District size as measured by average daily attendance was also included as an explanatory variable. This differs from population primarily due to differences in the number of public school pupils as a percentage of community population. The relationship between population and average daily attendance was not particularly significant, the simple correlation coefficient being less than .5. Once the separate effect of population was taken into account, district size was expected to be negatively related to the student-teacher ratio. There were two reasons for this. First, a large number of public school pupils in a community implies strong support for the school system. As small classes are usually preferred to larger ones, the community support was expected to be translated into small classes (Vincent 1969). Second, larger districts often find it possible to undertake special programs which may not be economically feasible in smaller ones. Many of these special programs are characterized by small classes thereby reducing the average class size.

The percentage of workers employed in white-collar occupations was expected to be negatively related to the student-teacher ratio. The concern for education which characterizes white-collar communities commonly takes the form of a demand for smaller classes and for specialized teaching services which lead to a lower number of pupils per teacher.

For reasons similar to those discussed with regard to teachers' salaries, the expected sign of the relationship between R and Z was in doubt. However, the negative sign with regard to salaries and state aid per pupil as a percentage of per pupil operating expenditures led us to anticipate a positive association.

Finally, the expectations with respect to the impact of formal agreements was not clear either. Teachers' organizations normally bargain for smaller classes, while school boards, faced with high salary demands and relatively fixed budgets, frequently offer pay increases in exchange for larger classes. Thus the sign of the relationship could not be determined on an a priori basis.

Determinants of Student-Teacher Ratio

Initially one might expect ability to pay as reflected in median family income or wealth to be a significant determinant of the student-teacher ratio (Mort and Furno 1960). This does not appear to be the case. Small class size appears to reflect a concern for education which is more closely related to the source of income than to the total amount. When Y was added to equation (3), the regression coefficient was smaller than the standard error.

Least-squares estimates of equation (3) yielded the following results:

$$Z = 11.8926 + .0001P^{***} - .0361W^{**} - .0005A^{***}$$
$$(3.1323) \qquad (2.1780) \qquad (3.1258)$$

$$+ .1453R^{***} + 1.2792U^{**}$$
$$(8.7369) \qquad (2.2728)$$

$R^2 = .4887$
t values in parentheses

*significant at the .10 level
**significant at the .05 level
***significant at the .01 level

The relationship between Z and U is positive and significant at the .05 level. The size of the regression coefficient suggests that collective contracts increase the student-teacher ratio by about 1.3

students per teacher. All of the other regression coefficients were significant at either the .05 or .01 level, and each had the expected sign.

Class size seems to increase by about one pupil as community population increases by 10,000 and decreases by one when average daily attendance increases by 2,000. An increase in the student-teacher ratio of .15 is associated with each one-point increase in R, while each one-point increase in W leads to a decrease in class size of approximately .04.

There is a serious problem with the models represented by equations (1) and (3). This difficulty, which is also embodied in the previous work on collective negotiations and salaries, arises from the failure of single-equation models to take into account the manner in which salaries and class size seem to be simultaneously determined. Large classes are generally regarded as an undesirable condition of employment by teachers. For this reason they are likely to demand higher salaries as compensation for accepting more students. This implies that large classes lead to higher salaries. On the other hand, school boards confronted with relative fixed budgetary constraints are often forced to increase the pupil-teacher ratio in response to higher salaries. This suggests that higher salaries cause large classes. There is something of a chicken-egg effect at work.

To complicate matters, teachers' organizations often respond to rank-and-file preferences and ask for smaller classes during collective negotiations. School boards in return are frequently willing to grant higher salaries to keep labor peace if teachers are willing to accept more pupils. Salaries and the student-teacher ratio appear to be simultaneously determined in negotiations as well as in an open market. Models which do not take this into account are inappropriate vehicles for explaining either.

In an effort to obtain more appropriate estimates of the parameters determining salaries and class size, a new model was constructed from equations (1) and (3). This was done by inserting Z into equation (1) and S into equation (3) to obtain

$$S = S(Y,W,A,M,E,R,U,Z)$$

$$Z = Z(P,W,A,R,U,S) \ .$$

(4)

Two-stage least-squares estimates of (4) were obtained with the following results:

$$S = 6432.0363 + .0715Y^{***} + 7.1433W^{**} + .0932A^{***}$$
$$(2.9215) \qquad (2.1476) \qquad (5.2172)$$

$$+ 10.7448M^* + 162.0494E^{***} - 10.7033R^{***}$$
$$(1.8361) \qquad (7.9800) \qquad (4.0881)$$

$$+ 163.1253U^{**} + 12.1297Z^{**}$$
$$(1.9936) \qquad (2.1734)$$

$R^2 = .7134$ \hfill t values in parentheses

*significant at the .10 level
**significant at the .05 level
***significant at the .01 level

and

$$Z = 6.8926 + .0001Y^{**} - .0185W^{***} - .0006A^{***}$$
$$(2.6444) \qquad (2.7627) \qquad (3.5864)$$

$$+ .0220R^{***} + 1.0540U^* + .0014S^*$$
$$(7.7772) \qquad (1.8434) \qquad (1.7759)$$

$R^2 = .5028$ \hfill t values in parentheses

*significant at the .10 level
**significant at the .05 level
***significant at the .01 level

These results confirm the relationship between formal contracts and salaries even after the influence of class size is taken into account. Somewhat less persuasive is the association between teachers' organizations and class size. However, the relationship is significant at the .10 level, and the size of the regression coefficient indicates that contracts increase the student-teacher ratio by about one. The positive relationship between class size and salaries is also confirmed. This is in sharp contrast with Thornton's findings, which in most cases did not show significance even at the .10 level between these latter two variables.

Conclusion

We believe our results help clarify the inconsistency in the findings of the most important earlier works on collective negotiations and salaries. As both Thornton, and Baird and Landon have claimed, the fault apparently lies more in the degree of aggregation in Kasper's data than in the research design of the other authors. Our findings strongly indicate that teachers' organizations do indeed increase salaries. This is true in the suburban areas into which collective negotiations have been spreading recently, as well as in the larger cities covered by other studies. Apparently, however, the magnitude of the increases are relatively small. Our estimates suggest that they average around $165.00 per year. This is consistent with the findings of Kasper, Thornton, and Baird and Landon. It is also well within the range which Lewis (1963) has suggested is typical of the impact of teachers' organizations in the private sector. If, as some writers have argued, there are significant differences in the distribution of bargaining power in the public and private sectors, it did not show up in the regressions. (See, for example, the discussion in reading 16.)

In addition, it appears that teachers' organizations are associated with a larger student-teacher ratio. This lends support to the common allegation that school boards are offering teachers higher salaries in exchange for larger classes and that these offers are being accepted. Certainly, there is nothing to suggest that teachers' organizations have had any success in reducing the number of pupils per classroom. However, this is consistent with the recommendation of the President's Commission on School Finance and offers a possibility of significant economies.

If teachers' associations are accepting larger classes for higher pay, the results of the estimates suggest some interesting conclusions concerning the terms of the "trade-off." Generally, our findings indicate that teachers' salaries are being increased by no more than $200.00, while the student-teacher ratio is being increased by about one. With a mean salary of $9,133.00 and an average of 21.3 students per teacher, average salary costs per pupil would appear to be approximately $430.00. It is doubtful whether the difference can be explained by any gains in fringe benefits which are not reflected in salary data. As long as teachers are willing to accept this arrangement, there would appear to be little cause for alarm among taxpayers over the rise of collective negotiations among public school faculties in their districts.

Finally, lest supporters of collective negotiations despair over the size of measured salary effects of formal contracts, it should be pointed out that our estimates may well understate the total influence of teachers' organizations on teacher pay. There is some evidence that unorganized districts have raised pay in response to higher salaries in neighboring areas or have increased salaries to discourage teacher militancy. The size of these "spillover" benefits is unknown. In our sample, since only one-third of the districts had contracts, they may be relatively small. Nevertheless, "spillover" effects combined with the direct impact may make the total effect somewhat more substantial.

References

Baird, Robert N., and Landon, John H. "The Effects of Collective Bargaining on Public School Teachers' Salaries: Comment." *Industrial and Labor Relations Review* 25, no. 3 (April 1972): 410-17.

Final Report of the President's Commission on School Finance. Washington, D.C.: U.S. Government Printing Office, 1972.

Kasper, Hirschel. "The Effects of Collective Bargaining on Public School Teachers' Salaries." *Industrial and Labor Relations Review* 24, no. 1 (October 1970): 57-72.

Lewis, H. G. *Unionism and Relative Wages in the United States.* Chicago: University of Chicago Press, 1963.

Mort, Paul R., and Furno, Orlando F. *Theory and Synthesis of a Sequential Simplex: A Model for Assessing the Effectiveness of Administrative Policies; Correlation Chart* (Institute Research Study no. 12). New York: Teachers College, Columbia University, 1960.

Thornton, Robert J. "The Effects of Collective Negotiations on Teachers' Salaries." *Quarterly Review of Economics and Business* 11, no. 4 (Winter 1971): 37-46.

Vincent, William S. "Class Size." *Encyclopedia of Educational Research* (4th ed.), edited by R. L. Ebel. New York: Macmillan, 1969.

Reading 23
Teacher Salaries and School Decentralization

Robert N. Baird and John H. Landon

Articles in education journals have recently expressed considerable interest in the major financial problems associated with public school reorganizations that would decentralize both the planning and operation of the educational program. For example, Callahan and Shalala (1969) recently reviewed how decentralization would affect financial resources available to the new districts by exploring the possible changes in property values, tax efforts, and state aid for three different forms of decentralization. Krughoff (1969) examined both the financial and qualitative changes that would likely be caused by the adoption of a voucher system which would channel public funds into privately operated schools. Paralleling these articles in education journals, a series of studies in the economic literature has been concerned with the determination of teachers' salaries. For example, Hellriegel et al. (reading 11) conducted a behavioral analysis of collective bargaining attitudes among teachers and found that lower relative salaries are associated with positive attitudes toward collective negotiations. Kasper (1970) studied average teacher salary and

Reprinted by permission from *Education and Urban Society* 4, no. 2 (February 1972), pp. 197-210. Copyright 1972 by Sage Publications.

percentage of teachers unionized, both by state, and found no consistent relationship between the two, but Thornton (1971), using data for 87 large school systems, found unionization significantly and positively related to teachers' salaries. In separate studies, Hirsch (1967) and Kershaw and McKean (1962) found that rigidities in salary schedules prevent teacher labor markets from reaching equilibrium and cause teacher shortages in particular fields of specialization.

We find these education and economic studies interesting for many different reasons, but a bridge between the two types of study is completely missing. The education studies fail to consider possible impact on teachers' salaries in the costs of school district reorganization, and the economics studies ignore school district organization as a determinant of these salaries. To us, this is a serious failing, and we shall attempt to correct it in this paper. In particular, this paper attempts to measure the effect of competition among school districts on the determination of teachers' salaries. We will conclude that local districts do compete strongly for first-year teachers and that the degree of competition is positively related to the number of districts within the community. Accordingly, any move to break up a large school district into several smaller independent districts will lead to increased competition and increased salaries.

The first major section of this paper discusses the principal determinants of teachers' salaries, giving special emphasis to the effect of interdistrict competition for personnel. The second major section presents the statistical tabulations that define the test of the proposed hypothesis. Lastly, conclusions and implications are presented in the third and final major section.

Determinants of Teachers' Salaries

We contend that the principal determinants of teachers' salaries are (1) the ability of the community to pay; (2) the willingness of the community to pay; (3) the supply of teachers to the community; and (4) the extent of district fragmentation (and resulting degree of competition) within the local area.

Ability to Pay

A community's willingness to provide education services will depend on the financial resources for this purpose available either locally or from state or federal grants. In areas where financial resources are large relative to the number of students to be educated, the sacrifice involved in providing educational services will be low. The value of taxable property in the community or the level of per capita or per student income constitute different measurements of this ability, with the choice of the appropriate criteria depending on tax options available to cities in the various states. While state aid affects ability to pay among states, the level of state aid is determined outside the local community. There are certainly strong pressures on the state from communities to provide high levels of state aid, and the response to these pressures probably depends in part on the ability of the state government to pay. However, at any moment in time, the relevant factor in salary determination is the amount of state aid actually forthcoming. In particular, it is the combination of the state aid in hand and the ability of the local district to raise money that determines the total school budget available for allocation.

Federal aid to public elementary and secondary schools amounts to only about 10 percent of all government spending for this purpose. It is of considerable importance only for areas with large military operations and for the District of Columbia. As with state aid, at any given time federal aid may be taken as fixed, and feedback and national ability to pay can be ignored. To the extent that federal spending is relevant to the issue of teachers' salaries, it is relevant only to the overall level and not to the distribution of salaries among the school systems. Only in the exceptional cases mentioned above would there be any likelihood of federal influence on relative pay levels. In our empirical work, we include only local ability to pay.

Willingness to Pay

Although ability to pay is important, it is the community's willingness to pay that actually provides the thrust necessary for the establishment of a high-quality educational program. The state may establish a minimum willingness to pay by setting teacher certification standards, pupil-teacher ratios, or per capita spending requirements, but maximum willingness is bounded only by the aspirations of the community.

The principal factors likely to affect substantially the willingness of a community to pay are the extent to which the parents are educated, the ratio of parents to nonparents in the community, and the age distribution of the population. While such factors as income and occupational distribution will also influence the esteem in which education is held, they are too highly correlated with education to be reasonably separate arguments.

Parental education as well as the general educational level of the community should influence the desired quality and quantity of public education. While it is true that aspirations for their children usually exceed the parents' own attainments, the level of these aspirations should be greater still among parents of higher educational backgrounds. Additionally, the ability to understand the needs and recognize the quality of an educational system should be greater among more educated communities. This understanding and recognition should result in a greater willingness to take on the burdens of supporting a high level of public education.

The greater the percentage of the population with a direct personal interest in the success of the educational system, the greater will be the collective desire for a good system. This desire should be manifest in a willingness to take on a greater tax burden to support the system. The ratio of parents to nonparents in the area is one reasonable index of the extent of such direct concern. Parents with children in the school system should feel more compelled to support the schools than do either childless parents or parents whose children are finished with their public school education.* Similarly, these parents should be more cognizant of educational problems and better able to evaluate school needs. It is also likely that the importance of private schools will influence willingness to pay for public education. The number of parents of children being privately educated should properly be added to the numbers of nonparents for the purpose of estimating probable support for public educational expenditures.

The age distribution of the population may exert an independent effect on the desire of the community to pay for public education. This may be true for a variety of reasons. The presence in the community of a large segment of retired persons living on fixed incomes may not only influence the relative voting strength of the nonparent population, but additionally may constrain the willingness of the whole community to increase the cost of living for these people

---

*This may not be true in communities where a large number of the nonparents have relatives in the public schools.

through general increases in the property tax. On the other hand, a substantial portion of very young parents may mean a large rental housing component that does not feel as directly the cost of supporting higher levels of public educational spending.

A large rental component in the local housing market may relate positively to willingness to pay, reflecting lower direct sensitivity to property taxes, or negatively, reflecting either lower attachment to the district among the rental community or fewer children. It is likely that the impact of this factor will vary with the type of community and the type of rental housing.

Area Supply of Teachers

It is useful and desirable to distinguish the factors which influence the supply of teachers in a geographic region (such as a Standard Metropolitan Statistical Area) from those whose primary effect is on the supply of individual school districts within these areas. Teacher supply in the region is likely to play a substantial role in determining the level of compensation teachers will receive at any point in time and (in a dynamic system) the speed with which salary adjustments will be made. Speed of adjustment will also reflect the rate at which the school systems are growing. Rapidly growing systems must be more sensitive to the competition of neighboring districts than are those whose sole concern is with the retention of the present supply. (This merely assumes some measure of inertia and a greater responsiveness to salary differences among new teachers and those who are moving anyway.)

The four factors which seem important in determining teacher supply for the region are the degree of geographic mobility of teachers; the extent to which present and prospective teachers are secondary wage earners in families; the demand for the talents of potential teachers in noneducational employment in the region; and the extent to which teachers are organized (i.e., unionized) and are willing to withhold services to back up salary demands. All of these factors and their interrelationships will influence the responsiveness of teachers to changes in compensation.

The mobility of teachers from region to region is affected by differences in certification requirements between regions and between states. Once a teacher is certified to teach in a particular geographic area and has met all of the area requirements, he is less likely to move outside the area than within it. The extent of this barrier to mobility is a function of the range of interregional differences. Such barriers tend to curtail mobility from low standard areas to high standard areas and between areas of any level when the requirements are substantially different.

Interregional mobility is also a function of differences in climatic conditions, life styles, and the strength of the ties of family and friendships. Strong preference for a particular climate, a particular size of city, a region of the country, or a way of life can limit the mobility of any group of people and thereby reduce their willingness to move to obtain a higher salary. Similarly, the strength of family and friendship ties in the aggregate will be negatively related to this willingness. The influence of these structural determinants should be weaker among teachers than among most other professions since their strength is likely to vary negatively with education.

Teachers who are secondary wage earners are tied to the location of the spouse's job. For such teachers, the decision to change locations must be based on the net change in total monetary and nonmonetary compensation of both husband and wife. This decreases the sensitivity to any given percentage change in teacher remuneration. Similarly, if the teaching job is considered as temporary (before the children arrive, to reach some target savings, to put the children through college, and so on), movement to a new community in response to a change in teacher salary alone is unlikely.

The opportunities for teachers in jobs outside education should also influence the responsiveness of salary to teacher supply in the area. These opportunities should affect some areas of teaching more than others. Other types of professional employment provide the closest alternative to a teaching career for teachers with skills demanded by other employers. To maintain an adequate teaching staff, a school district must establish a system of compensation which will attract and keep from alternative employment the necessary numbers of qualified individuals. Having staffed the schools with qualified teachers, a district presumably may increase the quality of the personnel by still further increases in compensation.

Institutional arrangements typically make it impossible to raise the starting salaries of teachers other than uniformly. Salary compensation for teachers with transferable skills, therefore, raises the level of all salaries. This is expensive for the district. The ability of the market mechanism to adjust supply by attracting relatively more personnel to the areas with the greatest combined demands of education and industry is seriously retarded.

The requirement for salary uniformity implies that a school system must choose between the high level of average compensation necessary to recruit qualified teachers in applied fields and lower general quality of teachers in these areas. As long as the uniformity constraint retards selective competition for personnel, the level of salaries must adjust to total supply, and there will be relative difficulty in obtaining personnel for various specialized areas of teaching.

The extent to which teachers are organized may also influence the wage required to obtain area teacher supply. A strong and militant teacher union can preclude the employment of any teachers at salary levels below their minimum demands. The regional teacher associations may recommend that teachers not consider employment in areas where salaries are below specific standards. Either of these types of teacher organization will tend to reduce sharply the number of teachers available at salaries below the suggested level.

Intra-Area Fragmentation

Available alternative employment within the teaching profession greatly affects the salary required to hire additional high-quality teachers for the district. This is the principal focus of this paper. Nearby school districts increase the alternatives available to the teacher without moving. In a region with several school districts, a secondary wage earner, a temporary worker, or a teacher with strong local ties has reasonable alternatives without leaving the area or the teaching profession. In fact, all the barriers to mobility discussed above will combine to confine the choice of many teachers to the local areas.

A large number of school districts not only increases the alternatives of present teachers but also presents incoming teachers with more options. When several systems are expanding, teachers with the highest qualifications will presumably locate in districts offering the highest levels of overall compensation. This should induce competition between districts in starting salary. In order to keep its present teachers or add well-qualified teachers to its staff, a district must remain competitive with surrounding districts.

A geographic concentration of population having a single public school system makes that system in a very real sense a "monopsonist," a single buyer of teachers' services. Teachers currently in the district can move within the profession only at the cost of geographic dislocation. Nonteaching employment and the private schools offer poor alternatives, at best. Accordingly, without growth, the district may pay salaries well below those of similar districts in other areas. Even in an expanding system, adequate staffing may be provided in the absence of competitive salaries by a normal influx of educators whose spouses find employment in the area.

Perhaps a simple illustration of how these forces can lead to the effect described is in order. Imagine a community with many school districts, including several small districts with a total of 10,000 students, and one district with 25,000. Differences in incomes, educational attainment, and other variables described in the three previous subsections might lead to different preferences for education between the districts. Suppose further that the desired student-teacher ratio in the smaller districts was 20 to 1, calling for 500 teachers. Suppose that the large district preferred a student-teacher ratio of 40 to 1 and thus required 625 teachers. The going wage for teachers in the community would then have to be high enough to attract 1,125 teachers to the area, and we would expect a considerable degree of competition between districts in vying for the more capable applicants. However, if for some reason the districts were to merge, the desired student-teacher ratio would likely be the result of a compromise that would weight more heavily the desires of the large district. Suppose that the compromise ratio is 35 students per teacher. With 35,000 students in the merged district, this requires a teaching staff of 1,000 teachers. The going rate for teachers then would only have to be high enough to attract this smaller number to the area and, more importantly, applicants would not be able to play one district against the other. The average salary in the second illustration could therefore be much lower than in the first.*

We anticipate, therefore, competition for teachers within metropolitan areas to be an important determinant of salary levels. The only influence likely to offset this intraregional competition is collu-

---

*A lower salary would result even if the teacher-student ratios of the merging districts were identical. Competition between the districts for the best of the available supply of educators would undoubtedly raise the level of compensation above that necessary to attract that many qualified educators to the region as a whole. The merged district would avoid this salary competition.

sion among local districts. To the extent that they agree on standard rates for incoming teachers, the districts in the area could avoid competitive salary increases. The probability of an effective buying cartel should decline as the number of districts increases and as the market for teachers becomes tight.

This analysis would be incomplete, however, without recognizing an additional factor bearing on the extent of monopsony, the comparability of the districts. If, for example, one district is far superior in terms of facilities, students, or in some other respect, substitutability will be decreased. However, as long as wage rates are not uniform and change over time, there is no reason to believe that salaries will not be influenced by competition as well.

Multiple Regression Analysis

In order to test the competitive hypothesis described above, we employed multiple regression analysis. That is, we assume that the basic teacher salary results from a weighted sum of the different forces described above. The weights of these forces are the regression coefficients of a multiple regression equation. The statistical technique by which estimates of these weights are derived yields coefficients that are normally distributed. Accordingly, an estimate for which the standard deviation is large (relative to the size of the estimate) is said to be unimportant or insignificant, and an estimate for which the standard deviation is relatively small is said to be important or significant in determining the basic teacher salary. For our study, we gathered data for 136 large school districts (over 25,000 students) for beginning teacher salary (designated in the following equation as S), the natural log of number of school districts in the same county (N) as a measure of competition between districts, the per capita income of the county as a proxy for ability to pay (I), and the percentage of school revenue raised from local sources (LS) and the effective tax rate for the district (TR) as measures of willingness to pay. The estimated equation based on these data was:*

---

*Data are taken from the National Education Association (1968a, 1968b), Standard Rate and Data Service (1968), U.S. Department of Commerce (1967, 1969), and U.S. Department of Health, Education, and Welfare (1967). A more complete set of regression results may be found in Landon and Baird (1971).

$$S = 4132 + 116.04 \, N + 242.32 \, I + 4.90 \, LS + 4.30 \, TR$$
$$(21.67) \qquad (64.30) \quad (2.01) \qquad (6.68)$$

$R^2 = .47$

The numbers in the equation are the weights or regression coefficients for the respective variables, and the numbers in parentheses are the standard deviations for the weights. The weights for the competition variable and the income variable are positive and highly significant (the weights are at least 1.96 times the size of the standard deviation indicating 95 percent confidence in the result), and the coefficient for percentage of revenue raised locally is positive and significant (weight is at least 1.28 times the standard deviation, indicating 90 percent confidence). Note that the variable for competition is not expressed as the number of districts in the county, but as the log of the number of districts. The equation therefore implies that an increase in the number of districts in the county of 1 percent will lead, *other things being equal,* to an annual increase in starting teachers' salaries of $116.04. Since this is a statistically significant figure, we feel that our previous arguments concerning the effect of competition among school districts are confirmed.

Conclusion

We have argued that economic theory predicts higher school teacher salaries in areas where many school districts compete for teacher services than in areas where there are only a few, or perhaps even just one, school districts. A statistical test using multiple regression analysis supports this theory. In terms of educational policy, the implication is quite obvious: decentralization of large school districts into more and more numerous and highly competitive school districts poses a hidden source of increased expenditures for the newly created districts. Failure to recognize this pressure for increased wages could easily result in a long series of financial headaches and frustrations in boards in the decentralized districts, and voters who do not understand what economic forces lay behind these pressures may not be sympathetic at the ballot box.

It should also be noted that the decentralization of school districts will not only affect the average teacher salary in the area, but also the variation of salaries in districts within the community. Under the present fixed schedules for salaries, assignment of staff to the more undesirable school must be at least partly a matter for coercion. New teachers in the district are particularly vulnerable to assignment in these schools. Under decentralization, especially with a voucher system, teachers will be given greater freedom in choosing their schools. Accordingly, schools in the less desirable neighborhoods will have to pay a financial premium to attract teachers, and the premium will be greater as the desired quality of instruction in those areas increases. Conversely, those schools in the better neighborhoods will probably find that more teachers want to work there than the schools are able to hire. As a result, salaries may be decreased to reduce the size of this excess supply.*

Of course, the fact that decentralization of school districts will lead to increased instructional costs should not be the primary consideration in developing new school district boundaries. A compelling reason for having a large number of school districts within any given area is that this permits educational curricula to be more closely tailored to the differing preferences of individual communities. Such advantages may more than offset increased personnel costs of the type studied in this paper. Similarly, unified hiring by area districts would offset the higher costs we predict for decentralized districts.

References

Callahan, J., and Shalala, D. "Some Fiscal Dimensions of Three Hypothetical Decentralization Plans." *Education and Urban Society* 2 (November 1969): 40-53.

Hirsch, W. Z. "Demand and Supply of Teachers in California." *California Management Review* 10 (Fall 1967): 27-34.

Kasper, H. "The Impact of Collective Bargaining on Public School Teachers." *Industrial and Labor Relations Review* 23 (October 1970): 57-72.

Kershaw, J. A., and McKean, R. N. *Teacher Shortages and Salary Schedules.* New York: American, 1962.

---

*This is simply a different manifestation of the problem that now plagues many districts that have the same salary schedule for all areas of teacher specialization. Since English teachers are offered the same salary as physics teachers with the same background, there is no simple means of curing surpluses of English teachers and shortages of physics teachers. Salary differentials could be used to solve this problem if districts abandoned fixed salary schedules.

Krughoff, R. "Private Schools for the Public." *Education and Urban Society* 2 (November 1969): 54-79.

Landon, J. H., and Baird, R. N. "Monopsony in the Market for Public School Teachers." *American Economic Review* 61 (December 1971): 966-71.

National Education Association. *Salary Schedules for Teachers, 1966-1967.* Washington, D.C.: The Association, 1968a.

National Education Association. *Selected Statistics of Local School Systems, 1966-1967.* Washington, D.C.: The Association, 1968b.

Standard Rate and Data Service. *Newspaper Circulation Analysis, 1967-1968.* Skokie, Ill.: The Service, 1968.

Thornton, R. "The Effects of Collective Negotiations on Teachers' Salaries." *Quarterly Review of Economics and Business* 11 (Winter 1971): 37-46.

U.S. Department of Commerce. *Census of Governments.* Washington, D.C.: U.S. Government Printing Office, 1967.

U.S. Department of Commerce. *Statistical Abstract of the United States.* Washington, D.C.: U.S. Government Printing Office, 1969.

U.S. Department of Health, Education, and Welfare. *Education Directory.* Washington, D.C.: U.S. Government Printing Office, 1967.

Reading 24

Negotiations at the Crossroads: Increased Professionalization or Reinforced Bureaucracy

Michael J. Murphy and David Hoover

It is often said that all militant teachers seek is increased wages and benefits; that is, teacher unionism is fundamentally a welfare movement. Like their industrial counterpart, the argument goes, teacher unions concentrate on improving wages and benefits, ignoring larger professional, organizational, or instructional issues. Although this favorite explanation of the motives behind teacher militancy continues dominant, there is a growing body of information which challenges this conventional thinking. From analyses of the behaviors and successes of the teacher unions over the last several decades, two facts emerge: (1) teachers' militancy has not had much effect on their economic returns; (2) collective bargaining procedures and resultant contracts have already had considerable impact on administrative and governance practices.

This is evident in the space allotted collective bargaining in the various administrator and school board journals, in the anguish of administrator groups over their collective bargaining impacted "roles," and in the huge commitments of time and money to con-

An earlier version of this reading appeared in *Teachers College Institute of Administrative Research* 14, no. 2 (February 1974).

tract negotiation and maintenance. Thus far, at least, the principal result of teacher bargaining has been more organizational than economic.

And there is reason to believe organizational restructuring will continue as the major output of teacher militancy and bargaining. Four principal factors cause us to discount conventional "bread and butter" assumptions in constructing a forecast of the impact of teacher unionism:

1. Although teacher unions will work to increase wages and benefits, they will be unable to introduce major distortions in income distribution systems.

2. The ideology of teaching stresses professional autonomy and hence discounts direction and control functions of administrators and supervisors (rights of management).

3. Through the contract medium, teachers have acquired substantial influence over rule definition. They are not likely to abandon (or be displaced from) this crucial organizational power.

4. Legal provisions notwithstanding, both rhetoric and behavior suggest that teachers consider all educational matters properly negotiable.*

It is our intent to elaborate on these propositions and to briefly submit possible functional and dysfunctional consequences of bargaining.

Teacher Unions and Wages

Trade unions in America have traditionally emphasized wages and benefits. Samuel Gompers, when asked to state the goals of American labor, reportedly said, "more, more, more now!" Preoccupation with economic benefits continues as the trademark of most private sector unions.†

---

*Legal provisions and court interpretations are moving in the direction of expanding definitions.

†This is not to say that labor in America has not engaged other issues, only that its "bread and butter" issue orientation has focused energy on securing higher wages and improved working conditions for its members.

It may be that teacher unions have also taken improved wages and working conditions as their primary objective, and so direct their energy. Or it may be that, as they are unions, we expect them to exhibit such behavior and thus view most union activities as means to larger economic ends. It may be that we are all conditioned by the widely circulated proposition that teacher militancy was a response to wage dissatisfaction.

Whatever the case, available evidence suggests that increased militancy and rapid institution of collective bargaining at best have had only marginal impact on teacher earnings. While it is true that in the thirty-five years between 1933-34 and 1968-69 teachers' average annual salary steadily rose from $1,227 to $8,272, this over 500 percent increase must be viewed in the context of changes in annual incomes generally. Such a comparison reveals that changes in teachers' incomes have been matched by changes in per capita income. Table 1 shows that the "salary-per capita ratio"* for each year has remained remarkably constant except for brief periods during the depression when teacher salaries declined more slowly than general income, and during World War II when teacher salaries lagged behind the upward surge in general income levels. Erick Lindman (1970), in revealing these and similar wage consistencies (e.g., in comparisons of average teacher salaries to "salaries and wages per employed person," and in state analyses), concludes that salaries paid teachers have kept pace with other salaries since the 1930s, but have shown no relative gain. It can be inferred from the work of Lindman and others that economic returns to teachers are a function of the larger economic system and not particularly subject to internal pressures generated by militant teachers.

Teacher Unions and Organizational Change

If unions have been unsuccessful in altering the wage status of teachers, can it be argued that the teacher organizations are impotent? We think not, and suggest that to be preoccupied with teacher union influence on wage rates is to miss important events associated

---

*Average annual salary of instructional staff divided by U.S. per capita personal income. Per capita income figures appear low because they are derived by dividing all personal income by the total population (not just wage earners).

Table 1
Ratio of the Average Annual Salary of Public School Instructional Staff to Per Capita Income Payments

Year	Salary in Dollars	Per Capita Income	Salary-Per Capita Income Ratio
1929-30	1420	703	2.02
1931-32	1417	529	2.68
1933-34	1227	375	3.27
1935-36	1283	472	2.72
1937-38	1374	573	2.40
1939-40	1441	556	2.59
1941-42	1507	719	2.09
1943-44	1728	1102	1.57
1945-46	1995	1234	1.62
1947-48	2639	1316	2.00
1949-50	3010	1384	2.17
1951-52	3450	1652	2.09
1953-54	3825	1804	2.12
1955-56	4156	1876	2.21
1957-58	4702	2045	2.30
1959-60	5174	2161	2.39
1961-62	5700	2264	2.52
1963-64	6240	2455	2.54
1965-66	6700	2765	2.42
1967-68	7630	3162	2.41
1968-69	8272	3421	2.42

Source: Per capita income payments, from U.S. Department of Commerce (1955 and 1969). Average annual salary of instructional staff, from U.S. Office of Education (1968) and National Education Association (1969-70).

with the growth of teacher unions. The unions' principal long-term impact in education will be organizational (e.g., the displacement of previously assumed administrator and school board decision prerogatives), not economic. There are several reasons for this.

Teacher unions do not function in the same organizational and ideological climate as their industrial counterparts. Teachers and their unions give no evidence of accepting Frederick Winslow Taylor's advice that an employee's duty is first and foremost to do as he is told by his boss.* Rather, teachers seem to view their occupation

---

*Taylor's "principles of scientific management" required acceptance of several assumptions: (1) management's prime function is to determine the best

as something of a "calling" (not merely supplying labor for a day's wages), with strong claims on the job definition processes. Further, educational systems do not have a specially recruited managerial elite like most corporations, the military, etc. Whereas most corporate managers need not have been assembly line workers, nor military officers infantrymen, educational managers must first have been teachers for at least three to five years. And finally, professional norms emphasize that decisions concerning clients' (pupils') educational well being must be left to teachers. Played out, these norms require that teachers seek to minimize instructional decision roles of parents, administrators, and school boards alike. Therefore, there is little reason to expect teacher unions to satisfy themselves with present organizational and governance arrangements if they possess means to alter them.

Educational Institutions as Rule Bureaucracies

Most would agree that in complex organizations there is need for control and capacity to monitor member performance. Anderson (1966) has identified four patterns of control which may exist in educational organizations:

1. Direct personal supervision and direction;
2. Impersonal mechanisms such as job standardization ("teacher proof" instructional packages) and performance records;
3. Bureaucratic rules; and
4. Professional standards.

Although many school organizations will entrust the control function to mechanisms in combination (e.g., direct supervision, bureaucratic rules, and professional standards), it is generally assumed that one pattern or mechanism is predominant. This is so because there are conflicts or redundancies among types which reduce the likelihood that they can function in concert. Bureaucratic

---

way to do a job and then see that it is done that way, (2) work could be most efficiently performed when division of labor and task routinization was maximized, (3) workers were primarily motivated by instrumental rewards (e.g., money wages). These assumptions are no longer generally accepted as valid.

rules and professional standards are largely incompatible as control strategies, for example. Job standardization reduces the utility of direct supervision.

Of possible control strategies, there has been little dependence in schools on impersonal mechanisms (job standardization). Direct personal supervision is generally impractical given ecological arrangements in schools. Teachers do their work in spatial isolation (i.e., classroom units). Administrators are unable to view much of a given teacher's work performance—probably only a few hours of it over the course of a year. The vast majority of work, therefore, goes on unobserved and unsupervised.

The trend in schools is toward increased dependence on bureaucratic rules to control behavior. This movement is encouraged by collective bargaining as teachers seek control of the rule-making process rather than dismantling it to substitute professional standards and autonomy as a way of life. In this instance of control by bureaucratic rules, work is directed not by supervisors, but by an explicit body of impersonal rules which prescribe and proscribe behavior.

The outcome of collective bargaining has generally been an increasingly complex body of rules and regulations which explicitly govern teacher behavior, rights and privileges of administrators and teachers, and minimum performance expectations. This codification of organizational authority in a body of rules (written contracts) has several side effects.

1. Direct authority of administrators and supervisors is reduced.

2. Undue emphasis is placed on minimum behavior standards.

3. Goal displacements occur, with rules becoming more important as ends than as means. As a consequence the organization may become less adaptive and less responsive to individual students.

4. Rules and regulations reduce individual teacher autonomy and the power of professional standards.

Teacher Unions as a Professional Influence

Although the organizational effect of collective bargaining has been to intensify the bureaucratic character of schools, it is equally capable of enhancing professional autonomy and decentralized policy making. Thus, it could become a force in shaping the school as a professional organization, with dependence on professional standards and a collegial rather than a hierarchical structure.

Ronald Corwin (1966) sees teacher militancy as a stage in professionalization. He specifies three key factors in a struggle toward a professional model: (1) the amount of autonomy to be gained for the vocation; (2) the ability to legitimize that autonomy with legal sanctions; and (3) the exclusive license to practice. Most would agree with Corwin that autonomy is a critical factor in professional practice. Inasmuch as the professional is expected to bring to bear a body of theory and research on the solution of a unique client's problem, it requires the autonomy to make a diagnosis and to carry out a prescription.

Corwin argues further that the professionalization of education will be fraught with conflict.

... In order to increase its autonomy, however, a vocational group must challenge the parties which have been in control. And unless these authorities are willing to voluntarily relinquish their hold, the vocation will defy them by objecting, criticizing or by legal action and more ambitious forms of militancy. Professionalization in this sense is a militant process—and a likely source of organizational conflict. (1966, p. 46)

In this context, it may be seen that education is passing through a critical period in its existence. On the one hand, emphasis by teacher organizations on expanding the control function of impersonal rules will lead to an increased bureaucratization of the school. The result will be less flexibility and less professional behavior. There are professionalizing side benefits which accompany increased rule dependence, however: (1) the absolute authority of administrators and supervisors has been reduced—a necessary prerequisite to a collegial organization; (2) the decision-making process in schools is becoming more democratized.* Thus, depending in large measure on how teacher unions exercise their options, schools may be increasingly bureaucratized or emerge as the long advocated professional model.

_____

*There is evidence which suggests that in schools with active union-building representatives, teachers feel more involved in the essential decision-making process of the schools. See, for instance, Goldberg and Harbotkin (1970), and Ellman (1973).

References

Anderson, James G. "Bureaucratic Rules: Bearers of Organizational Authority." *Educational Administration Quarterly* 2 (1966): 7-34.

Corwin, Ronald G. *Staff Conflicts in the Public Schools.* Columbus: Ohio State University Press, 1966.

Ellman, Neil G. *The Role of the United Federation of Teachers Chapters in the Union and Their Respective Schools.* Ph.D. dissertation, Teachers College, Columbia University, 1973.

Goldberg, Albert I., and Harbotkin, Lisa. "The Teachers Union Chapter in the Elementary School." *Teachers College Record* LXXI (May 1970): 647-54.

Lindman, Erick L. "Are Teachers' Salaries Improving?" *Phi Delta Kappan* (April 1970): 420-22.

National Education Association. *Estimates of School Statistics.* Washington, D.C.: The Association, 1969-70.

U.S. Department of Commerce. *Survey of Current Business.* Washington, D.C.: U.S. Government Printing Office, 1955 and 1969.

U.S. Office of Education. *Digest of Educational Statistics.* Washington, D.C.: U.S. Government Printing Office, 1968.

Reading 25

Collective Bargaining and School Finance Reform

Michael J. Murphy, Clifford Barton, and Richard P. Mills

Collective Bargaining and School Finance

For a variety of reasons, the task of relating school finance reform and collective bargaining is a difficult one. Finance reform proposals come in many variants and shades. Each of these approaches (e.g., full state funding, power equalizing, shared cost) may impact bargaining systems somewhat differently. Full state funding, for instance, establishes the state as the educational fiscal unit. Because bargaining units usually conform to fiscal units, this plan virtually compels statewide bargaining. Bargaining implications of shared cost models are more subtle.

School finance reforms are still in the proposal state. Nowhere are they implemented. Empirical validation of consequences is, as yet, impossible. No literature illuminating the interaction of collective bargaining and revenue source systems has had time to develop. As a consequence, collective bargaining problems, if any, posed by reform models, and reform problems, if any, posed by collective bargaining, are poorly understood.

Reprinted by permission from *Teachers College Research Bulletin* 15, no. 3 (March 1975), pp. 3-11.

Education is what economists call a highly labor intensive industry. By that they mean the delivery of educational service is mainly a function of labor (people work) rather than machine work. The production of goods and services in all sectors is a function of the expenditure of labor and capital (i.e., machinery). In capital intensive industries people are employed, by and large, to make managerial decisions and to tend the machinery. On the other extreme, labor intensive industries (such as education) hire people not only to make managerial decisions, but to perform most production and service tasks as well.

The meaning of this to educational finance reform is that most of the educational dollar is spent to pay people. In all, about 85 percent of a district operating budget is wage related (Levin 1972). Therefore, when we talk about educational finance reform, we must inevitably talk also about the amount and the ways people working for school districts are paid.

In its simplest form, collective bargaining is a bilateral decision process through which organized employees and employers set wages, benefits, and working conditions. Since the wages that teachers are paid and the services they perform in large measure determine the cost of education, and because wage rates and conditions of work are now usually established bilaterally through collective bargaining, it is obvious that the process of collective bargaining lies in the thick of educational finance reform issues. Yet bargaining reform moves in one orbit, finance reform in another.* The intimate relationship between the two is seldom explored.

There are a number of finance reform alternatives now vying for popular support. They range from systems in which the state would assume full funding to more modest proposals leading to redistribution of certain property tax revenues. The plans most often discussed are:

1. *Full State Funding.* In its most basic form, full state funding means that the state picks up the tab for educational costs out of its own treasury. Under this system, state funds are usually distributed to school districts according to some costs/needs formula. The two

---

*There are two bills now before the United States Congress to establish a federal regulatory system for teacher bargaining similar in scope to provisions of the National Labor Relations Act which governs private sector bargaining.

simplest distribution formulas are cost reimbursement and per student capita allowances. In a cost reimbursement system, the state would simply assume the fiscal obligations of the school district as they are incurred. In a per student capita system, the state would fix a per student expenditure level. The district revenue would be student enrollment multiplied by this amount. Full state funding proposals are generally more complex than these two illustrations. Reimbursement proposals, for instance, usually include expenditure ceilings. Per student capita systems nearly always acknowledge the differential costs of educating different types of students (e.g., handicapped, disadvantaged). Some indexing or weighting formula, often complex, is usually recommended (see Levin 1972; Sherman 1974).

2. *Power Equalizing.* Power equalizing systems employ mechanisms to equalize the taxing power of school districts in the state (see Coons 1970). Usually this is accomplished by replacing the actual tax base of a school district (i.e., assessed valuation per pupil) with a computational tax base which would be the same for all school districts. As long as they maintain a minimum expenditure level, districts can choose their own tax rate. The revenue they receive is computed from the following formula:

$$\text{Revenue} = \text{tax rate} \times \text{computational tax base.}$$

Surpluses or deficiencies between the revenue required by the above formula, and the actual amount of money raised by a given tax rate accrue to the state. Thus, if a district elects a $200 tax rate, and that tax rate raises less than the formula amount the state makes up the difference. Conversely, if a tax rate of $200 raises more than the formula amount, the state takes the surplus for redistribution to poorer districts. The formula for state aid is as follows:

$$\begin{aligned} \text{State aid} = &\ (\text{computational tax base} \times \text{tax rate}) \\ &- (\text{real tax base} \times \text{tax rate}). \end{aligned}$$

Power equalizing proposals may contain differential cost weighting equations as in full state funding programs.

3. *Shared Cost.* Shared cost proposals also guarantee revenue generating power to local districts, usually through a minimum tax base established by the state. Thus, if the assessed value per pupil is

below some established level, the state minimum is substituted. Revenue is then calculated on the substitution tax base, with the state contributing the difference between revenue actually raised with a given tax and revenue called for in the substitution formula. Shared cost differs from power equalizing principally in that there is no negative equalizing rate, i.e., districts whose assessed value per pupil exceeds the state guarantee may retain all money raised.

Consequences of Reform Proposals to Bargaining

If full state funding were enacted, the union would have more to gain by pressuring the legislature for a larger share for its district (Simon 1973); and if it were not for the fact that the scope of bargaining might tend to expand into so-called administrative and policy areas, we might see boards and unions forming coalitions to bargain with the legislature. There is some historical precedence for such a coalition. Over the years the State Teacher Associations and School Board Associations joined forces to press for funding changes at the state level.

If power equalizing was the alternative selected by the legislature, unions would have to push their local district for high tax rates, and they would get nowhere in the more affluent communities because of prohibitively high tax rate increments that would be required under the power equalizing idea. The union would be better off seeking a change to full state funding by lobbying at the state level, or using their power in the state capital to modify power equalizing formulas.

Shared cost models do not threaten wage rates in affluent districts the way power equalizing does. Nevertheless, unions will be quick to recognize the advantage in applying pressure to increase the state guaranteed minimum assessed value per student. In that the majority of teachers may work in districts likely to fall below the minimum, there will be substantial pressure to raise it, thereby raising district revenue and allowing higher wage rates. As the minimum assessed value per pupil level is raised more districts will be affected by it, hence the pressure for upward movement will be increased. Since teachers in districts whose revenue is not affected by the minimum guarantee (i.e., affluent districts) have no reason to oppose increases in minimum guaranteed levels, there should be no internal conflict over union policy to lobby for increased minimum guarantee levels, and to devote union resources toward this end.

Though major reform proposals are quite different in form, and in their immediate consequence to district budget practices, they would all seem to set in motion forces leading to greater state level union activity. The state union will become relatively stronger, and a consequence of its strength may be the transfer of bargaining decisions to the state level.

Forces That Point Toward Bargaining Centralization

Teacher associations at the present time bargain at the district level because local boards create budgets and make educational policy (within the guidelines laid down by the State Department of Education). The net effect of reform which centralizes finance decisions will be to cause unions and school boards to press for more centralized or statewide salary bargaining. Unions will quickly sense that the source of wage increases is no longer local government. School boards, fearing greater union monopoly of the educational dollar, will press for statewide salary controls. This situation will join with other pressures, unrelated to the finance reform issue, that point in the direction of centralized collective bargaining in education.

A major reason for the interest in centralized bargaining is the discovery by both unions and school boards that the bargaining process consumes enormous quantities of time and energy. Negotiations and contract administration are year round concerns that crowd out other administrative duties. In cases where bargaining is conducted by members of the district's regular staff (such as assistant superintendent, personnel director, or the superintendent), these officers report spending up to one-third of their time preparing for and engaging in contract negotiations, and maintaining the contract during its life. In that most administrators are not trained in bargaining, boards are often hurt by their lack of expertise in negotiation. In his survey of settlements in New York state, Myron Lieberman (1971) found many badly written and, thus, costly contracts which he attributed to inexperience on both sides. When districts employ outside professional bargainers to conduct their negotiation, on the other hand, the cost is considerable. One hundred dollars an hour until midnight, two hundred after, is a common fee structure. Over the course of bargaining, a sizeable negotiators' fee is generated.

There is some evidence that school systems and teacher unions are already engaged in what is referred to in the private sector as a *pattern bargaining* process; that is, a contract with one district in a region sets the settlement pattern for all school systems in the region (Sommi 1974). Once the pattern is established, school districts refuse to pay more than the established wage rate and the unions refuse to settle for less. In essence, pattern bargaining sets regional contracts. Other developments along these lines lie in the use of BOCES units in New York to provide bargaining service to multiple affiliated school districts. Similar forms of regional cooperatives are appearing elsewhere in the country.

The burden of bargaining is not on the districts alone. In spite of their apparent rich experience and resource base, teacher unions and associations are similarly taxed by the fragmented (i.e., district level) bargaining systems now in operation. Bargaining occurs at the same time throughout the state, and so a statewide union must service simultaneously the many district bargaining units. Their bargaining experts must be on the move constantly to be of assistance to as many of their constituents as possible. In reality, the state organization must choose on some priority system which districts it can afford to advise during the bargaining season. The rest may get supporting documents and resource materials but are otherwise left to their own bargaining means.

One solution to this difficult process of local bargaining is regional, or statewide bargaining. The factors described above, when added to the special nature of the educational finance reform question, seem to make more centralized alternatives irresistible.

Alternative Collective Bargaining Models

If some other system develops or is deliberately created, what could it look like? At least three models are available: *regional bargaining, statewide bargaining,* and a *two tier system* with some issues negotiated at the local level while others are settled by state negotiators.

Many observers have suggested that it would be to the advantage of local boards to adopt joint or regional bargaining arrangements where two or more boards unite to face the union and negotiate a single contract. They could then afford the cost of a full-time professional negotiator, thus saving some of the costs of negotiation as well as the costs of living with contracts that are negotiated by amateurs. To those who say that the board would have to give up its autonomy, Myron Lieberman points out that board autonomy does not lie in this particular area anyway, since regional patterns of settlement exist already.

So far the regional bargaining model is not related to the aims of school finance reform but is a defensive posture for districts. The key is what happens when we start to define regions. If regions contained districts with similar costs for the same educational resources, such a solution would probably be acceptable to the courts (Simon 1973). It might also legitimize disparities of the sort that finance reform seeks to eradicate. Why do resources cost more in some regions? There are factors of distance from supply, different population densities, the need for costly transportation systems, the presence of those groups declared to be in need of more costly educational services and so on. In spite of these items, the one factor that accounts for most of the cost differential between districts is teacher salaries. Teachers receive salary increments automatically for length of service and for additional credit hours of teacher education courses. Older teachers who have more credits are more costly, and by the tacitly accepted criterion, they are better teachers. A regionalization plan that supported existing salary costs would compensate a district for having better teachers.

There are other obstacles to regional bargaining. In New York, for example, the Taylor Law definition of a bargaining party applies to districts but not groups of districts. A more difficult problem appears in the area of ratification of agreements reached through joint bargaining. The system would collapse if some local boards commonly rejected all or part of every contract. The obvious solution would be the delegation of board powers to the joint bargaining group, but this would be illegal at least in New York, and probably elsewhere.

Other objections come from the unions. Union leaders in New York County were reluctant to enter joint bargaining arrangements because they felt they had more to gain from confronting individual boards. Another powerful objection was that local leaders would not give up hard won positions of authority as they would have to do if bargaining were conducted over their heads.

Statewide bargaining would be the ultimate extension of regional bargaining. Statewide bargaining would have a stabilizing effect on costs because the power of the union could no longer be used to create interdistrict wage disparities for "whipsawing" purposes. Ironically statewide bargaining does not mean that interdistrict disparities would be removed altogether. In fact, negotiations would tend to legitimize disparities that did get into the contracts because the courts would be reluctant to overturn the results of collective bargaining (Simon 1973).

What would happen to teacher salaries? They might rise in the short run, but without the spur of uncontrolled interdistrict disparities and competition the rate of increase could be slowed. Technically, the more expert staffs and more efficient use of information, characteristic of larger bargaining units, would have the same effect.

The two tier alternative would: (1) place responsibility for pricing and controlling expensive education costs at the state level; and (2) place responsibility for raising the funds with the legislature.

A two tier system would also allow greater bargaining expertise to be concentrated on economic issues, while expertise in educational issues could be concentrated on educational problem-solving bargaining. It would permit that local boards, administrators, teachers, and the public be freed to deal with the content of educational programs in the districts.

While there are many difficulties with a two tier statewide system, they may not outweigh the advantages. One problem area is the definition of the bargaining units. At the state level the two sides in the bargaining relationship must be defined by law in such a way that neither side has major built-in weaknesses nor excessive power. It has been noted often that unions in the public service area should be more constrained than those in the private sector because they are in control of government services and so can distort the political process because they possess greater power than other groups (Wellington and Winter 1970).

Related to the question of local control is the situation of the local unions under a two tier system. Salary is a major issue for unions, and if this matter is taken out of the hands of local unions would they not collapse? The question is of interest to the public, because if local unions withered, the state organization would bargain not only for salary but for other matters as well; they would probably press to enlarge the scope of state level bargaining regardless of any limiting legislation. The local board in that extreme case might be relegated to the role of observer in important decision making. One solution lies in the legislative distinctions that could be drawn between the scope of bargaining issues at the two levels. If local boards were required to bargain with local unions over a wide scope of nonsalary issues, the local union would be stronger in relationship to the state organization, and would thus have an interest in preventing state level intrusion into local issues. We have already noted the reluctance of unions in one New York county to relinquish bargaining authority. A two tier system could be devised to take advantage of this reluctance, so that the local union would in a sense join with the board in the common task of maintaining local control.

If local boards, on the other hand, insist upon excluding most noneconomic items from bargaining on the grounds that they are management prerogatives or policy questions reserved to the board, they may well weaken local bargaining and begin an inevitable drift to statewide bargaining.

Ratification of the master contract, which appeared to be a problem in a joint or regional bargaining model described earlier, need not be under a two tier system because the legislature itself could ratify the economic settlement. Unlike the case of bargaining cooperatives or multi-employer bargainings in private industry, approval from local boards and union locals is not required. There is no veto power in this model.

We have already referred to the unequal distribution of teacher talent and thus teacher salary costs. If the state simply assumes the costs of local salaries, nothing would prevent districts from hiring the best and most expensive teachers. In other words, to attain equity, the districts should be under a market constraint also. Some countries such as New Zealand meet the problem by means of statewide assignment of teachers—a method with little appeal here. Teachers could be paid incentives to move to other districts. Another solution would be for either state level collective bargaining or political bargaining, as in reapportionment, to set, within some reasonable range, both the number of staff positions and the total salary allocation that would be available to each local district either by class of district or by some weighted formula. The local district could then distribute that total amount in any way it wanted by hiring teachers with various combinations of experience and training. If the local district were unable to reallocate any leftover funds, it would not be in its best interest to hire only inexperienced teachers, and encourage high turnover, a fear expressed by unions and individual teachers.

Perhaps the most crucial problem posed by a two tier bargaining system, however, is the interaction between cost (economic issues) and program (educational issues). Budget constraints are program constraints, but the reverse case is not necessarily true. District staffing patterns could be determined by the state contract, for instance, even though the contract covered only "economic" issues.

Conclusion

An examination of school finance reform and collective bargaining leads to the following conclusions:

1. Greater state involvement in fiscal support, spending level determinations, or control of revenue inputs will most certainly have consequences on the bargaining system.

2. Fiscal reform, and the underlying equity motivation of the reform movement, will lead to increasing policy attention being given to collective bargaining, with a probable drift toward more centralized systems.

3. Pressure for more centralized bargaining (i.e., larger units) is already sufficiently strong to encourage experimentation with regional bargaining cooperatives, and the like. Most of the present reform proposals, we believe, would add to these pressures making bargaining reform a likely coordinate of finance reform.

4. More centralized bargaining formats have much to recommend them. They use scarce bargaining resources more efficiently and probably lead to more rapid maturity of the system. Service disruptions caused by impasse or job action are less likely since bargaining "mistakes" will be reduced. Local district personnel, time, and money resources now consumed in bargaining can be released for other purposes.

References

Coons, John E., et al. *Private Wealth and Public Education.* Cambridge, Mass.: Harvard University Press, 1970.

Levin, Betsy, et al. *Public School Finance: Present Disparities and Fiscal Alternatives.* Washington, D.C.: The Urban Institute, 1972.

Lieberman, Myron. "The Impact of the Taylor Act upon the Governance and Administration of Elementary and Secondary Education." New York:

New York State Commission on the Quality, Cost and Financing of Elementary and Secondary Education, 1971.

Sherman, Joel. "Program Weightings for State Funding." Trenton: New Jersey Education Reform Project, 1974.

Simon, Larry G. "The School Finance Decision: Collective Bargaining and Future Finance Systems." *Yale Law Journal* 82, no. 3 (January 1973): 406-26.

Sommi, John. "Management's Response: Bargaining Between Boards of Education and Teacher Union in Rockland County, New York." Ed.D. dissertation, Teachers College, Columbia University, 1974.

Wellington, Harry H., and Winter, Ralph K., Jr. "Structuring Collective Bargaining in Public Employment." *Yale Law Journal,* 79, no. 5 (April 1970).

Reading 26

Political Implications of Public Employee Bargaining

Thomas M. Love and George T. Sulzner

From 1956 to 1968, union membership among government employees (federal, state, and local) grew from 915,000 to 2,155,000, a gain of 135.5 percent (Cohany and Dewey 1970). During the same period, another large segment of government employees formed associations for the purpose of collective bargaining or persuaded existing associations to include collective bargaining among their activities. By the end of 1968, this group of organizations represented an additional 2 to 2.5 million employees.* Though comprehensive figures for 1969 and 1970 are not yet available, everything indicates continued growth of collective bargaining in the public sector. Already, the rapid spread of employee organization has unleashed enormous pressures on a largely unsuspecting and thus unprepared public.

Reprinted by permission from *Industrial Relations* 11, no. 1 (February 1972), pp. 18-33.

*The major associations that have been involved in collective bargaining are the National Education Association and the American Nurses Association, but associations of policemen, social workers, and many smaller groups have also been active.

The legal, economic, and managerial implications of this growth in public employee organization have stimulated interest and comment among scholars and practitioners and have given rise to a rapidly expanding literature.* Relatively few questions, however, have been asked about the political implications of union growth in the public sector, and where such questions have been raised they have been treated as peripheral matters. Yet it would appear obvious that politics is central to the new labor-management relationships taking place in governmental units.[†] Government governs its workers as well as its citizens; the union leader deals with elected officials as well as with professional management; the two-party labor agreement may involve the informal participation of other parties, and so forth.

This paper seeks to partially remedy this gap in the literature by focusing on two broad areas—enterprise structure and pressure tactics —where substantial public/private differences exist. These differences, when viewed from a political perspective, give rise to a host of unresearched questions and dilemmas which have generally been ignored by theoreticians and practitioners alike. While we are concerned here more with conceptualization than with research design, we have cast some of our concerns in the form of hypotheses in the belief that they can be tested and that the results would have important implications both for labor relations specifically and the conduct of government generally.

Public vs. Private Bargaining: Similarities and Differences

The purpose of labor organization is essentially political:[‡] it enables workers to participate meaningfully in the decision processes

---

*The following sources provide an overall review of the topic: Anderson (1968); Kruger and Schmidt (1969); Moskow, Loewenberg, and Koziara (1970); Ocheltree (1969); Roberts (1968); Walsh (1969); Warner (1965); Warner and Hennessy (1967); and Woodworth and Peterson (1969).

[†]Dotson (1956) has developed a theory of public employment which is founded on the essentiality of recognizing the political nature of labor-management relations in government. His ideas, however, have been largely ignored by other students of public employment. Some of his concepts are highlighted in the last segment of this essay.

[‡]To permit an extensive application of democratic principles and to widen the scope of analysis, we have chosen Peter Bachrach's (1967) broad definition of the word "political": decision making which significantly affects societal val-

which establish the circumstances of their work and, to a considerable extent, their life. The notion that labor is not simply a commodity reflects an underlying value system that accords to men the right to give their consent to the terms and conditions of their employment. Individual bargaining is too weak a means to effective participation in these decisions, and government structures in modern society can provide only highly indirect participation to workers. Meaningful participatory democracy for workers seems achievable only through self-organization and collective action.

The means of labor organization are also political. Everyone accepts the word "political" in reference to the labor movement's various attempts to influence local, state, and national governmental bodies, but the collective bargaining process itself can also be considered a political activity.* Collective bargaining is a decision-making process which brings workers (as represented by their labor organization) and management together for the purpose of reaching mutual agreement concerning the rules governing the conduct of work. Collective bargaining, in other words, functions as a system of governance (i.e., a political system) at the work place. Whether the particular economic enterprise is publicly or privately owned does not change the basic fact that collective bargaining performs a political function. Labor and management groups in both sectors take formal positions on job-related issues; they marshall facts and seek to sway public opinion; they manipulate power; they may employ quasi-judicial third parties; they write legally binding agreements; and their decisions affect broad segments of society.

What probably does matter a good deal is the fact that the private bargainers operate in the market system and, theoretically, are held socially responsible by market forces. Public bargainers, on the other hand, operate outside the market system, which means that

ues. Where a narrower sense of the word is required, it is modified in a way such as "traditional political tactic."

Our views on the political nature of collective bargaining have also been strongly influenced by Peter F. Drucker (1950).

*It is also common to use the word "political" in describing unions' *internal* decision processes such as election of officers, policy making at conventions, and determination of bargaining demands. Strong political differences within a union can have a disruptive effect upon collective bargaining but such problems are not unique to the public sector and they are not considered in this paper.

these market forces do not contain them. Yet public bargainers are held socially responsible by more direct means—by the set of rules and devices that comprise representative government. Accordingly, different kinds of enterprise *structures* have evolved in the two sectors. A most striking example of this difference is that effective power and authority in private enterprise is vested in management, whereas management in public enterprise shares its power and authority with the legislature and with the judiciary. There are additional differences between structures in the public and private sectors: some public officials are elected and some appointed; local politics may be partisan or nonpartisan; and several agencies may share in the managerial decisions that affect workers.

In addition to the structural differences between the two sectors, major differences exist in the *pressure tactics* used to support bargaining positions. Certain tactics—such as the strike or threatened strike, the generation of publicity, and threats by management to change working conditions or eliminate jobs—are common to both sectors. But other pressure tactics—lobbying, support for particular candidates for public office, and control over patronage—are either unique to the public sector or are not very directly related to the bargaining activities of private labor organizations. For example, a public employee union could concurrently engage in some kind of job action, say a refusal to perform nonessential work, plus lobbying. Both activities could be employed in connection with a bargaining demand such as a proposed wage increase. In contrast, only the job action would be available to a private sector union.*

Political Structures and Public Employee Bargaining

Political Structures and Union Influence

The notion that the way in which community political systems are structured exerts an influence over policy independent of the mix of socioeconomic factors in a community is not an unusual one in

---

*Most private sector unions have objectives that involve activities at the executive, legislative, or judicial levels of government. An effort to secure an increase in the minimum wage closely parallels the example given above. Such objectives and activities, however, are usually independent of collective bargaining.

political science.* "The political weight of organized city employees in a particular city," Edward C. Banfield and James Q. Wilson (1966, p. 214) write, "depends largely upon the nature of that city's political structure, and especially upon the degree to which influence is centralized." Banfield and Wilson contend that in cities where party organization is strong, the political demands of all other organizations must necessarily be channeled through the party structure, where they are usually open to substantial modification. Because of this, Banfield and Wilson conclude that, "Where party organization is strong, the city administration is in a relatively good position to resist the demands of the organized employees. . . . On the other hand, where party organization is weak or altogether absent, the political weight of organized employees is relatively large and might be decisive."† The thrust of the Banfield-Wilson position can be reduced to the following hypotheses: (1) *city employees are likely to exert the most influence in communities whose political structure includes a council-manager form of government, nonpartisan elections, and an at-large election system.* (These institutional forms may be called *reformed structures.*) And (2) *city employees are likely to exert the least influence in communities whose political structure includes a mayor-council form of government, partisan elections, and a ward electoral system.* (These may be referred to as *unreformed structures.*)

The expected effect of reformed and unreformed structures upon the political influence of city employees is by no means subject to general agreement, however. Based upon a study of 200 American cities, Robert L. Lineberry and Edmund P. Fowler (1967) state:

Our data suggest that when a city adopts reformed structures, it comes to be governed less on the basis of conflict and more on the basis of a rationalistic theory of administration. The making of public policy takes less account of the

---

*Philip Coulter (1970) provides a useful summary and analysis of the literature that examines public policy outcomes in American community political systems.

†Banfield and Wilson state that: "In many small nonpartisan cities, especially ones which elect their councils on the at-large system, organized city employees . . . may be the only, and at any rate by far the largest, city-wide organization."

enduring differences between White and Negro, business and labor, Pole and W.A.S.P.

Reformed governments, they contend, minimize access to minority groups because of their centralized, bureaucratized, and "depoliticized" methods of decision making. On the other hand, a mayor-council or unreformed government, with its greater decentralization, "permits a multiplicity of access points for groups wishing to influence decision makers. It may also increase the possibilities for collaboration between groups and a bureaucratic agency, a relationship which has characterized administrative patterns in the federal government." Thus, Lineberry and Fowler seem to argue precisely the opposite of Banfield and Wilson. Appropriate hypotheses representing their views would be: (1) *city employees are likely to exert the most influence in communities whose political structure includes a mayor-council form of government, partisan elections, and a ward election system*; and (2) *city employees are likely to exert the least influence in communities whose political structure includes a council-manager form of government, nonpartisan elections, and an at-large election system.*

An accurate determination of which of the above two views is more nearly correct would be no mean finding. For example, political structures which consistently favor organized government employees could easily put enormous pressure on shadow parties* and provoke them to request a more formal role in collective bargaining.

---

*We have chosen this term to denote third-party pressure groups who represent workers or other groups that are not part of the bargaining unit but who may have a vested interest in the outcome of collective bargaining in the unit. Such groups may become informally involved in the bargaining but they would not be a signatory to the labor agreement. For example, an organization of principals might be consulted during negotiations between a teachers' union and the school board over a proposed change of the transfer rights of teachers. Similar possibilities exist with respect to civil rights groups, parent organizations, etc. Other *unions* may also have a vested interest in the bargaining demands of any given union. For example, inter-union pay ratios and pay parity provisions create a direct link between otherwise separate negotiations. The term "interest groups," though it is more familiar, does not fit our purposes because it does not imply any special connection to collective bargaining.

Bargaining in the presence of shadow parties has been referred to as "multilateral bargaining." See McLennan and Moskow (1969).

This would undoubtedly complicate the bargaining process, as well as substantially change the nature of government itself.

Locus of Authority Within Government

In comparison to private enterprise where bargaining authority is generally fixed at the level of professional management and where decisions taken at that level are not usually overturned at a higher level, the decision structure in government is highly varied. In government, decisions might be taken: (1) by the legislature *or* by some agency in the executive branch; (2) by an elected official *or* by a professional manager; or (3) by a top executive officer *or* by a lower level labor relations expert.* Also in government, it is not unusual to find the locus of decision authority shifting from one level to another in response to political pressures.

The problem for government then is how to make collective bargaining *efficient* (i.e., how to accomplish agreement while minimizing expense, effort, interruption of production, frustration, and anything else that interferes with the achievement of enterprise goals) in the context of such complexity. Collective bargaining cannot be very efficient in the absence of considerable expertise, or under rigid time constraints, or where there is no identifiable and stable locus of decision authority on either side of the bargaining table. Moreover, collective bargaining seems certain to be inefficient if it is conducted by legislative bodies. There is no question that ultimate policy-making authority rests with the legislature, but the fact is that legislators usually lack the inclination, the expertise, and the time to devote to this one important but small aspect of their work.

For these reasons there is a growing tendency to "professionalize" the bargaining function in public enterprise either by hiring persons who have gained their expertise in the private sector or by developing skilled negotiators from among existing staff members. In either case, however, the existence of a higher authority offers the constant temptation to unions to circumvent the management negotiator and seek to deal directly with elected officials. Moreover, if

---

*The actual decision structure is both vertically and horizontally more complex and contains more elements than we have presented here. We have abstracted from reality to illustrate the public policy problems inherent in this situation.

one side or the other is not sincere in the first place it can easily exploit this situation—the union by playing one element of management against another, and the employer by disclaiming authority at all levels.

Political Implications

There is, therefore, a dilemma posed by the conflicting demands of time and expertise on the one side and authority on the other side. This is a serious problem, and it has been given much attention in the literature, mainly from the perspective of bargaining efficiency (see Derber 1969). However, the political aspects of the situation viewed from the perspective of democratic theory have not received the attention they deserve. One question that should be asked is whether the attempt to institutionalize collective bargaining procedures in government would, in effect, remove the public from any decisional role in a policy area that has a direct bearing on the lives of citizens. That this concern already exists in other policy areas is demonstrated by the far-ranging discussion of concepts such as ombudsmen, participatory democracy, citizen control of the schools, and the community action antipoverty strategy. But, so far at least, there appears to be little scholarly attention given to the possibility that collective bargaining among government employees may intensify the problem. Certainly, decisions pertaining to employee job interests, through their effects upon costs and services, are crucial to the public as well as to the employees. The problem can be expressed in the form of the following hypothesis: *the "professionalization" of collective bargaining will intensify the forces of bureaucracy and elitism in government, and result in a further erosion of the citizen's capacity to govern his affairs through access to the machinery of government on a basis of equality with other citizens.**

It is possible to conceive of developments, however, which could preserve democracy in the sense used above. That is, citizens may react to the "professionalization" of collective bargaining by transforming their shadow parties into more formal and potent

---

*We are referring to professional elites who, due to their unique skills, possess power and influence in society which exceeds that of most citizens. The underlying theory of this and other types of democracy is discussed in Bachrach (1967). The classic exposition of this theme within organizations remains that of Robert Michels (1966).

mechanisms for participation in the affairs of government. And, while the individual citizen would still not deal directly with his government, it is theoretically possible that he would have equality vis-à-vis his peers and there could be equality among political organizations. An example of such arrangements closely related to this discussion is the "bargaining" among civil rights groups, unions, construction companies, and government, over the issue of equal access to jobs in the construction industry. Thus, an alternative hypothesis that appears to be as plausible as the one previously presented is that: *the "professionalization" of collective bargaining in the public sector will lead to the development of third-party formal participation in employer-employee decisions.*

A third possibility, of course, is that attempts to "professionalize" the bargaining process may ultimately fail. Specifically, we can hypothesize that: *where management authority is diffuse, difficult to locate, and likely to shift both vertically and horizontally through the management structure, unions will seek to deal directly with elected officials.* Under such conditions, elected officials would be playing a larger role in bargaining and since these officials, in contrast to professional management, can be assumed to be responsive to citizen groups, the issue of citizen participation would remain troublesome but perhaps less severe than under the circumstances described earlier.

Finally, this discussion leads to consideration of the pressure tactics that a public employee organization might apply. Presumably, the strike is not the only tactic or even the major tactic that could be effectively applied to elected officials. The nature of other kinds of tactics and the implications of their use is explored in the sections which follow.

Pressure Tactics

It is axiomatic that some forms of pressure tactics will accompany collective bargaining wherever it is found. The very existence of independent and separate positions at the bargaining table implies differences of outlook, motivation, subgoals (if not goals), and values that cannot be resolved by appeal to fact or reason. Thus, both parties marshal whatever forces they can command in support of their positions.

The Strike in Relation to Other Tactics

For reasons that are less clear, strikes have come to be regarded as the only significant pressure tactic available to employees.* Perhaps this is because strikes are immediately visible and dramatic, with effects more easily measured than is the case with other tactics. Even in the private sector, however, where the strike is legally sanctioned, it is actually utilized in only a small minority of bargaining situations that take place every year. Numerous other pressure tactics exist and, taken together, they are much more frequent occurrences. Such tactics include placing advertisements in newspapers, calling news conferences, shifting attitudes and demeanor at the bargaining table, conducting mass meetings and strike votes, threatening to strike, slowing the pace of work, refusing to abide by the rules, obstructing production by strict adherence to rules, and manipulating the grievance procedure.

As indicated earlier, there are a greater number of alternatives to the strike[†] in the public sector, of which lobbying and participation in elections are probably most important. (Public employee and employer "power assets" are discussed in Belasco 1966.) Moreover, since public employee bargaining entails issues which are central to the public interest and which are also frequently controversial (educational policy, police and sanitation services, etc.), the publicity generating techniques available to public labor organizations are likely to create greater pressure than they do when used by private sector unions. This means that there is a dual system of pressure tactics available to public employees—political and economic.

This dual system of pressure tactics is accorded oblique recognition in the literature in the course of an argument over the appropriate scope for strike activity in public employment. Wellington and Winter (reading 15; the argument is restated and expanded in Wellington and Winter 1970), on the one hand, argue that in most cases

---

*We argue thusly because there is a massive literature concerning strikes in professional journals, magazines, newspapers, and other media. At the same time, almost no space or time is devoted to other pressure tactics.

[†]The industrial relations specialist commonly employs the phrase "alternatives to the strike" to refer to methods of dispute settlement such as mediation, factfinding, and arbitration. We ignore these processes here, not because they are unimportant or inappropriate to the public sector, but because we wish to focus attention upon other alternatives.

union power in the private sector is restrained by market forces before the use of such power imposes intolerable social costs, but that such limitations to union power are not effective in the public sector because it is outside of the scope of the market. They conclude that: "If public employee unions are free to strike as well as to employ the usual methods of political pressure, interest groups with competing claims and different priorities will be put at a competitive disadvantage and the political process will be distorted" (1970, p. 808). For this reason they urge that strikes be banned in the public sector until steps can be taken to protect the "normal" political process.*

Burton and Krider (reading 16), on the other hand, argue that limitations on the right to strike will not necessarily protect the "normal" political process. The essence of their argument is that political power is not distributed evenly among all groups that compete in the political process. For example, they contend that public sector craft employees may benefit from close ties with politically powerful private sector craft unions. In the absence of the right to strike, other public employees would be at a decided disadvantage at the bargaining table. They also argue that public sector strikes are, in effect, political weapons that cannot be distinguished operationally from other political weapons. Having refuted strike prohibitions on the grounds of their political inappropriateness, Burton and Krider argue that the strike should be allowed in the public sector except where essential services are provided.

While the two sets of authors differ in the scope of sanctioned strike activity and while the political system enters into their considerations, they view political pressure tactics as given and take the strike as the main public policy variable. We contend that this structures the analysis in a manner which is inconsistent with the existence of a dual system of pressure tactics. Such an analysis takes explicit account of the costs of strikes, but leaves out the costs or gains of lobbying or electioneering. We contend, therefore, that the public sector analytical model should treat political pressure tactics

---

*They recommend contingency planning and partial operation to reduce the costs of strikes and also recommend various changes in the political process (such as more explicit budgeting practices) that would increase public awareness of the costs of the union bargaining proposals.

as variables and that efforts should be undertaken to develop better data on such tactics.*

Problems in Applying Traditional Bargaining Rules to the Public Sector

We wish to narrow our focus now to consider specific situations where the use of certain strategies is usually seen as being injurious to effective collective bargaining. Moskow, Loewenberg, and Koziara (1970, pp. 267-68) employ the terms "end run" lobbying and "carom" lobbying to describe such situations. "End run" lobbying occurs while negotiations are in progress and where management is represented by a labor relations expert. It is an attempt to use political pressure on elected officials to undermine the position of the management negotiator. "Carom" lobbying is similar in all respects except that it takes place after *tentative* agreement has been reached with the management negotiator.

While it seems obvious that such behavior would interfere with the successful development of collective bargaining in the public sector, the rules of conduct which might govern these cases are not so obvious. A step toward such rules is suggested by Anderson (1967, pp. 37-38), who writes:

Good faith bargaining requires that public employee organizations should not attempt to improve on the terms of the bargain before the legislative body . . . if it agreed to forego such improvement during negotiations in consideration of other benefits granted.

He continues:

Similarly, public bargaining representatives, who have agreed with local union representatives on the terms of a new labor agreement, should not renege on their promise to recommend acceptance of the proposal to the full legislative body (city council or county board) nor should they ask their fellow members of the legislative body to take them off the hook.

These are conceptually sensible guidelines, but they are likely to be difficult to place into operation since they inevitably lead to some

---

*The best statement about the limited degree of knowledge that political scientists possess concerning the political activities of labor is contained in Scoble (1963).

form of public intervention. Should the parties be required to make and to live up to a pledge to "forego such improvement" or to "not renege on their promise"? If so, should public intervention be in the form of statutory, agency, or judicial rules? Can rules be formulated which avoid conflict with the constitutional right of employees and their organizations to engage in political activities?

Looking to the private sector for guidelines in this area is of little help. Broadly speaking, strikes are prohibited both before the point of impasse and during the life of an agreement. While such a rule concerning strikes could logically be carried over to the public sector, it is less clear how the use of other available tactics should be handled. For example, is there any appropriate rule for situations where, instead of striking, the public union applies traditional political pressure against a key councilman to get him to influence the management negotiators? Or suppose an important legislative committee chairman exerts his influence to persuade the union to modify its demands?

Consider also the posture of the law *after* agreement is reached and formally authorized by all parties. Should any or all political action by public employee organizations be similarly circumscribed during the life of the agreement?

Pressure Tactics and the Political System

In our society, the constitution, statutes, and the courts have permitted private employee organizations, as organizations, to engage in a rather wide array of political activities including lobbying, endorsing candidates, and making financial contributions to candidates. The major exception to this general rule is that federal law does not permit labor organizations to make contributions in connection with federal elections. The courts have also ruled that a labor organization may not use a member's dues for political purposes if the individual member objects to such use. This law, however, allows labor organizations to create political adjuncts, such as the AFL-CIO's Committee on Political Education, for the purpose of collecting *voluntary* contributions from members and using these monies to support candidates for public office.

The questions which underlie these private sector policies did not become matters of wide concern until after the labor movement became extensively organized and until after it developed an ambitious political agenda. It is likely, therefore, that similar attention will be focused upon public employee organizations as they become better organized and as their political impact grows.* An illustration of the type of public policy questions which might arise is provided by excerpts from a *New York Times* editorial. Concerning endorsements of candidates for political office by the Patrolmen's Benevolent Association, *The Times* commented:

As arbiters, policemen should certainly not be committed *en bloc* to the support of particular candidates, nor do they have the right to put political officials in a position of being obligated to them. (July 14, 1970, p. 34)

The same editorial was critical of the action of a group of patrolmen who picketed a police station in protest of the use of policemen to guard foreign consulates and U.N. missions:

The proper deployment of the police force is not a matter for collective bargaining; it is the responsibility of the appropriate police and city authorities. The police picketing—however good-humored—constituted highly unprofessional conduct.

The issues raised by the editorial are both potentially serious and enormously complicated. Electioneering or other political involvement by public employees might be detrimental to the public interest in the following ways: (1) it could lead to interference with the merit system; (2) it could impair the impartial performance of services; and (3) it could lead to alliances between political and union elites and consequent perpetuation of power in their hands. Whether or not such problems would actually arise depends upon factors such as municipal political structures, merit system regulations, the strength of internal union democracy, the nature of political activity among other groups, and the extent to which new issues lead to shifts among groups. Obviously, the extent to which electioneering and other political actions by public employees are harmful to the public interest demands immediate and thoughtful consideration.

---

*At the federal level, the Hatch Act and Civil Service regulations prohibit civil service employees from playing active roles in elections. Similar legislation exists at the state level. These prohibitions, however, appear to apply to individual employees rather than to employee organizations.

A viable public policy in this area will also have to consider the following: first, it is probably necessary to distinguish between the rights of an individual public employee and the rights of his labor organization. For example, the individual may need to be protected from political interference with the merit system, but it seems unlikely that labor organizations require such protection. Second, if careful study reveals that the public interest is damaged by public employee political action, such damage must be balanced against the costs of restricting the political rights of such employees. Interest groups exist to express preferences on issues vital to their members. Hence, the imposition of arbitrary restrictions on public employee organizations but not on private unions or other groups would appear to be both unfair and a repudiation of the normal political process. Finally, it is necessary to consider whether there is something unique in the job functions of, say, policemen (as opposed to teachers, sanitationmen, clerks, etc.) that might create "obligations" which would warrant treating them differently on this issue.

As in the case of electioneering, the picketing issue requires society to balance the benefits which flow from the existence of political rights such as free speech with the harm which their exercise might create in specific instances. Labor law in the private sector has faced this problem and, while the law is quite intricate, it generally holds that picketing is allowable as long as it is a peaceful, informational, and primary activity. Is there any reason why the private sector law should not apply in this situation?* The most obvious reason for a positive answer to this question is that allowing the police to picket may weaken their resolve to protect the public against violation of the picketing laws by other unions. Even if this should occur, it is not immediately clear that limitations upon the constitutional rights of policemen are the appropriate remedy.

A Possible Base for Public Bargaining Guidelines

The foregoing discussion clearly shows the need for guidelines that would recognize and protect the legitimate interests of both the

---

*A news item in the *New York Times* indicated that the police picketing with which their editorial was concerned would have been lawful under such standards. "Police Pickets Protest Consulate Duty," *New York Times*, July 14, 1970, p. 25.

state and its citizens as public employees raise their political profile. We believe that Dotson (1956) has begun such a formulation in his "theory of public agency." He strives to provide in his theory a practical basis for public policy, appropriate for the use of legislators, administrators, and adjudicators alike. The methodological premise of Dotson's theory is that it "must be based in the practical needs and resources of the parties."

His theory summarizes the needs of government as being: (1) faithful performance by employees; (2) freedom to determine manpower needs and utilization; (3) flexibility of policy, especially substantive policy which should follow majority will; and (4) maintenance of certain functions without interruption. For securing and preserving its interests, the government may exercise both economic power (its ability to raise revenue and its immunity from competition) and political power (its sovereignty and the presumption of its representing the public interest).

The needs of public employees are also four-fold: (1) reasonable working conditions; (2) minimum security against life's vicissitudes; (3) psychological satisfaction from participation in managerial decisions; and (4) preservation of political status. The employee, too, possesses economic power (the services he offers and may withhold either individually or in concert with his fellows) and political power (his vote and the ability to affect public policy from the inside).

Substantively, then, Dotson views public employment as a "political connection between the *state* and a *group* of citizens." He argues that like any other connection between the government and a group of citizens: (1) it must be rationalized in the context of public law; (2) the position of the parties must be regulated by a fundamental law (the Constitution); and (3) the public character of public employment means that all public employment must be subject to the same system of principles. However, public employment is a specific aspect of the totality of citizen-state relationships and, as such, has its own subordinate principles and rules. Dotson attempts to capture these principles in his "theory of public agency." It is based on three interrelated concepts that he has entitled "democratic effectiveness," "compensatory right," and "equitable advantage." We will discuss only the first two here.

The concept of "democratic effectiveness" has two parts, one emphasizing the public nature of the relationship and the other the requirements of efficient execution of policy. Dotson notes that this concept "holds that the government must be able to satisfy its practical needs. The state," he continues, "must be empowered to take such measures as are necessary to protect its interests and the public welfare. But this is not to say that it may take any measure at all, for any interest or any welfare." He concludes that "where there are compelling reasons, and after showing that the abridgment is indispensable to an essential need, the government may override the ordinary attributes of its employees." Simply, the government must be permitted to govern, but it must govern responsibly.

The essence of the concept of "compensatory right" is embodied in the idea that if the fundamental rights of one party to a relationship are invaded by the other, jural compensation should be due. Corresponding to the principle of eminent domain, "the standard of 'compensatory right' in public employment means that any party who is required through public employment to give up rights 'with which he has no desire to part' shall be 'left whole' by a right to compensation."

In practical terms, then, under the "theory of public agency" the government would have to build a case of exceptional need before it could restrict the political participation of public employees. Thus, the general disestablishment of the political rights of public employees that occurred in the Hatch Acts of 1939 and 1940 would not be compatible, as Dotson observes, with his "theory of public agency." There is a reasonable balance in Dotson's approach to public employment that, unfortunately, is absent from current laws. If flexibility and discrimination are important characteristics of viable policy in this area, then Dotson's thinking indicates the direction future research should take.

Conclusion

It is regrettable, although understandable, that public employee organization and bargaining progressed so rapidly as to preclude sufficient consideration of the many salient differences existing between the public and private sector. Intense grass roots pressure for the exercise of rights that were inherently unassailable left little time for reflection, and it is not too surprising that public sector labor relations quickly took on most of the trappings of its private counterpart. We can only hope that it is not yet too late for a reassessment of public employee bargaining—a reassessment aimed at discovery and recognition of the unique characteristics of this process and the development of policy guidelines and regulations keyed to these differences.

In a positive vein, the present situation might be seen as providing a unique opportunity to reconstruct the law and practice of labor relations in both sectors. We have argued, however, that this will require fresh perspectives in looking upon the problem. Only in this manner will it be possible to open up new alternatives where real differences exist and to avoid double standards where such differences do not exist.

References

Anderson, Arvid. "The U.S. Experience in Collective Bargaining in Public Employment." *Collective Bargaining in the Public Service: Theory and Practice,* edited by Kenneth O. Warner. Chicago: Public Personnel Association, 1967.

Anderson, Howard J. (ed.). *Public Employee Organization and Bargaining.* Washington, D.C.: Bureau of National Affairs, 1968.

Bachrach, Peter. *The Theory of Democratic Elitism: A Critique.* Boston: Little, Brown, 1967.

Banfield, Edward C., and Wilson, James Q. *City Politics.* New York: Vintage, 1966.

Belasco, James A. "Collective Bargaining in City X." *Government Labor Relations in Transition,* edited by Keith Ocheltree. Chicago: Public Personnel Association, 1966.

Cohany, Harry P., and Dewey, Lucretia. "Union Membership Among Government Employees." *Monthly Labor Review* XCIII (July 1970): 15-30.

Coulter, Philip. "Comparative Community Politics and Public Policy: Problems in Theory and Research." *Polity* 3 (Fall 1970): 23-43.

Derber, Milton. "Who Negotiates for the Public Employer." *Perspective in Public Employee Negotiation,* edited by Keith Ocheltree. Chicago: Public Personnel Association, 1969.

Dotson, Arch. "A General Theory of Public Employment." *Public Administration Review* 16 (Summer 1956): 197-211.

Drucker, Peter F. *The New Society: The Anatomy of Industrial Order.* New York: Harper & Row, 1950.

Kruger, Daniel H., and Schmidt, Charles T., Jr. *Collective Bargaining in the Public Service.* New York: Random House, 1969.

Lineberry, Robert L., and Fowler, Edmund P. "Reformism and Public Policies in American Cities." *American Political Science Review* 61 (September 1967): 710-16.

McLennan, Kenneth, and Moskow, Michael H. "Multilateral Bargaining in the Public Sector." *Proceedings*, Twenty-First Annual Meeting, Industrial Relations Research Association. Madison, Wis.: Industrial Relations Research Association, 1969.

Michels, Robert. *Political Parties*. New York: Free Press, 1966.

Moskow, Michael H.; Loewenberg, J. Joseph; and Koziara, Edward C. *Collective Bargaining in Public Employment*. New York: Random House, 1970.

Ocheltree, Keith (ed.). *Perspective in Public Employee Negotiation*. Chicago: Public Personnel Association, 1969.

Roberts, Harold S. *Labor Management Relations in the Public Service*. Honolulu: University of Hawaii, 1968.

Scoble, Harry. "Organized Labor in Electoral Politics: Some Questions for the Discipline." *Western Political Quarterly* 16 (September 1963): 666-85.

Walsh, Robert E. (ed.). *No Government Today: Unions vs. City Hall*. Boston: Beacon Press, 1969.

Warner, Kenneth O. (ed.). *Developments in Public Employee Relations: Legislative, Judicial, Administrative*. Chicago: Public Personnel Association, 1965.

Warner, Kenneth O., and Hennessy, Mary L. *Public Management at the Bargaining Table*. Chicago: Public Personnel Association, 1967.

Woodworth, Robert T., and Peterson, Richard B. *Collective Negotiation for Public and Professional Employees*. Glenview, Ill.: Scott, Foresman, 1969.